The Uniformed Services Employment and Reemployment Rights Act

BNA Books Authored by the
ABA Section of Labor and Employment Law

Age Discrimination in Employment Law, 2009 Supplement

Covenants Not to Compete: A State-by-State Survey

The Developing Labor Law

Discipline and Discharge in Arbitration

Elkouri & Elkouri: How Arbitration Works

Employee Benefits Law

Employee Duty of Loyalty: A State-by-State Survey

Employment Discrimination Law

Employment Termination: Rights and Remedies, 2003 Supplement

Equal Employment Law Update

The Fair Labor Standards Act

The Family and Medical Leave Act

How ADR Works

How to Take a Case Before the NLRB

International Labor and Employment Laws

Labor Arbitration: A Practical Guide for Advocates

Labor Arbitration: Cases and Materials for Advocates

Labor Arbitrator Development: A Handbook

Labor Union Law and Regulation

Occupational Safety and Health Law

The Railway Labor Act

Tortious Interference in the Employment Context: A State-by-State Survey

Trade Secrets: A State-by-State Survey

The Uniformed Services Employment and Reemployment Rights Act

Wage and Hour Laws: A State-by-State Survey

For details on these and other related titles, please visit the BNA Books
Web site at **bnabooks.com** or call **1-800-960-1220** to request a catalog.
All books are available on a 30-day free examination period.

The Uniformed Services Employment and Reemployment Rights Act

Editors-in-Chief

George R. Wood
Littler Mendelson, P.C.
Minneapolis, MN

Ossai Miazad
Outten & Golden, LLP
New York, NY

Federal Labor Standards Legislation Committee
Section of Labor and Employment Law
American Bar Association

AMERICAN BAR ASSOCIATION
Section of
Labor and Employment Law

BNA Books, *A Division of BNA,* Arlington, VA

Library of Congress Cataloging-in-Publication Data

The Uniformed Services Employment and Reemployment Rights Act / editors-in-chief, George R. Wood, Ossai Miazad.
    p. cm.
  ISBN 978-1-57018-846-6
  1. United States. Uniformed Services Employment and Reemployment Rights Act of 1994. 2. Veterans--Employment--Law and legislation--United States. 3. Veterans--Legal status, laws, etc.-- United States. I. Wood, George R. II. Miazad, Ossai.
  KF3460.U53 2009
  344.73′0114--dc22

                    2009046924

Published by BNA Books
1801 S. Bell Street, Arlington, VA 22202
bnabooks.com

ISBN 978-1-57018-846-6
Printed in the United States of America

CONTRIBUTORS

EDITORS-IN-CHIEF

GEORGE R. WOOD
Littler Mendelson, P.C.
Minneapolis, MN

OSSAI MIAZAD
Outten & Golden, LLP
New York, NY

CHAPTER AUTHORS

Chapter 1

DAVID BALL
Schottenstein Zox & Dunn
   Co., LPA
Columbus, OH

BERNIE MAZAHERI
Morgan & Morgan
Orlando, FL

Chapter 2

MICHAEL FISCHER
Quarles & Brady LLP
Milwaukee, WI

Chapter 3

JOHNATHAN R. CARTER
Littler Mendelson P.C.
Fayetteville, AR

Chapter 4

REBECCA J. JACOBS
Ulmer & Berne LLP
Columbus, OH

RACHELLE L. WILLS
Littler Mendelson P.C.
San Francisco, CA

Chapter 5

HARVEY C. BERGER
Pope, Berger & Williams, LLP
San Diego, CA

DAVID M. JAFFE
CVS Caremark Corporation
Woonsocket, RI

Chapter 6

TODD K. BOYER
Littler Mendelson P.C.
San Jose, CA

KATHRYN PRUSS ZELTWANGER
Armstrong Holdings, Inc.
Butler, PA

Chapter 7

KRISTEN ASHWORTH
Burr & Forman LLP
Mobile, Alabama

KRIS CATO
McAngus Goudelock & Courie,
   LLC
Columbia, SC

Chapter 8

HARVEY C. BERGER
Pope, Berger & Williams, LLP
San Diego, CA

DAVID M. JAFFE
CVS Caremark Corporation
Woonsocket, RI

Chapter 9

STEVEN M. BERNSTEIN
Fisher & Phillips LLP
Tampa, FL

BRYAN SMITH
Littler Mendelson P.C.
Minneapolis, MN

Chapter 10

CHRISTOPHER F. CARIÑO
Brouse McDowell
Akron, OH

RICHARD C. "CHIP" MCWILLIAMS,
JR.
Littler Mendelson P.C.
Atlanta, GA

Chapter 11

TRACY STOTT PYLES
Littler Mendelson P.C.
Columbus, OH

Brandon M. Shelton
Ogletree, Deakins, Nash, Smoak
   & Stewart, P.C.
Charlotte, NC

FOREWORD

Since 1945 the ABA Section of Labor and Employment Law has expanded its stated purposes in response to the evolution of the field. Currently, they include the following: (a) to study and report upon continuing developments in the field of labor and employment law; (b) to provide a forum for members of the Association interested in the field of labor and employment law to meet and confer; (c) to assist the professional growth and development of practitioners in the field of labor and employment law; (d) to establish and maintain working liaison with state, federal, and, where applicable, multi-national agencies having jurisdiction over matters affecting labor and employment law toward achieving procedural reform and administrative due process; (e) to study and report upon proposed and necessary legislation and rule making within the field encompassed by the jurisdiction of this Section; (f) to promote justice, human welfare, industrial peace, and the recognition of the supremacy of law in labor-management relations and the employment relationship; and (g) to establish, moderate, and sponsor seminars, workshops, forums, and other programs promoting the advancement of knowledge and practice in the field of labor and employment law.

Through the publication of books such as *The Uniformed Services Employment and Reemployment Rights Act* and through annual and committee meeting programs designed to provide a forum for the exchange of ideas, the Section has pursued these stated goals. Gradually, the Section has built a library of comprehensive legal works intended for the use of the Section membership as well as the bar generally.

The Section of Labor and Employment Law is pleased to provide this treatise on the Uniformed Services Employment and Reemployment Rights Act as part of its library of books published by BNA Books. The combined efforts of many individual authors from the Federal Labor Standards Legislation Committee of the Section are reflected in this book.

The Section wishes to express its appreciation to the committee, and in particular to editors-in-chief, George R. Wood and Ossai Miazad, and to the chapter authors. This group has tried to accomplish two primary objectives: (1) to be equally balanced and nonpartisan in its viewpoints, and (2) to ensure the book is of significant value to the practitioner, student, and sophisticated nonlawyer.

The views expressed herein do not necessarily represent the views of the American Bar Association, or its Section of Labor and Employment Law, or any other organization, but are simply the collective, but not necessarily the individual, views of the authors. Information on the affiliation of government employees who contributed to this work is for informational purposes and does not constitute any official endorsement of the information provided herein.

NORA L. MACEY
Chair

GORDON E. KRISCHER
Chair-Elect

Section of Labor
and Employment Law
American Bar Association

December 2009

PREFACE

The Uniform Services Employment and Reemployment Rights Act (USERRA or the Act) is a federal statute granting employees rights with respect to leaves of absence from employment to serve in the United States armed forces. In consideration of the sacrifices made by those Americans who serve in the military, Congress made USERRA intentionally broad in its coverage. Unlike the Family and Medical Leave Act, USERRA provides no limits on its coverage based on the size of employer's workforce. The significance of this breadth cannot be understated. USERRA effectively applies to all companies within the United States who have employees, whether one or thousands.

Beginning in 1940, the federal government enacted a series of laws governing leaves of absences from employment to serve in the military. Starting with the Selective Training and Service Act of 1940, Congress sought to provide employees with, among other things, the right to take leave from employment to serve in the military. Over time, these various legislative enactments became confusing and difficult to interpret and apply. In enacting USERRA, Congress addressed the concern that existing veteran's rights statutes were overly complex and ambitious, leaving veterans and employers confused as to their rights and responsibilities. It enacted USERRA in large part to clarify, simplify and where necessary, strengthen existing laws governing veterans' rights.

Thus, while not the first such statute of its kind, USERRA as enacted in 1994 is Congress's most recent attempt to provide rights to those Americans serving in our armed services. USERRA is comprehensive in its application. Like most statutes, however, it cannot and does not contemplate every situation employers and employees face with respect to military leave. Understanding USERRA's inner-workings is important to both employers and employees in order to facilitate the intent of the law.

Congress made clear that USERRA's provisions supersede any state laws providing fewer rights to employees. In essence, USERRA establishes a "floor" of rights below which no state—or employer—may go. While states may grant employees more rights than those under USERRA, they cannot take away any of USERRA's provisions. Any attempt to do so is specifically preempted by the Act. Practitioners thus need to keep in mind that examination of USERRA's provisions may only be half the necessary analysis. Relevant state statutes and laws need to be analyzed to determine the full rights and obligations of employers and employees for military leave purposes.

Basic Provisions

USERRA seeks to protect employee reinstatement rights based on the concept of maintaining an employee's "seniority" while on leave for military service. Known as the "escalator provision," this aspect of USERRA allows an employee to return from military service to the position the employee would have attained had he or she remained "continuously employed" during the leave period. USERRA—and the regulations that the United States Department of Labor have adopted to implement USERRA— make clear that this escalator may go up, stay at the same level the employee had at the start of the leave, or go down. Thus, employees subject to a layoff or termination due to a reduction in force during a period of military leave are not granted greater rights than those employees not on USERRA leave.

Reinstatement, however, is not the only seniority right protected. Where employers grant other rights to employees based on seniority, an employee on military leave has these rights protected. The seniority rights at issue are not simply those granted by a union collective bargaining agreement or strict seniority-based system of employment. Seniority rights are defined as those rights the employee accrues due to the passage of time. While determining and applying these rights may be easier where a collective bargaining agreement or strict seniority system of employment is in place, the protections granted under USERRA for seniority rights is not limited to these settings.

In addition to protecting employment rights based on seniority, USERRA requires employers to grant employees on military leave those *non-seniority* rights provided to employees taking a comparable leave of absence who are of similar seniority, status and pay to the employee on military leave. In effect, the employee taking military leave is to be given the equivalent of "most-favored-nation" status, i.e., the best of any non-seniority based rights granted to similar employees taking similar leaves of absence.

Finally, USERRA provides certain protections to protected employees' pension benefit rights, both during a leave of absence and upon re-hire. Employees on a leave of absence under USERRA are entitled to be treated as having no break in service while on leave and are granted the right to obtain or make up missed contributions to the their pension benefit plan.

Significantly, Congress limited USERRA's application to those employees who effectively receive an honorable discharge (or an equivalent discharge). While employers may still employ persons who are dishonorably discharged, those persons are not entitled to most of USERRA's protections.

USERRA imposes obligations on employees as well as employers. An employee taking a leave of absence for military service, and thereafter seeking a return to work, must meet requirements such as proper notice for the leave and proper notice for returning to work.

Like most federal statutes protecting certain employee rights, USERRA contains provisions protecting employees against discrimination, harassment, and retaliation due to an employee's attempt to seek military service, military status, actual employee's military service, complaint about discrimination based on military status, and/or participation in an investigation regarding an of the same.

Structure of the Book

This treatise is an attempt by various practitioners (both those representing employers and those representing employees) to provide a balanced view of USERRA and its rights/obligations. This approach allows for greater education, since practitioners from 'both sides of the aisle' are providing their views of the Act and its implementation.

Chapter 1 of the treatise provides a history of USERRA and its predecessors. It briefly reviews the prior statutes in this area on a federal level and how those statutes (and the cases that interpret them) are to be squared with USERRA.

Chapter 2 discusses which employers and employees are covered by USERRA. While USERRA's application is broad, it is clear that USERRA is not without boundaries with respect to its coverage: there are situations where employers will not be required to cover certain persons taking military leave. Issues such as "successor-in-interest" employers are also discussed.

Chapter 3 outlines the entitlements employees have to take leave under USERRA. The requirements placed on both employers and employees regarding leave requests are discussed in detail.

Chapter 4 analyzes the issues of scheduling leaves and the notice requirements USERRA imposes.

Chapter 5 discusses the issue of the pay and benefits to which an employee is entitled to when taking a leave of absence under USERRA. Although leave under USERRA is unpaid, circumstances exist under which persons taking leave under USERRA are entitled to paid leave. In addition, a number of employers, particularly larger employers, provide certain amounts of paid leave for persons taking military leave. The treatise discusses these options for employers.

Chapter 6 analyzes the issue of reinstatement following an employee's release from military service. The obligations of employees and employers with respect to reinstatement are discussed, along with the position to which a returning employee is to be returned under various circumstances.

Chapters 7 and 8 review the issue of healthcare and non-healthcare benefits to which an employee properly requesting and returning from military leave are entitled to receive.

Chapter 9 discusses how USERRA interrelates with other statutes, both those on the federal level and those enacted by various states. Understanding how these statutes interrelate is important to fully understanding an employer's obligations to its employees who take military leave.

Chapter 10 discusses the discrimination, harassment, and retaliation protections USERRA provides to employees. A full understanding of these protections is critical to fully understand an employee's rights under USERRA.

Finally, Chapter 11 reviews the remedies provided under USERRA and enforcement mechanisms USERRA provides to enforce these rights.

Acknowledgments

The editors wish to thank all of those who made very significant contributions to this treatise. These include those members of the American Bar Association's Subcommittee on USERRA within the Federal Labor Standards Legislation Committee of the ABA Section of Labor and Employment Law who contributed significant time, energy and resources to preparing the subcommittee midwinter meeting reports and/or to preparation of this treatise as listed in the Board of Editors. A special thanks goes to Tim Darby at BNA, who worked hard to help develop the treatise and prepare it for publication.

We hope that this treatise allows readers to better understand USERRA and its requirements. We will continue to cover developments as case law with respect to USERRA emerges and, possibly, amendments to the statute are made; we hope that through such developments requirements under the law will become ever clearer.

GEORGE R. WOOD
OSSAI MIAZAD
Editors-in-Chief

Minneapolis, MN
New York, NY
November 2009

SUMMARY TABLE OF CONTENTS

DETAILED TABLE OF CONTENTS

CHAPTER 1

BRIEF HISTORY OF THE UNIFORMED SERVICES EMPLOYMENT AND REEMPLOYMENT RIGHTS ACT

I. OVERVIEW

Statutorily protected job security for armed services members has a long history, dating back to the Selective Training and Service Act of 1940.[1] From 1940 to today, Congress has sought to protect the reemployment rights of

---

[1] *See* Petty v. Metropolitan Gov't, 538 F.3d 431, 439 (6th Cir. 2008).

veterans.[2] The Uniformed Services Employment and Reemployment Rights Act (USERRA or the Act),[3] enacted in 1994 pursuant to the War Powers Clause,[4] represents Congress's most recent effort to create a comprehensive statutory scheme to provide civilian reemployment rights for those who serve in the armed forces.

Congress enacted USERRA in part because of a concern that "existing veteran's rights statutes [were] overly complex and ambitious, leaving veterans and employers confused as to their rights and responsibilities."[5] In enacting USERRA, Congress sought "to clarify, simplify, and where necessary, strengthen the existing veterans' employment and reemployment rights provisions."[6] Accordingly, USERRA seeks "to encourage non-career service in the uniformed services by eliminating or minimizing the disruption to civilian careers and employment which can result from such service"; "to minimize the disruption to the lives of persons performing [such] services"; and "to prohibit discrimination against persons because of their service."[7]

A brief review of Congress's prior enactments of statutorily protected leaves from civilian employment will provide needed background to understanding USERRA's enhanced provisions.

---

[2]Tilton v. Missouri Pac. R.R.,. 376 U.S. 169, 170, 84 S. Ct. 595, 597 (1964).

[3]*38 U.S.C. §§4301–4334.

[4]U.S. Const. art. I, §8, cl. 11.

[5]*Petty*, 538 F.3d at 439 (citing Francis v. Booz, Allen & Hamilton, Inc., 452 F.3d 299, 304) (4th Cir. 2006).

[6]*Id.*

[7]Smith v. U.S. Postal Service, 540 F.3d 1364, 1366 (Fed. Cir. 2008) (quoting 38 U.S.C. §4301(a)).

II. Pre-USERRA Legislation

A. Selective Training and Service Act

The Selective Training and Service Act of 1940 (STSA)[8] was aimed primarily at draftees and voluntary enlistees in World War II. It was premised on Congress's belief that an individual obligated or willing to serve the United States in its hour of need should not be penalized by loss of previous employment rights upon reentry into civilian life.[9] Several of the STSA's key provisions are still found in USERRA, albeit in a more expansive fashion.

Under the STSA, a private employer was required to restore a veteran who had satisfactorily completed military service to the veteran's former position or to "a position of like seniority, status, and pay unless the employer's circumstances [had] so changed as to make it impossible or unreasonable to restore the veteran."[10] Further, the veteran was to be restored to employment "without loss of seniority."[11] In order to trigger reemployment rights under STSA, the veteran was required to show that the individual had "left his civilian employment *in order to perform* the military service, and not for some different object."[12]

In 1946, the Supreme Court first interpreted the STSA's guarantee of reemployment "without loss of seniority" by reference to what has become known as the "escalator principle."[13] In *Fishgold v. Sullivan Drydock & Repair Corp.*, the Supreme Court observed that a veteran "does not step back on the seniority escalator at the point he stepped

---

[8]54 Stat. 885 (1940);50 U.S.C.S. App. §301.

[9]*See* Lapine v. Town of Wellesley, 304 F.3d 90, 98 (1st Cir. 2002).

[10]Accardi v. Pennsylvania R.R. Co., 383 U.S. 225, 226, 86 S. Ct. 768, 770 (1966) (citing STSA §8(c), 54 Stat. 885 (1940)). USERRA has broken these provisions into several separate sections. *See* 38 U.S.C. §4313(A), §4312(D)(1).

[11]*Id.* at 227 (citing STSA §8(b)(B)) 54 Stat. 885 (1940). *See* 38 U.S.C. §4313(a), §4316.

[12]*Lapine,* 304 F.3d at 98 (emphasis in original). *See* 38 U.S.C. §4312(a).

[13]*See* Fishgold v. Sullivan Drydock & Repair Corp., 328 U.S. 275, 284-85, 66 S. Ct. 1105, 1111 (1946).

off. He steps back on at the precise point he would have occupied had he kept his position continuously during the war."[14] In other words, a veteran "acquires not only the same seniority he had; his service in the armed services is counted as service in the plant so that he does not lose ground by reason of his absence."[15] On the other hand, "[n]o step-up or gain" is to be awarded a veteran.[16]

B. Selective Service Act of 1948

The 1940 Selective Training and Service Act was essentially reenacted as the Selective Service Act of 1948.[17]

C. Universal Military Training Service Act

In 1951, the Selective Service Act was renamed the Universal Military Training and Service Act (UMT).[18] In addition to extending veterans' reemployment rights into the post-World War II era, UMT for the first time "provided civilian reemployment protection to reservists who were called up from their civilian jobs to perform active or training duty."[19] In enacting UMT, Congress specifically noted that it intended to provide "the same reemployment rights and benefits [for reservists] as are provided for persons inducted or enlisted in the Armed Forces."[20] UMT also expressly codified the "escalator principle" developed by the Supreme Court in *Fishgold*.[21]

The following year, in 1952, the Armed Forces Reserve Act of 1952 expanded UMT's protections to include the National Guard.[22]

---

[14]*Id.*

[15]*Id.* at 285.

[16]*Id.* at 286.

[17]*See* Foster v. Dravo Corp., 420 U.S. 92, 96 n.6, 95 S. Ct. 879, 882 n.6 (1975).

[18]*See id.*

[19]*Lapine*, 304 F.3d at 98.

[20]*Id.* (citing H.R. Rep. No. 82-271 (1951), *reprinted in* 1951 U.S.C.C.A.N. 1472, 1502).

[21]*See Tilton*, 376 U.S. at 175.

[22]*See Lapine*, 304 F.3d at 98 n.8.

D. Military Selective Service Act

In 1967, UMT was renamed the Military Selective Service Act of 1967.[23] Four years later, the Act was renamed, simply, the Military Selective Service Act.[24]

E. Veterans' Reemployment Rights Act

Enacted as part of the Vietnam Era Veterans' Readjustment Act of 1974, the Veterans' Reemployment Rights Act (VRRA) is USERRA's immediate predecessor.[25] The VRRA carried forward the STSA's "nexus requirement," i.e., that to trigger the statute's protections, the employee must leave civilian employment "in order to perform" military duty.[26]

III. The Uniformed Services Employment and Reemployment Rights Act

A. 1994 Enactment

In enacting USERRA, Congress was responding to the Supreme Court's decision in *Monroe v. Standard Oil Co.*,[27] which had interpreted the VRRA's nexus requirement to mean that "claims for anti-military employment discrimination would lie only if the employee could show that the discrimination was 'motivated *solely* by reserve status.'"[28] In the House report accompanying USERRA, Congress observed that the court in *Monroe* had "misinterpreted the original legislative intent" of USERRA's predecessor statutes.[29] Accordingly, under USERRA "the employee need only show

---

[23]*See Foster,* 420 U.S. at 96 n.6.
[24]*See id.*
[25]*See* Velazquez-Garcia v. Horizon Lines, 473 F.3d 11, 16 n.6 (1st Cir. 2007).
[26]*Lapine,* 304 F.3d at 101.
[27]452 U.S. 549 (1981).
[28]*Velazquez-Garcia,* 473 F.3d at 16 (citing *Monroe v. Standard Oil,* 452 U.S. at 559).
[29]H.R. Rep. No. 103-65(I), at 24 (1994), *reprinted in* 1994 U.S.C.C.A.N. 2449, 2457).

that military service was *'a* motivating factor,'" not "the 'sole motivating factor' test of *Monroe.*"[30]

While expressly overturning *Monroe,* USERRA's legislative history specifically states that the "extensive body of case law" under its predecessor statutes "would remain in full force and effect to the extent consistent" with USERRA.[31] Accordingly, in 2005, the United States District Court for Colorado, in *Duarte v. Agilent Technologies, Inc.,* relied on two 1948 decisions for the propositions that termination of a reemployed veteran "due to the employer's adverse economic circumstances" is a permissible termination "for cause," and that more generally "the test which must be applied is whether or not the discharge by the employer was a reasonable one under the circumstances."[32]

In addition, USERRA's legislative history expressly states that it was enacted to affirm holdings in several cases providing specific rights to employees who may take military leave. For example, the House Report on USERRA specifically adopts the rationale of a Third Circuit Court of Appeals decision regarding application of employer policies providing the greatest benefits to employees taking military leave:

> The Committee intends to affirm the decision in *Waltermyer v. Aluminum Co. of America,* 804 F.2d 821 (3rd Cir. 1986) that, to the extent the employer policy or practice varies among various types of non-military leaves of absence, the most favorable treatment accorded any particular leave would also be accorded military leave, regardless of whether the non-military leave is paid or unpaid. Thus, for example, an employer cannot require servicemembers to reschedule their work week because of a conflict with reserve or National Guard duty, unless all other employees who miss work are required to reschedule their work.[33]

---

[30] *Velazquez-Garcia,* 473 F.3d at 16–17. USERRA's regulations, adopted in 2005, outline the burden of proof scheme for discrimination claims. *See* 20 C.F.R. §§1002.22, .23.

[31] *See Smith,* 540 F.3d at 1366 (citing S. Rep. No. 102-203, at 27 (1991)).

[32] *See* Duarte v. Agilent Techs., Inc., 366 F. Supp. 2d 1039, 1046 (D. Colo. 2005) (citing Ruesterholtz v. Titeflex, Inc., 166 F.2d 335 (3d Cir. 1948); Kemp v. John Chatillon & Sons, Inc., 169 F.2d 203, 206 (3d Cir. 1948)).

[33] H.R. Rep. 103-65(I) at 33 (1994 U.S.C.C.A.N. at 2466).

The House Report also states that USERRA was enacted to affirm prior interpretations of the escalator principle such that the employee need not show that he would have been promoted had the employee not been absent for military service; it is enough for the employee to demonstrate a "reasonable certainty," meaning, according to prior decisions, a "high probability" that the promotion would have occurred:

> The Committee intends to affirm the interpretation of "reasonable certainty" as "a high probability," (*see Schilz v. City of Taylor, Michigan*, 825 F.2d 944, 946 (6th Cir. 1987)), which has sometimes been expressed in percentages. *See Montgomery v. Southern Electric Steel Co.*, 410 F.2d 611, 613 (5th Cir. 1969) (90 percent success of probationary employees becoming permanent meets reasonable certainty test); *Pomrening v. United Air Lines, Inc.*, 448 F.2d 609, 615 (7th Cir. 1971) (86 percent pass rate of training class meets reasonable certainty test).[34]

The House Report contains discussion of a number of other pre-USERRA decisions, which provides further indications of Congress's legislative intent in enacting USERRA.[35]

B. USERRA's Structure and Administration

Structurally, USERRA has four primary components.

- First, 38 U.S.C. §4312 "guarantees returning veterans a right of reemployment after military service."[36]
- Second, 38 U.S.C. §4313 "prescribes the position to which such veterans are entitled upon their return."[37]
- Third, 38 U.S.C. §4311 "prevents employers from discriminating against returning veterans on account of their military service."[38]

---

[34]*Id.* at 31 (1994 U.S.C.C.A.N. at 2464).
[35]*See id.* at 19–36 (1994 U.S.C.C.A.N. at 2452–69).
[36]538 F.3d at 439.
[37]*Id.*
[38]*Id.*

- Fourth, 38 U.S.C. §4316 "prevents employers from firing without cause any returning veterans within one year of reemployment."[39]

As the Sixth Circuit noted in *Petty v. Metropolitan Government*, "At times, the interplay among these provisions has caused some confusion."[40] Some courts had held that "to recover for a reemployment violation under Section 4312, a plaintiff also must show discrimination under Section 4311," whereas others had concluded "that recovery under Section 4312 is separate from and not in any way dependent upon Section 4311."[41] The *Petty* Court embraced the Eighth Circuit's approach, according to which Section 4312 governs reemployment rights "at the instant of seeking reemployment," independently of Section 4311, which bars discrimination against those who have returned from military service "after reemployment has occurred."[42] The Sixth Circuit further clarified that Section 4311 protects not only those who were absent for military service. It also prohibits retaliation "against individuals, whether service members or not, who testify or give statements on behalf of a USERRA claimant."[43]

Since USERRA's passage, courts have consistently held that claims arising out of events that took place prior to USERRA's enactment must be determined based on the USERRA predecessor statute in effect at the time.[44]

C. 1998 Amendments

In 1998, Congress enacted the Veterans Programs Enhancement Act of 1998, making substantial changes to the

---

[39] *Id.*

[40] *Id.*

[41] *Id.* (comparing Curby v. Archon, 216 F.3d 549, 557 (6th Cir. 2000) with Wrigglesworth v. Brumbaugh, 121 F. Supp. 2d 1126, 1133–39 (W.D. Mich. 2000).

[42] *Id.* at 439–40 (citing Clegg v. Arkansas Dep't of Corr., 496 F.3d 922, 930 (8th Cir. 2007).

[43] *Id.* at 440 n.4 (citing Coffman v. Chugach Support Servs., 411 F.3d 1231, 1234 (11th Cir. 2005)).

[44] *See* Machulas v. Dept. of the Air Force, 109 M.S.P.R. 165, 170 (Merit Systems Protection Board 2008) and cases cited therein.

jurisdiction and venue provisions of USERRA.[45] Specifically, the amended Act confirmed that, with "the validity of USERRA's abrogation of state sovereign immunity … in doubt" after the Supreme Court's decision in *Seminole Tribe v. Florida*,[46] private actions against state employers must be brought in state court, even if against "an arm of the State" such as a state university.[47]

D. 2005 Regulations

It was not until 2005 that the Department of Labor, in consultation with the Department of Defense, issued regulations implementing USERRA.[48] These regulations went into effect on January 18, 2006.[49] The preliminary summary of the regulations declared, among other things, that "Congress intended that the only time-related defense that may be asserted in defending against a USERRA claim is the equitable doctrine of laches."[50] The regulations provide needed guidance to practitioners with respect to applying USERRA's protections.

E. 2008 Amendments

In 2008, Congress enacted the Veterans' Benefits Improvement Act of 2008 (VBIA), which established certain time limits for the Department of Labor's Veterans' Employment and Training Service to notify complainants of their rights;[51] for complaint investigation and resolution;[52] and for the Office of Special Counsel or Attorney General to determine whether to provide legal representation to the claimant and to notify the complainant in writing of such

---

[45]*See* Townsend v. University of Alaska, 543 F.3d 478, 482 (9th Cir. 2008).
[46]517 U.S. 44, 116 S. Ct. 1114 (1996).
[47]*Townsend*, 543 F.3d at 482–84.
[48]20 C.F.R. §1002 (2005) (published at 70 Fed. Reg. 75246 (Dec. 19, 2005)).
[49]70 Fed. Reg. at 75246.
[50]*Id.*
[51]38 U.S.C. §4322(c)(1) (5 days).
[52]38 U.S.C. §4322(f) (90 days).

decision.[53] In addition, the VBIA addressed USERRA's statute of limitations, explicitly providing that no federal or state statute of limitations applies to claims under USERRA.[54] Finally, the VBIA modifies certain requirements for reporting by the Secretary of Labor[55] and requires training for federal human resources personnel.[56]

---

[53]38 U.S.C. §4324(a)(2)(B) (60 days).

[54]38 U.S.C. §4327(b) ("If any person seeks to file a complaint or claim with the Secretary, the Merit Systems Protection Board, or a Federal or State court under this chapter alleging a violation of this chapter, there shall be no limit on the period for filing the complaint or claim"). This obviously significant amendment of USERRA largely went unnoticed.

[55]*See* 38 U.S.C. §4332.

[56]*See* 38 U.S.C. §4335.

USERRA COVERAGE ISSUES

I. Overview

Unlike many leave statutes, the Uniform Services Employment and Reemployment Rights Act (USERRA or the Act) covers all employers—regardless of size—whose employees are, or may be, absent from work because of "service in the uniformed services."[1] USERRA covers both voluntary and involuntary service for both active and/or inactive duty (such as annual National Guard training).[2] It also covers absences for examinations required to determine fitness for duty and funeral honors duty performed by National Guard or reserve members.[3] Finally, under the Public Health Security and Bioterrorism Preparedness and Response Act of 2002,[4] employees providing medical and health services as part of the National Disaster Medical System (NDMS) during a national emergency are, for the time during which such service is being provided, also covered by USERRA.[5]

---

[1] *See* 38 U.S.C. §§4303(3)–(4), 4311(a). While USERRA's leave provisions (38 U.S.C. §§4312–16) covers those employees who take, or reasonably seek to take, leave for service in the uniformed services, USERRA's discrimination section (38 U.S.C. §4311) covers all employees who complain about, or participate in the investigation of, a claim of discrimination based on military service.

[2] *See* 38 U.S.C. §4303(13).

[3] *See id.*

[4] Pub. L. 107–188, Title II, §201(a), 116 Stat. 5974, 637 (2002).

[5] *See* 20 C.F.R. §1002.5(l). An otherwise eligible employee can forfeit USERRA protection for a number of reasons, each covered elsewhere in this treatise, including a failure to comply with USERRA eligibility requirements involving notice (*see* Chapter 4); the length of the individual's service in the uniformed services (*see* Chapter 6); the nature of separation from service (i.e., whether discharge was other than honorable) (*see* Chapter 6); and the length of time elapsed between the employee's discharge from service and his or her declaration of an intent to return to work (*see* Chapter 6). This chapter is concerned solely with the threshold question of which employees are potentially eligible for USERRA coverage, which must be determined prior to any assessment of that employee's USERRA rights.

Section II of this chapter discusses the definition of a "covered employer" under USERRA. Section III discusses how USERRA defines a "covered employee." Finally, Section IV discusses the qualifying types of military service under USERRA.

II. Covered Employers

A. Introduction

USERRA defines an employer as "any person, institution, organization, or other entity that pays salary or wages for work performed or that has control over employment opportunities."[6] This term not only includes the federal government and all states,[7] but also includes "a person, institution, organization, or other entity to whom the employer has delegated the performance of employment-related responsibilities," as well as any of its or their successors in interest.[8] Reflecting the fact that USERRA's definition of "employee" covers applicants as well as current employees, the statute's definition of "employer" also reaches entities that have denied initial employment to an individual.[9] Finally, "employer" includes an employee benefit pension

---

[6]38 U.S.C. §4303(4)(A); 20 C.F.R. §1002.5(d)(1). For certain civilian employees of the Department of Defense who serve in military technician positions—and who are known as non-dual-status technicians—the term "employer" means the adjutant general of the state in which the technician is employed. See 38 U.S.C. §4303(4)(B) and 20 C.F.R. §1002.5(d)(2); see also 10 U.S.C. §10217 (defining a non-dual-status technician).

[7]"State" in this context includes not only the 50 states of the United States, but also "the District of Columbia, the Commonwealth of Puerto Rico, Guam, the Virgin Islands, and other territories of the United States (including the agencies and political subdivisions thereof)." 38 U.S.C. §4303 (14); see also 20 C.F.R. §1002.39. Actions against states brought by individuals must be brought "in a State court of competent jurisdiction in accordance with the laws of the State." 38 U.S.C. §4323(b)(2); see also Risner v. Ohio Dep't of Rehab. and Corr., 577 F. Supp. 2d 953, 960–61 (N.D. Ohio May 20, 2008) (collecting cases confirming jurisdictional limitations on private party plaintiffs bringing a USERRA claim against a state). Jurisdictional matters involving when and under what circumstances USERRA claims can be brought against states are addressed more fully in II.E. of this chapter.

[8]See id., 38 U.S.C. §4303(4)(A).

[9]See 38 U.S.C. §4303(4)(A)(v); see also 38 U.S.C. §4311(a).

plan,[10] for individuals that the plan does not actually employ, insofar as the plan has an obligation to provide such individuals with pension benefits.[11] As the Department of Labor (DOL) states in the Preamble to its USERRA regulations, "[i]n comparison to the ADA, the ADEA, and Title VII of the Civil Rights Act, USERRA's definition of 'employer' is quite different and much broader."[12]

B. Basic Coverage Standard

Unlike Title VII, USERRA does not base its coverage of an employer on an employer having a certain number of employees; even employers of just a single employee are subject to and must comply with USERRA's provisions.[13]

As with the Family and Medical Leave Act (FMLA), also administered by the DOL, the broad reach of the term *employer* under USERRA means that individual managers and supervisors, as well as the entities that employ them, may be considered "employers" and held liable under the Act.

In *Brandsasse v. City of Suffolk*,[14] for example, the court held that the City's personnel director—the individual who had allegedly denied the plaintiff's request for an accommodation that would allow him to reconcile his military obligations with a City-mandated promotional exam—was an employer within the meaning of USERRA. Because the personnel director had authority over hiring and firing, the court reasoned, she was a "person ... to whom the employer has delegated the performance of employment-related

---

[10]The definition of what constitutes an employee benefit pension plan is adopted from Section 3(2) of the Employee Retirement Income Security Act (ERISA); *see* 29 U.S.C. §1002(2); *see also* 20 C.F.R. §1002.5(d)(3).

[11]*See* 38 U.S.C. §4303(4)(C); 20 C.F.R. §1002.5(d)(3).

[12]*See* Veterans' Employment & Training Service, 70 Fed. Reg. No. 242, at 75246 (Dec. 19, 2005).

[13]*See* 38 U.S.C. §4303(4)(A); 20 C.F.R. §§ 1002.5(d)(1), .34(a); *see also* Cole v. Swint, 961 F.2d 58, 60 (5th Cir. 1992) (interpreting and applying the VRRA and rejecting employer's argument that it does not apply to "small or casual employers"; distinguishing Title VII and other laws establishing a minimum threshold number of employees before coverage is triggered).

[14]72 F. Supp. 2d 608 (E.D. Va. 1999).

responsibilities" under 38 U.S.C. Section 4304(4), and therefore potentially liable to the plaintiff.[15]

Other courts addressing the issue of potential individual liability under USERRA have generally reached a similar result.[16] In one case, a court declined to do so, but only because the supervisor who had been named as a defendant did not himself have the power to hire and fire the plaintiff, despite having been the person who was responsible for carrying out the decision to do so.[17]

C. Religious Institutions and Indian Tribes

Even when an individual or an entity fits within the broad USERRA definition of an employer, it does not always follow that every such employer is subject to USERRA's provisions. As with other employment statutes, for example, USERRA cannot be applied against employees of a religious institution when the nature of the relationship between that institution and the employee in question risks involving the government in questions of religious doctrine.[18]

USERRA also contains no explicit enforcement mechanism that might allow its application against Indian tribes; the statute's enforcement provisions generally allow for enforcement against a state, private employer, or federal agen-

---

[15]See id. at 618. The court also noted that the City, too, was potentially liable as "an entity that pays salaries or wages for work performed and controls employment opportunities through its agents," including the personnel director. See id.

[16]See, e.g., Risner v. Ohio Dep't of Rehab. and Corr., 577 F. Supp. 2d 953, 966–67 (N.D. Ohio 2008) (noting the broad statutory definition of "employer" under USERRA in concluding that two individually named defendants were proper parties); Palmatier v. Michigan Dep't of State Police, 981 F. Supp. 529 (W.D. Mich. 1997) (distinguishing between impermissible suits brought against state officials in their official capacities and USERRA-mandated, permissible suits brought against such officials in their individual capacities); Jones v. Wolf Camera, 1997 WL 22678, at *1–2 (N.D. Tex. Jan. 12, 1997) (denying motion to dismiss on ground that pleadings alone provide insufficient basis to conclude that individual defendants do not meet the definition of an "employer" under USERRA); Novak v. Mackintosh, 919 F. Supp. 870, 878 (D.S.D. 1996) (finding that the definition of "employer" under the VRRA more closely tracks the definition in the Fair Labor Standards Act than the definition in Title VII and therefore holding that VRRA imposes joint and several liability upon employers as both individuals and entities).

[17]See Brooks v. Fiore, No. 00-803GMS 2001 WL 1218448 (D. Del. Oct. 11, 2001).

[18]See generally NLRB v. Catholic Bishop, 440 U.S. 490 (1979).

cy.[19] As the DOL acknowledged in the preamble to USERRA's regulations, it does not follow that just because "USERRA likely applies to Native American tribal employers" that it can therefore be enforced against them; "there is a difference between the right to demand compliance with the law and the means to enforce it."[20] "[J]udicial enforcement of the Act against an Indian tribe," the Department continued, "depends on whether the tribe has waived its immunity, and such a waiver 'cannot be implied but must be unequivocally expressed.'"[21]

Even if USERRA does not apply to Indian tribes acting in their governmental capacity on purely internal matters, it presumably would apply to a tribal employer as long as application of USERRA did not involve the tribe's exercise of governmental power and thereby interfere with tribal self governance.[22]

D. Application of USERRA to Foreign Employers

In 1998, USERRA was amended to make clear that when a United States employer operates directly in a foreign country, or controls an entity incorporated or otherwise organized in a foreign country, actions taken by that employer operating abroad, as well as actions taken by its foreign entity, will be imputed to the U.S. employer for purposes of USERRA.[23] The question of whether an employer "controls" an entity, for purposes of determining whether that entity is subject to USERRA, is "based upon the interre-

---

[19]See 38 U.S.C. §§4323–25.

[20]70 Fed. Reg. at 75252 (citing Kiowa Tribe of Oklahoma v. Manufacturing Techs, Inc., 523 U.S. 751, 754 (1998)).

[21]Id. (quoting Santa Clara Pueblo v. Martinez, 436 U.S. 49, 58 (1978)).

[22]Compare Reich v. Great Lakes Indian Fish & Wildlife Comm'n, 4 F.3d 490, 495 (7th Cir. 1993) (Fair Labor Standards Act (FLSA) does not apply to wildlife officer of tribe because such an officer is similar to a police officer and therefore exercising governmental power), with Reich v. Mashantucket Sand & Gravel, 95 F.3d 174 (2d Cir. 1996) (OSHA applies to a tribal-owned construction company, even though the company takes direction from the tribe's Tribal Council, because its activities are of a commercial rather than governmental character).

[23]See 38 U.S.C. §4319(a); 20 C.F.R. §1002.34(c).

lation of operations, common management, centralized control of labor relations, and common ownership or financial control of the employer and the entity."[24]

Similarly, when a foreign employer has a physical location or branch in the United States (including U.S. territories or possessions), it must comply with USERRA with regard to those of its employees who are located in the United States (or U.S. territory or possession).[25] USERRA, however, does not apply to foreign operations of entities that are not controlled by a U.S. employer.[26] USERRA also does not apply when compliance with its terms would violate the law of the foreign country in which a workplace is located.[27]

E. Public Employers

As noted above,[28] USERRA's broad definition of "employer" extends to public as well as private employers, without distinction or exception. But while public entities may be "employers" under USERRA, their status as public employers nevertheless raises unique issues affecting the scope of USERRA coverage.

1. The Federal Government

The introductory section of USERRA includes a provision stating that "[i]t is the sense of Congress that the Federal Government should be a model employer in carrying out the provisions of this chapter."[29] In keeping with this goal, the scope of federal employers covered by the statute is extremely broad.[30]

---

[24]*See* 38 U.S.C. §4319(c).
[25]*See* 20 C.F.R. §1002.34(b).
[26]*See* 38 U.S.C. §4319(b).
[27]*See* 38 U.S.C. §4319(d); 20 C.F.R. §1002.34(c).
[28]*See* the introduction to Part II, *supra.*
[29]38 U.S.C. §4301(b).
[30]USERRA prescribes unique reemployment and enforcement mechanisms for federal employees. *See* 38 U.S.C. §4314 (reemployment) and 38 U.S.C. §§4324–25 (enforcement).

Having included the federal government within its definition of "employer,"[31] USERRA goes on to make clear in turn that the term "Federal Government" includes "any Federal executive agency, the legislative branch of the United States, and the judicial branch of the United States."[32] The term "Federal executive agency" is itself in turn defined as including the U.S. Postal Service and Postal Rate Commission, "any nonappropriated fund instrumentality of the United States,"[33] any military department with respect to the civilian employees of that department, and any Executive agency (subject to certain limited exceptions).[34]

The Executive agency exceptions are for those agencies "referred to in section 2302(a)(2)(C)(ii) of title 5,"[35] which includes "the Federal Bureau of Investigation, the Central Intelligence Agency, the Defense Intelligence Agency, the National Geospatial-Intelligence Agency, the National Security Agency, and, as determined by the President, any Executive agency or unit thereof the principal function of which is the conduct of foreign intelligence or counterintelligence activities."[36] The heads of each of these agencies, however, is nevertheless charged with "prescribe[ing] procedures for ensuring that the rights under [USERRA] apply to the employees of such agency"[37] and complying with USERRA's reemployment provisions "to the maximum extent practicable."[38] To the extent that an employee working for one of these agencies is denied reemployment to which the employee would have otherwise been entitled under USERRA's reemployment provisions,

---

[31]38 U.S.C. §4303(4)(A)(ii).

[32]38 U.S.C. §4303(6).

[33]In the report on USERRA submitted by the House Committee on Veterans' Affairs, examples given of "nonappropriated fund instrumentalities of the United States"— entities whose funds come from profits rather than from Congress—included military exchanges and officers' clubs. *See* H.R. Rep. No. 103-65, *reprinted in* 1994 U.S.C.C.A.N. 2449, 2455.

[34]*See* 38 U.S.C. §4303(5).

[35]*Id.*

[36]5 U.S.C. §2302(a)(2)(C)(ii).

[37]38 U.S.C. §4315(a).

[38]*Id.* §4315(b).

that employee is ensured employment in "a position in a federal executive agency" if the employee's former agency formally determines that reemployment of the employee within the employee's former agency would be "impossible or unreasonable."[39] In order to exercise this right, such an employee must submit an application to the Director of the Office of Personnel Management seeking such employment.[40]

Even when a federal employee may be covered under USERRA, that employee may not have a means of enforcing his USERRA rights. In *Conyers v. Merit Systems Protection Board*,[41] for example, the Federal Circuit Court of Appeals upheld a decision by the Merit Systems Protection Board (MSPB)[42] denying the claim of a Transportation Security Administration (TSA) employee who alleged that the TSA violated USERRA by failing to select him for a TSA position. The MSPB had held that it did not have jurisdiction over the complaint because the TSA is given authority to make appointments "notwithstanding any other provision of law,"[43] which the MSPB had interpreted as including USERRA.

2. States

Prior to its amendment in 1998, USERRA allowed federal district courts to exercise jurisdiction over all USERRA actions, including those brought by a person against a state employer.[44] Following its amendment in 1998, however, USERRA mandates that actions brought against states by individuals must be brought "in a State court of competent ju-

---

[39]*Id.* §4315(e).

[40]*See id.,* §4315(e)(3).

[41]388 F.3d 1380 (Fed. Cir. 2004).

[42]USERRA complaints made by federal employees are litigated before the MSPB, with a right of appeal to federal appellate court. *See* 38 U.S.C. §4324(a).

[43]49 U.S.C. §44935.

[44]*See* Pub. L. No. 103-353, §2, 108 Stat. 3149, 3165 (1994), *amended by* Pub. L. No. 105-368, §211(a), 112 Stat. 3315, 3329 (1998).

risdiction in accordance with the laws of the State."[45] Actions can only be brought against states in federal district court when those actions are brought by the United States.[46]

3. Political Subdivisions of States

Solely for purposes of the enforcement rights provided under USERRA Section 4323, the term *private employer* includes a political subdivision of a state.[47] Because Section 4323 allows individuals to bring suit against "private employers" in federal district court, it necessarily follows, as a result of Section 4323(j), that political subdivisions of a state, such as counties and cities, may be sued by private individuals in federal district court. The Eleventh Amendment's protections do not extend to such political subdivisions of a state.[48]

F. Successors in Interest

USERRA's definition of *employer* expressly includes "any successor in interest to a person, institution, organization, or other entity referred to in this subparagraph."[49]

---

[45]38 U.S.C. §4323(b)(2). *See also* Townsend v. University of Alaska, 543 F.3d 478 (9th Cir. 2008) (discussing 1998 USERRA amendments and confirming limitation on an individual plaintiff's ability to sue a state in federal court); McIntosh v. Partridge, 540 F.3d 315 (9th Cir. 2008) (individual suit against a state or state official acting in official capacity must be brought in state court); Risner v. Ohio Dep't of Rehab. and Corr., 577 F. Supp. 2d 953, 960–61 (N.D. Ohio (2008) (collecting cases confirming jurisdictional limitations on private party plaintiffs bringing USERRA claims against a state). The legislative history of the 1998 amendments makes clear that Congress was attempting to address the problem posed by the U.S. Supreme Court's decision in *Seminole Tribe v. Florida,* 517 U.S. 44 (1996), which limited Congressional power to abrogate a state's sovereign immunity. *See, e.g.,* 144 Cong. Rec. H1396-02, H1398 (daily ed. March 24, 1998) (Statement of Rep. Evans); *see also* Velasquez v. Frapwell, 160 F.3d 389 (7th Cir. 1998) (USERRA unconstitutional to the extent that it purports to authorize suits in federal court against states by private individuals; applying *Seminole Tribe*).
[46]*See* 38 U.S.C. §4323(b)(1).
[47]*See id.,* §4323(j).
[48]*See* Hopkins v. Clemson Agric. College, 221 U.S. 636, 645 (1911) ("neither public corporations nor political subdivisions are clothed with that immunity from suit which belongs to the State alone by virtue of its sovereignty").
[49]38 U.S.C. §4303(4)(A)(iv).

While the statute does not further define what is meant by the term *successor in interest*, USERRA's regulations and legislative history do. The House Committee on Veterans' Affairs had indicated that it intended the term *successor in interest* to be interpreted consistent with the Eighth Circuit's decision in *Leib v. Georgia Pacific Corp.*,[50] a Veterans' Reemployment Rights Act (VRRA) case in which defendant Georgia Pacific had refused to reemploy the plaintiff upon his honorable discharge from the Air Force.[51]

In *Leib*, Georgia Pacific acquired the company for which the plaintiff worked while he was serving in the military. Rejecting the employer's claim that successorship should be examined under an "ownership and control" test that looks for common ownership and control between the successor and its predecessor, the Eighth Circuit opted for a "business continuity" test that looks to the actual business activities being conducted before and after the change in control.[52] Elaborating on the factors that should be examined under this analysis, the court focused on "whether there is (1) substantial continuity of the same business operations, (2) use of the same plant, (3) continuity of workforce, (4) similarity of jobs and working conditions, (5) similarity of supervisory personnel, (6) similarity in machinery, equipment, and production methods, and (7) similarity of products or services."[53] Consistent with the direction provided by Congress, the DOL adopted the *Leib* factors when defining "successor in interest."[54]

The House Committee on Veterans' Affairs also specified that it is irrelevant whether a successor in interest is or is not actually aware that one or more employees absent for

---

[50]925 F.2d 240 (8th Cir. 1991).

[51]*See id.*

[52]*See id.* at 245.

[53]*Id.* at 247.

[54]*See* 20 C.F.R. §1002.35. The only *Leib* factor not adopted by the DOL is the sixth: "similarity in machinery, equipment, and production methods," presumably because it is itself subsumed under the factor mandating an assessment regarding the relative "similarity of jobs and working conditions."

military service worked for its predecessor.[55] Again, the applicable USERRA regulation reflects this intent, stating that "it is not necessary for an employer to have notice of a potential reemployment claim at the time of merger, acquisition, or other form of succession."[56]

The federal courts have had limited experience determining who may be a successor-in-interest employer. The first attempt, which arose prior to the DOL's USERRA regulations, came in *Coffman v. Chugach Support Services*.[57] While the plaintiff was on active duty, his employer lost a government contract and was replaced by another company. The successor hired 97 of the 100 employees who had been working for the predecessor company, but did not hire the plaintiff upon his completion of military service. The employee sued under USERRA. Upholding the district court's decision granting summary judgment for the defendant, the Eleventh Circuit ruled that "one of the fundamental requirements for consideration of the imposition of successor liability is a merger or transfer of assets between the predecessor and successor companies."[58]

The next year, in 2006, the district court for the Eastern District of Louisiana reached the opposite conclusion in another case involving a change of contractors during the period when an employee was on military leave.[59] Noting that neither the *Leib* test nor the applicable USERRA regulations address a required transfer of assets between predecessor and successor, the court noted that the regulations had been issued after *Coffman* was decided.[60] Quoting Section 1002.36 of those regulations, the court noted that its inclusion of the phrase "or other form of succession" as the recognition of "a residual category in which a party can become a successor-in-interest without a merger or acquisi-

---

[55]*See* H.R. Rep. No. 103-65, *reprinted in* 1994 U.S.C.C.A.N. 2449 at 2454.
[56]20 C.F.R. §1002.36.
[57]411 F.3d 1231 (11th Cir. 2005).
[58]*Id.* at 1237.
[59]*See* Murphree v. Communications Techs., Inc., 460 F. Supp. 2d 702 (E.D. La. 2006).
[60]*See id.* at 707–08.

tion."[61] "Thus," the court concluded, "while the existence of a merger or transfer of assets can be relevant, it is not determinative of the successor-in-interest rule."[62]

Finally, in *Reynolds v. RehabCare Group East, Inc.*,[63] the United States District Court for the Southern District of Iowa rejected the plaintiff's claim that a rehabilitation company was her successor-in-interest employer. The plaintiff had worked for a rehabilitation company that provided services to a nursing home on a contract basis. While the plaintiff was on military leave, her employer lost that contract and the defendant entered into a new contract with the nursing home. The district court rejected the plaintiff's claim that this change in suppliers was sufficient to establish a successor-in-interest employer under USERRA.[64]

G. Joint Employment Hiring Halls

While USERRA does not expressly refer to joint employers, the statute includes within its definition of *employer* "a person, institution, organization, or other entity to whom the employer has delegated the performance of employment-related responsibilities."[65] The DOL therefore had little trouble, when issuing its implementing regulations, including joint employers within the definition of employer, noting that in cases in which one entity may pay an individual's wages while a second entity controls the individual's day-to-day employment opportunities, "both employers share responsibility for compliance with USERRA."[66] Quoting the same statutory language, the DOL also extended

---

[61]*Id.*; *see also* the discussion of 20 C.F.R. §1002.36 at *supra*, n.55.

[62]*Id.* at 708.

[63]590 F. Supp. 2d 1107 (S.D. Iowa 2008). The district court issued a prior ruling on a motion for a preliminary injunction, which ruling is found at 531 F. Supp. 2d 1050 (S.D. Iowa 2008).

[64]*See* 590 F. Supp. 2d at 1122. *Reynolds* is currently on appeal to the United States Court of Appeals for the Eighth Circuit. One of the editors, Mr. Wood, represents the defendant in that matter.

[65]38 U.S.C. §4303(4)A)(i).

[66]20 C.F.R. §1002.37.

this principle to hiring halls, stating that "[a] hiring hall therefore is considered the employee's employer if the hiring and job assignment functions have been delegated by an employer to the hiring hall."[67]

USERRA's legislative history supports the inclusion of joint employers, including hiring halls, within the definition of *employer*. Commenting on the meaning of this term under USERRA, the House Report states that it

> includes not only what may be considered a "traditional" single employer relationship, but also (1) those under which a service-member works for several employers in industries such as construction, longshoring, etc., where the employees are referred to employment, and (2) those where more than one entity may exercise control over different aspects of the employment relationship.[68]

III. Covered Employees

A. Introduction

Mirroring and complementing its definition of the term *employer*, USERRA includes an equally broad definition of the term *employee*, which is defined as "any person employed by an employer."[69] In practice, that definition proves deceptively simple. For example, individuals who are not yet "employed by an employer" but who have applied for such employment are nevertheless covered by USERRA's anti-discrimination provision, which not only prohibits discrimination against employees but also against individuals who have applied for "initial employment."[70] Other individuals who are clearly employees under the statutory definition are, because of the "brief, nonrecurrent" nature of their employment prior to going on leave, not entitled to the same panoply of rights available to other employees on

---

[67]*Id.* §1002.38.

[68]H.R. Rep. No. 103-65, *reprinted in* 1994 U.S.C.C.A.N. 2449, 2454.

[69]38 U.S.C. §4303(3).

[70]*Id.* §4311(a); *see also* 20 C.F.R. §1002.40 (addressing protections against discrimination for applicants).

military leave.[71] Reflecting USERRA's application to U.S. employers operating abroad and to foreign employers operating within the United States,[72] USERRA's definition of *employee* includes "any person who is a citizen, national, or permanent resident alien of the United States employed in a workplace in a foreign country by an employer that is an entity incorporated or otherwise incorporated in the United States or that is controlled by an entity organized in the United States," with the determination of whether an employer controls an entity being based upon the "interrelations of operations, common management, centralized control of labor relations, and common ownership or financial control of the employer and the entity."[73]

B. Temporary Employees

As the broad definition of *employee* suggests, USERRA applies to temporary and seasonal employees.[74] But consistent with application of the escalator principle—which attempts to place an employee upon return from leave in the position that most closely approximates the position the employee would have held if he or she had never taken military leave[75]—USERRA qualifies an employee's right to return to a previously held job or workplace if the employee was in a temporary position at the time when leave began. The statute therefore makes clear that "[a]n employer is not required to reemploy a person" under USERRA if "the employment from which the person leaves to serve in the uniformed services is for a brief, nonrecurrent period and there is no reasonable expectation that such employment will continue indefinitely or for a significant period."[76] Re-

---

[71]*See* 38 U.S.C. §4312(d)(1)(C), and *infra* at Part III, Section B.
[72]*See* Part II, Section D.
[73]38 U.S.C. §4303(3); *id.* §4319(c).
[74]*See* 20 C.F.R. §1002.41.
[75]*See generally* 38 U.S.C. §4313.
[76]38 U.S.C. §4312(d)(1)(C); *see also* 20 C.F.R. §1002.41. The positions falling within the scope of this exclusion are not specifically described.

gardless of whether an employee is classified as occupying such a position and is thereby without the reemployment rights otherwise provided by USERRA, all employees—including those occupying such temporary positions—are covered under USERRA's antidiscrimination provisions.[77] Similarly, employees taking military leave, regardless of the nature of the employment position they hold immediately prior to the beginning of that leave, are entitled to non–seniority-based benefits to the same extent that such benefits are provided to similarly situated employees on comparable, non-military leave.[78]

Whether an employee is truly "temporary" for purposes of USERRA's exception to an employer's otherwise applicable reemployment obligations will be determined by the facts and circumstances of an employee's employment position rather than on the basis of how that position is labeled. The legislative history indicates that such a determination should be guided by the concepts outlined in *Stevens v. Tennessee Valley Authority*, a Sixth Circuit case decided under the VRRA.[79]

In *Stevens*, the Tennessee Valley Authority refused to reemploy an hourly construction worker upon his completion of military service because a collective bargaining agreement stated unequivocally that construction workers are to be classified as temporary employees. While the Sixth Circuit acknowledged that "an employer is free to create both temporary and non-temporary positions," it simultaneously cautioned that an employer "cannot do so simply by designating a particular position as 'temporary,' if, in fact, the characteristics of that position make it non-temporary."[80] What counts in determining whether a position is temporary, the Sixth Circuit continued, "is whether, regard-

---

[77]38 U.S.C. §4311(d); *see also* 20 C.F.R. §1002.41.
[78]*See* 70 Fed. Reg. 75253, citing 38 U.S.C. §4316(b)(1)(B).
[79]H.R. Rep. No 103-65, *reprinted in* 1994 U.S.C.C.A.N. 2449, 2455 (citing *Stevens*, 687 F.2d 158 (6th Cir. 1982)).
[80]687 F.2d at 161.

less of the contract of employment, there was a reasonable expectation that the employment would be continuous and for an indefinite time."[81]

The mere fact that an employee is hired for a fixed term, therefore, is not determinative; if it were, an at-will employee would invariably enjoy greater protections than an employee under contract.[82] Similarly, the Sixth Circuit noted that "a seasonal employee who is hired for a short period only, but nevertheless has a reasonable expectation of reemployment on a regular basis in the future, enjoys a right to reemployment."[83] Even an employee subject to periodic layoffs would not be temporary if that employee were to retain previously earned seniority during the layoffs.[84]

As stated in the preamble to USERRA's regulations, probationary or apprenticed employees—who may not be "permanent," but who are not temporary simply because their positions remain unsettled and conditional—are entitled to reemployment.[85] If the apprentice or probationary period requires actual training or observation, "the employee should be allowed to complete the apprenticeship or probationary period following reemployment."[86] If the returning employee successfully completes this trial period, "the employee's pay and seniority should reflect both the pre- and post-service time in the apprenticeship or probationary period, plus the time served in the military."[87]

An employee is not required to prove that a position is other than temporary; rather, the employer must shoulder the burden of proving "the brief or nonrecurrent nature of

---

[81]*Id.*

[82]*See id.* at 162.

[83]*Id.*

[84]*See id.*

[85]*See* 70 Fed. Reg. at 75272.

[86]*Id.*

[87]*Id.* Application of the escalator principle, in this and other contexts, is discussed more fully in Chapter 6 of this treatise.

the employment without a reasonable expectation of continuing indefinitely or for a significant period."[88]

C. Independent Contractors

USERRA does not apply to independent contractors,[89] which begs the question of how to determine who qualifies as an independent contractor under the statute.

USERRA's legislative history points toward an answer by indicating that the statute's definition of *employee* should be applied "in the same expansive manner as under the Fair Labor Standards Act,[90] except that temporary employees are not covered."[91] In the regulatory preamble, the DOL refers to that legislative history in explaining why USERRA's regulations prescribe the broad "economic reality" test, rather than the more narrowly tailored "degree of control" test, in determining whether an individual is an independent contractor or an employee.[92] The "degree of control" test focuses primarily on the hiring party's right to control the manner and means by which work is to be accomplished.[93] Conversely, the "economic reality" test focuses on "whether the individual is economically dependent on the business to which he or she renders service or is, as a matter of economic fact, in business for him- or herself."[94]

Applying the "economic reality" test, the applicable USERRA regulation outlines six factors to consider in determining whether an individual is an employee or an independent contractor, making clear that, in doing so, "[n]o

---

[88] *See* 38 U.S.C. §4312(d)(2); *see also* 20 C.F.R. §1002.41 (characterizing establishment of the "temporary" nature of an employment position as an "affirmative defense").

[89] *See* 20 C.F.R. §1002.44(a).

[90] 29 U.S.C. §203(e).

[91] H.R. Rep. No 103-65, *reprinted in* 1994 U.S.C.C.A.N. 2449, 2454.

[92] 70 Fed. Reg. at 75254.

[93] *See id.* at 75253-54 (quoting Nationwide Mut. Ins. Co. v. Darden, 503 U.S. 318 (1992)).

[94] *See id.* at 75254 (quoting Bartels v. Birmingham, 332 U.S. 126, 130 (1947)).

single one of these factors is controlling, but all are relevant" in making that determination.[95] Those six factors are:

(1) The extent of the employer's right to control the manner in which the individual's work is to be performed;

(2) The opportunity for profit or loss that depends upon the individual's managerial skill;

(3) Any investment in equipment or materials required for the individual's tasks, or his or her employment of helpers;

(4) Whether the service the individual performs requires a special skill;

(5) The degree of permanence of the individual's working relationship; and,

(6) Whether the service the individual performs is an integral part of the employer's business.[96]

D. Former Employees

Although USERRA's definition of "employee" does not distinguish current from former employees, the legislative history confirms that the statutory definition of *employee* was intended to cover former employees as well.[97] Acknowledging this legislative history in the Preamble to USERRA's regulations,[98] the DOL's interpretation of "employee" states expressly that "'[e]mployee' includes the former employees of an employer."[99] This extension of the term "employee" to former employees ensures protection for those individuals who are administratively terminated during a military leave. While the DOL permits such terminations,[100] the conse-

---

[95]20 C.F.R. §1002.44(c).

[96]*See id.*, §1002.44(b).

[97]*See* H.R. Rep. No 103-65, *reprinted in* 1994 U.S.C.C.A.N. 2449, 2454 (citing Bailey v. USX Corp., 850 F.2d 1506, 1509 (11th Cir. 1988)); *see also* S. Rep. No. 103-158 at 41 (1993).

[98]70 Fed. Reg. at 75249 ("Congress intended that the term employee would include former employees of an employer"; citation omitted).

[99]20 C.F.R. §1002.5(c).

[100]*See* 20 C.F.R. §1002.149 and discussion of the same in the Preamble to the regulations at 70 Fed. Reg. 75263 (Dec. 19, 2005).

quent designation of an individual as terminated, or as a "former employee," does not undermine that individual's entitlement to the same USERRA protections that would otherwise be available to the individual.

E. Family Members of Employees

Broad as the definition of "employee" is under USERRA, it does not extend protections and benefits to family members of individuals who are on military leave. Under the 2008 National Defense Authorization Act, however, covered family members—including spouses, parents, and children, and also including next of kin under certain circumstances—are entitled to take protected leave from employment under the federal FMLA if those employees would otherwise be eligible for FMLA leave.[101] The fiscal year 2010 Defense Authorization Act further amended the FMLA to broaden coverage of the provisions added to that law in the 2008 National Defense Authorization Act dealing with qualifying exigency leave and military caregiver leave, extending qualifying exigency leave provisions to active duty members. The legislation also extended military caregiver leave provisions to family members of veterans.[102]

IV. COVERED FORMS OF SERVICE IN THE UNIFORMED SERVICES

A. Introduction

One purpose of USERRA is "to encourage noncareer service in the uniformed services by eliminating or minimizing the disadvantages to civilian careers and employment

---

[101] *See* 29 U.S.C. §2612 and 29 C.F.R. §§825.126–27. A discussion of family military leave is beyond the scope of this treatise.

[102] *See* the discussion of this topic in ABA SECTION OF LABOR AND EMPLOYMENT LAW, THE FAMILY AND MEDICAL LEAVE ACT, 2010 CUMULATIVE SUPPLEMENT (Gail C. Coleman ed., BNA Books 2010).

which can result from such service ... minimiz[ing] the disruption to the lives of persons performing services in the uniformed services," and "prohibit[ing] discrimination against persons because of their service in the uniformed services."[103] Determining what constitutes "service in the uniformed services" under USERRA, therefore, is integral to determining whom USERRA covers and protects.

USERRA makes clear that "service in the uniformed services" can be voluntary or involuntary.[104] It includes active duty, active duty for training, initial active duty for training, inactive duty training, and full-time National Guard duty.[105] "Service in the uniformed services" also includes "a period for which a person is absent from a position of employment for the purpose of an examination to determine the fitness of the person to perform any such duty."[106] And "service in the uniformed services" includes "a period for which a person is absent from employment for the purpose of performing funeral honors duty as authorized by section 12503 of title 10 or section 115 of title 32."[107]

B. Covered "Uniformed Services" Under USERRA

Only service in one of the covered "uniformed services" is protected service under USERRA. USERRA defines the "uniformed services" as:

> [T]he Armed Forces, the Army National Guard and the Air National Guard when engaged in active duty for training, inactive duty training, or full-time National Guard duty, the commissioned corps of the Public Health Service, and any other category of persons designated by the President in time of war or national emergency.[108]

---

[103]38 U.S.C. §4301.

[104]*See* 38 U.S.C. §4303(13).

[105]*See id.*

[106]*Id.*

[107]*Id.* The two statutory sections referred to above prescribe the terms under which reservists and members of the National Guard perform funeral honors duty.

[108]38 U.S.C. §4303(16); *see also* 20 C.F.R. §1002.5(o)

While USERRA begins by expressing the intent of encouraging noncareer service in the military,[109] and while the DOL acknowledges that USERRA is "most often understood as applying to National Guard and reserve military personnel,"[110] the statutory definition of "uniformed services" expresses Congress's intent that USERRA "cove[r] all categories of military training and service" and therefore protect "persons serving in the active components of the Armed Forces" as well as individuals serving in the National Guard or the reserves.[111]

C. Applicants for Service in the Uniformed Services

Just as USERRA applies to applicants for employment as well as employees, so too does it apply to employees who are applying to one of the covered uniformed services. The statute's broadly worded antidiscrimination provision makes clear that applicants to serve are entitled to the same protections as those covered individuals who are already serving in the uniformed services:

> A person who is a member of, applies to be a member of, performs, has performed, applies to perform, or has an obligation to perform service in a uniformed service shall not be denied initial employment, reemployment, retention in employment, promotion, or any benefit of employment by an employer on the basis of that membership, application for membership, performance of service, application for service, or obligation.[112]

The DOL underscored this point in the regulatory preamble, which specifically references applicants for service in the uniformed services as among those individuals protected by USERRA.[113] Coverage of applicants for service is also implicit in the inclusion, within the statutory definition of "service in the uniformed services," of "a period for

---

[109]*See* 38 U.S.C. §4301(a)(1).
[110]20 C.F.R. §1002.6.
[111]*Id.*
[112]38 U.S.C. §4311(a).
[113]*See* 70 Fed. Reg. at 75249; *see also* 20 C.F.R. §1002.18.

which a person is absent from a position of employment for the purpose of an examination to determine the fitness of the person to perform any such duty."[114] Individuals sent for such examinations will ordinarily be prospective recruits, with the outcome of the examination determining the applicant's eligibility for service in the uniformed services. Upon return from such an examination, an applicant is entitled to the same prompt employment that USERRA mandates for all eligible employees returning from a military leave.[115]

D. Service in the National Disaster Medical System

In the wake of the September 11, 2001, terrorist attacks and the ensuing anthrax scare, Congress in June 2002 passed the Public Health Security and Bioterrorism Preparedness and Response Act of 2002, which extends USERRA protection to individuals serving as intermittent disaster-response appointees of the National Disaster Medical System (NDMS) when the Secretary of Health and Human Services activates that system.[116] The same protections are also conferred by the NDMS on individuals who "participat[e] in a training program authorized by the Assistant Secretary for Preparedness and Response or a comparable official" from the Department of Health and Human Services, the Department of Homeland Security, the Department of Defense, or the Department of Veterans Affairs.[117]

---

[114]38 U.S.C. §4303(13); *see also* Part IV, Section A, of this chapter, *supra.*

[115]*See* 38 U.S.C. §4313(a) and 20 C.F.R. §§180–81. The nature of an employer's reemployment obligation under USERRA is also discussed more fully in chapter 6 of this treatise.

[116]*See* 42 U.S.C. §300hh-11; *see also* 20 C.F.R. §1002.5(l), 20 C.F.R. §1002.5(o), and 20 C.F.R. §1002.6 (addressing extension of USERRA protection to intermittent disaster response appointees).

[117]*See* 42 U.S.C. §§300hh-11(d)(3), 11(a)(2)(B). The USERRA regulations designate this section as 42 U.S.C. §300hh-11(e) rather than as 42 U.S.C. §300hh-11(d); *see* 20 C.F.R. §1002.5(l). Subsequent to the implementation of the final USERRA regulations in December 2005, however, 42 U.S.C. §300hh-11(a) was deleted and the remaining sections of 42 U.S.C. §300hh-11 were renumbered by the passage of Pub. L. No. 109-417 (2006), §301(a)(2).

Although not included within USERRA's own statutory definition of "uniformed services,"[118] service by such individuals "shall," under the statutory scheme creating the NDMS, "be deemed 'service in the uniformed services' for purposes of [USERRA], pertaining to employment and reemployment rights of individuals who have performed service in the uniformed services" under USERRA.[119] NDMS members covered by this provision are also entitled to "[a]ll rights and obligations . . . and procedures for assistance, enforcement, and investigation" provided by USERRA.[120]

The NDMS is designed to work in conjunction with state and local entities in developing a coordinated response to major peacetime disasters by providing health services, health-related social services, and related auxiliary services to victims of such disasters through a network of civilian medical teams and hospitals.[121] An example of a disaster that has involved the NDMS is Hurricane Katrina in the fall of 2005; the NDMS played a major role in providing medical relief and services to victims of Katrina in Louisiana, Mississippi, and Texas.

Because of the nature of those services provided under the auspices of the NDMS, and the rapidity with which individuals providing them might be called into the field, such individuals may often be unable to provide advance notice of an absence from employment. The same Act that extended USERRA to certain NDMS members also makes clear that NDMS members who are not able to provide advance notice of their need for leave are excused from providing such notice if, as with employees performing military service in one of the "uniformed services," they are unable to

---

[118]See 38 U.S.C. §4303(16); see also Part IV, Section B, of this chapter, supra.
[119]42 U.S.C. §300hh-11(d)(3)(A).
[120]Id.
[121]See 42 U.S.C. §300hh-11(a)(3); see also the description of the NDMS at 20 C.F.R. §1002.05(f) and in the Preamble to USERRA's regulations at 70 Fed. Reg. at 75247–48 (Dec. 19, 2005).

provide notice because of "necessity."[122] For NDMS members, however, such a qualifying "necessity" need not be a qualifying "military" necessity as determined by the Secretary of Defense. Rather, as determined by the Secretary of Health and Human Services and in consultation with the Secretary of Defense, necessity for NDMS members excuses USERRA's advance notice request for taking leave.[123] As with a determination of "military necessity" under USERRA, a determination of "necessity" by the Secretary of Health and Human Services is not subject to judicial review.[124]

---

[122]*Compare* 38 U.S.C. §4312(b) (addressing "military necessity" which, under USERRA, would excuse an employee's otherwise applicable obligation to provide advance notice of military leave) *with* 42 U.S.C. §300hh-11(d)(3)(B) (equating "necessity" for purposes of service in the NDMS with "military necessity" under USERRA for purposes of excusing the provision of notice). For further discussion regarding the provision of notice under USERRA, see Chapter 4 of this treatise.

[123]*Id.*

[124]*See id.*

LEAVE ENTITLEMENTS UNDER USERRA

I. Overview

Under the Uniformed Services Employment and Reemployment Rights Act of 1994 (USERRA or the Act), all public and private sector employers are required to provide leaves of absence to employees who perform, on a voluntary or involuntary basis, service in the uniformed services.[1] Unlike most other federal leave statutes, USERRA applies to all employers, regardless of the number of persons employed.[2] One of USERRA's main purposes is to provide non-career service members with the basic guarantee that they will have jobs with their employers upon return from military service.[3] To that end, USERRA covers leave for "service" performed in a "uniformed service."[4] "Service" includes active duty, inactive and active duty training, full time National Guard duty, any time spent undergoing fitness-for-duty examinations, funeral honors duty, and duty performed by intermittent employees of the National Disaster Medical System in training exercises or in response to public health

---

[1] See 38 U.S.C. §§4301 et seq.
[2] See id., §4303(4)(A).
[3] See id., §4301(a)(1).
[4] See id., §4303(13).

3-2 USERRA Ch. 3 I.

emergencies.[5] This protection covers full-time, part-time, probationary, or seasonal employees as well as temporary employees unless they have no realistic expectation of on-going employment.[6] Most states regulate military leave in some manner, with many providing similar or additional protections to employees with military service obligations.[7] USERRA supersedes less generous state laws that seek to limit or condition the rights the Act provides.[8] However, where state- or employer-provided rights or benefits are more generous than the provisions of USERRA, whether pursuant to state law, policy, practice, plan, contract, or agreement, USERRA will not preempt claims for the more generous rights and benefits.[9] Employees returning from military leave are provided additional protection beyond mere reinstatement. If the employee's period of service during the leave was between 30 and 180 days, the employee may not be terminated, except for cause, within 180 days of reemployment.[10] If the leave was more than 180 days, the employee may not be terminated without cause within one year after the date of reemployment.[11]

II. FIVE-YEAR SERVICE PERIOD

USERRA grants employees who have military service obligations a total of five years of leave while employed by a particular employer.[12] Employees who work for more than

---

[5] *See id.* The "uniformed services" include the Armed Forces, the Army National Guard and the Air National Guard, the Commissioned Corps of the Public Health Service and any other category of persons the President may designate in time of war or national emergency. *See id.*, §4303(16).

[6] *See id.*, §4303(3).

[7] *See* Appendix E, State Military Leave Laws.

[8] *See* 38 U.S.C. §4302(b).

[9] *See id.*, §4302(a)

[10] *See id.*, §4316(c)(1); 20 C.F.R. §1002.247(a). The term "cause" is defined in the U.S. Department of Labor's regulations adopted pursuant to USERRA. *See* 20 C.F.R. §1002.248. "Cause" means "conduct that would constitute cause for discharge" or the application of "other legitimate, nondiscriminatory reasons" for discharge. *See id.*

[11] *See* 38 U.S.C. §4316(c)(2); 20 C.F.R. §1002.247(b).

[12] *See* 38 U.S.C. §4312(a)(2).

one employer may have up to five years of service for each employer.[13] This five-year limit obviously is substantial. USERRA, however, also provides that certain types of military service do not count towards the five-year limit, thereby extending that limit beyond five years in a number of circumstances.[14] There are four basic categories of service that do not count toward the five-year limit under USERRA:

1. Service that is required beyond five years to complete an initial period of obligated service;[15]

2. A period during which employees are unable to obtain orders of release, through no fault of their own, before the expiration of the five-year period;[16]

3. The period that is needed to fulfill additional training requirements as certified in writing by the Secretary of Defense to be necessary for professional development or completion of skill training;[17]

4. The period during which members of the uniformed services are ordered to active duty during a war or national emergency as declared by the President or Congress or other active duty orders.[18]

III. USE OF VACATION OR PAID TIME OFF

Under USERRA, it is unlawful to force employees to use vacation or other paid time off benefits for covered military obligations.[19] At the same time, USERRA requires that

---

[13]*See id.*, §§4303(3), (4)(A), 4312(a).

[14]*See id.*, §4312(c).

[15]*See id.*, §4312(c)(1). This exception would apply if, for example, an individual enlisted in a program where the initial service obligation was six years long. At the end of this period of service, the employee would be considered to have exhausted his five-year leave period under USERRA and, despite the six-year term of service, would be permitted to seek reinstatement assuming the employee meets USERRA's other reinstatement obligations.

[16]*See id.*, §4312(c)(2).

[17]*See id.*, §4312(c)(3). This includes periods of Reserve and National Guard training in which many employees participate. Thus, employers may not count this annual service obligation toward the five-year limit.

[18]*See id.*, §4312(c)(4).

[19]*See id.*, §4316(d).

an employer permit its employees to use paid time off if they so request.[20] USERRA, however, has been interpreted as permitting an employer to provide certain categories of service members with benefits not provided to non-service members.

In *Welshans v. United States Postal Service*,[21] the United States Court of Appeals for the Federal Circuit held that the United States Postal Service's (USPS) military leave policy did not violate USERRA where it afforded additional protections to reserve members that non-reserve members did not receive. The plaintiff, a reservist in the United States Army and a USPS employee, filed an appeal with the Merit Systems Protection Board claiming that the USPS improperly charged him for military leave in violation of USERRA. Specifically, the plaintiff claimed that charging him with military leave for non-workdays is a USERRA violation. After the Board dismissed his claim, he appealed. On appeal, the Federal Circuit held that the USPS's military leave policy did not violate USERRA. The policy granted reservists sick leave, annual leave, and military leave, while non-reservists were entitled only to sick leave and annual leave. The court held that "[r]egardless of whether non-workdays are charged against military leave, such leave is a benefit available only to employees serving in the military. USERRA prohibits discrimination against reservists because of their service; there is nothing in the statute to prevent an agency from granting them benefits not available to other employees."[22]

The breadth of USERRA's obligations with respect to leave entitlements—and the possible problems employers face who fail to honor those entitlements—is demonstrated by the Sixth Circuit Court of Appeals' decision in *Koehler v.*

---

[20] *See id.*
[21] 550 F.3d. 1100 (Fed. Cir. 2008).
[22] *See id.*

PepsiAmericas, Inc.[23] The plaintiff, one of the defendant's salespeople, enlisted in the Army Reserves. On several occasions over the next several years, the plaintiff was called to active duty with less than one day's notice. The defendant charged the plaintiff with either unexcused absences or personal time off for the absences. In addition, although the defendant had a policy granting certain employees on military leave a pay differential, the defendant refused to provide this pay to the plaintiff. At one point, the defendant paid the plaintiff the pay differential and then later reversed the payment and withdrew the amount from the plaintiff's bank account without his permission. Based on these actions, the district court found, and the Sixth Circuit agreed, that the defendant had violated USERRA by charging the plaintiff for absences that were related to his military service. The Sixth Circuit also held that requiring the plaintiff to use paid time off was a USERRA violation. Indeed, the violations were considered willful and defendant was ordered to pay liquidated damages.[24]

---

[23]268 F. Appx. 396 (6th Cir. 2008).
[24]*See id.* at **6–8.

Chapter 4

SCHEDULING LEAVES AND PROVIDING LEAVE NOTICE

I. Notice

A. USERRA's General Notice Requirement

To be eligible for leave under the Uniformed Services Employment and Reemployment Rights Act (USERRA), and to obtain USERRA's reemployment rights, an employee is required to provide his or her employer with advance notice that he or she will be absent from work due to upcoming military service.[1] Notice of military service may be given orally or in writing.[2] An employee is not obligated to provide the notice in any particular format and employers may not impose any particular notice requirements on employees.[3]

Alternatively, an "appropriate officer" from the employee's service branch may provide notice of military service to the employer on the employee's behalf.[4] USERRA's regulations define an "appropriate officer" as "a commissioned, warrant, or non-commissioned officer authorized to give such notice by the military service concerned."[5] Notice provided by an officer from the employee's service branch may also be made orally or in writing.[6]

Unlike the Family and Medical Leave Act,[7] USERRA contains no time frames within which an employee must notify his employer of upcoming military service.[8] The Department of Defense (DOD), however, recommends that service men and women provide at least 30 days' notice to their civilian employers when feasible.[9] USERRA's regulations advise employees to provide notice "as far in advance as is reasonable under the circumstances"[10] and adopt the DOD's 30-day recommendation.[11]

To date, no cases have directly addressed the issue of the amount of advance notice an employee must provide under USERRA. Courts, however, have considered whether an employer's requirement that an employee complete certain forms in connection with upcoming military service violates USERRA's notice provision. These cases suggest that

---

[1] See 38 U.S.C. §4312(a); 20 C.F.R. §1002.85(a).
[2] See 20 C.F.R. §1002.85(c).
[3] See id.
[4] 38 U.S.C. §4312(a)(1); 20 C.F.R. §1002.85(b).
[5] 20 C.F.R. §1002.85(b).
[6] See 38 U.S.C. §4312(a)(1).
[7] See 29 C.F.R. §825.302.
[8] See 38 U.S.C. §4312(a)(1); 20 C.F.R. §1002.85(d).
[9] See 32 C.F.R. §104.6(a)(2)(i)(B).
[10] See 20 C.F.R. §1002.85(c).
[11] See id., §1002.85(d).

employers may require employees to complete certain forms to document upcoming military leave provided that the forms are not intended to serve as prerequisites to an employee's exercise of USERRA rights.

In *Brooks v. Fiore*,[12] the employer maintained a pay differential policy for employees called to military service. Pursuant to this policy, the employer agreed to pay employees the difference between an employee's military pay and the employee's regular pay, provided, however, that the employee complete a form requesting leave. The employee asserted that the employer had violated USERRA's notice requirement because of the obligation to complete a form to obtain paid leave. The United States District Court for the District of Delaware rejected the employee's claim, reasoning that USERRA's notice provision did not prohibit employers from "requiring certain notification procedures or documentation of military leave," as long as those procedures did not impose formal notice requirements in order to take leave under USERRA.[13] Because the form in question dealt with voluntary pay provided by the employer, and was not intended to impose notice requirements on employees in order to take leave under USERRA, no actionable claim existed for violation of Section 4312's notice requirement.[14]

Similarly, in *Boelter v. City of Coon Rapids*,[15] the United States District Court for the District of Minnesota considered whether an employer violated USERRA's notice provision by requiring firefighters taking military leave to complete a form in order to track hours under a state statute governing pay requirements for government employees on military leave. The court rejected the plaintiffs' claim that the form violated USERRA's notice requirement. Because the form was not intended to provide notice of military ser-

---

[12] 2001 WL 1218448 at *10 (D. Del. Oct. 11, 2001).
[13] *Id.*
[14] *See id.*
[15] 67 F. Supp. 2d 1040, 1051 (D. Minn. 1999).

vice under USERRA, but rather was used to document the plaintiffs' eligibility for paid military leave under a separate state statute, no USERRA violation existed.[16]

Two circumstances exist under USERRA where the giving of advance notice of military leave is excused. Each will be discussed in turn.

B. Excusing the Requirement of Advance Notice Because of "Military Necessity"

The first instance where advanced notice of a military leave is excused is where notice is not given because of "military necessity."[17] The determination of whether "military necessity" exists is not made by the employee or his employer; nor is it a term that may be defined by the courts.[18] Rather, a designated military authority makes the decision regarding whether "military necessity" exists.[19] Such decisions are not subject to judicial review.[20]

USERRA'S regulations[21] direct employers and employees to the DOD's regulations, which define "military necessity" as follows:

> A mission, operation, exercise or requirement that is classified, or a pending or ongoing mission, operation, exercise or requirement that may be compromised or otherwise adversely affected by public knowledge is sufficient justification for not providing advance notice to an employer.[22]

USERRA's regulations paraphrase this definition.[23] Ultimately, an employer may not know at the time an employee is absent from work that the employee has gone on military

---

[16] See id.

[17] See 38 U.S.C. §4312(b); 20 C.F.R. §1002.86.

[18] See 20 C.F.R. §1002.86(a), which states that the determination of "military necessity" is not subject to judicial review once made by the appropriate designated military authority. Presumably, this lack of judicial review means that the courts may not, in the first instance, interpret the phrase "military necessity."

[19] See id.

[20] See id.

[21] See id.

[22] 32 C.F.R. §104.3.

[23] See 20 C.F.R. §1002.86(a).

leave and that advance notice was not required due to military necessity. Employers, therefore, are cautioned to be patient with this process and simply place the employee on leave pending the receipt of additional information, which may be no more than a statement from the appropriate designated military authority that "military necessity" precluded advance notice in a particular instance.

Also, in certain cases, the United States Department of Homeland Security may make a determination, in consultation with the Secretary of Defense, that advance notice of intermittent disaster response appointees under the National Disaster Medical System is precluded by "medical necessity."[24] Once again, an employer may not know this fact until after the employee has left work unexpectedly and without notice, and must be patient with the process.

C. Excusing the Requirement of Advance Notice Because It Is Unreasonable or Impossible

The second instance in which advance notice is not required under USERRA is where the giving of such notice is either "impossible" or "unreasonable" under "all relevant circumstances."[25] USERRA's regulations help to define several situations in which it may be "impossible or unreasonable" for an employee to give advance notice.[26] These include situations where the employer or its representative is unavailable to give the required notice and where the employee is required to report for military service "in an extremely short period of time."[27] These are just several examples of where it may be impossible or unreasonable to provide advance notice; the list is not exhaustive.[28]

---

[24]See 42 U.S.C. §300hh-11(e)(3)(B); 20 C.F.R. §1002.86(a).
[25]38 U.S.C. §4312(b).
[26]See 20 C.F.R. §1002.86(b).
[27]Id.
[28]See id.

II. Scheduling Leaves

A. An Employee Is Not Required to Accommodate Employer's Scheduling Needs When Taking Military Leave

USERRA makes clear that an employee is not required to schedule his military leave at a time that is most convenient for the employer. In fact, USERRA prohibits an employer from refusing to grant military leave, or denying reemployment, because of the timing of the leave request or the inconvenience/burden it imposes on the employer.[29] This principle is reflected in both the statute and the implementing regulations. Section 4312(h) of USERRA sets forth the basic principle:

> In any determination of a person's entitlement to protection under this chapter, the timing, frequency, and duration of the person's training or service, or the nature of such training or service (including voluntary service) in the uniformed services, shall not be a basis for denying protection of this chapter if the service does not exceed the limitations set forth in subsection (c) and the notice requirements established in subsection (a)(1) and the notification requirements established in subsection (e) are met.[30]

Section 1002.104 of USERRA's regulations expands upon this principle and provides instructions for employers who believe that their operations will be adversely impacted by the employee's leave. If an employer has concerns about the timing, frequency, or duration of the military leave, the employer must address these issues with the appropriate *military* authority, not with the employee.[31] Section 1002.104 provides as follows.

> **§1002.104 Is the employee required to accommodate his or her employer's needs as to the timing, frequency or duration of service?**
>
> No. The employee is not required to accommodate his or her employer's interests or concerns regarding the timing, frequency, or

---

[29] *See* 38 U.S.C. §4312(e)(1).
[30] 38 U.S.C. §4312(h).
[31] *See* 20 C.F.R. §1002.104.

duration of uniformed service. The employer cannot refuse to reemploy the employee because it believes that the timing, frequency or duration of the service is unreasonable. However, the employer is permitted to bring its concerns over the timing, frequency, or duration of the employee's service to the attention of the appropriate military authority. Regulations issued by the Department of Defense at 32 CFR 104.4 direct military authorities to provide assistance to an employer in addressing these types of employment issues. The military authorities are required to consider requests from employers of National Guard and Reserve members to adjust scheduled absences from civilian employment to perform service.

DOD Regulation Section 104.4, referenced in USERRA Regulations Section 1002.104, provides as follows:

It is DOD policy to support non-career service by taking appropriate actions to inform and assist uniformed Service members and former Service members who are covered by the provisions of 38 U.S.C. chapter 43, and individuals who apply for uniformed service of their rights, benefits, and obligations under 38 U.S.C. Chapter 43. Such actions include:

(a) Advising non-career Service members and individuals who apply for uniformed service of their employment and reemployment rights and benefits provided in 38 U.S.C. chapter 43, as implemented by this part, and the obligations they must meet to exercise those rights.

(b) Providing assistance to Service members, former Service members and individuals who apply for uniformed service in exercising employment and reemployment rights and benefits.

(c) Providing assistance to civilian employers of non-career Service members in addressing issues involving uniformed service as it relates to civilian employment or reemployment.

(d) Considering requests from civilian employers of members of the National Guard and Reserve to adjust a Service member's scheduled absence from civilian employment because of uniformed service or make other accommodations to such requests, when it is reasonable to do so.

(e) Documenting periods of uniformed service that are exempt from a Service member's cumulative 5-year absence from civilian employment to perform uniformed service as provided in 38 U.S.C. chapter 43 and implemented by this part.

(f) Providing, at the Service member's request, necessary documentation concerning a period or periods of service, or providing a written statement that such documentation is not available, that will assist the Service member in establishing civilian reemployment rights, benefits and obligations.[32]

To date, no opinions have construed or applied Section 1002.104. The only case law that addresses employers' scheduling needs predates the enactment of USERRA.

In these earlier cases, a number of federal circuits addressed the needs of the employer with respect to the taking of military leave by fashioning a "reasonableness" test. The test weighed various factors in order to determine whether the employee was entitled to protection under the law, generally focusing on what is "reasonable both in the context of the reservist's military obligation and the requirements of the employer."[33] For example, the Third Circuit Court of Appeals articulated the reasonableness test as follows:

> In explaining the reasonableness standard, the Third Circuit identified various factors by which to judge reasonable conduct: (1) the nature of the employee's military obligation; (2) the employee's ability to schedule the leave at another time; (3) the length of the requested leave; (4) whether the employee's request was to extend a current leave, or for a discrete term; (5) the promptness of the request; (6) the employee's good faith; and (7) advice given by a military legal officer.
> Second, the Third Circuit identified certain employer concerns that bear on reasonableness: (1) the employer's legitimate needs; (2) the employer's need for the particular employee and its ability to find a substitute; (3) the work load during the leave period; (4) the extra cost of accommodating the leave; and (5) the clarity of the company's policy regarding reserve leaves.[34]

The United States Supreme Court, however, rejected the reasonableness test in 1991 in *King v. St. Vincent's Hospital*.[35] The Court examined whether a request for a three-year leave of absence was per se unreasonable under the

---

[32]32 C.F.R. §104.4.

[33]Lee v. Pensacola, 634 F.2d 886, 888 (5th Cir. 1981).

[34]Eidukonis v. Southeastern Pa. Transp. Auth., 757 F. Supp. 634, 137 LRRM 2349 (E.D. Pa. 1991) (remanded by Eidukonis v. Southeastern Pa. Transp. Auth., 873 F.2d 688, 694 (1989)).

[35]502 U.S. 215, 112 S. Ct. 570, 116 L.Ed.2d 578 (1991).

Veterans' Reemployment Rights Act (VRRA).[36] The Eleventh Circuit had held that such a request was per se unreasonable, thereby resulting in the employee not being entitled to protection under the law.[37] The Supreme Court discussed the split among the Circuits with respect to the reasonableness requirement.[38] In reversing the Eleventh Circuit, the Supreme Court concluded that the absence of any conditions on the length of service in Section 2024(d) of the VRRA was deliberate and that no limit could be implied.[39] The Court was not unsympathetic to the employer's concerns about the length of the leave, but recognized that the statutory right to leave was unconditional:

> We may grant that the congressionally mandated leave of absence can be an ungainly perquisite of military service, when the tour of duty lasts as long as King's promises to do, and if we were free to tinker with the statutory scheme we could reasonably accord some significance to the burdens imposed on both employers and workers when long leaves of absence are the chosen means of guaranteeing eventual reemployment to military personnel.[40]

The policy behind *King* was reaffirmed several years later when USERRA was enacted.[41] Where an employee is entitled to military leave by statute, the employer's inconvenience may not result in the employee being deprived of his statutory protection.[42]

---

[36] *See id.* at 217. The particular provision of the Veterans' Reemployment Rights Act at issue in *King* was 38 U.S.C. §2024(d).

[37] *See id.* (citing Lee v. Pensacola, 634 F.2d 886, 889 (5thCir. 1981)).

[38] *See id.* at 218, n.7.

[39] *See id.* at 221–22.

[40] *Id.* at 220.

[41] *See* 38 U.S.C. §4312(a) and (b).

[42] *See id.*; *King*, 502 U.S. 221–22. Following *King*, but still prior to the enactment of USERRA, at least one court recognized that an employee's statutory protection under the VRRA could not be impacted by the inconvenience suffered by the employer. *See, e.g.*, Cole v. Swint, 961 F.2d 58, 60, 140 LRRM 2447 (5th Cir. 1992) (affirming district court's judgment that employer violated Veterans Reemployment Rights Act by terminating ranch foreman who asked for a Saturday off in order to drill with his Guard Unit on the basis that the day off would "create a problem").

B. Employer May Not Preface the Taking of Military Leave Upon Obtaining the Employer's Permission

As with the issue of employer convenience, USERRA's regulations make clear that an employer may not preface the taking of military leave upon the employee obtaining the employer's permission for such a leave. This is succinctly stated in the regulations:

> **§ 1002.87 Is the employee required to get permission from his or her employer before leaving to perform service in the uniformed services?**
>
> No. The employee is not required to ask for or get his or her employer's permission to leave to perform service in the uniformed services. The employee is only required to give the employer notice of pending service.[43]

Accordingly, with respect to scheduling, an employee need only provide notice of the pending service. The employer has no option to approve or reject the employee's leave. If concerns exist with respect to the timing of the leave, the employer must address those only with the appropriate military authority.

---

[43]20 C.F.R. §1002.87.

CHAPTER 5

PAY AND BENEFITS DURING LEAVE

I. INTRODUCTION

Employees who take military leave under the Uniformed Services Employment and Reemployment Rights Act (USERRA or the Act) are entitled to a number of benefits including, but not limited to, the preservation of both pension plan and health plan benefits as well as other non–seniority-based rights typically given to similarly situated employees on other types of leave.[1] This chapter discusses those rights in detail in addition to providing information about how employers should characterize an employee's leave during that time.

II. CHARACTERIZING AN EMPLOYEE'S STATUS WHILE ON MILITARY LEAVE

Employees on military leave are deemed to be on furlough or leave of absence.[2] Employers are permitted to place such employees in a "terminated" status and hire an employee to backfill the employee on military leave, but upon return, the employer must rehire the employee on military leave even if it means terminating the replacement employee.[3] USERRA does not require that employers or pension plans grant retirement credits for military service that pre-dates the employee's employment with that employer or that they treat employees with military service better than those who did not serve.[4]

III. NON-SENIORITY RIGHTS AND BENEFITS WHILE ON MILITARY LEAVE

While on military leave, and regardless of how the employer characterizes the employee's status (i.e., terminated vs. on leave), the employee is entitled to all of the

---

[1] In order to qualify for any rights and benefits under USERRA, an individual must meet five threshold requirements. The employee must have: (i) held a civilian job before service; (ii) provided the civilian employer with advance notice of military leave (that is, unless notice was otherwise excused under the Act); (iii) served less than five cumulative years in the military; (iv) neither been dishonorably discharged nor released from the military under other punitive conditions, and (v) either reported back or applied for reemployment in a timely manner. *See* 38 U.S.C. §§4312, 4313, 4316; Douglas M. Selwyn, *The Uniformed Services Employment and Reemployment Rights Act and Employee Health Benefits,* 46 HOUS. LAW 28, 29 (Sep./Oct. 2008) [hereinafter *Selwyn*].

[2] *See* 20 C.F.R. §1002.149 (2009).

[3] *See id.*, §1002.139(a).

[4] *See* Steelman v. Oklahoma Police Pension & Ret. Sys., 128 P.3d 1090, 1095 (Okla. Ct. App. 2005).

non-seniority-based rights and benefits[5] the employer generally provides to other employees on a furlough or leave of absence who have similar seniority, status, and pay.[6] These rights and benefits include those in effect at the beginning of the employee's leave and any benefits established after that leave begins.[7] In keeping with the breadth of the rights provided under USERRA, if non-seniority benefits vary, the employee on military leave must be given those benefits provided to any person on a leave that is "comparable" with the person's military leave.[8]

There is debate as to which benefits fall within the category of those that must be provided when a leave is considered "comparable." One view is that USERRA's language is broad and the rights and benefits to be provided include even those benefits provided by law according to a statute or rule.[9] This would include, by way of example, health care benefits paid at the regular employer/employee rates, as required by the Family and Medical Leave Act (FMLA). An alternative view is that this provision of USERRA applies only to rights and benefits voluntarily provided by an employer for employees on a leave of absence.[10] Under this view, only those items an employer voluntarily provides—such as paid leave for FMLA purposes—would qualify for inclusion as a

---

[5]USERRA defines the terms "benefit," "benefit of employment," and "rights and benefits" broadly to include "any advantage, profit, privilege, gain, status, account, or interest (other than wages or salary for work performed) that accrues by reason of an employment contract or agreement or an employer policy, plan, or practice and includes rights and benefits of under a pension plan, a health plan, an employee stock ownership plan, insurance coverage and awards, bonuses, severance pay, supplemental unemployment benefits, vacations, and the opportunity to select work hours or location of employment." 38 U.S.C. §4303(2).

[6]See 20 C.F.R. §§1002.149, .150(a). The regulations make clear that the non-seniority-based benefits to be provided to such employees includes those in effect when the employee was hired, along with all non-seniority-based benefits that are added or modified at any time during the person's employment.

[7]See id., §1002.150(a).

[8]Id. §1002.150(b).

[9]See Veterans' Employment and Training Service, 70 Fed. Reg. 75246, 75263 (Dec. 19, 2005).

[10]See id. This view is supported by the definition of "rights and benefits" under Section 4303(2), which includes items that "accrue[] by reason of an employment contract or agreement or an employer policy, plan, or practice." See 38 U.S.C. § 4303(2). There is no mention of "rights and benefits" required by statute or rule in this definition.

right or benefit to which an employee on military leave would be entitled. The Department of Labor (DOL) refused to decide this dispute when it issued USERRA's final regulations, deciding instead to state that the application of this provision would be decided on a "case-by-case" basis.[11]

A. How to Determine Non-Seniority Benefits

To determine the benefits to provide to an employee on military leave, employers should consider other types of leave that are most comparable to military leave. Among the criteria used to determine what constitutes a "comparable" type of leave are the duration and purpose of the leave, along with the ability of the employee to choose when to take the leave.[12]

Due to its potential duration, FMLA[13] leave is perhaps the most similar to military leave. Thus, if an employer provides certain benefits to an employee on FMLA leave, it must provide the same benefits to an employee on military leave. For example, vacation accrual during a leave is generally considered to be a non-seniority benefit that must be provided by an employer to an employee on a military leave of absence only if the employer provides the same benefit to similarly situated employees on comparable leaves of absence.[14] If the employer permits an employee on FMLA leave to accrue vacation during that leave, the employer must provide the same benefit to employees on military leave.[15]

---

[11]See id.
[12]See 20 C.F.R. §1002.150(b).
[13]29 U.S.C. §§2601–2654.
[14]See 20 C.F.R. §1002.150(c).
[15]As stated above, whether USERRA's non-seniority-based benefits provision applies to those benefits an employer is forced to provide an employee taking a leave required by statute or rule is an undecided question.

B. Pay While on Leave

Ordinarily, an employee on military leave is not entitled to compensation from his civilian employer.[16] If, however, the employer pays employees who take other types of comparable leave, the employer is required to provide the same benefit to employees on military leave.[17] Moreover, upon request, an employer must permit an employee to use any accrued vacation, annual leave, or similar leave with pay during the period of military leave, but the employer cannot require it.[18] The employee is not, however, permitted to use sick leave during military leave unless the employer allows other employees to use sick leave for any reason, or allows other similarly situated employees on comparable furlough or leave of absence to use accrued paid sick leave.[19]

C. Employees May Forfeit Right to Non-Seniority Benefits

Under some circumstances, an employee can forfeit his or her right to non-seniority benefits. For example, if an employee takes military leave *and* knowingly provides written notice of intent not to return to the position of employment after the military leave expires, the employee forfeits any right to non-seniority rights and benefits.[20] However, the employee's written notice of an intent not to return to work does not waive any other rights to which the employee is otherwise entitled under USERRA, including reemployment.[21]

---

[16]*See* 38 U.S.C. §4303(2); 20 C.F.R. §§1002.149–.151.
[17]*See* 20 C.F.R. §1002.150(b).
[18]*See id.*, §1002.153(a), (b).
[19]*See id.*, §1002.153(a).
[20]*See id.*, §1002.152.
[21]*See id.*

IV. EMPLOYEES' HEALTH BENEFITS PROTECTED DURING MILITARY LEAVE

USERRA requires that employers provide employees on military leave with continued access to health benefits.[22] Specifically, an employee on military leave has two distinct rights with respect to health benefits under USERRA:

1. the right to continue preexisting coverage at certain rates, depending on the length of the leave; and

2. the opportunity to participate in the employer's health plan upon return to his or her civilian job without meeting initial eligibility requirements.[23]

A. Impact of Military Leave on Health Benefits—38 U.S.C. §4317

USERRA Section 4317 is the exclusive source of an employee's rights with respect to health benefits. Section 4317 supersedes the more general provisions of USERRA—dealing with rights and benefits of employees—that may conflict with Section 4317.[24] In addition, the Secretary of Labor, in consultation with the Secretary of Defense, may prescribe regulations to implement USERRA's provisions applicable to States, local governments, and private employers.[25]

1. A USERRA Health Plan

The ambit of a "health plan" under the Act is broad, and encompasses any "insurance policy or contract, medi-

---

[22]*See* 38 U.S..C. §4317; 20 C.F.R. §§1002.163–.171.

[23] *See id.*

[24] *See* 38 U.S.C. §4316(b)(5). This includes those rights and benefits found in Section 4316(a).

[25]The Secretary issued regulations on Dec. 15, 2005, that became effective on Jan. 16, 2006. Specifically, Sections 1002.163 through 1002.171 of the regulations implement Section 4317 of the Act. *See* 70 Fed. Reg. 75,246, at 75,265 (Dec. 19, 2005) (to be codified at 20 C.F.R. pt. 1002).

cal or hospital service agreement, membership or subscription contract, or other arrangement under which health services for individuals are provided, or the expenses of such services are paid."[26] Additionally, the regulations provide that USERRA applies to health plans covered under the Employee Retirement Income Security Act (ERISA) and those that otherwise are exempt from ERISA coverage—e.g., plans initiated or maintained by governmental entities or by churches for their employees.[27] A USERRA "health plan" also includes multiemployer health plans (the special characteristics of such plans will be discussed below), cafeteria plans, and other flexible arrangements.[28]

However, there is no indication whether the term "health services" under USERRA is congruent with "medical care" under I.R.C. Section 213. If the terms share the same or a similar meaning, USERRA would entitle an employee to maintain coverage for dental treatment, vision therapy, drug and alcohol treatment, and the like. Given the intent of the Act, it would be prudent to assume, at a minimum, that dental insurance and vision insurance are covered "health services."

2. USERRA versus COBRA Coverage

As of this publication, neither Section 4317 nor the regulations to implement health benefits under the Act has been interpreted by any state or federal court. Accordingly, there is little guidance to determine what potential issues may arise with respect to an employee's health benefits under the Act versus those granted under the Consolidated Omnibus Budget Reconciliation Act (COBRA) and how potential issues will subsequently be resolved. To gain a better

---

[26]38 U.S.C. §§4303(7); 20 C.F.R. §1002.5(e).
[27]See id., §1002.163(b).
[28]See id., §1002.163(c).

understanding of USERRA, therefore, it is prudent to compare the Act with COBRA.[29]

The health plan provisions under USERRA share similarities, in many respects, with those of COBRA. USERRA, however, is not identical to COBRA. USERRA and COBRA are similar in that neither Act requires the employer to establish a health plan (if one is not already in place), nor must it provide any particular type of coverage if it chooses to establish a plan.[30] Additionally, both Acts extend continuing coverage to the employee (or former employee, as the case may be with COBRA) as well as his or her dependents.

Unlike COBRA, USERRA's regulations provide plan administrators with significant leeway when implementing its health plan provisions.[31] This flexibility flows from a distinct difference between USERRA and COBRA. Unlike COBRA, employers must comply with USERRA's health plan provisions.[32] Accordingly, the DOL chose not to unduly burden small employers that otherwise would not have to comply with COBRA-like compliance guidelines but for USERRA.[33]

B. Employers Subject to Health Plan Provisions of USERRA

USERRA broadly defines who is an "employer" to include any third party (e.g., plan administrator, insurance company) that has assumed responsibility to administer employee health plans on behalf of the employer.[34] The pres-

---

[29]The Consolidated Omnibus Budget Reconciliation Act of 1985 (COBRA) was enacted to allow former employees to maintain access to affordable private health insurance.

[30]*See Selwyn, supra* note 1, at 29.

[31]*See* 70 Fed. Reg. at 75,266.

[32]*Compare* I.R.C. §4890B(d)(2) (COBRA coverage does not apply to plans established or maintained by churches, the federal government, or small employers with fewer than 20 employees), *with* 38 U.S.C. §4303(4)(A) (the term "employer" specifically includes the federal government and excludes neither small employers nor churches from the general definition).

[33]*See* 70 Fed. Reg. at 75,267.

[34]38 U.S.C. §4303(4); 20 C.F.R. §1002.5(d).

ence of a written agreement—that a third party has undertaken responsibilities on behalf of the employer—is not dispositive in determining whether liability extends to such third parties under USERRA.[35] For example, a third party who merely performs ministerial tasks at the request of the employer will not be deemed an "employer" subject to USERRA liability for noncompliance.[36] Additionally, a "hiring hall" may, under certain circumstances, be considered an employer for the purposes of USERRA liability.[37]

1. *"In Connection With Employment" Requirement*

USERRA's health plan provisions apply only if the service member's coverage was received in connection with his or her employment.[38] If the service member was covered as a dependent or spouse under another family member's policy, USERRA will not apply with respect to such coverage.[39] Furthermore, the mere fact that a service member used compensation from services rendered to purchase a policy independent from one provided by the employer will not extend USERRA rights to cover that independent policy.[40] Further, policies a service member obtains in connection with a professional association, club, or other organization are not governed by USERRA.[41] Finally, retirees and service members who are dependents under another person's health plan are not entitled to USERRA's COBRA-like coverage because their policies were not received in connection with their employment.[42] However, even though these individuals are not entitled to continuing coverage under

---

[35]*See* 70 Fed. Reg. at 75,266.
[36]The Regulations provide limited guidance as to what is considered a "purely ministerial" task (e.g., maintaining the employer's files, preparing forms to submit to a government agency. *See* 20 C.F.R. §1002.5(d)(1)(i).
[37]*See* 20 C.F.R. §1002.38.
[38]*See* 38 U.S.C. §4317(a)(1).
[39]*See* 70 Fed. Reg. at 75,266.
[40]*See id.*
[41]*See id.*
[42]*See id.*

USERRA, they may be entitled to reinstatement of health plan coverage after military service under the Service Members Civil Relief Act.[43]

C. Dependents Entitled to Coverage

USERRA provides that individuals who are absent from employment have the right to elect to continue coverage for their dependents.[44] While dependents are entitled to continuing coverage under USERRA, they are not vested with an independent right to elect continuing coverage as they may have under COBRA.[45] The absence of this election right for dependents may be problematic when the service member does not elect to continue coverage, and the subsequent lapse in coverage violates a custody or child support agreement.[46] However, even though an independent election right for dependents does not arise from the Act itself, the Department of Labor's interpretative regulations provide that plan administrators may provide COBRA-like notice, election, and waiver procedures, at their discretion.[47]

D. Length of Time for Continuing Coverage

Section 1002.164 of the regulations determines the length of time an employee is entitled to continue coverage. If an employee elects to continue coverage under the pre-existing policy during military service, an employer is obligated to provide such coverage under the policy for a

---

[43]*See* 50 U.S.C. App. 594.

[44]38 U.S.C. §4317(a)(1).

[45]In contrast to USERRA, COBRA entitles "qualified beneficiaries" a separate right to elect to continue coverage under an existing policy. By way of example, if an employee under COBRA does not elect to continue coverage, the employee's spouse or dependent children may nevertheless elect to continue coverage for themselves. *See* I.R.C §4980B(F)(1), (5)(B); Treas. Reg. §45.4980B-6.

[46]*See* 70 Fed. Reg. at 75,266.

[47]*See id.*

maximum of 24 months.[48] Accordingly, the employer may terminate the employee's coverage when the employee's service time exceeds 24 contiguous months. However, if the employee's service time is less than 24 months, the employer does not have to offer continuing coverage under the pre-existing policy for the entire 24-month period. Instead, the employer may terminate coverage on the last day the service member is required to apply for reemployment and fails to do so.[49] The 24-month period commences on the first date of the employee's absence for the purpose of performing military service.[50] The length of time an employee may elect to continue coverage during service time will be the same for his or her dependents as well.

It is important to note that USERRA explicitly entitles an employee to continue coverage already in existence; it does not, however, entitle the employee to initiate coverage upon departure from employment for military service.[51]

E. Procedures for Implementing the Right to Continue Coverage Under USERRA

USERRA Regulation Section 1002.165 describes what is required of plan administrators and fiduciaries to implement an employee's election right to continue coverage. USERRA does not impose extensive requirements or procedures to ensure compliance. To the contrary, plan administrators may implement reasonable procedures to ensure compliance, but they are not required to do so.[52] While Section 1002.165 does not provide much detail in terms of what procedures are reasonable, it does state that such pro-

---

[48]38 U.S.C. §4317(a)(1)(A); 20 C.F.R. §1002.164.

[49]The relevant date for determining when the service member must apply for reemployment to avoid termination of continuing coverage is provided under Sections 1002.115–1002.123 of USERRA'S regulations. *See* 20 C.F.R. §1002.164(a)(2).

[50]This date is similar to a "qualifying event" under COBRA that triggers an employee's "election period." *See* I.R.C. §4980B(f)(3).

[51]*See* 20 C.F.R. §1002.164(c).

[52]*See id.*, §1002.165.

cedures (if implemented) must comport with the notice requirements under Section 4312(b).[53] Accordingly, where military necessity[54] prevents the service member from giving the employer notice that he or she is leaving for military duty, or where giving such notice would be impossible or unreasonable, plan requirements may not be imposed to deny the service member continuing coverage.[55]

Compliance with this notice provision puts an employer who does not receive advance notice of an employee's military leave and election to continue coverage in an unusual predicament: It could carry the coverage and pay premiums even though the employee does not wish to continue coverage or cancel the plan and risk potential USERRA liability.

1. *Retroactive Reinstatement*

To remedy the dilemma posed above, Section 1002.167 entitles a plan administrator to cancel coverage if the employer does not receive notice of the employee's election to continue coverage premised on excusal of notice under Section 4312(b).[56] When an employee does not affirmatively elect to continue the plan during military service, and the failure to give notice is excused, an employer is generally entitled to cancel the coverage.[57] However, if the employee subsequently invokes the right to continue coverage, the

---

[53]There are a few reasons why the Secretary was averse to implementing a strict set of procedural requirements or operating procedures to implement the service member's election right. First, compliance with such requirements may be unduly burdensome on small employers that are subject to USERRA and exempt from COBRA. Second, individual plans are best suited to determine election rules to implement their respective plans' unique features. And third, nothing prohibits a plan from developing COBRA-like time frames and election periods so long as they comport with Section 4312(b). See 70 Fed. Reg. at 75,267.

[54]"Military necessity" exists and therefore excuses an employee's failure to give notice when "a mission, operation, exercise or requirement that is classified, or a pending or ongoing mission, operation, exercise or requirement [sic] may be compromised or otherwise adversely affected by public knowledge." 32 C.F.R. §104.3

[55]See 70 Fed. Reg. at 75,266.

[56]See 20 C.F.R. §1002.167(a).

[57]See id.

employer must retroactively reinstate the coverage provided the employee makes full payment of all unpaid amounts.[58] This may provide an employee on military leave a cost-effective option—the employee may apply for reinstatement "after the fact"—when the cost of paying premiums is less than medical costs without coverage.[59]

2. Reinstatement for Non-Electing Employees

Employees who provide their employers with advance notice of departure, but initially elect to terminate coverage, may change their minds and have coverage retroactively reinstated in a similar manner as an employee who seeks reinstatement because his or her plan was excused under the notice provision.[60] Section 1002.167(b) of the regulations addresses a situation in which an employee leaves employment for uniformed service in excess of 30 days and provides advance notice of the military service but does not elect continuing coverage.[61] A plan administrator who has developed reasonable rules regarding the election of continuing coverage may cancel the employee's health plan coverage, but must reinstate that coverage upon the employee's subsequent election and full payment within the time periods established by the plan, without imposition of administrative costs.[62] On the other end of the spectrum, a plan administrator who has not developed rules regarding the employee's election right may also cancel the employee's plan, but must reinstate it under the same general requirement as a plan that has implemented regulations.[63]

---

[58]*See id.* §1002.167(b).
[59]*See Selwyn, supra* note 1, at 30.
[60]Employees that (i) do not give notice and (ii) do not fall under the §4212(b) exception are not entitled to retroactive reinstatement under USERRA.
[61]*See* 70 Fed. Reg. at 75,267.
[62]*See id.*
[63]*See id.*

F. Cost of Continuation of Coverage

A plan may require an individual who elects to continue plan coverage to pay a premium for such coverage. Indeed, a service member who elects to continue employer-provided coverage may be required to pay 102 percent—representing both the employee and the employer's share—of the premium.[64] However, continuing coverage for the employee's first 30 days of military service during a leave of absence shall not exceed the employee's share of the coverage if any such share existed—i.e., if the employee did not have to pay for the coverage prior to military service, he gets the first 30 days for free.[65]

USERRA does not provide specific guidance concerning the timing of payments for the continuation of coverage or the termination of coverage for failure to make payments. Plan administrators are entitled to develop reasonable procedures for payment, consistent with the plan's terms.[66] Plan administrators also are permitted to develop reasonable procedures to handle either scenario.[67] In either scenario, the Secretary suggests that it may be reasonable for the health plan administrator to adopt COBRA-compliant rules.[68] Under COBRA, the employee is generally entitled to a 45-day grace period for making his or her initial payment after an election to continue coverage and a 30-day grace period for each payment thereafter.[69]

---

[64]USERRA's regulations do not specifically compare the 102% figure to the "applicable premium" under COBRA (which is also 102%), but plan administrators presumably calculate the number in the same manner. *See Selwyn, supra* note 1, at 30.

[65]This provision was imposed to protect the dependents of Reserve Component members because, under the military health care system, such dependents were not entitled to coverage unless the member's service exceeded 30 days. *See* H.R. REP. No. 103–65, pt. 1, at 34 (1993).

[66]*See* 20 C.F.R. §1002.166(c); 20 C.F.R. §1002.167(c).

[67]*See id.*

[68]*See* 20 C.F.R. §1002.166(c).

[69]*See* I.R.C. §4980B(f)(2)(C), (B)(iii).

G. Reinstatement Rights

Section 1002.168 of the regulations provides that when an employee's health plan is terminated during service time, the plan must subsequently be reinstated—to ensure there is no gap in the employee's coverage—upon his or her reemployment after service.[70] The employer may be liable if the imposes an exclusion or waiting period when one would not have been imposed if the employee had not taken military leave.[71] Additionally, if dependents were covered under the employee's health plan before its termination, their coverage must also be reinstated upon the service member's reemployment.[72]

While there is a general right to plan reinstatement upon reemployment, the employer will not be liable for imposing an exclusion or waiting period for injuries or illnesses that were aggravated or incurred during service.[73] The Secretary of Veterans' Affairs determines whether such conditions exist.[74] This limited exception obviously does not apply to dependents that could not have incurred any conditions by reason of service.[75]

1. Insurance Company Liability

If an employer delegates the responsibility of administering health coverage to an insurance company, the former still may be liable for noncompliance with USERRA for not negotiating for the employee's automatic reinstatement

---

[70]Section 1002.168(a) provides employees with a reinstatement right upon reemployment. Note, however, that health plans terminated by reason of failing to give advance notice of leave that were not excused under USERRA are not entitled to automatic reinstatement.

[71]See 20 C.F.R. §1002.168(a).

[72]See id.

[73]See 70 Fed. Reg. at 75,268.

[74]See id.

[75]There is no authority for determining whether dependents who were also performing service would be subject to exclusion. Additionally, since many conditions may be latent, and therefore not present for years after service, there may be potential issues regarding health coverage for these conditions long after service time.

right.[76] Additionally, the latter may be held liable under USERRA for failing to modify the plan at the request of the employer to comply with USERRA because the third party has sufficient control over the employee's USERRA rights.[77]

2. Upon Reinstatement and Not Sooner

Under USERRA, an employee is entitled to "prompt reemployment" after a timely application.[78] "Prompt" does not necessarily mean "immediate"—i.e., the employer has up to two weeks to reemploy the employee after he submits an application for reemployment.[79] Accordingly, the employee's right to immediate reinstatement of coverage does not vest until he or she is actually reemployed.[80] Therefore, an employer will not be subject to liability for failure to reinstate the plan during the period between applying for reemployment and actual reemployment.[81]

3. Returning Employees Do Not Have Right to Delay Reinstatement

Although Section 1002.168 of the regulations grants a returning employee the right to automatic reinstatement, Section 1002.169 does not grant a returning employee the corollary right to delay reinstatement: If the employee wishes to delay reinstatement until sometime after reemployment, the employer does not have to oblige.[82] But nothing in the regulation prohibits the employer from accommodating the employee's request to delay reinstatement.[83]

---

[76]See 70 Fed. Reg. at 75,268.
[77]See S. REP. No. 103–158, at 42 (1993).
[78]See 20 C.F.R. §1002.181.
[79]See id.
[80]See 70 Fed. Reg. at 75,268.
[81]See id.
[82]See 20 C.F.R. §1002.169.
[83]The regulations provide flexibility to employers in this situation. However, there is no indication of what an employee must do to ask for or delay reinstatement. This could create problems—if there is a delay due to the employee's request, could the employer be subject to liability if the employee later relinquishes his wish to delay reinstatement?

H. Multiemployer Health Plans

Under USERRA, the employer does not have to provide an employee with continuing coverage during service if the employee would have lost such coverage in connection with employment without regard to service time (for example, if the employer were to go out of business or terminate the plan).[84] Section 1002.170 of the regulations, however, modifies this general rule with respect to *multiemployer* health plans. If the employee is a member of a multiemployer health plan, USERRA requires continuing coverage under the plan even if the employer goes out of business or otherwise discontinues participation in the plan while the employee is performing military service.[85] This regulation may put an employee who left work for military service in a better position than if the employee had never left his or her civilian job.

1. Liability for Employer Contributions

Generally, during a period of service, the employer is not obligated to make contributions to the health plan on the employee's behalf.[86] However, upon return, the employee is no longer obligated to pay 102 percent—which previously may have included both the employee and the employer's share—of the premium to continue coverage. Accordingly, it is necessary to determine who is liable for paying premiums on behalf of the employer who no longer participates in a multiemployer health plan to continue coverage for the employee. Liability for payment of the employer's share under the plan upon return is allocated in the following order:

---

[84]Stated another way, if the employer goes out of business or terminates health plans for all employees while the service member is performing military duty, the employer will not be subject to liability for canceling the service member's plan while he or she is performing duty. *See* 70 Fed. Reg. at 75,269.

[85]*See id.*

[86]Under Section 1002.166, the employer does not have to pay the employer's share of the premium to continue coverage on behalf of the employee after the first 30 days of service.

1. Liability for contributions to the plan is allocated as provided by the multiemployer health plan's sponsor.[87]
2. If the sponsor does not provide for the allocation of responsibility, such responsibility lies with the last employer before the employee's service time.[88]
3. When the former employer is no longer functional (without respect to whether the plan allocates responsibility to the non-functional former employer), then responsibility is allocated to the plan itself.[89]

2. Multiemployer "Bank Plans"

Employers may subscribe to health plans commonly referred to as "credit bank," "dollar bank," or "hour bank" plans within the multiemployer health plan community. By way of example only, these plans allow employees who work a certain number of hours during a given period to "bank" excess credits and apply them to later payments for insurance premiums.[90] In Section 1002.171 of the regulations, the Secretary provides guidance on how these multiemployer plans may comply with USERRA. Under this section, a bank plan may freeze an employee's credits during service time—and therefore require the employee to pay the full amount of premiums during service time—so the employee may later apply these stored credits upon reinstatement to continuing coverage.[91]

Conversely, the plan does not have to freeze the employee's credits. The plan may permit the employee to apply stored credits (assuming he or she has accumulated them prior to military service) to continue coverage—in lieu of monetary premium payments—until they have been

---

[87]See 20 C.F.R. §1002.170
[88]See id.
[89]See id.
[90]See 70 Fed. Reg. at 72,569.
[91]See 20 C.F.R. §1002.171(a)(2).

exhausted. When the employee's credits have been exhausted, to continue coverage during service time, the employee must subsequently pay his or her allocable premium to maintain coverage. Accordingly, when the employee subsequently returns from service without any stored credits, the plan must allow the service member to pay for continuing coverage until the employee's credits are sufficiently restored under the plan.[92] Since an employee may not fully comprehend the consequences of his or her actions with respect to these technical plans, the regulations encourage employers or plan administrators to provide guidance to employees in determining what action may be prudent.[93] The regulations do not, however, address whether an employee or plan administrator may be liable for failing to counsel employees with respect to their options under these types of plans.

V. Pension Plan Benefits

USERRA specifically prohibits discrimination against military service members with respect to pension plans.[94] In other words, an employer must treat any employee who becomes reemployed after a period of military service as if the employee had remained continuously employed with respect to any employee pension benefit plans.[95]

A. Covered Plans

USERRA covers both ERISA and non-ERISA plans. Thus, USERRA covers employee pension benefit plans that provide retirement income to employees or defer employee

---

[92]*See id.,* §1002.171(a)(1).

[93]*See id.,* §1002.171(b).

[94]*See* 38 U.S.C. §4318(a)(1)(A); Steelman v. Oklahoma Police Pension & Ret. Sys., 128 P.3d 1090, 1095 (Okla. Ct. App. 2005).

[95]*See* Scott v. Absolute Insulation, No. 06-1174, 2007 U.S. Dist. LEXIS 68599, at *6 (W.D. Pa., Sept. 17, 2007).

income for a period extending to or beyond the term of employment, as well as non-ERISA plans such as those sponsored by a state, government entity or religious institution for its employees.[96] USERRA does not, however, cover pension benefits provided by a Federal Thrift Savings Plan.[97] Where state laws and pension plan terms conflict with USERRA, they are specifically preempted.[98]

B. Treatment of Returning Employees

Upon reemployment, an employee must be treated as if there had been no break in service with respect to participation, vesting, and accrual of benefits.[99] Each period of service shall, upon reemployment, be deemed to constitute service with the employer maintaining the plan for the purpose of determining the non-forfeitability of the person's accrued benefits and for determining the accrual of benefits under the plan.[100] As discussed above, in some cases, the employee may wait up to 90 days before applying for reemployment and, so long as the employee applies for reemployment within the designated time period, the period between the employee's conclusion of military service and his reemployment shall also be counted as continuous service for purposes of determining participation, vesting, and accrual of pension benefits under the plan.[101] Furthermore, any employee who is hospitalized for, or convalescing for up to two years from, an illness or injury incurred or aggravated during service must be treated as having continuous service with the employer for purposes of determining the participation, vesting, and accrual of pension benefits.[102] Moreover, when a qualified employee dies while perform-

---

[96]See 20 C.F.R. §1002.260(a).
[97]See 38 U.S.C. §4318(a)(1)(B); 20 C.F.R. §1002.260(b).
[98]E.g., Wrigglesworth v. Brumbaugh, 129 F. Supp. 2d 1106, 1112 (W.D. Mich. 2001).
[99]See 38 U.S.C §4318(a)(2)(A).
[100]See id., §4318(a)(2)(B).
[101]See 20 C.F.R. §1002.259(a).
[102]See id., §1002.259(b).

ing military service, the employee's survivors are entitled to any additional benefits that would be provided under the plan had the employee resumed employment with the employer maintaining the plan and then terminated employment on account of death.[103] Thus, for example, if a plan provides for accelerated vesting, ancillary life insurance benefits, or other survivor benefits that are contingent upon an employee's termination of employment on account of death, the plan must provide such benefits to the beneficiary of an employee who dies during qualified military service.[104]

C. Funding the Pension Plan

1. Employer's Obligations

An employer is liable to the pension benefit plan to fund any obligation of the plan to provide benefits that are attributable to the employee's military leave.[105] With respect to defined contribution plans, once the employee is reemployed, the employer must allocate the amount of its make-up contribution for the employee, the employee's make-up contributions, and the employee's elective deferrals in the same manner and to the same extent that it allocates the amounts for other employees during the military leave.[106]

With respect to a defined benefit plan, the employee's accrued benefit will be increased for the period of service once he is reemployed and, if applicable, has repaid any amounts previously paid to him or her from the plan and made any employee contributions that may be required under the plan.[107]

---

[103]See 26 U.S.C. §401(a)(37).
[104]http://www.roa.org/site/PageServer?pagename=law-review__0843   (last   visited May 13, 2009).
[105]See 38 U.S.C. §4318(b)(1).
[106]See 20 C.F.R. §1002.261.
[107]See id.

2. Timing of Employer Contributions

The employer is not required to make its contribution until the employee becomes reemployed.[108] For plans in which the employee is not required or permitted to contribute, the employer must make the contribution attributable to the employee's period of service no later than 90 days after the date of reemployment, or when plan contributions are normally due for the year in which the military leave occurred, whichever is later.[109] If it is impossible or unreasonable for the employer to make the contribution within this time period, the contribution must be made as soon as practicable.[110]

3. Employee Obligations and Requirements

If an employee is enrolled in a contributory plan, he is allowed, but not required, to make up his missed contributions or elective deferrals during a time period starting with the date of reemployment and continuing for up to three times the length of the employee's immediate past period of military leave, with the repayment period not to exceed five years.[111] Make-up contributions or elective deferrals may only be made during this period and while the employee is employed with the post-service employer.[112] If the employee does not become reemployed or terminates employment before he is able to make up the missed elective deferrals and the employer matches, the benefit is lost.[113] Additionally, an employee is entitled to make "make-up" contributions along with his annual contributions from pre-

---

[108]*See id.*, §1002.262(a).

[109]*See id.*

[110]*See id.*

[111]*See* 38 U.S.C. § 4318(b)(2).

[112]*See id.*

[113]Samuel F. Wright, *Am I Permitted to Make Up Missed Employee Contributions to My Pension Plan Account after Leaving the Employ of My Pre-Service Employer?* http://www.roa.org/site/PageServer?pagename=law_review_0741 (last visited May 13, 2009).

tax dollars, and the employer should note this on W-2 statements.[114]

If the employer's plan is contributory and the employee does not make up contributions or elective deferrals, the employee will not receive the employer match or any accrued benefit attributable to his or her contribution, because the employer is required to make contributions that are contingent on, or attributable to, the employee's contributions or elective deferrals only to the extent that the employee makes up his or her payments to the plan.[115] Any employer contributions that are contingent on, or attributable to, the employee's make-up contributions or elective deferrals must be made according to the plan's requirements for employer matching contributions.[116]

The employee is not required to make up the full amount of employee contributions or elective deferrals that were missed during the period of service.[117] If the employee does not make up all of the missed contributions or elective deferrals, the pension may be less than if he or she had done so.[118] Any vested accrued benefit in the pension plan that the employee was entitled to before the military leave remains intact regardless of whether the employee chooses to be reemployed after leaving uniformed service.[119]

An adjustment will be made to the amount of contributions or elective deferrals the employee will be able to make to the pension plan for any contributions or elective deferrals the employee actually made to the plan during the period of military leave.[120] The employee is not required, or

---

[114]*Marc. J. Soss, Pre-Tax Dollars for Make-Up Pension Contributions,* http://www.roa.org/site/PageServer?pagename=law_review_82 (last visited May 13, 2009). Once the employee's make-up contributions reach the level where an employer would have been required to make matching contributions, the employer is required to make such matching contributions. *See* 20 C.F.R. §1002.262(c).

[115]*See* 20 C.F.R. §1002.262(c).

[116]*See id.*

[117]*See id.,* §1002.262(d).

[118]*See id.*

[119]*See id.,* §1002.262(e).

[120]*See id.,* §1002.262(f).

even permitted, to make up a missed contribution that exceeds the amount the employee would have been permitted or required to contribute had he remained continuously employed during the period of service.[121]

If the plan is a defined benefit plan and the employee received a distribution of all or part of the accrued benefit in connection with his military service before reemployment, the employee must be allowed to repay the withdrawn amounts upon reemployment.[122]

4. Contribution Amounts

If the employee becomes reemployed by the preservice employer, the amount of pension benefit will depend on the type of pension plan.[123] In a non-contributory defined benefit plan, where the amount of the pension benefit is determined according to a specific formula, the employee's benefit will be the same as though he or she had remained continuously employed during military leave.[124] In a contributory defined benefit plan, the employee will need to make up contributions to have the same benefit as if he had remained continuously employed during the military leave.[125] In a defined contribution plan, the benefit may not be the same as if the employee had remained continuously employed, even though the employee and the employer make up any contributions or any elective deferrals attributable to the period of service, because the employee is not entitled to forfeitures and earnings or required to experience losses that accrued during the period or periods of service.[126] In other words, USERRA does not require the employer to replace the interest or earnings that other employees who had been continuously employed

---

[121]See 38 U.S.C. §4318(b)(2).
[122]See 20 C.F.R. §1002.264.
[123]See id., §1002.265.
[124]See id., §1002.265(a).
[125]See id., §1002.266(b).
[126]See id., §1002.266(c).

earned on the employer's or employee's contributions during the employee's military leave.[127]

D. Multiemployer Plans

Under a multiemployer pension benefit plan,[128] the last employer that employed the employee before the period of service is responsible for making the employer contribution to the multiemployer plan, if the plan sponsor does not provide otherwise.[129] If the last employer is no longer functional, the plan must nevertheless provide coverage to the employee.[130]

1. Notice to Plan Administrator

An employer that contributes to a multiemployer plan and reemploys the employee pursuant to USERRA must provide written notice of reemployment to the plan administrator within 30 days after the date of reemployment.[131] The returning service member should notify the reemploying employer that he or she has been reemployed pursuant to USERRA.[132]

2. Employee Entitlements Under Multiemployer Plan

The 30-day period within which the reemploying employer must provide written notice to the multiemployer plan does not begin until the employer has knowledge that the employee was reemployed pursuant to USERRA.[133] The employee is entitled to the same employer contribution

---

[127]*Pension Rights,* http://www.roa.org/site/PageServer?pagename=law_review_04 (last visited May 13, 2009).

[128]A plan in which more than one employer is required to contribute and which is maintained pursuant to one or more collective bargaining agreements between one or more employee organizations and more than one employer. *See* 20 C.F.R. §1002.266.

[129]*See* 20 C.F.R. §1002.266(a).

[130]*See* 38 U.S.C. §4318(b)(1).

[131]*See id.,* §4318(c).

[132]*See* 20 C.F.R. §1002.266(b).

[133]*See id.,* §1002.266(b).

whether he is reemployed by the pre-service employer or by a different employer contributing to the same multiemployer plan, provided that the pre-service employer and the post-service employer share a common means or practice of hiring the employee, such as common participation in a union hiring hall.[134] In the case of a multiemployer plan, this provision would enable the plan to pursue its existing remedies under ERISA for failure to make the required contributions in the event that neither the plan nor the collective bargaining agreement pursuant to which the plan is maintained provides for any such funding obligations.[135] But this does not affect the plan's obligation to comply with USERRA and make its contributions to the returning employee.

E. How to Calculate Pensions

In many pension benefit plans, the employee's compensation determines the amount of contribution or the retirement benefit to which he is entitled.[136] Where the employee's rate of compensation must be calculated to determine pension entitlement, the calculation must be made using the rate of pay that the employee would have received but for the period of military leave.[137] Where the rate of pay the employee would have received is not reasonably certain, such as where the compensation is based on commissions earned, the average rate of compensation during the 12-month period before to the period of military leave must be used.[138] Where the rate of pay the employee would have received is not reasonably certain and the employee was employed for fewer than 12 months before the period of military leave, the average rate of compensation

---

[134]*See id.,* §1002.266(c).
[135]Kelly v. W.G. Tomko, Inc., No. 4: CV 06-2072, 2007 U.S. Dist. LEXIS 20251, at *10–11 (M.D. Pa. Mar. 22, 2007).
[136]*See* 20 C.F.R. §1002.267.
[137]*See* 38 U.S.C. §4318(b)(3).
[138]*See id.,* §4318(b)(3).

must be derived from this shorter period of employment that preceded service.[139]

VI. Conclusion

Substantial care must be taken by employers when examining issues related to an employee's rights with respect to plan benefits during a military leave and after reinstatement. The rules applicable to these issues are specific and, in many cases, complex. Additionally, both USERRA and COBRA must be examined for compliance.

---

[139]See 20 C.F.R. §1002.267(b)(2).

Chapter 6

REINSTATEMENT RIGHTS AND OBLIGATIONS

I. Rights of a Returning Employee

The Uniformed Services Employment and Reemployment Rights Act (USERRA or the Act)[1] provides an employee returning from military service with various job protections if that employee meets certain requirements. Generally, an employee returning from service is entitled to:

- prompt reinstatement;
- seniority credit, including certain pension credits;
- status;
- protection from dismissal without "cause"; and
- training or retraining.

A. Prompt Reinstatement

After receiving a timely application for reemployment (see Section III(B)(5) below), an employer is required to act on such application in a prompt manner.[2] Although not defined in the statute, the phrase "prompt manner" has been defined by the United States Department of Labor (DOL) in its regulations implementing USERRA to mean "as soon as practicable under the circumstances of each case."[3] The regulations make clear, however, that absent unusual circumstances, reemployment must occur within two weeks of the employee's application for reemployment.[4]

It is important to note that the employer may not make an employee returning from military service employee wait for a vacancy. In fact, it may be necessary for the employer to lay off another employee in order to provide a job for a returning employee.[5] This topic is discussed in more detail at Section V(A) below.

---

[1] 38 U.S.C. §§4301–4335.
[2] *See id.*, §§4301(a)(2); 4313(a).
[3] *See* 20 C.F.R. §1002.181.
[4] *See id.*
[5] *See* Cole v. Swint, 961 F.2d 58 (5th Cir. 1992); Goggin v. Lincoln St. Louis, 702 F.2d 698 (8th Cir. 1983); Fitz v. Board of Educ. of Port Huron Area Schs., 662 F. Supp. 10

If the employer unreasonably delays the employee's return to employment, the employer must pay the employee back pay to compensate for any lost wages.[6] The employee, however, has a duty to mitigate damages and must seek alternate employment if the employer denies reinstatement. The employee's earnings from the alternate employment (if he finds any) will be compared, on a pay-period-by-pay-period basis, with what the employee would have earned from the violating employer, plus interest.[7] Overtime pay earned from the alternate employment will not be weighed against the wages the employee would have earned from the violating employer.[8]

B. "Seniority" Rights Under USERRA

1. General Principles

A returning employee is entitled to be treated, for purposes of seniority and any seniority-based rights or benefits, as if he or she had been continuously employed during the period of service.[9] Thus, for example, if an employee with five years of employment leaves for two years of uniformed service, the employee, upon reinstatement, is entitled to be treated as if he or she had been continuously employed by the employer for seven years for purposes of seniority and any seniority-based rights and benefits. The U.S. Supreme Court has dubbed this concept the "escalator principle," a term the DOL has since adopted.[10]

(E.D. Mich. 1985); Anthony v. Basic Am. Foods, 600 F. Supp. 352 (N.D. Cal. 1984); Green v. Oktibbeha County Hosp., 526 F. Supp. 49 (N.D. Miss. 1981).

[6]See 38 U.S.C. §4323(d)(1)(B).

[7]See Dyer v. Hinky Dinky, Inc., 710 F.2d 1348 (8th Cir. 1983).

[8]See Hembree v. Georgia Power Co., 637 F.2d 423 (5th Cir. 1981).

[9]See 38 U.S.C. §4316(a). If a right or benefit is considered to be a non-seniority-based right or benefit, the right or benefit is governed by Section 4316(b)(1).

[10]See Fishgold v. Sullivan Drydock & Repair Corp., 328 U.S. 275 (1946); 20 C.F.R. §1002.191.

2. *Applicable System of Seniority; Definition of "Seniority"; Escalator Principle*

USERRA does not create its own system of seniority—it simply applies itself to the system already put in place by the employer. It is important to note that USERRA defines "seniority" more loosely than it might be defined in other employment contexts. Under USERRA, "seniority" is defined as "longevity in employment together with any employment benefits that accrue with, or are determined by, longevity in employment."[11] If an employer does not have a formal seniority system, such as one established through collective bargaining, the custom and practice of the employer determines the employee's entitlement to any employment benefits that accrue with, or are determined by, longevity in employment.[12] For example, regardless of whether an employee handbook labels a promotion as one due to "merit," USERRA requires that the promotion opportunity be examined to determine whether it is one that accrues due to longevity in employment. If 95 percent of the employees considered for promotion to such a position ultimately are promoted, it is possible that advancement to this position would be considered "seniority-based."

The escalator principle applies to all other rights and benefits of seniority to which the returning employee would have been entitled if continuously employed.[13] The test to determine whether a right or benefit qualifies as "seniority-based" is two-pronged:

1. The right or benefit must have been intended to be a reward for length of service, not a form of short-term compensation, and

---

[11]38 U.S.C. §4303(12); 20 C.F.R. §1002.211.
[12]*See* 20 C.F.R. §1002.211.
[13]*See* 38 U.S.C. §4316(a).

2. It must be "reasonably certain" that the employee would have attained the right or benefit had he been continuously employed.[14]

Important to this seniority analysis is the principle that USERRA "does not prohibit lawful adverse job consequences that result from the employee's restoration on the seniority ladder. Depending on the circumstances, the escalator principle may cause an employee to be reemployed in a higher or lower position, laid off, or even terminated."[15] Thus, the escalator for an employee returning from military leave may go up, down, or stay the same. Similarly, application of the escalator principle may result in a reemployment position that involves transfer to another shift or location, more or less strenuous working conditions, or changed opportunities for advancement.[16]

3. Vacation Accrual—Is It Seniority-Based?

Prior to the adoption of the DOL's regulations implementing USERRA, the question regularly arose whether vacation accrual is considered a seniority-based benefit under USERRA. The DOL's answer to this question in the USERRA regulations is "no."[17] Relying on the United States Supreme Court's decision in *Foster v. Dravo,*[18] the DOL has determined that vacation is not a seniority-based benefit under USERRA because vacation is considered "a form of short-term compensation for work performed."[19] Thus, vacation accrual is subject only to the rules applicable to non–seniority-based benefits under USERRA, which are discussed below.

---

[14]20 C.F.R. §1002.212; *see* Foster v. Dravo Corp., 420 U.S. 92 (1975).

[15]20 C.F.R. §1002.194.

[16]*See id.; see also* Woodard v. New York Health & Hosps. Corp., 554 F. Supp. 2d 329 (E.D.N.Y. 2008).

[17]*See* Veterans' Employment and Training Service, 70 Fed. Reg. 75246–75263 (Dec. 19, 2005).

[18]420 U.S. 92 (1975).

[19]70 Fed. Reg. at 75263 (citing *Foster*).

4. Pension Plans

USERRA and its regulations defined an "employee pension benefit plan" more broadly than the Employee Retirement Income Security Act (ERISA).[20] In addition to covering pension plans subject to ERISA, USERRA specifically states that it applies to any "employee pension benefit plan,"[21] including those plans sponsored by a state, other government entity, or a church.[22] Thus, a pension benefit plan that is not qualified under ERISA would still be subject to USERRA's provisions. The only exception is that Federal Thrift Savings Plans are not covered by USERRA.[23]

Although USERRA applies to all pension plans, the statute and its regulations differentiate between different types of plans and contain differing rules depending on the type of plan involved.[24] The applicable rules are specific to each type of plan, but essentially boil down to a single, general principle: The employer (and the plan administrator) must treat the employee for pension benefit purposes as if he had never left.[25]

a. Breaks in Service

A typical issue confronted by employers whose employees take extended leaves of absence is whether the leave constitutes a "break in service" for purposes of determining an employee's right to benefits, vesting, and the timing of benefit payments. Fortunately for employers, USERRA provides an answer for employees who are reinstated following a military leave: The employer and the plan must treat the employee as if he had been continuously employed for the purposes of determining when the employee qualifies for

---

[20] See 38 U.S.C. §4318(a)(1)(A).
[21] Id.
[22] See id.
[23] See 38 U.S.C. §4318(a)(1)(B).
[24] See id., 38 U.S.C. §4318(2).
[25] See id.

pension benefits and for determining the amount of the monthly pension check.[26] In other words, an employee who properly seeks reinstatement after a military leave has no "break in service" for purposes of an employee pension benefit plan.[27]

b. Make-up Payments/Contributions[28]

Another issue facing employers with respect to extended leaves of absence is whether, to what extent, and when the employer is required to make up contributions to a defined benefit plan, or permit an employee to make up contributions to a defined contribution plan, upon return to work. Once again, USERRA provides employers with specific guidance on this issue.

For defined benefit plans (i.e., those in which an employee is not required or permitted to contribute), an employer need not make contributions to the plan while the employee is away on an eligible military leave.[29] Upon an employee's reinstatement following an eligible military leave, however, the employer is *required* to make up any contributions to the plan that the employee would have received if continuously employed by the later of the following two dates: (1) 90 days after the date of reemployment or (2) when the plan contributions are normally due for the year in which the military service was performed.[30]

For defined contribution plans (i.e., where an employee is permitted to make contributions), no contributions are due from the employee or the employer during the period of military service.[31] Once again, upon reinstatement from an eligible leave, an employee is permitted—but not

---

[26]*See id.,* §4318(a)(2)(A)–(B); 20 C.F.R. §1002.259.

[27]*See id.*

[28]For purposes of make-up payments/contributions, the types of plans will be referred to as "defined benefit" and "defined contribution" plans, but the reader must remember that USERRA does not limit these definitions to qualified plans under ERISA.

[29]*See* 20 C.F.R. §1002.262(a).

[30]*See id.*

[31]*See* 20 C.F.R. §1002.262(b).

required—to make up the contributions the employee missed while on military leave.[32] The employee has three times the period of military service—up to a maximum of five years—within which to make up these contributions.[33] These make-up contributions are in addition to any contributions the employee is entitled to make to the plan upon return to work, including any "catch up" contributions that employees over the age of 50 are permitted to make under certain plans. The employer will then note such make-up contributions on the employee's W-2, thus putting the IRS on notice that such contributions are make-up contributions (in pre-tax dollars), not excess contributions (which would be taxed).

If an employee chooses to make up missed contributions under a defined contribution plan, the employer is also required to make matching payments to the employee's account if provided for by the rules of the plan.[34] These matching contributions, however, are not due until such time as the employee's make-up contributions reach the level where the plan calls for a matching contribution.[35] If the employee does not make up the contributions, or falls short of the matching number within the make-up period, the employer is not required to make a matching contribution.[36]

5. *"Status"*

In several places, USERRA uses the phrase "seniority, status and pay."[37] While seniority and pay are either defined or more generally understood, USERRA does not define the word "status." Courts, therefore, have applied the

---

[32] *See id.*
[33] *See id.* In effect, a military leave longer than 16.5 months will trigger the five-year limitation under this section.
[34] *See* 20 C.F.R. §1002.262(c).
[35] *See id.*
[36] *See id.*
[37] *See* 38 U.S.C. §§4313(a)(2)(A), (a)(3)(B).

word's ordinary and common meaning.[38] The following have all been held to be elements of "status" for USERRA purposes:

- being the supervisor versus being the supervisee;
- working days versus working nights;
- working in a part of the company where there is a better chance at being promoted or earning commissions; and
- location or commuting distance.[39]

USERRA's regulations also provide some guidance, stating that an employee's status in the reemployment position could include "opportunities for advancement, general working conditions, job location, shift assignment, rank, responsibility, and geographical location."[40]

6. Dismissal Only for "Cause" Under Certain Circumstances

USERRA provides certain employees returning from military service with the right to be dismissed only for "cause."[41] This protection prevents an employer from terminating employment for reasons other than "cause" during one of two relevant time periods, which are based on the period of the employee's military service. If the period of service is 31–180 days, the employee is protected for 180 days.[42] If the period of service is 181 days or more, the employee is protected for one year.[43] A period of service less than 31 days is not protected under the "cause" provision of

---

[38]See Duarte v. Agilent Techs., Inc., 366 F. Supp. 2d 1039 (D. Colo. 2005).

[39]See Smith v. United States Postal Serv., 540 F.3d 1364 (Fed. Cir. 2008); Clegg v. Arkansas Dep't of Corr., 496 F.3d 922 (8th Cir. 2007); Ryan v. Rush-Presbyterian-St. Luke's Medical Ctr., 15 F.3d 697 (7th Cir. 1994); Monday v. Adams Packing Ass'n, 85 LRRM 2341 (M.D. Fla. 1973); Reynolds v. Rehabcare Group East, Inc., 531 F. Supp. 2d 1050 (S.D. Iowa 2008); Hackett v. Minnesota, 120 Lab. Cas. (CCH) 11,050 (D. Minn. 1991); Armstrong v. Cleaner Servs., Inc., 79 LRRM 2921 (M.D. Tenn. 1972); Britton v. Department of Agric., 23 M.S.P.R. 170 (1984).

[40]20 C.F.R. §1002.193.

[41]See 38 U.S.C. §4316(c); 20 C.F.R. §1002.247.

[42]See 38 U.S.C. §4316(c)(2).

[43]See id., §4316(c)(1).

USERRA, but would be subject to USERRA's general discrimination rules.[44]

However, the definition of "cause" under USERRA is not as broad as in other legal contexts. "Cause," for USERRA purposes, is defined as employee "conduct" or the application of "other legitimate non-discriminatory criteria" to an employee's circumstances.[45] If the discharge is for conduct, the employer must show that it is reasonable to discharge the employee for the conduct in question and that the employee had notice (either on an express or fairly implied basis) that the conduct would constitute cause for discharge.[46] If the discharge is for another legitimate, non-discriminatory reason, the employer bears the burden of showing that the reason was, in fact, legitimate and nondiscriminatory.[47]

Employers must also understand that the prohibitions against discrimination found in Section 4311 apply regardless of whether an employee is properly discharged for "cause." Thus, an employer who properly discharges an employee for "cause" under Section 4316(c) may still be liable for discrimination against that employee under Section 4311.[48] If the employee establishes that his uniformed service was a motivating factor, then the adverse action was unlawful unless the employer can prove that the employee would have experienced the same adverse action for a reason unrelated to his uniformed service.[49]

---

[44]*See id.*, §4311.
[45]20 C.F.R. §1002.248.
[46]*See id.*
[47]*See id.* This is, in effect, the same standard applicable to claims under discrimination statutes such as Title VII of the Civil Rights Act of 1964. *See, e.g.,* McDonnell Douglas Corp. v. Green, 411 U.S. 792 (1973). The difference, however, is that the employer under USERRA bears the entire burden of persuasion, whereas under Title VII, it only bears the burden of production.
[48]20 C.F.R. §1002.22.
[49]*Id.*

7. *Training/Retraining*

Once an employee is reinstated, the employer is required to make reasonable efforts, at no cost to the employee, to provide adequate training to qualify the employee for the position the employee would have attained if he had remained continuously employed.[50] The employer is not required to reemploy the employee on his return from service if the employee cannot, after reasonable efforts by the employer, qualify for the appropriate reemployment position.[51]

The regulations defined "qualified" to mean that

(1) ...the employee has the ability to perform the essential tasks of the position. The employee's inability to perform one or more non-essential tasks of a position does not make him or her unqualified.

(2) Whether a task is essential depends on several factors, and these factors include but are not limited to:
(i) The employer's judgment as to which functions are essential;
(ii) Written job descriptions developed before the hiring process begins;
(iii) The amount of time on the job spent performing the function;
(iv) The consequences of not requiring the individual to perform the function;
(v) The terms of a collective bargaining agreement;
(vi) The work experience of past incumbents in the job; and/or
(vii) The current work experience of incumbents in similar jobs.[52]

What amounts to "reasonable efforts" by an employer is discussed below in Section IV(C).

---

[50] *See* 38 U.S.C. §4313(a), 20 C.F.R. §1002.198.
[51] *See* 20 C.F.R. §1002.198.
[52] *Id.*

II. THE EMPLOYEE'S OBLIGATION TO PROVIDE DOCUMENTATION PRIOR TO REINSTATEMENT

An employee absent for qualified military service for more than 30 days is required, upon request from his employer, to provide documentation showing that (1) the application for reemployment is timely; (2) the employee has not exceeded the five-year service limitations of Section 4312(a)(2); except as permitted by Section 4312(c); and (3) the employee did not receive a disqualifying discharge.[53] The employer, however is not permitted to delay or deny reemployment if the requested documentation does not exist at the time the request is made or is not readily available at that time.[54] In effect, the employer must reemploy the employee and await the documentation. If the documentation shows that the employee was not entitled to reemployment because he did not meet USERRA's standards for reinstatement, the employer may terminate the employee. Any rights or benefits to which the employee would have been entitled to under USERRA are then lost.[55]

Although the types of documents available to determine whether an employee is eligible for reemployment will vary from case to case, in general an employer may request one or more of the following documents:

1. A DD (Department of Defense) 214 Certificate of Release or Discharge from Active Duty;
2. A copy of duty orders prepared by the facility where the orders were fulfilled carrying an endorsement indicating completion of the described service;

---

[53]*See* 38 U.S.C. §4312(f)(1); 20 C.F.R. §1002.121.

[54]*See* 38 U.S.C. §§4312(f)(3)(A), (f)(4); 20 C.F.R. §1002.122. However, if an employee has been absent from employment for more than 90 days, the employer may require the employee to provide the requested documentation before treating that person as not having incurred a break in service for pension purposes. *See id.*

[55]*See* 38 U.S.C. §4312(f)(3)(A).

3. A letter from the commanding officer of a Personnel Support Activity or someone of comparable authority;
4. A certificate of completion from military training school;
5. A discharge certificate showing character of service;
6. A copy of extracts from payroll documents showing periods of service; and/or
7. A letter from National Disaster Medical System (NDMS) Team Leader or Administrative Officer verifying dates and times of NDMS training or Federal activation.[56]

III. An Employee's Criteria and Obligations When Seeking Reinstatement

A. The Employee Must Be an Employee

Perhaps the most important criterion in determining when USERRA rights attach is often overlooked as obvious: In order to have USERRA rights, an individual must first have been an employee.

USERRA initially defines an "employee" as "any person employed by an employer."[57] This definition is so broad as to be unhelpful and there does not appear to be case law that offers any substantive guidance as to its meaning in this context. The United States Supreme Court, however, has addressed similar definitions of *employee* in other contexts.[58] In these contexts, the Supreme Court has held that "when Congress has used the term 'employee' without defining it, we have concluded that Congress intended to describe the conventional master-servant relationship as understood by

---

[56] *See* 20 C.F.R. §1002.123.

[57] *See* 38 U.S.C. §4303(3).

[58] *See, e.g.,* Nationwide Mut. Ins. Co. v. Darden, 503 U.S. 318 (1992); Community for Creative Non-Violence v. Reid, 490 U.S. 730 (1989).

agency doctrine."[59] There is also guidance from other areas of employment law. For example, the Internal Revenue Service's guidelines for determining independent contractor versus employee status can assist in quantifying the factors to consider in determining if someone is an employee.[60]

However, it appears as if the federal agencies responsible for enforcing USERRA take the position that partners or shareholders (i.e., owners) of a business are *not* employees under USERRA.[61] This stance is contrary to the position taken by the U.S. Supreme Court in addressing whether shareholders are considered employees under various employment discrimination statutes. In *Clackamas Gastroenterology Associates v. Wells*,[62] the Supreme Court held that the determination of whether a shareholder is an employee or an employer is a facts-and-circumstances test focused mainly on common-law control issues.

The *Clackamas* Court also found that the Equal Employment Opportunity Commission's (EEOC's) Compliance Manual contained a useful, although not exhaustive, list of factors that a court should consider when determining whether a shareholder is an employee:

1. Whether the organization can hire or fire the individual or set the rules and regulations of the individual's work;

2. Whether and, if so, to what extent the organization supervises the individual's work;

---

[59]*Darden*, 503 U.S. at 322.

[60]*See* IRS, INDEPENDENT CONTRACTOR (SELF-EMPLOYED) OR EMPLOYEE, *available* at http://www.irs.gov/businesses/small/article/0,,id=99921,00.html (June 15, 2009).

[61]Representatives of the Employer Support of the Guard and Reserves (ESGR) organization, which is part of the Department of Defense, have commented that USERRA would not cover shareholders and partners of businesses. While not binding on the ESGR, the DOD, or the DOL, these statements indicate the direction in which these agencies may go with this issue.

[62]538 U.S. 440, 447 (2003). The Supreme Court has also addressed the question of whether partners are employees, and found that, like shareholders, partners are to be viewed as employees or not employees depending on the facts and circumstances of the given situation. *See, e.g.*, Hishon v. King & Spalding, 467 U.S. 69, 80 (1984) ("An employer may not evade the strictures of Title VII simply by labeling its employees as 'partners'").

3. Whether the individual reports to someone higher in the organization;
4. Whether and, if so, to what extent the individual is able to influence the organization;
5. Whether the parties intended that the individual be an employee, as expressed in written agreements or contracts; and
6. Whether the individual shares in the profits, losses, and liabilities of the organization.[63]

While the Court did not decide whether the shareholders in question were employees, it did comment on factors it considered important in the analysis of whether the individual is an employee:

> Some of the District Court's findings—when considered in light of the EEOC's standard—appear to weigh in favor of a conclusion that the four director-shareholder[s] ... are not employees of the clinic. For example, they apparently control the operation of their clinic, they share the profits, and they are personally liable for malpractice claims. There may, however, be evidence in the record that would contradict those findings or support a contrary conclusion under the EEOC's standard.... For example, ... the four director-shareholders receive salaries, ... must comply with the standards established by the clinic, ... and ... report to a personnel manager.[64]

Although *Clackamas* focused on the Americans with Disabilities Act, the Court indicated that its precepts should be applied to a number of other federal employment discrimination statutes.[65] Additionally, the Congressional Report issued when USERRA was passed indicates that "employee" was purposely defined "expansively" in order to reach the greatest number of affected employees.[66]

Given the above, it is important when dealing with even an owner of a business to consider whether that person still qualifies as an "employee" under USERRA. Wheth-

---

[63]*See Clackamas*, 538 U.S. at 449, 450 (quoting 2 EEOC, COMPLIANCE MANUAL §§605:0008–605.00010 (2000)).

[64]*Id.* at 451 n.11.

[65]*See id.* at 443 n.3.

[66]H. REP. No. 103-65, 1994 U.S.C.C.A.N. 2449.

er common-law standards are applicable to USERRA is not yet known, but it seems likely that, given the proper circumstances, the Supreme Court or lower federal courts would apply these common-law standards to USERRA as well.

Practitioners should be aware that more than just full-time or part-time workers are covered by USERRA. Certain temporary workers also may be protected. Indeed, unless the position of employment is for a "brief non-recurrent period" without a "reasonable expectation that the employee will continue indefinitely or for a significant period," the individual may likely be considered an employee.[67] Coupled with this is the requirement that the *employer* prove that there was no expectation of continued employment.[68]

USERRA also applies to the hiring of employees. If an employee is called to service between the time an offer of employment is made and the proposed starting date of the employment, the offer must be held open while the employee performs his uniformed service and re-extended when the employee returns.[69]

B. Additional Criteria for USERRA Coverage

An employee returning from military leave must meet five criteria in order to be eligible for reemployment:

- The employee must have left his job for the purpose of performing service in the uniformed services;
- The employee must give employer prior notice of absence (unless notice is impossible or unreasonable or precluded due to military necessity);
- The employee's cumulative periods of service, relating to that particular civilian employer, must not

---

[67]*See* 38 U.S.C. §4312(d)(1)(C); 20 C.F.R. §1002.41; *see also* Stevens v. Tennessee Valley Auth., 687 F.2d 158 (6th Cir. 1982).

[68]*See* 38 U.S.C. §4312(d)(2)(C).

[69]*See id.*, §4311(a); 20 C.F.R. §1002.40.

have exceeded the five-year limit (subject to certain exceptions);

- The employee must have been released from the period of service without receiving a disqualifying discharge; and
- The employee must make a timely application for reemployment.

1. An Employee Must Have Left Employment to Perform Service in the Uniformed Services

In order to qualify for reinstatement, an employee must have left his position for the purpose of performing service in the uniformed services.[70] If the employee leaves for any other reason and then performs the service, he is not entitled to reemployment rights under USERRA.[71] Whether the service is voluntary (because the employee enlisted or volunteered for it) is irrelevant. Similarly, if the employee uses the absence for other purposes (such as working at another position when permitted by the military during the service) or takes additional time prior to beginning service to prepare for that service, these additional reasons do not disqualify the employee from taking the leave or being reinstated.[72]

a. Laid-Off or Furloughed Employees

If an employee is laid off or furloughed such that he is subject to recall, the employee is considered to still have an employment relationship with the employer and has all applicable rights under USERRA.[73] If the employee would have been recalled to work while he was performing qualified military service, but was unable to work due to this ser-

---

[70] See 38 U.S.C. §4312(a).
[71] See id.; 20 C.F.R. §1002.73 .74.
[72] See 20 C.F.R. §1002.73.
[73] See id., §1002.42.

vice, the employee is entitled to employment when he returns from service.[74] A similar analysis applies to employees who are on strike or leave of absence.[75] The one qualifier is that, in all of these instances, the employee still must have given prior notice to his employer.

2.   *Prior Notice of Absence*

a.   *General Rule*

USERRA requires that an employee seeking military leave give his employer prior notice of an absence, regardless of the category or duration of the period of service.[76] The notice can be written or oral,[77] although written is obviously preferred, both by employers and employees. Providing written notice, and the employee's retention of a copy of the written notice, avoids a dispute later over whether an employee gave notice, and thus meets that criterion for USERRA protection. It also eliminates the risk that the employee's oral notice to one manager will be overlooked.

Notice can be given either by the employee or by an appropriate officer of the uniformed service in which the employee's service is to be performed.[78] An "appropriate officer" is defined as a commissioned, warrant, or noncommissioned officer authorized to give such notice by the military service concerned.[79] As a practical matter, this generally means someone in the employee's chain of command or the unit administrator for the employee's unit or headquarters company. Among the National Guard and Reserves, the company or battalion commanding officer will often send a letter to the employers of all of the individuals who will be absent from work for a particular duty.

---

[74]*See id.,* §1002.42; *see also* Colon v. Shawnee County of Shawnee, 815 F.2d 594 (10th Cir. 1987).
[75]*See* 20 C.F.R. §1002.42.
[76]*See* 38 U.S.C. §4312(a)(1).
[77]*See id.*
[78]*See* 38 U.S.C. §4312(a)(1); 20 C.F.R. §1002.85.
[79]*See* 38 U.S.C. §4312(a)(1); 20 C.F.R. §1002.85; 32 C.F.R. §104.3.

b. Prior Notice

A question often arises as to what constitutes "prior" notice. "Prior" is not defined in USERRA or the corresponding regulations. By normal statutory interpretation rules, therefore, "prior" simply has its common meaning, which is "earlier."[80] Although "prior" may mean that an employee can advise his employer of the need for leave and simply walk off the job immediately, as a practical matter it is better to give an employer as much lead time as possible. Indeed, the Department of Defense (DOD) and DOL recommend that an employee treat "prior" as meaning "as soon as possible after receiving orders" and *not* "as the employee is packing up to go."[81]

c. Exceptions to Prior Notice Requirement

Circumstances obviously exist where prior notice of the need for a leave cannot be given. USERRA waives the requirement of notice under two distinct circumstances: (i) where the giving of notice "is precluded by military necessity"; or (ii) where, "under all of the relevant circumstances, the giving of such notice is otherwise impossible or unreasonable."[82] With respect to the issue of military necessity, USERRA provides that this determination is to be made pursuant to DOD regulations and is not be subject to judicial review.[83]

---

[80]BLACK'S LAW DICTIONARY, 1074–75 (5th ed. 1979).

[81]*See, e.g.,* 32 C.F.R. §104.6(a)(2)(i)(B) (DOD "strongly recommends that advance notice to civilian employers be provided at least 30 days prior to departure for uniformed service when it is feasible to do so."); ESGR, TIPS FOR NATIONAL GUARD AND RESERVE MEMBERS, *available at* http://www.esgr.org/files/factsheet/TIPS%20RC.pdf ("The earlier you inform your boss about drill schedules, annual training plans, and any extra time-off requirements, the easier things will go. . . . Giving employers the maximum lead-time enables them to make plans to accommodate your absence").

[82]38 U.S.C. §4312(b).

[83]*Id.*

d. Sample Letter to Employer: Notice of Active-Duty Absence

Although there is no requirement that the notice be in writing, a sample notification letter is included as Exhibit 1.

3. *An Employee May Take a Cumulative Total of Five Years of Service While Employed By a Particular Employer*

USERRA protects an employee's employment with a particular employer for a cumulative total of five years of uniformed service.[84] The amount of time it takes an employee to accumulate this total is irrelevant.[85] Further, the relevant query is the duration of the periods of service, not the duration of the employee's total leave of absence from work.[86] This is an important distinction, as an employee is generally entitled to time prior to starting each period of military service, and recovery time after each period of service ends, which does not count towards the five-year limit.[87]

USERRA's five-year limit, however, is subject to a number of broad exceptions. Section 4312(c) lists various categories of service that do *not* count toward the five-year limit, but for which the employee is still entitled to receive leave.[88] The exemptions most often used are listed below:

1. Service beyond five years that is necessary to complete an initial period of obligated service.[89] An example would be enlistment in the Navy nuclear program, which has an initial enlistment period of six years.

2. The employee expects to leave active duty before the five-year limit but is unable to through no fault of his own.[90] An example would be a sailor who is

---

[84]*See* 38 U.S.C. §4312(a)(2).
[85]*See id.*
[86]*See* 20 C.F.R. §1002.100.
[87]*See id.* §1002.73; 38 U.S.C. §4312(e).
[88]*See* 38 U.S.C. §4312(c).
[89]38 U.S.C. §4312(c)(1).
[90]*See id.*, §4312(c)(2).

Exhibit 1. Employee's Active-Duty Absence Notification Letter to Employer[91]

[Employee's Home Address]

[Date]

[Employer's Business Address]

Send by Certified Mail, Return receipt requested

Dear Sir/Madam:

I will perform service with the [**service**] beginning on [**date**] and ending on [**date**]. My absence from work for this period of military service is protected by the Uniformed Services Employment and Reemployment Rights Act, Title 38, United States Code Sections 4301-33.

My last day at work with you before I begin my military service will be [**date**]. I expect to return to work with you on or about [**date**]. **Note: Make sure your return date complies with Title 38, United States Code Section 4312.* [During my absence, I can be reached at {give mailing address and telephone number, if known}] [During my absence, _____, telephone number (____) _____-_____, will know how to reach me.]

[I {do} {do not} desire to take _____ days of paid {vacation, annual leave, etc.} as the first _____ days of my absence.] Please be advised that I may not be required to use vacation pay or time for military absence from my workplace, per Title 38, United States Code Section 4316(d).

[I {do} {do not} desire to continue my health care insurance, per Title 38, United States Code Section 4317.

If you have any questions about the provisions of the Uniformed Services Employment and Reemployment Rights Act, the National Committee for Employer Support of the Guard and Reserve, toll-free telephone number 1-800-336-4590, will be happy to answer them.

Sincerely,

[Signature]

Original Received for Employer by:

_____

[Printed Name and Signature]

---

[91]http://esgr.org/site/USERRA/SampleLettersForms/tabid/177/Default.aspx.

scheduled to leave active duty on a certain date but is at sea on that date.

3. Reserve and National Guard training periods.[92] An example would be the two- or three-week annual training periods and weekend training.

4. The employee is involuntarily called to active duty or involuntarily retained on active duty ("stop lossed")—the involuntary period does not count toward the five-year limit.[93] An example would be someone called to activity duty to serve in Iraq or Afghanistan.

5. The employee volunteers to serve on active duty for an operational mission for which other personnel have been involuntarily called to active duty—the service may be exempt from the five-year limit if the relevant service Secretary certifies in writing that it should be exempt.[94] An example would be someone who volunteers to serve in Iraq or Afghanistan.

6. The employee volunteers for active duty service that the relevant service Secretary certifies should be exempt because it was in support of a critical mission or requirement.[95]

7. The employee is called into federal service as a member of the National Guard.[96]

4. The Employee's Discharge or Release From Service Must Not Be Disqualifying

For USERRA protections to attach, the employee's discharge or other release from the uniformed service must be under honorable conditions. If the employee receives a dishonorable, bad-conduct, or other than honorable discharge, or if the employee is dropped from the rolls of the

---

[92]*See id.,* §4312(c)(3).
[93]*See id.,* §4312(c)(4)(A), (B).
[94]*See id.,* §4312(c)(4)(C).
[95]*See id.,* §4312(c)(4)(D).
[96]*See id.,* §4312(c)(4)(E).

relevant armed force, the employee loses his rights under USERRA.[97]

5. The Employee Must Make Timely Application for Reemployment

a. General Rule

An employee returning from eligible military service must apply for reemployment within a specified time limit after completing the period of service. The length of this deadline varies depending on the employee's length of service:

1. If the period of service is less than 31 days, the employee must report to work at the start of the work-shift on the first full calendar day following the completion of the period of service and a reasonable time for safe travel home, plus eight hours of rest.[98]
2. If the period of service was 31–180 days, the employee has two weeks to apply for reemployment.[99]
3. If the period of service was more than 180 days, the employee has 90 days to apply for reemployment.[100]

If the employee is hospitalized or convalescing from a service-related illness or injury, the application period can be extended for up to two years.[101]

b. Sample Letter to Employer: Employee's Request for Reinstatement

There is no special language or form that must be used to apply for reemployment. The application can be written or oral and can be as simple as a phone call, email, or letter

---

[97] See 38 U.S.C. §4304.
[98] See id., §4312(e)(1); 20 C.F.R. §1002.115.
[99] See id.
[100] See id.
[101] See id., §4312(e)(2)(A).

to the employee's former boss stating that he has returned from service and is ready to return to work. Although there is no official form, a sample reemployment application letter is included below as Exhibit 2.

IV. An Employer's Reinstatement Obligations

A. In General

For the most part, the employer's obligations correspond to the employee's rights. *See supra* Section II.

B. To What Position Must the Employer Restore the Employee?

If the employee's period of service is less than 91 days, USERRA provides that an employer must reinstate the employee to the position in which the employee would have been continuously employed without interruption.[102] USERRA provides some relief to the employer, however, in the event that the employee is not qualified to perform the duties of the position described above after reasonable efforts have been made to qualify the person for such position.[103] In this instance, the employer may return the employee to the position that the employee held when he left for uniformed service.[104] In most instances, given the short period of service, this means that the employee will return to the job that he left.

If the employee's period of service is more than 90 days, the employer must reinstate the employee either to: (1) the position to which the employee would have been continuously employed without interruption; (2) the position of employment in which the employee was employed on the date the period of service commenced; or (3) a posi-

---

[102]*See id.*, §4313(a)(1)(A). Once again, this is referred to as the "escalator principle." *See supra* note 11.

[103]*Id.* §4313(a)(1)(B).

[104]*See id.*; 20 C.F.R. §1002.191.

Exhibit 2. Employee's Request for Reinstatement Notification Letter to Employer[105]

[Employee's Home Address]

[Date]

[Employer's Business Address]

Send by Certified Mail, Return receipt requested

RE: Application for Reinstatement—Uniformed Services Employment and Reemployment Act (USERRA), Title 38, U.S. Code Section 4312

Dear Sir/Madam:

On [**date**], I entered active duty with the [**service**]. On [**date**], I was honorably released from active duty.

Please accept this letter as a formal request to be reinstated in my former job. With your permission, I plan to report to work on [**date**]. Please call me at the number listed below if this date is not convenient. Pursuant to the Uniformed Services Employment and Reemployment Rights Act, Title 38, United States Code Sections 4301–4335, I am entitled to be reinstated as soon as possible to my former position.

In the Department of Defense, there is an organization known as "Employer Support of the Guard and Reserve" (ESGR). ESGR's mission is to gain and maintain employer support for Guard and Reserve service by recognizing outstanding support, increasing awareness of the law, and resolving conflicts through mediation. If you have any questions about USERRA or employer support, you can find information on ESGR's Web site at www.esgr.mil. You also can call the ESGR, toll-free, at 1-800-336-4590, or contact ESGR via e-mail USERRA@osd.mil.

Sincerely,

[Signature]

Original Received for Employer by:

_____

[Printed Name and Signature]

---

[105]http://esgr.org/site/USERRA/SampleLettersForms/tabid/177/Default.aspx.

tion of like seniority, status, and pay, the duties of which the person is qualified to perform, but only if the person is unable to perform the duties of (2) after reasonable efforts to qualify the person for that position.[106]

In practice, determining which position the employee should be returned to may be based on many factors. The starting point is the escalator principle (discussed *supra* in Section I.B.2.) and the analysis begins with a question: Which job position would the employee have reasonably been expected to attain by the time he applied for reemployment if the employee had been continuously employed for the entire period of his absence? Once this has been determined, the employer may need to consider several other factors before deciding on an appropriate reemployment position. Such factors may include the employee's length of service, qualifications, and disability, if any.[107] The seniority rights, status, and pay of a particular position include those established or changed by a collective bargaining agreement, employer policy, or employment practice and can be found in agreements, policies, and practices in effect at the beginning of the employee's service, and any changes that may have occurred during the period of service.[108]

The ability to effectively make this decision may vary depending on whether the employer operates under a system of strict seniority or a more merit-based system. In general, USERRA's reinstatement requirements for employers work well where the employee's position is more dependent on issues of seniority, such as under a collective bargaining agreement or a strict seniority system for advancement. The reinstatement decision, however, is more difficult for employers who apply merit to advancement decisions. For these employers, the issue of what position the employee

---

[106]*See* 38 U.S.C. §4313(a)(2)(A)–(B).

[107]*See* 20 C.F.R. §1002.192.

[108]*See id.*, §1002.193(a); *see* Smith v. United States Postal Serv., 540 F.3d 1364 (Fed. Cir. 2008); Clegg v. Arkansas Dep't of Corr., 496 F.3d 922 (8th Cir. 2007); Rogers v. Department of Army, 88 M.S.P.R. 610 (2001).

would have attained had he been continuously employed can be difficult. Employers applying such criteria would be wise to document the positions that an employee on military leave reasonably would have been in line to obtain while on leave. This permits employers to at least consider, in the abstract, whether the employee on military leave would be entitled to this position upon reinstatement.

Occasionally, promotions or other increases in status, seniority, or pay may be contingent upon an employee's performance on certain skills tests or other examinations. In such cases, the employer must give the returning employee the opportunity to take such skills tests or other examinations after the employee has had a reasonable amount of time to adjust to reemployment and understand the requirements of the examination and the promotional position.[109] What constitutes a "reasonable amount of time" will vary from case to case. Employers should consider a number of factors, including, but not limited to: (1) the length of time the returning employee was absent from work, (2) the level of difficulty of the test itself, (3) the typical time necessary to prepare or study for the test, (4) the duties and responsibilities of the reemployment position and the promotional position, and (5) the nature and responsibilities of the employee while serving in the uniformed service.[110]

If the employee successfully passes the skills test or exam, and there is otherwise a reasonable certainty that he would have been promoted (or made eligible for promotion) had he not been absent for uniformed service, then the promotion (or eligibility for promotion) must be made effective as of the date it would have occurred had employment not been interrupted by uniformed service.[111]

---

[109] See 20 C.F.R. §1002.193(b).
[110] See id.
[111] See id.

C. Accommodation for Disabilities

When making the reinstatement decision, an employer is required to make reasonable efforts to accommodate the disability of an employee who suffered an illness or injury during eligible military service.[112] If a disabled employee is not qualified to be employed in the positions of employment the person would have attained with continuous employment, he is entitled to reemployment in one of two possible positions: (1) any position that is equivalent in seniority, status, and pay to the continuous employment position (if the person can be qualified after reasonable training efforts by the employer); or (2) the position that is the nearest approximation to the position he otherwise would have had in terms of seniority, status, and pay consistent with the circumstances of such employee's case.[113]

The legislative history of USERRA explains Congress's concerns and logic.

> Section 4313(a)(3) would address the issue of the position to be granted a serviceperson disabled while in military service, regardless of length of service, and who is not qualified for the "escalator" position after reasonable efforts to accommodate the disability. That obligation would be to reemploy the returning employee in an equivalent position in terms of seniority, status and pay for which the person is qualified or can become qualified with reasonable efforts by the employer. If no such position exists, the nearest approximate position in terms of seniority, status and pay would be required to be found. If a position other than the "escalator" position is offered to a returning disabled employee, full company seniority is always to be accorded the disabled serviceperson, regardless of whether seniority follows an employee under other circumstances. *See Hembree v. Ga. Power Co.*, 637 F.2d 423 (5th Cir. 1981); *Ryan v. City of Phila.*, 559 F. Supp. 783 (E.D. Pa. 1983), *aff'd.* 732 F.2d 147 (3rd Cir. 1984).[114]

USERRA's regulations define "reasonable efforts" as "actions, including training provided by an employer that

---

[112]*See* 38 U.S.C. §4313(a)(3).
[113]*See id.*, 38 U.S.C. §4313(a)(3)(A); 20 C.F.R. §§1002.225, .226.
[114]H. REP. No. 103-65, 1994 U.S.C.C.A.N. 2449, 2464–65.

do not place an undue hardship on the employer."[115] "Undue hardship" is defined as:

> an action requiring significant difficulty or expense, when considered in light of (1) The nature and cost of the action . . .; (2) The overall financial resources of the facility or facilities involved in the provision of the action; the number of persons employed at such facility; the effect on expenses and resources, or the impact otherwise of such action upon the operation of the facility; (3) The overall financial resources of the employer; the overall size of the business of an employer with respect to the number of its employees; the number, type, and location of its facilities; and, (4) The type of operation or operations of the employer, including the composition, structure, and functions of the work force of such employer; the geographic separateness, administrative, or fiscal relationship of the facility or facilities in question to the employer.[116]

In the commentary to the regulations, the DOL seeks to expand its views of what efforts to accommodate an employee's disability would constitute reasonable efforts at such accommodation.

> Such accommodations may include placing the reemployed person in an alternate position, on "light duty" status; modifying technology or equipment used in the job position; revising work practices; or shifting job functions. The appropriate level of accommodation depends on the nature of the service member's disability, the requirements for properly performing the job, and any other circumstances surrounding the particular situation.[117]

The DOL goes on to state that

> [i]n identifying an alternate position for a disabled service member, the focus should be on the returning service member's ability to perform the essential duties of the job. The position must be one that the person can safely perform without unreasonable risk to the person or fellow employees. The disabled service member is required to provide information on his education and experience, the extent of the disability, and his present capabilities. The employer then has the duty to disclose all positions that the service member may be qualified to perform. Because the employer has greater knowledge of the various positions and their requirements in the organization, the employer, and not the service member, is

---

[115] 20 C.F.R. §1002.5.
[116] *Id.*
[117] 70 Fed. Reg. 75,246, 75,277 (December 19, 2005).

exclusively responsible for accommodating the disability by identifying suitable positions within the service member's abilities and capabilities.[118]

Many practitioners may be tempted to treat USERRA'S disability provisions as the same as those under the Americans With Disabilities Act (ADA). While the analysis may be similar, the DOL has specifically declined to simply apply the ADA's regulations to the disability provisions of USERRA.[119] USERRA's definition of a disability is broader than the definition of a disability under the ADA and therefore requires more accommodation consideration during reinstatement.[120] USERRA's disability provisions, however, apply only during reinstatement.[121] Finally, because USERRA applies to all employers, regardless of size, it is broader than the ADA, which applies only to employers with at least 15 employees.

The EEOC has issued guidance on the applicability of, and the interaction between, the disability provisions of USERRA and the ADA.[122]

V. An Employer's Affirmative Defenses to Reinstatement

An employer is not required to reemploy a returning employee if the employer can establish any of the following:

1. The employer's circumstances have so changed that reemployment is impossible or unreasonable.

2. In the case of a person who is entitled to reemployment under §4313(a)(3) (disability), §4313(a)(4) (unable to qualify for a position), or §4313(b)(2)(B) (two or more persons entitled to

---

[118]*Id.*

[119]*See id.*

[120]*See* 38 U.S.C. §4313; 20 C.F.R. §§1002.198, .225, .226.

[121]*See* 38 U.S.C. §4312(a)(3).

[122]*See* EEOC, Veterans With Service-Connected Disabilities in the Workplace and the Americans with Disabilities Act (ADA), *available at* http://www.eeoc.gov/facts/veterans-disabilities.html (last modified Mar. 28, 2008).

the same position), such employment would impose an undue hardship on the employer.

3. The employment from which the employee left to serve in the uniformed services was for a brief, non-recurrent period, and there was no reasonable expectation that such employment would continue indefinitely or for a significant period.[123]

The employer bears the burden of proof with respect to each of these defenses.[124] Consequently, an employer's ability to establish any of these defenses will depend on the circumstances of each case and may be limited.

A. Employer's Changed Circumstances Make It Impossible or Unreasonable to Rehire

This affirmative defense is a narrow exception and the burden on the employer is significant. The mere fact that an employee's job has been filled does not make it impossible or unreasonable for the employer to reemploy the employee.[125] Nor does the lack of an open position at the time an employee seeks reemployment permit an employer to deny employment. It is possible that the employer may need to lay off another employee in order to reemploy the returning employee.[126]

Courts have generally held that this affirmative defense is only applicable "where reinstatement would require creation of a useless job or where there has been a reduction in the work force that reasonably would have included the veteran."[127] The regulations cite the example of an employ-

---

[123]See 38 U.S.C. §4312(d)(1).

[124]See id., §4312(d)(2).

[125]See 20 C.F.R. §1002.139.

[126]See id.; see also Cole v. Swint, 961 F.2d 58 (5th Cir. 1992); Goggin v. Lincoln St. Louis, 702 F.2d 698 (8th Cir. 1983); Anthony v. Basic Am. Foods, 600 F. Supp. 352 (N.D. Cal. 1984); Murphree v. Communications Techs., Inc., 460 F. Supp. 2d 702 (E.D. La. 2006); Fitz v. Board of Educ. of Port Huron Area Schs., 662 F. Supp. 1011 (E.D. Mich. 1985), aff'd, 802 F.2d 457 (6th Cir. 1986).

[127]Davis v. Halifax County Sch. Sys., 508 F. Supp. 966, 969 (E.D. N.C. 1981); see Watkins Motor Lines, Inc. v. de Galliford, 167 F.2d 274 (5th Cir. 1948); H. Rep. No. 103-65, 1994 U.S.C.C.A.N. 2449, 2458.

er being unable to reemploy an employee because "there has been an intervening reduction in force that would have included that employee."[128]

B. Undue Hardship for Disability, Training, More Than One Employee Returning to a Position

The defense of an undue hardship is only applicable where a person is not qualified for any appropriate position due to disability or another bona fide reason even after the employer has made reasonable efforts to help the person become qualified.[129]

C. Employment for a Brief, Non-Recurrent Period Without Reasonable Expectation That Employment Would Continue for a Significant Period

USERRA does not define "significant period"; nor do the DOL regulations or commentary offer an example of a position that would be considered as falling within this exception. However, a temporary or seasonal job does not necessarily qualify as brief, non-recurrent, and without reasonable expectation that the employment would continue for a significant period. Courts have held that USERRA provides protections for temporary or seasonal jobs if there was a reasonable expectation that the job would be available again.[130]

VI. CONCLUSION

USERRA imposes requirements on employers and employees alike with respect to reinstatement. Determinations as to reemployment, and the seniority rights and benefits to

---

[128]20 C.F.R. §1002.139.

[129]See 70 Fed. Reg. 75,246, 75,262 (December 19, 2005).

[130]See, e.g., Stevens v. Tennessee Valley Auth., 687 F.2d 158 (6th Cir. 1982); see also 20 C.F.R. §1002.41.

which an employee is entitled upon reinstatement, must be made with the utmost care, both by employers and employees.

Chapter 7

PAY AND NON-HEALTHCARE BENEFIT ISSUES UPON REINSTATEMENT OF EMPLOYMENT

I. Introduction

As part of the reinstatement process under the Uniformed Services Employment and Reemployment Rights Act (USERRA), employers and employees must consider the compensation and benefits to which a returning employee is entitled. In general, USERRA divides these issues into two categories: (1) those to which an employee is entitled based on his or her seniority with the employer (seniority-based benefits); and (2) non-seniority-based benefits the employee may be entitled to receive (non-seniority-based benefits).[1]

USERRA Section 4316 sets forth the general rule with respect to the pay and benefits a returning employee is entitled to receive upon reinstatement:

> A person who is reemployed under [USERRA] is entitled to the seniority and the other rights and benefits determined by seniority that the person had on the date of the commencement of service in the uniformed services plus the additional seniority and rights and benefits that such person would have attained if the person had remained continuously employed.[2]

In essence, when determining the rights and benefits to which an employee is entitled upon reinstatement, an employer must first decide what rights and benefits are based on "seniority." The employer must then decide the "seniority" rights and benefits to which the employee would have been entitled had he or she remained "continuously employed."

II. The Definition of a "Seniority" Right or Benefit

USERRA defines the word "seniority" as meaning "longevity in employment together with any benefits of employment which accrue with, or are determined by, longevity in employment."[3] USERRA's regulations reiterate this longevity requirement and provide factors for determining whether a right or benefit is seniority-based or not:

> A seniority-based right or benefit is one that accrues with, or is determined by, longevity in employment. Generally, whether a right

---

[1] See 38 U.S.C. §§4313(a), 4316(a). Although not specifically delineated in either section, the use of an employee's seniority-based rights and benefits as the critical factor is evident from the language of each section. USERRA's regulations also speak in terms of seniority-based benefits. See 20 C.F.R. §§1002.210–.213.

[2] 38 U.S.C. §4316(a); see 20 C.F.R. §1002.210. As USERRA's regulations make clear, the escalator principle found in USERRA's reinstatement provisions (See 38 U.S.C. §4313) also applies to the determination of rights and benefits to which an employee may be entitled upon reinstatement. See 70 Fed. Reg. at 75275 (December 18, 2005). Thus, if the escalator goes down, an employee's rights and benefits may decrease. See id.

[3] 38 U.S.C. §4303(12).

or benefit is seniority-based depends on three factors:

(a) Whether the right or benefit is a reward for length of service rather than a form of short-term compensation for work performed;

(b) Whether it is reasonably certain that the employee would have received the right or benefit if he or she would have remained continuously employed during the period of service; and

(c) Whether it is the employer's actual custom or practice to provide or withhold the right or benefit as a reward for length of service. . . .[4]

A. What Is a "Reasonable Certainty"?

In applying the factors set forth in Section 1002.212, a key question is when an employee would have been reasonably certain to receive the right or benefit if continuous employment had been maintained. Anticipating this issue, USERRA's regulations define "reasonable certainty" as "a high probability that the employee would have received the seniority or seniority-based benefit if he or she had been continuously employed."[5] While still subject to some interpretation,[6] the remainder of Section 1002.213 provides some additional guidance regarding what is meant by a "reasonable certainty":

(i) The employee claiming that he or she would have been reasonably certain to receive the benefit need not show with "absolute certainty" that he or she would have received the benefit;

(ii) An employee will be considered reasonably certain to have received the benefit if the employee can demonstrate that other employees with similar seniority received the right or benefit; and

(iii) An employer cannot withhold a right or benefit based on an assumption that a series of unlikely events could have prevented the employee from gaining the right or benefit.[7]

---

[4]20 C.F.R. §1002.212. Section 1002.212 also makes clear that "provisions of an employment contract or policies in the employee handbook are not controlling if the employer's actual custom or practice is different from what is written in the contract or handbook." *Id.* Thus, substance, rather than form, will be examined with respect to whether a benefit is truly based on seniority.

[5]20 C.F.R. §1002.213.

[6]Obviously, the issue of when something has a "high" probability of occurring is subject to interpretation. Rather than establishing a set percentage or threshold, USERRA's regulations (like many other regulations) left the meaning of the word "high" undefined.

[7]*See* 20 C.F.R. §1002.213.

III. Determining Seniority-Based Benefits in Employment

While USERRA's regulations make clear that an employer is not required to use a system of awarding rights and benefits that is based on seniority,[8] the use of such a system clearly makes the decision of whether a right or benefit is seniority-based easier. Where all decisions are made based on an employee's seniority, deciding what benefits are seniority-based should be relatively easy.

More difficult determinations, however, arise in those settings where rights and benefits are not based on seniority—or the decision whether a right or benefit is seniority-based is unclear. These may occur, for example, where an employer (without a seniority system) pays annual bonuses, provides "merit" pay increases, or makes advancement decisions based in part on an employee's tenure with the company, to name several. While none of these situations involves seniority-based rights per se, they are situations in which the facts and circumstances surrounding the benefit can cause them to be considered seniority-based.[9] Careful examination of all surrounding circumstances should be the first order when faced with the issue of whether these types of benefits in a non-seniority-based employment setting are to be considered seniority-based under USERRA.

USERRA's regulations also specifically provide that a seniority-based benefit may be one that is statutorily prescribed, rather than voluntarily provided.[10] For example, the regulations specifically provide that an employee returning from a USERRA leave is entitled to have the time he was absent counted toward calculations of the months employed and hours worked under the Family and Medical

---

[8] *See id.*, §1002.211.

[9] *See id.*, §1002.212(c). For example, if an employer regularly awards merit increases to 98% of its employees, this fact may make the "merit" increase look more like a seniority-based benefit. *See id.* The title "merit" will not be determinative in the decision regarding whether the benefit is seniority-based or not. *See id.*

[10] *See id.*, §1002.210.

Leave Act (FMLA).[11] Failure to do so could result in a violation of the FMLA.[12]

IV. Non-Seniority-Based Benefits

USERRA makes clear that, for non-seniority-based benefits, an employee returning from a military leave of absence is to be treated like any other employee who is on (and returning from) a leave of absence or furlough.[13] Thus, if certain non-seniority-based benefits are not provided to persons generally returning from a leave of absence or furlough, they need not be provided to the employee on a military leave of absence.[14]

An exception to this general rule is found in what may be referred to as USERRA's "me, too" principle, which provides that an employee on military leave "must be given the most favorable treatment accorded to any comparable form of leave."[15] In essence, an employee on military leave must be provided with the most favorable treatment accorded to employees on any type of comparable leave voluntarily provided by the employer.[16] In determining whether a leave is comparable to leave under USERRA, the regulations state that "the duration of the leave may be the most significant factor to compare."[17] Other factors include the purpose of

---

[11] *See id.*

[12] *See id.*

[13] *See* 38 U.S.C. §4316(b)(1)(B).

[14] *See id.* Under 38 U.S.C. §4316(b)(3), a person deemed to be on a leave of absence or furlough while serving in the armed services "shall not be entitled under [Section 4316] to any benefits which the person would not otherwise be entitled to if the person had remained continuously employed." Under 38 U.S.C. §4316(b)(4), a person on military leave may be required to pay for the employee cost, if any, of any seniority-based benefits, but only to the extent other employees are required to pay those costs under another leave.

[15] *See* 20 C.F.R. §1002.150(b). The phrase "me, too, principle" is a creation of the authors and is not part of USERRA, its regulations, or any legislative history known to the authors.

[16] *See id.*

[17] 20 C.F.R. §1002.150(b). The regulations provide one example: A funeral leave of two days' duration will not be considered "comparable to an extended military leave." *Id.*

the leave and the ability of the employee to choose when to take the leave.[18]

V. Pay Upon Reinstatement to Employment

In general, an employee's pay upon reinstatement under USERRA will be determined in large part by the position to which the employee is reinstated.[19] USERRA, however, divides this determination into two categories, depending on the length of the employee's military service.[20] For those employees whose military service lasts 90 days or less, USERRA makes no mention of pay issues, presumably because of the relatively short duration of the leave.[21] Where an employee's military service lasts more than 90 days, USERRA specifically requires that the employee be placed in a position that involves considerations of "seniority, status and pay."[22] While this distinction may cause some to ponder about whether considerations of seniority, status and pay are appropriate for leaves lasting 90 days or less, USERRA's regulations make clear that any reemployment position under USERRA includes a consideration of such elements as "like seniority, status and pay."[23]

VI. Case Law Interpreting Reinstatement Issues

Several cases have interpreted the issues, under USERRA, surrounding the questions of the proper reinstatement position, pay, and benefits. These are considered in turn.

---

[18]See id.
[19]See 38 U.S.C. §4313(a).
[20]See id.
[21]See id., §4313(a)(1).
[22]See id., §4313(a)(2).
[23]See 20 C.F.R. §1002.193.

In *Long v. Ellis Environmental Group, LC,*[24] the defendant-employer Ellis Environmental Group employed the plaintiff-employee, a Naval Reservist, as Vice President of Construction, when he received orders to deploy to Iraq.[25] After the plaintiff notified the employer of his active military leave of absence, the employer sent him a letter acknowledging his reemployment rights and pledging to pay him $2,000 per month as a retainer during his deployment.[26]

During the plaintiff's eight-month deployment, the employer promoted another worker to the Vice President of Construction position.[27] The employer notified the plaintiff of the promotion by email and mentioned that it hoped that the plaintiff would return to the employer for a possible promotion.[28] Upon the plaintiff's return from deployment, the employer offered the plaintiff reemployment in only one position, the newly created position of Senior Vice President of Air Force Programs, which paid the same salary as his last position and required him to relocate to another state.[29] The plaintiff, feeling that the offer violated his rights under USERRA, rejected the offer.[30] The employer subsequently offered the plaintiff the new position with a higher salary and without the relocation requirement.[31] However, the plaintiff rejected that offer and resigned.[32]

The plaintiff brought suit alleging, *inter alia,* that the employer violated his rights by failing to reemploy him in the position he would have held—or in a "position of like seniority, status, and pay,"—but for his active duty.[33] The

---

[24]Long v. Ellis Envtl. Group, LC, 2007 U.S. Dist. LEXIS 23784 (N.D. Fla. Mar. 30, 2007).

[25]*Id.* at *1.

[26]*Id.*

[27]*Id.*

[28]*Id.* at *2.

[29]*Id.*

[30]*Id.* at *3.

[31]*Id.*

[32]*Id.*

[33]*Id.*

parties disagreed as to whether the plaintiff's former Vice President of Construction position was of like "status" to the new position of Senior Vice President of Air Force Programs under Section 4313.[34] The United States District Court for the Northern District of Florida considered six factors to determine whether the jobs were of like status, including: (1) opportunities for advancement, (2) general working conditions, (3) job location, (4) shift assignment, (5) rank, and (6) responsibility.[35] The court closely scrutinized the plaintiff's former job duties as they existed at this time of his deployment, and compared them to the later-offered job.[36] Granting the employer's motion for summary judgment, the court determined that both positions involved similar duties and that the new position did not have less desirable working conditions than the former job.[37]

In *Acker v. Greenville Surgery Center,*[38] Greenville Surgery Center (Greenville) employed the plaintiff, a military member, as an orderly.[39] Greenville terminated the plaintiff in June 2004 after three consecutive "no call/no show" absences.[40] The plaintiff claimed that he had orally advised his supervisors that he would be on military leave during this time period.[41] Upon returning from military service, the plaintiff received a COBRA letter informing him of his termination.[42] The plaintiff brought reinstatement and discrimination claims under USERRA.[43]

---

[34] 38 U.S.C. §4313(a)(2)(A) (known as the "escalator provision," this section states that a returning employee must return to a "position of employment in which the person would have been employed if the continuous employment of such person with the employer had not been interrupted by such service, or a position of like seniority, status and pay, the duties of which the person is qualified to perform").

[35] Long v. Ellis Envtl. Group, LC, 2007 U.S. District LEXIS 23784 at *6; *see also* 20 C.F.R. §1002.194.

[36] *Long,* 2007 U.S. Dist. LEXIS at *6.

[37] *Id.*

[38] 2008 U.S. Dist. LEXIS 3129 (D.S.C. 2008).

[39] *Id.* at *1.

[40] *Id.*

[41] *Id.*

[42] *Id.*

[43] *Id.*

The U.S. District Court for the District of South Carolina denied Greenville summary judgment on these claims,
determining that fact issues precluded it from granting
Greenville's motion.[44] First, denying Greenville's motion on
the reinstatement claim, the court reiterated that, despite
Greenville's policy requiring written notice of leaves,
USERRA permits an employee to provide verbal notice of a
need for military leave.[45] Greenville, therefore, was not entitled to summary judgment on this basis.[46] Further, the court
rejected Greenville's argument that, even if Acker was on
military leave, he did not seek reinstatement within the required time period under USERRA.[47] Given that Greenville
sent Acker a COBRA notice stating that his employment
was terminated after the "no call/no shows," it was reasonable for Acker not to report back to work after receiving the
COBRA notice.[48] At the very least, this created a fact issue
that could not be resolved on summary judgment.[49]

In *Serricchio v. Wachovia Securities, LLC*,[50] plaintiff-
employee worked as a commission-based broker for Prudential Securities, Inc. (Prudential) when he was called to
active duty after the September 11, 2001, events.[51] When
the plaintiff reported for duty, he had a number of accounts that had generated more than $75,000 in annual
commission income.[52]

The plaintiff was on active duty for approximately two
years, during which time Prudential underwent major
changes, selling its brokerage business to Wachovia Corporation (Wachovia), which dealt with less-wealthy and lower-
volume clients through a national telephone customer ser-

---

[44]*Id.* at *4.
[45]*Id.* at *3.
[46]*Id.*
[47]*Id.* at *4.
[48]*Id.*
[49]*Id.*
[50]556 F. Supp. 2d 99 (D. Conn. 2008).
[51]*Id.* at 102.
[52]*Id.*

vice rather than through individual brokers.[53] Moreover, the plaintiff's former clients either had been assigned to the national call center or had left.[54]

After the plaintiff was honorably discharged in fall 2003, through his counsel, he wrote a letter to Wachovia requesting reinstatement in accordance with USERRA[55] and also listing a number of actions taken by Wachovia and Prudential that he felt damaged his career.[56] After meeting with the plaintiff, Wachovia offered him reinstatement to a financial advisor position with the return of his remaining accounts, a $2,000 per month advance against his commissions, and the opportunity to cold-call for new client accounts.[57] After receiving this offer, he left the office and did not return.[58] Six months later, Wachovia terminated him for job abandonment.[59]

The plaintiff sued Wachovia and Prudential alleging, *inter alia*, that the defendants violated USERRA by failing to promptly reinstate him to an appropriate position under Section 4313(a).[60] The United States District Court for the District of Connecticut first noted, over defendants' objection, that the plaintiff properly applied for and pursued reemployment with diligence, because his letter to the employer specifically requested reinstatement.[61] The court next analyzed whether the defendants offered the plaintiff a position that he would have attained had he not been ab-

---

[53]*Id.* at 103.
[54]*Id.*
[55]*Id.*
[56]*Id.* at 105.
[57]*Id.* at 103.
[58]*Id.*
[59]*Id.*
[60]28 U.S.C. §4313(a) ("[A] person entitled to reemployment under section 4312, upon completion of a period of service in the uniformed services, shall be promptly reemployed in a position of employment").
[61]Serricchio v. Wachovia Securities, LLC, 556 F. Supp. 2d 99, 105 (D. Conn. 2008). The court found that the plaintiff's letter requesting reinstatement was not a conditional request for reinstatement, but instead was Serricchio's attempt to "red flag" additional USERRA rights implicated in his reinstatement. *Id.*

sent.[62] The plaintiff raised sufficient factual disputes to preclude summary judgment by arguing that Wachovia had not provided him equivalent earning opportunities because Wachovia was not diligent in maintaining his clients and the plaintiff could not rebuild his business through cold-calling alone.[63] Finally, the court noted that Wachovia did not have a duty to preserve the plaintiff's exact book of business during his leave.[64] Rather, Wachovia was required to provide him the opportunity to reenter the workplace with comparable earning potential and advancement to that which his previous book would have provided, regardless of what clients were in the book of business.[65] Accordingly, the court denied Wachovia's motion for summary judgment on the plaintiff's USERRA claim.[66]

In *Woodard v. New York Health and Hospitals Corp.*,[67] the New York City Health and Hospitals Corporation (HHC) employed the plaintiff-employee as an Associate Director when she took military leave just after the September 11, 2001, attacks.[68] The plaintiff had joined the United States Army reserves approximately 10 years before HHC hired her.[69] Shortly after the September 11 attacks, the plaintiff was ordered to begin military duty.[70]

After two and a half years of active duty, the plaintiff sent HHC Human Resources a letter requesting reemployment.[71] In response, although her prior position was still available, HHC directed the plaintiff to report to a related division of HHC, the Quality Management and Clinical Affairs (QMCA), due to QMCA staffing concerns.[72] Previously

---

[62]*Id.* at 106.
[63]*Id.*
[64]*Id.* at 108.
[65]*Id.*
[66]*Id.* at 114.
[67]554 F. Supp. 2d 329 (E.D.N.Y. 2008).
[68]*Id.* at 334.
[69]*Id.* at 335.
[70]*Id.* at 339.
[71]*Id.* at 340–41.
[72]*Id.* at 341.

a manager with HHC, in her position with QMCA, the plaintiff found herself with the primary responsibilities of attending meetings, transcribing minutes, and preparing quarterly board reports.[73]

The plaintiff filed suit against HHC under USERRA, alleging HHC discriminated against her based on her military service in the form of reduced pay increases,[74] as well as substituting her prior managerial functions for secretarial functions.[75] HHC filed a motion for summary judgment on both counts.[76]

The United States District Court for the Eastern District of New York determined Woodard's claim of a reduced pay increase was moot, despite evidence that she had been deprived of half of her pay increase at the time it was due, because she eventually received a full retroactive pay increase.[77] Noting that USERRA does not provide punitive or statutory penalties,[78] the court found the plaintiff's receipt of a full pay increase removed any injury that could be addressed by the court had the court determined that the HHC had discriminated against her by deferring her pay increase on account of her military service.[79]

---

[73]*Id.* at 342.

[74]*See* 38 U.S.C. §4311 ("An employer may not discriminate in employment against or take any adverse employment action against any person because such person (1) has taken an action to enforce a protection afforded any person under this chapter, (2) has testified or otherwise made a statement in or in connection with any proceeding under this chapter, (3) has assisted or otherwise participated in an investigation under this chapter, or (4) has exercised a right provided for in this chapter. The prohibition in this subsection shall apply with respect to a person regardless of whether that person has performed service in the uniformed services").

[75]38 U.S.C. §4313(a)(2)(A) (Returning employee must be placed "in the position of employment which the person would have been employed if the continuous employment of such person with the employer had not been interrupted by such service or a position of like seniority, status, and pay, the duties of which the person is qualified to perform").

[76]*See Woodard,* 554 F. Supp. 2d at 347.

[77]*See id.* at 354.

[78]*See id.* (citing Morris-Hayes v. Board of Educ., 423 F.3d 153, 160 (2d Cir. 2005) holding that a Section 1983 suit for damages is unavailable to enforce the rights created by USERRA, because "USERRA provides a comprehensive remedial scheme to ensure the employment and reemployment rights of those called upon to serve in the armed forces of the United States")).

[79]*See id.* at 354–55.

Further, the court determined HHC was entitled to summary judgment on the plaintiff's Section 4313 claim that HHC failed to reemploy her in a position of similar status.[80] The court noted that while the plaintiff may sincerely believe that her new role was secretarial and not managerial, her supervisors' and coworkers' testimony indicated that the new position was, in fact, managerial in nature,[81] and carried the same pay and seniority as the prior position.[82] The court also noted that the plaintiff failed to demonstrate any evidence that HHC treated her differently than it treated other similarly situated employees or that it failed to provided her with the benefits she was supposed to accrue during her military leave.[83] Accordingly, the court determined that HHC's changes to plaintiff's responsibilities were properly based on the legitimate needs of HHC, not on the plaintiff's military leave.[84] As such, the court concluded that HHC acted properly when it assigned her a new role with the QMCA,[85] and granted HHC summary judgment on all of the plaintiff's claims.[86]

In *Johnson v. Preston Cycles, LLC,* [87] Preston Cycles employed the plaintiff-employee, a military member, in a sales position.[88] The plaintiff left work for 30 days for military duty.[89] The U.S. District Court for the District of South Carolina stated that USERRA protected the plaintiff from being discharged, except for cause, after reemployment.[90] Despite this protection, the employer immediately and

---

[80]*See id.* at 356–57.
[81]*See id.* at 355.
[82]*See id.* at 356.
[83]*See id.* at 357.
[84]*See id.*
[85]*See id.*
[86]*See id.* at 360.
[87]2008 U.S. Dist. LEXIS 92454, 2008 WL 4908191 (D.S.C. 2008).
[88]*See id.* at *2.
[89]*See id.*
[90]*See id.* at *1.

wrongfully terminated the plaintiff upon his return from military service.[91]

In considering the company's summary judgment motion, the court explained that "cause" under USERRA means "any reason for discharge that is not arbitrary or made in order to avoid the statute's requirement that military service members not be discharged because of their protected military service."[92] The employer explained that it terminated the plaintiff "for cause" because: (1) the plaintiff was identified, before his leave, as an employee with low sales and the company was reducing its workforce; and (2) that the plaintiff violated the office email policy by using it for personal use and offensive email.[93]

The plaintiff, not disputing the company's charges, provided evidence from which a jury could conclude that his military service was the true reason for his termination, including: (1) plaintiff's supervisor frequently made negative comments about his military duty; (2) on the day the plaintiff returned from military duty, someone else sat at his desk; and (3) the financial manager submitted an affidavit in the case explaining that when the plaintiff was on military leave, his supervisor stated that the company would terminate the plaintiff upon his return.[94] The court, in concluding that a reasonable jury could find that the company's stated reasons for terminating the plaintiff were not the true reasons, explained that the jury could also find that the company did not terminate the employee "for cause," as required under USERRA.[95] Therefore, the court denied the defendant's summary judgment motion.[96]

---

[91] *See id.*
[92] *Id.*
[93] *Id.* at *2.
[94] *Id.*
[95] *Id.* at *3.
[96] *Id.*

VII. Protection Against Termination of Employment Upon Reinstatement

Except for cause, a person reemployed by an employer under USERRA shall not be discharged within one year after the date of such reemployment if his period of service was more than 180 days;[97] if his period of service was more than 30 days but less than 181 days, the protection provided for "cause" dismissals is reduced to 180 days.[98] Military leaves of 30 days or less are provided no protection against dismissals.[99]

In *Johnson v. Preston Cycles, LLC,*[100] the United States District Court for the District of South Carolina denied defendant-employer's motion for summary judgment on the grounds that a reasonable jury could find that the employer's stated reasons for plaintiff-employee's termination were false and did not constitute for-cause termination under Section 4316(c).[101] The employer provided two justifications for the termination: employee's low sales before his last 30-day military duty, coupled with a move to reduce workforce due to a downturn in business; and employee's use of his office email account while on military leave to forward a non–work-related and offensive email to other employees in violation of company policy.[102]

While the plaintiff neither disputed the offensive nature of the email nor offered contrary evidence regarding his low sales, the court found that he offered sufficient evidence from which a jury could find that the termination was not for either of the employer's proffered reasons.[103] The evidence included: frequent comments by a supervisor that his weekend military duty was causing the plaintiff to

---

[97] 38 U.S.C. §4316(c)(1).
[98] *Id.*, §4316(c)(2).
[99] *See id.*
[100] 2008 U.S. Dist. LEXIS 92454 (D.S.C. 2008).
[101] *Id.* at *3–4; 38 U.S.C. §4316(c).
[102] *Id.*
[103] *Id.* at *5.

miss sales and have low sales numbers;[104] finding another salesperson at his desk (discrediting the notion that the employer sought to reduce its workforce);[105] actions that appeared as if the supervisor was looking for a reason to terminate the plaintiff;[106] attendance by the supervisor at a lengthy meeting, after which the plaintiff was told he was being terminated for low sales numbers;[107] and the plaintiff's submission of an affidavit from the financial manager, confirming a conversation with the supervisor indicating that the plaintiff would be terminated upon his return from military duty for failing to give advance notice of the military duty requirement.[108] Accordingly, the court denied the defendant summary judgment.[109]

In addition to alleging a violation of Section 4313(a),[110] the plaintiff in *Serricchio v. Wachovia Securities, LLC,* brought suit against his employer for constructive discharge without cause under Section 4316(c)(1).[111] The plaintiff argued that he had gone from a financially comfortable position to one in which he had virtually no book of business and had to cold-call new clients to pay off his $2,000 per month advance.[112] Given his pessimism, in contrast with the defendant's optimism for future prospects, the court found a triable issue of fact, ruling that reasonable jurors could find that a reasonable person would have felt compelled to resign.[113]

---

[104]*Id.*

[105]*Id.*

[106]*Id.*

[107]*Id.*

[108]*Id.* at *6.

[109]*Id.*

[110]*See* Serricchio v. Wachovia Securities, LLC, 556 F. Supp. 2d 99, 109 (D. Conn. 2008); *See also Serricchio* dicussion *infra* at nn. 50–66.

[111]38 U.S.C. §4316(c)(1) ("A person who is reemployed by an employer under this chapter shall not be discharged from such employment, except for cause— (1) within one year after the date of such reemployment, if the person's period of service before the reemployment was more than 180 days").

[112]*Serricchio,* 556 F. Supp. 2d at 109.

[113]*See id.*

A. Employee Pension Plans

A returning employee under USERRA must be treated as not having incurred a break in service with the employer who maintains the employee's pension plan.[114] During the employee's absence due to military service, the employer is liable for funding any obligation owed by the employee to the pension plan, and shall allocate the amount of employer contribution in the same manner and to the same extent such allocation occurs for other employees.[115] In the case of defined contribution plans, the employer is not responsible for making up for any of the employee's earnings and forfeitures missed while in service.[116] For thrift plans and cash or deferred arrangements, the returning employee may make contributions up to the amount he or she would have been allowed to had his or her employment not been interrupted, as long as the employee makes such contributions within a time period equal to three times the period he was in military service, up to five years maximum.[117]

To compute an employer's liability, the employee's compensation shall be computed at a rate the employee would have received but for the military service.[118] If that rate is not reasonably certain, then the calculation must be made on the basis of the employee's average rate of compensation during the 12-month period immediately preceding such service.[119]

---

[114]See 38 U.S.C. §4318(a)(2)(A).
[115]See id., 38 U.S.C. §4318(b)(1).
[116]See id.
[117]See id., §4318(b)(2).
[118]See id., §4318(b)(3)(A).
[119]See id., §4318(b)(3)(B).

CHAPTER 8

USERRA AND HEALTH CARE BENEFITS

I. Introduction

The Uniformed Services Employment and Reemployment Rights Act of 1994 (USERRA or the Act) provides that qualifying individuals shall have continuing access to health benefits.[1] An employee who leaves work to perform military service (employee or service member) has two distinct rights with respect to health benefits under USERRA:

(1) the right to continue preexisting coverage; and
(2) the opportunity to participate in the employer's health plan upon return to the civilian job without meeting initial eligibility requirements.[2]

The scope and effect of these rights is the subject of this chapter and detailed below.

II. Impact of Military Leave on Health Benefits (38 U.S.C. Section 4317)

Section 4317 of USERRA is the exclusive source of an employee's rights under the Act with respect to health benefits; accordingly, this section supersedes more general provisions of USERRA—dealing with rights and benefits of employees, generally—that may conflict with Section 4317.[3] In addition to the Act, the Secretary of Labor (in consultation with the Secretary of Defense) can prescribe regulations to implement the provisions of the Act applicable to States, local governments, and private employers.[4]

---

[1] In order to qualify for any rights under USERRA, an individual must meet five threshold requirements. Accordingly, he or she must have: (1) held a civilian job before service; (2) provided the civilian employer with advance notice of military leave (that is, unless notice was otherwise excused under the Act); (3) served less than five cumulative years in the military; (4) neither been dishonorably discharged nor released from the military under other punitive conditions, and (5) either reported back or applied for reemployment in a timely manner. *See* Douglas M. Selwyn, *The Uniformed Services Employment and Reemployment Rights Act and Employee Health Benefits*, 46 Hous. Law 28, 29 (2008) [hereinafter *Selwyn*].

[2] *Id.*

[3] *See* 38 U.S.C. §4316(b)(5)

[4] The Secretary issued regulations on December 15, 2005, that became effective on January 16, 2006. Specifically, Sections 1002.163 through 1002.171 of the regulations im-

A. A USERRA Health Plan

The ambit of a "health plan" under the Act is broad, and encompasses any "insurance policy or contract, medical or hospital service agreement, membership or subscription contract, or other arrangement under which health services for individuals are provided, or the expenses of such services are paid."[5] Additionally, the regulations provide that USERRA applies to health plans covered under ERISA, and those that otherwise are exempt from ERISA coverage—e.g., plans initiated or maintained by governmental entities or churches for their employees.[6] A USERRA "health plan" also includes multiemployer health plans (and the special characteristics of such plans are discussed below), cafeteria plans, and other flexible arrangements.

However, there is no indication whether "health services" under USERRA is congruent with "medical care" under Internal Revenue Code Section 213. If the terms share the same or a similar meaning, USERRA would entitle an employee to maintain coverage for dental treatment, vision therapy, drug and alcohol treatment, and the like. Given the intent of the Act, it would be prudent to assume, at the minimum, that dental insurance and vision insurance are covered "health services."

B. USERRA Coverage Compared to COBRA

As of May 2009 there has been no case law to interpret Section 4317 or the regulations to implement health benefits under the Act. Accordingly, there is little guidance in determining what potential issues may arise with respect to an employee's health benefits under the Act, and how po-

---

plement Section 4317 of the Act. *See* Veterans' Employment and Training Service, 70 Fed. Reg., 75246, 75265 (Dec. 19, 2005).
    [5] 38 U.S.C. §§4303(7); *see also* 20 C.F.R. 1002.5(e).
    [6] *See* 20 C.F.R. §1002.163(b).

tential issues will subsequently be resolved. But, to gain a better understanding of USERRA, it is prudent to compare the Act with the Consolidated Omnibus Budget Reconciliation Act (COBRA).[7]

The health plan provisions under USERRA share similarities, in many respects, to those of COBRA. USERRA, however, is not identical to COBRA. USERRA and COBRA are similar in that both Acts neither require the employer to establish a health plan (if one is not already in place), nor must it provide any particular type of coverage if it chooses to establish a plan.[8] Additionally, both Acts extend continuing coverage to the employee (or former employee, as the case may be with COBRA) as well as his or her dependents.

Unlike COBRA, the Secretary of Labor (Secretary) provides plan administrators a significant amount of leeway to implement USERRA.[9] The flexibility to implement USERRA flows from a distinguishable variation between the two Acts: no employees are exempt from compliance with USERRA.[10] Accordingly, since small employers are not exempt from USERRA compliance, the Secretary chose not to unduly burden such employers that otherwise would not have to comply with COBRA-like compliance guidelines but for USERRA.[11]

---

[7]The Consolidated Omnibus Budget Reconciliation Act of 1985 (COBRA) was enacted to allow former employees to maintain access to affordable private health insurance.

[8]*See Selwyn, supra* note 1, at 29.

[9]*See* Veterans' Employment and Training Service, 70 Fed. Reg. at 75266.

[10]*Compare* IRC §4890B(d)(2) (COBRA coverage does not apply to plans established or maintained by churches, the federal government, or small employers with fewer than 20 employers) *with* 38 U.S.C. §4303(4)(A)(the term "employer" specifically includes the federal government, and excludes neither small employers nor churches from the general definition).

[11]*See* 70 Fed. Reg. at 75267.

III. EMPLOYERS SUBJECT TO THE HEALTH PLAN PROVISIONS OF USERRA

The term "employer" under USERRA, as previously discussed above, is broadly defined. The term also includes any third party (e.g., plan administrator, insurance company) that has assumed responsibility to administer employee health plans on behalf of the employer.[12] And the presence of a written agreement—that a third party has undertaken responsibilities on behalf of the employer—is not dispositive in determining whether liability extends to such third parties under USERRA.[13] However, a third party who merely performs ministerial tasks at the request of the employer will not be deemed an "employer" subject to USERRA liability for noncompliance.[14] Additionally, a "hiring hall" may, under certain circumstances, be considered an employer for the purposes of USERRA liability.[15]

IV. "IN CONNECTION WITH EMPLOYMENT" REQUIREMENT

USERRA's health plan provisions only apply if the service member's coverage was received in connection with his or her employment.[16] *If the service member was covered as a dependent or spouse under a family member's policy, USERRA will not apply with respect to such coverage.*[17] Furthermore, the mere fact that a service member used compensation from services rendered to purchase a policy independent from one provided by the employer will not extend USERRA rights to cover that independent policy.[18] And policies received by a

---

[12]*See* 38 U.S.C. §4303(4); 1002.5(d).

[13]*See* 70 Fed. Reg. at 75266

[14]The Regulations provide limited guidance as to what is considered a "purely ministerial" task (e.g., maintaining the employer's files, preparing forms to submit to a government agency). *See* 20 C.F.R. §1002.5(d)(1)(i).

[15]*See* 20 C.F.R. §1002.38.

[16]*See* 38 U.S.C. §4317(a)(1).

[17]*See* Veterans' Employment and Training Service, 70 Fed. Reg. at 75266.

[18]*See id.*

service member in connection with a professional association, club, or other organization also will not be governed by USERRA.[19]

Neither dependents nor retirees that have a policy are entitled to continuing coverage under USERRA because their policies were not received in connection with their employment. However, even though these individuals are not entitled to continuing coverage under USERRA, they may be entitled to reinstatement of health plan coverage after military service under the Service Members Civil Relief Act.[20]

V. Dependents Entitled to Coverage

USERRA provides that individuals who are absent from employment have the right to elect to continue coverage for their dependents.[21] While dependents are entitled to continuing coverage under USERRA, they are not vested with an independent right to elect for continuing coverage.[22] The absence of this election right for dependents may be problematic when the service member does not elect to continue coverage, and the subsequent lapse in coverage violates a custody or child support agreement.[23] However, even though an independent election right for dependents does not emanate from the Act itself, Section 1002.165 provides that plan administrators may provide COBRA-like notice, election, and waiver procedures, at their discretion.[24]

---

[19] See id.

[20] See 50 U.S.C. App. 594.

[21] See 38 U.S.C. §4317(a)(1).

[22] In contrast to USERRA, COBRA entitles "qualified beneficiaries" a separate right to elect to continue coverage under an existing policy. By way of example, if an employee under COBRA does not elect to continue coverage, the employee's spouse or dependent children may nevertheless elect to continue coverage for themselves. See I.R.C §4980B(F)(1) and (5)(B); I.R.S. Regs. §45.4980B-6.

[23] See Veterans' Employment and Training Service, 70 Fed. Reg. at 75266.

[24] See id.

VI. Length of Time for Continuing Coverage

Section 1002.164 of the regulations determines the length of time an employee is entitled to continue coverage. If an employee elects to continue coverage under the pre-existing policy during military service, an employer is only obligated to provide such coverage under the policy for a maximum of 24 months.[25] Accordingly, the employer may terminate the employee's coverage when the employee's service time exceeds 24 contiguous months. However, if the employee's service time is less than 24 months, the employer does not have to offer continuing coverage under the pre-existing policy for the entire 24-month period: the employer may terminate coverage on the day after the service member fails to apply for reemployment.[26] The maximum 24-month period commences on the date of the employee's absence for the purpose of performing military service.[27] The length of time an employee may elect to continue coverage during service time will be the same for his or her dependents as well.

The statute explicitly entitles an employee to continue coverage already in existence; it does not, however, entitle the employee to initiate coverage upon departure from employment for military service.[28]

VII. Procedures for Implementing the Right to Continue Coverage Under USERRA

Section 1002.165 details what is required of plan administrators and fiduciaries to implement an employee's

---

[25] See 38 U.S.C. §4317(a)(1)(A); 20 C.F.R. §1002.164.

[26] The relevant date for determining when the service member must apply for reemployment to avoid termination of continuing coverage is provided under Sections 1002.115–123 of these regulations. See 20 C.F.R. §1002.164(a)(2).

[27] This date is similar to a "qualifying event" under COBRA that triggers an employee's "election period." See I.R.C. §4980B(f)(3)

[28] See 20 C.F.R. §1002.164(c).

election right to continue coverage. USERRA does not impose an extensive set of requirements or procedures to ensure compliance. To the contrary, plan administrators may implement reasonable procedures to ensure compliance, but they are not required to do so.[29]

While Section 1002.165 does not provide much detail in terms of what procedures are reasonable, the regulation does specifically state that such procedures (if implemented) must comport with the notice requirements under Section 4312(b).[30] Accordingly, where military necessity[31] prevents the service member from giving the employer notice that he or she is leaving for military duty, or where giving such notice would be impossible or unreasonable, plan requirements may not be imposed to deny the service member continuing coverage.[32] Compliance with this notice provision puts an employer who does not receive advance notice of an employee's military leave and election to continue coverage in an unusual predicament: they could carry the coverage and pay premiums even though the employee does not wish to continue coverage, or cancel the plan and risk potential USERRA liability.

A. Retroactive Reinstatement

To remedy the dilemma posed above, Section 1002.167 entitles a plan administrator to cancel coverage if the employee does not receive notice of the employee's election to

---

[29]*See id.*, §1002.165.

[30]There are a few reasons why the Secretary was averse to implementing a strict set of procedural requirements or operating procedures to implement the service member's election right. First, compliance with such requirements may be unduly burdensome on small employers that are subject to USERRA and exempt from COBRA. Second, individual plans are best suited to determine election rules to implement their respective plans' unique features. And third, nothing prohibits a plan from developing COBRA-like time frames and election periods so long as they comport with Section 4312(b). *See* Veterans' Employment and Training Service, 70 Fed. Reg. at 75267.

[31]"Military necessity" exists and therefore excuses an employee's failure to give notice when "a mission, operation, exercise or requirement that is classified, or a pending or ongoing mission, operation, exercise or requirement [sic] may be compromised or otherwise adversely affected by public knowledge." 32 C.F.R. §104.3.

[32]*See* Veterans' Employment and Training Service, 70 Fed. Reg. at 75266.

continue coverage premised on excusal of notice under Section 4312(b).[33] When an employee does not affirmatively elect to continue the plan during military service, and the failure to give notice is excused, an employer is generally entitled to cancel the plan.[34] However, if the employee subsequently invokes the right to continue coverage, the employer must retroactively reinstate the plan provided the employee makes full payment of all unpaid amounts.[35] This may provide an employee on military leave with a cost-effective option—the employee may apply for reinstatement "after the fact"—when the cost of paying premiums is less than medical costs without coverage.[36]

B. Reinstatement for Non-Electing Employees

Employees who provide their employers with advance notice of departure but initially elect to terminate coverage may change their mind and have coverage retroactively reinstated in a similar manner as an employee that seeks reinstatement because his or her plan was excused under the notice provision.[37] Subsection (b) of Section 1002.167 addresses a situation in which an employee leaves employment for uniformed service in excess of 30 days and provides advance notice of the military service, but does not elect continuing coverage.[38] A plan administrator that has developed reasonable rules regarding the election of continuing coverage may cancel the employee's health plan coverage, but must reinstate it upon the employee's subsequent election and full payment within the time periods established by the plan, without imposition of administrative

---

[33]See 20 C.F.R. §1002.167(a).

[34]See id., §1002.167(a).

[35]See id., §1002.167(b).

[36]See Selwyn, supra note 1, at 30.

[37]Employees who (1) do not give notice and (2) do not fall under the Section 4212(b) exception, are not entitled to retroactive reinstatement under USERRA.

[38]See Veterans' Employment and Training Service, 70 Fed. Reg. at 75267.

costs.[39] On the other end of the spectrum, a plan administrator who has not developed rules regarding the employee's election right may also cancel the employee's plan, but it must be reinstated under the same general requirement as a plan that has implemented regulations.[40]

VIII. Cost of Continuation Coverage

A plan may require an individual who elects to continue plan coverage to pay a premium for such coverage. Indeed, a service member who elects to continue employer-provided coverage may be required to pay 102%—representing both the employee and the employer's share of the premium.[41] However, continuing coverage for the employee's first 30 days of military service shall not exceed the employee's share of the coverage if any such share existed—i.e., if the employee did not have to pay for the coverage prior to military service, he gets the first 30 days for free.[42]

USERRA does not provide specific guidance concerning the timing of payments for the continuation of coverage or the termination of coverage for failure to make payments. Plan administrators are entitled to develop reasonable procedures for payment, consistent with the plan's terms.[43] Plan administrators are permitted to develop reasonable procedures to handle either scenario.[44] In either scenario, the Secretary suggests that it may be reasonable for the health plan administrator to adopt COBRA-compli-

---

[39] See id.

[40] See id.

[41] USERRA's regulations do not specifically compare the 102% figure to the "applicable premium" under COBRA (which is also 102%), but plan administrators presumably calculate the number in the same manner. See Selwyn, supra note 1, at 30.

[42] This provision was imposed to protect the dependents of Reserve Component members because, under the military health care system, such dependents were not entitled to coverage unless the member's service exceeded 30 days. See H.R. Rep. No. 103-65, Pt. 1, at 34 (1993).

[43] See 20 C.F.R. §1002.166(c); 20 C.F.R. §1002.167(c).

[44] See id.

ant rules.[45] Under COBRA, the employee is generally entitled to a 45-day grace period for making his or her initial payment after an election to continue coverage, and a 30-day grace period for each payment thereafter.[46]

IX. Reinstatement Right

Section 1002.168 provides that when an employee's health plan is terminated during service time, the plan must subsequently be reinstated—to ensure there is no gap in the employee's coverage—upon his or her reemployment after service.[47] The employer may be liable if the plan imposes an exclusion or waiting period when one would not have been imposed if the employee had not otherwise left work for military service.[48] Additionally, if dependents were covered under the employee's health plan before its termination, their coverage must also be reinstated upon the service member's reemployment.[49]

While there is a general right to plan reinstatement upon reemployment, the employer will not be liable for imposing an exclusion or waiting period for injuries or illnesses that were aggravated or incurred during service time.[50] The Secretary of Veterans' Affairs will determine whether such conditions exist.[51] This limited exception obviously does not apply to dependents that could not have incurred any conditions by reason of service.[52]

---

[45]See 20 C.F.R. §1002.166(c);

[46]See I.R.C. §§4980B(f)(2)(C);(B)(iii).

[47]Section 1002.168(a) provides employees with a reinstatement right upon reemployment. Note, however, that health plans terminated by reason of failing to give advance notice of leave that were not excused under USERRA are not entitled to automatic reinstatement.

[48]See 20 C.F.R. §1002.168(a).

[49]See id.

[50]See 70 Fed. Reg. at 75268.

[51]See id.

[52]There is no authority for determining whether dependents that were also performing service would be subject to exclusion. Additionally, since many conditions may be latent, and therefore not present for years after service, there may be potential issues regarding health coverage for these conditions long after service time.

A. Insurance Company Liability

If an employer delegates the responsibility of administering health coverage to an insurance company, the former may be liable for noncompliance with USERRA for not negotiating for the employee's automatic reinstatement right.[53] Additionally, the latter may be held liable under USERRA for failing to modify the plan at the request of the employer to comply with USERRA because the third party has sufficient control over the employee's USERRA rights.[54]

B. Upon Reinstatement and Not Sooner

Under USERRA, an employee is entitled to "prompt reemployment" after a timely application.[55] "Prompt" does not necessarily mean "immediate"—i.e., the employer has two weeks to reemploy the employee after submitting an application for reemployment.[56] Accordingly, the employee's right to immediate reinstatement of coverage does not vest until he or she is actually reemployed.[57] Therefore, an employer will not be subject to liability for failure to reinstate the plan during the period of applying for reemployment and actual reemployment.[58]

C. Returning Employees Do Not Have a Right to Delay Reinstatement

While Section 1002.168 grants a returning employee the right to automatic reinstatement, Section 1002.169 does not grant a returning employee the corollary right to delay reinstatement: if the employee wishes to delay reinstatement until sometime after reemployment, the employer

---

[53] *See* 70 Fed. Reg. at 75268.
[54] *See* S. Rep. No. 103-158, at 42 (1993).
[55] *See* 20 C.F.R. §1002.181.
[56] *See id.*
[57] *See* 70 Fed. Reg. at 75268.
[58] *See id.*

does not have to oblige.[59] But nothing in the regulation prohibits the employer from accommodating the employee's request to delay reinstatement.[60]

X. Multi-Employer Health Plans

Under USERRA, the employer does not have to provide an employee with continuing coverage during service if the employee would have lost such coverage in connection with employment irrespective of service time.[61] However, Section 1002.170 varies this general rule with respect to multiemployer health plans. If the employee is a member of a multiemployer health plan, USERRA requires continuing coverage under the plan even if the employer goes out of business, or otherwise discontinues participation in the plan while the employee is performing military service.[62] This regulation may put an employee who left work for military service in a better position than if the employee had never left his or her civilian job.

A. Liability for Employer Contributions

Generally, during service time, the employer is not obligated to make contributions to the health plan.[63] However, upon return, the employee is no longer obligated to pay 102 percent—which previously may have included both the employee and the employer's share—of the premium

---

[59]See 20 C.F.R. §1002.169.

[60]The regulations permit flexibility to employers in this situation. However, there is no indication of what an employee must do to ask for or delay reinstatement. This could create problems—if there is a delay due to the employee's request, could the employer be subject to liability if the employee later relinquishes his wish to delay reinstatement?

[61]Stated another way, if the employer goes out of business or terminates health plans for all employees while the service member is performing military duty, the employer will not be subject to liability for cancelling the service member's plan while he or she is performing duty. See 70 Fed. Reg. at 75269.

[62]See id.

[63]Under Section 1002.166, the employer does not have to pay the employer's share of the premium to continue coverage on behalf of the employee after the first 30 days of service.

to continue coverage. Accordingly, it is necessary to determine who is liable for paying premiums on behalf of the employer who no longer participates in a multiemployer health plan to continue coverage for the employee. Liability for payment of the employer's share under the plan upon return is allocated in the following order:

(1) Liability for contributions to the plan is allocated as provided by the multiemployer health plan's sponsor.[64]

(2) If the sponsor does not provide for the allocation of responsibility, such responsibility lies with the last employer before the employee's service time.[65]

(3) When the former employer is no longer functional (irrespective of whether the plan allocates responsibility to the non-functional former employer), then responsibility is allocated to the plan itself.[66]

B. Multi-Employer "Bank Plans"

Employers may subscribe to health plans commonly referred to as "credit bank," "dollar bank," or "hour bank" plans within the multiemployer health plan community. By way of example only, these plans allow employees who work a certain amount of hours during a given period to "bank" excess credits and apply them to later payments for insurance premiums.[67] In Section 1002.171, the Secretary provides guidance on how these multiemployer plans may comply with USERRA. Under this section, a bank plan may freeze an employee's credits during service time—and therefore require the employee to pay the full amount of premiums during service time—so the employee may later

---

[64]20 C.F.R. §1002.170.
[65]Id.
[66]Id.
[67]See 70 Fed. Reg. at 72569.

apply these stored credits upon reinstatement to continuing coverage.[68]

Conversely, the plan does not have to freeze the employee's credits. The plan may permit the employee to apply stored credits (assuming he or she has accumulated them prior to military service) to continue coverage—in lieu of monetary premium payments—until they have been exhausted. When the employee's credits have been exhausted, to continue coverage during service time, the employee must subsequently pay his or her allocable premium to maintain coverage. Accordingly, when the employee subsequently returns from service without any stored credits, the plan must allow the service member to pay for continuing coverage until the employee's credits are sufficiently restored under the plan.[69] Since an employee may not fully comprehend the consequences of their actions with respect to these technical plans, the regulations encourage employers or plan administrators to provide guidance to employees in determining what action may be prudent.[70] The regulations do not, however, address whether an employee or plan administrator may be liable for failing to counsel employees with respect to their options under these types of plans.

---

[68]20 C.F.R. §1002.171(a)(2).
[69]20 C.F.R. §1002.171(a)(1).
[70]20 C.F.R. §1002.171(b).

CHAPTER 9

INTERRELATIONSHIP WITH OTHER LAWS AND EMPLOYER PRACTICES

I. OVERVIEW

The Uniformed Services Employment and Reemployment Rights Act (USERRA or the Act) contemplates interaction with a variety of federal, state, and local laws, along with various employer policies. Where a state or local law or employer policy provides greater benefits than USERRA, the employee remains entitled to those benefits.[1] However, any state or local law or employer policy that purports to limit, reduce, or eliminate a right or benefit provided by USERRA, or that establishes additional prerequisites to the exercise of such rights or benefits, is explicitly superseded.[2] An employer that chooses to confer a benefit exceeding USERRA requirements in one area may not attempt to offset its commitment by reducing or limiting USERRA rights in another area.[3]

---

[1] See 38 U.S.C. §4302(a); 20 C.F.R. §§1002.7(a), (c).

[2] See 38 U.S.C. §4302(b); 20 C.F.R. §1002.7(b).

[3] See 20 C.F.R. §1002.7(d). For example, USERRA regulations suggest that an employer may choose to provide a fixed amount of paid military leave each year to members of the National Guard or Reserve. The fact that it voluntarily chooses to confer this benefit, however, does not allow the employer to refrain from providing unpaid military leave once the paid leave is exhausted. Id.

Section II of this chapter deals with the interaction between USERRA and other federal laws. It is important to note that many states and the District of Columbia have chosen to enact provisions extending additional benefits to covered servicemembers employed in the public sector,[4] while others have chosen to extend some protections to all employees, regardless of whether they are employed in the public or private sector.[5] For example, some states have chosen to extend coverage to temporary employees, while others require public employers to continue the pay of servicemembers. This chapter does not attempt to cover those provisions in detail, but rather provides a general overview of some of the more common elements. Finally, Section III discusses the interplay of employer policies with USERRA.

The statutory provisions primarily covered in this chapter include 38 U.S.C. Sections 4301, 4302, 4322, and 4323. The provisions of the DOL Regulations primarily addressed in this chapter are located at 20 C.F.R. Section 1002.7.

II. INTERRELATIONSHIP WITH OTHER LAWS

A. General Principles

As a federally mandated leave and anti-discrimination law, USERRA must interact with a number of other federal, state, and local employment statutes. Consequently, USERRA coexists with anti-discrimination laws such as Title VII of the Civil Rights Act of 1964 (Title VII), as well as federal leave statutes such as the Family and Medical Leave Act

---

[4]Delaware, the District of Columbia, Maryland, Massachusetts, North Dakota, Ohio, South Dakota, Tennnessee, and West Virginia.

[5]Alabama, Alaska, Arizona, Arkansas, California, Colorado, Connecticut, Florida, Georgia, Hawaii, Idaho, Illinois, Indiana, Iowa, Kansas, Kentucky, Louisiana, Maine, Massachusetts, Michigan, Minnesota, Missouri, Montana, Nebraska, Nevada, New Hampshire, New Jersey, New Mexico, New York, North Carolina, Oklahoma, Oregon, Pennsylvania, Rhode Island, South Carolina, Texas, Utah, Vermont, Virginia, Washington, Wisconsin, Wyoming. Congress has also enacted military leave laws applicable to Puerto Rico. Each of these states provides various protections; examination of a particular state's laws is required to determine the applicable rights/obligations.

(FMLA),[6] neither enhancing nor diminishing employee rights under such laws.

The Act expressly contemplates this interrelationship by emphasizing that it does not "supersede, nullify or diminish any Federal or State law (including any local law or ordinance), contract, agreement, policy, plan, practice or other matter that establishes" greater rights or benefits for those engaging in military service.[7] That being said, the Act makes clear that it does supersede "any State law (including any local law or ordinance), contract, agreement, policy, plan, practice or other matter that reduces, limits, or eliminates in any manner any right or benefit provided" thereunder.[8]

Put simply, "USERRA establishes a floor, not a ceiling, for the employment and reemployment rights and benefits of those it protects."[9] This leaves states with the ability to grant employees greater rights than those provided by USERRA, and allows employers to increase an employee's rights and benefits beyond those provided under USERRA, while precluding both states and employers from limiting any right or benefit guaranteed by the Act.[10]

Thus, in any situation triggering USERRA rights and obligations, other state and federal laws, as well as an employer's policies, may come into play, and thus the potential applicability of additional rights and obligations must be evaluated.

---

[6]29 U.S.C. §§2601–2654.

[7]38 U.S.C. §4302(a). As an example, USERRA's regulations make clear that, while the Act does not require an employer to pay for time spent away from work in uniformed service, a policy, plan or practice providing such benefits would be entirely permissible. 20 C.F.R. §1002.7(c).

[8]38 U.S.C. §4302(b). For illustrative purposes, USERRA's regulations suggest that, "an employment contract that determines seniority based only on actual days of work in the place of employment would be superseded by USERRA, which requires that seniority credit be given for periods of absence from work due to service in the uniformed services." 20 C.F.R. §1002.7(b).

[9]20 C.F.R. §1002.7(a).

[10]See id.

B. Federal Laws

1. Family and Medical Leave Act

a. General Principles

The FMLA is a federal law that provides an "eligible" employee of a covered employer with the right to take up to 12 work weeks of unpaid, job-protected leave on an annualized basis for, among other things the birth or care of a newborn child, placement of a child for adoption or foster care purposes, or the serious health condition of the employee or a close family member.[11] The FMLA was enacted in 1993 and is codified at 29 U.S.C. Sections 12601–2654, and at 5 U.S.C. Sections 16381–6387 relating to federal civil service employees.

Recent FMLA amendments covering leave in connection with servicemembers and their family members substantially increase the interrelationship between the FMLA and USERRA. Those developments are discussed in detail in Sections II.B.1.e and II.B.1.f, below.

b. Covered Employers and Eligible Employees

Under the FMLA, the term "employer" "means any person engaged in commerce or in any industry or activity affecting commerce who employs 50 or more employees for each working day during each of 20 or more calendar workweeks in the current or preceding calendar year."[12] This term includes "any person who acts, directly or indirectly, in the interest of an employer to any of the employees of such employer."[13] Thus, individuals, including managers

---

[11]See ABA Section of Labor and Employment Law, The Family and Medical Leave Act (Michael J. Ossip & Robert M. Hale et al. eds., 2006 & Gail C. Coleman et al. eds., Cumulative Supp. BNA Books 2009).

[12]29 U.S.C. §2611(4)(A)(i).

[13]Id., §2611(4)(A)(ii).

and supervisors, can be held personally liable to eligible employees for violations of the statute.[14]

This definition is further restricted by the definition of an eligible employee. To be eligible for leave under the FMLA, an employee must have: (1) worked for the employer for at least 12 months, although this time need not be consecutive; (2) worked at least 1,250 hours during the 12-month period immediately preceding the commencement of leave; and (3) worked at a work site that employs 50 or more employees within 75 surface miles of the site.[15]

USERRA's coverage is far more broad than that of the FMLA, extending to all public and private employers, regardless of size.[16] Covered employees are defined simply as "person[s] employed by an employer."[17] In addition, USERRA typically applies to individuals, including managers and supervisors, so that, as under the FMLA, individuals can be personally liable for violations of the statute.[18]

USERRA, however, does exclude certain temporary employees. Under the Act, "[a]n employer is not required to reemploy a person if . . . the employment from which the person leaves to serve in the uniformed services is for a brief, non-recurrent period, and there is no reasonable expectation that such employment will continue indefinitely or for a significant time."[19]

One area of overlap between USERRA and the FMLA occurs in connection with employees who slip below minimum FMLA eligibility requirements due to USERRA-pro-

---

[14]See Mitchell v. Chapman, 343 F.3d 811, 829–30 (6th Cir. 2003), cert. denied, 542 U.S. 937 (2004); Mueller v. J.P. Morgan Chase & Co., 2007 U.S. Dist. LEXIS 20828, at *67 (N.D. Ohio Mar. 23, 2007); Smith v. Genesis Ventures I, 2006 U.S. Dist. LEXIS 89285, at *15–16, (E.D. Pa. 2006); Brown v. CBK, 2005 U.S. Dist. LEXIS 31960, at *5-11 (W.D. Tenn. Nov. 28, 2005). In the public employer context, the result may be different. See Lombardi v. Hinsdale Sch. Dist. 86 Bd. of Trs., 463 F. Supp. 2d 867, 870–72, (N.D. Ill. 2006); but see Modica v. Taylor, 465 F.3d 174, 186–87 (5th Cir. 2006).

[15]29 C.F.R. §825.110(a), (b).

[16]See 20 C.F.R. §1002.34(a).

[17]38 U.S.C. §4303(3).

[18]See, e.g., Brandsasse v. City of Suffolk, Va., 72 F. Supp. 2d 608, 617–18 (E.D. Va. 1999).

[19]38 U.S.C. §4312(d)(1)(C).

tected service commitments. Recognizing this issue, the Department of Labor has opined that leave occasioned by military service is deemed equivalent to hours worked for purposes of determining eligibility for FMLA leave.[20]

For example, an employee on military leave may fall short of the threshold FMLA eligibility requirements of 1,250 hours worked. The DOL's memorandum states that an employer must count time the individual would have worked had he or she not been called to duty toward the 1,250-hour requirement for FMLA eligibility. To determine the hours that would have been worked during the period of military service, the employee's pre-service work schedule can generally be used for calculations.

The same holds true for the FMLA's 12-month eligibility requirement with respect to total length of service. Take the example of an employee with 10 months of service who is subsequently ordered to serve in the military for 10 months, at which point he or she returns to work. Upon reemployment, the employee is considered to have been employed by the employer for more than the required 12 months for FMLA eligibility purposes.[21]

c. Qualifying Events

Aside from recent FMLA amendments pertaining to caregiver and qualifying exigency leave, there is not a great deal of intersection between the FMLA and USERRA when it comes to qualifying events for leave. Generally speaking, under the pre-amendment provisions of FMLA, the following circumstances qualified an employee for leave:

- birth of a child and the need to care for the newborn child;

---

[20]*See generally* U.S. Dep't of Labor, FMLA Special Rules for Returning Reservists (USERRA), Memorandum from Eugene Scalia, Solicitor of Labor, *at* www.dol.gov/esa/whd/FMLA/userra.htm.

[21]*See id.*

- placement of a child with the employee for adoption or foster care;
- the need to care for a child, spouse, or parent with a serious health condition; or
- the employee's own serious health condition that prevents the employee from performing the functions of his position.[22]

Under USERRA, the performance of the following duties on an involuntary or voluntary basis constitutes "service in the uniformed services": active duty; active duty for training; initial active duty for training; inactive duty training; full-time National Guard Duty; and absence from work for an examination to determine an individual's fitness for any of the aforementioned types of duty.[23]

The following discussion addresses the 2008 FMLA amendments, which provide for FMLA caregiver and qualifying exigency leave.

(i) Caregiver Leave

On January 28, 2008, the FMLA was amended to provide for two new forms of leave that create significant overlaps with USERRA. Provisions establishing military "caregiver" leave took effect immediately, while those pertaining to "qualifying exigency" leave were implemented upon the effective date of final regulations that took effect on January 16, 2009.[24]

Pursuant to the 2008 amendments, an eligible employee who is the spouse, son, daughter, parent, or next of kin of a "covered servicemember" is entitled to take up to 26 work weeks of FMLA-protected caregiver leave during a single 12-month period to care for the service member. For the purposes of these amendments, a *covered servicemember* is

---

[22]*See* 29 U.S.C. §§2612(a)(1)(A)–(D); §§825.112(a)(1)–(4).
[23]38 U.S.C. §4303(13).
[24]*See* The Family and Medical Leave Act of 1993, 73 Fed. Reg. 67,934 (Nov. 17, 2008) (amending and revising 29 C.F.R. pt. 825).

defined as "a current member of the Armed Forces, including a member of the National Guard or Reserves, who is undergoing medical treatment, recuperation, or therapy, is otherwise in an outpatient status, or is otherwise on the temporary disability retired list, for a serious injury or illness incurred in the line of duty on active duty."[25] Thus, military caregiver leave is *not* limited to members of the National Guard or Reserves who are on active duty or have been called to active duty status, as is the case with "qualifying exigency" leave, discussed below.

The final regulations provide for changes in two important definitions. First, for purposes of caregiver leave, the definition of a "son or daughter" was expanded to apply to a covered servicemember's "biological, adopted, or foster child, stepchild, legal ward, or a child for whom the servicemember stood *in loco parentis*," regardless of age."[26]

Second, to avoid potentially inconsistent state law definitions, the new regulations define "next of kin of a covered servicemember" as the servicemember's nearest blood relative (other than the covered servicemember's spouse, parent, son, or daughter, who are already entitled to leave for this purpose) in the following order of priority: blood relatives who have been granted legal custody of the servicemember, brothers and sisters, grandparents, aunts and uncles, and first cousins.[27]

Family members sharing the same level of familial relationship (i.e., all siblings), are considered next of kin and are entitled to take military caregiver leave to care for the covered servicemember. A covered servicemember also may expressly designate a blood relative to serve as his only next

---

[25]29 U.S.C. §2611(16).

[26]29 C.F.R. §825.122(h). Prior to the 2008 amendments, the FMLA definition of *son or daughter* included only those (1) under 18 years of age, or (2) 18 years of age or older and incapable of self-care because of a mental or physical disability. *See* 29 C.F.R. §825.113(c)(2007) (current version at 29 C.F.R. §§835.122(c),h. If this definition were applied to military caregiver leave, adult children would not be able to take leave to care for a parent who is a covered servicemember.

[27]*See* 29 C.F.R. §825.122(d).

of kin for military caregiver leave. An employer may request reasonable documentation (i.e., a simple written statement or other document) to confirm the employee's family relationship to a covered servicemember.[28]

Eligible employees are entitled to a combined total of 26 work weeks for military caregiver leave and leave for any other FMLA-qualifying reason during the same "single 12-month period," provided that they take no more than 12 work weeks of leave because of a qualifying exigency or for any other FMLA-qualifying reason.[29] A "single 12-month period" begins on the date an employee first uses such leave and ends 12 months after that date.[29A]

By way of example, assume that an employee takes 16 work weeks of military caregiver leave to care for a spouse, child, parent, or next of kin. Later, in that same 12-month period, the employee wishes to take time off to bond with a newly adopted child. Because the law allows up to 26 work weeks of leave in a 12-month period for caregiver leave or in combination with other types of FMLA leave, that employee will be allowed to take up to 10 additional weeks off to care for the child in that same 12-month period, so long as the employee otherwise qualifies for FMLA leave.[30]

Military caregiver leave is to be applied on a per-covered-servicemember, per-injury basis. In other words, an eligible employee may be entitled to take more than one period of 26 workweeks of leave during his employment if the leave is to care for different covered servicemembers *or*

---

[28]*See* 29 C.F.R. §825.122(j)

[29]*Id.*, §825.127(c).

[29A]*Id.*, §825.127(c)(1).

[30]At present, there is some debate as to how the amount of leave an employee may take under the FMLA is affected by whether "caregiver" leave comes before or after any other FMLA leave. Assistant Secretary of Labor Victoria Lipnic has stated that an employee may be entitled to a maximum of 38 weeks of FMLA leave if an employee's caregiver leave were to come after the employee's regular 12 weeks of FMLA leave. *See* Bureau of National Affairs Daily Labor Report, January 15, 2009, available at http://news.bna.com/dlln/DLLNWB/split__display.adp?fedfid=11312358&vname=dlrnotallissues&wsn=508680000&searchid=8181833&doctypeid=1&type=date&mode=doc&split=0&scm=DLLNWB&pg=0. Assistant Secretary Lipnic also stated that, if the caregiver leave comes first, the employee would be limited to 26 weeks total of leave under the FMLA. *See id.*

to care for the same servicemember with a *subsequent* serious injury or illness, so long as the employee takes no more than 26 work weeks of leave (for any FMLA-qualifying reason) within any "single 12-month period."[31]

The regulations explicitly allow an employee to split the 26 weeks of leave for different reasons. For example, an eligible employee may, during the single 12-month period, take 18 weeks of FMLA leave to care for a covered servicemember and eight weeks of FMLA leave because of the employee's own serious health condition, so long as the employee does not take more than 12 weeks of leave due to his own serious health condition or for any other FMLA-qualifying reason.

Employees are permitted to take military caregiver leave on an intermittent basis not only in situations where it is medically necessary for treatment of the servicemember but also where the employee is needed only intermittently—such as where other care is usually available or care responsibilities are shared with another family member or third party.[32]

If military caregiver leave also qualifies as leave to care for a family member with a serious health condition during the "single 12-month period," the employer must designate the leave as military caregiver leave.[33] In other words, the two forms of FMLA leave do not run concurrently and, therefore, the leave time should not be counted both as leave to care for a covered servicemember and for a family member with a serious illness.

A husband and wife who are eligible for FMLA and who work for the same covered employer (even if they work at different work sites, in different operating divisions, or are located more than 75 miles apart) may be limited to a combined total of 26 work weeks of FMLA leave during a

---

[31]29 C.F.R. §825.127(c)(2).
[32]*See id.,* §825.124(c).
[33]*Id.,* 29 C.F.R. §825.127(c)(2), §825.127(c)(4).

"single 12-month period." If one spouse is ineligible for FMLA leave, however, the other spouse would be entitled to the full 26 weeks.[34]

An employer may request that an employee seeking military caregiver leave obtain medical certification that the servicemember's serious illness or injury was "incurred in the line of duty on active duty in the Armed Forces."[34A]

In addition to the general certification requirements for other types of FMLA-qualifying leave, the health care provider may certify that the servicemember is undergoing medical treatment, recuperation or therapy for a serious injury or illness that was incurred in the line of duty.[34B] An employer may also request clarification of the certification, but it may not request second or third opinions or recertifications.[35]

The final regulations clarify that there is no temporal proximity requirement between the time of illness and the treatment, recuperation, or therapy, except that the covered servicemember must be a current member of the Armed Forces, National Guard, or Reserves or on the temporary disability retired list.[36]

The definition of *covered servicemember* includes *current* members of the Regular Armed Forces, National Guard or Reserves, as well as members of the Regular Armed Forces, National Guard or Reserves who are on the temporary disability retired list.[37] By definition, therefore, *former* members of the Armed Forces, National Guard or Reserves, and members on the *permanent* disability retired list are not considered to be covered servicemembers.

---

[34]29 C.F.R. §825.127(d).
[34A]29 C.F.R. §§825.310(a), (b)(2).
[34B]*Id.*, §§825.310(b)(2), (4).
[35]*Id.* §825.310(d)–(e).
[36]*See id.*, §825.127(a).
[37]*See id.*, 29 U.S.C. §2611(16).

(ii) Qualifying Exigency Leave

The January 2008 FMLA amendments provide that an employee may take up to 12 weeks of unpaid leave for one or more "qualifying exigencies" if the employee's spouse, child, or parent (covered military member) is a member of one of the U.S. Armed Forces' reserve components or the National Guard on active duty or call-to-active-duty status. The amendments, however, did not define the term "qualifying exigency," and employers were not required to provide such leave, until that phrase was defined by the amended FMLA regulations on January 16, 2009.

Those regulations now define the term "qualifying exigency" by providing a non-exhaustive list of qualifying circumstances.[38] To be eligible for such leave, the covered military member must be a member of the military Reserves or National Guard when called to active duty and not already on active duty in the regular Armed Forces.[39] Although the term "active duty" commonly refers to those serving in the regular U.S. Armed Forces, the DOL has made clear that qualifying exigency leave is *not* available to those whose family members serve in the regular military. Rather, such leave applies *only* to reservists and National Guard members. Additionally, leave is only available for covered relatives of National Guard members who are called to active *federal* service by the President, and is therefore not available to those in the National Guard who are recalled to state service by the governor of the member's respective state.

The final regulations clarify the meaning of "qualifying exigency" by providing a list of specific examples along with a catch-all provision covering any agreed-upon "additional activities." An eligible employee may take FMLA leave while the covered military member is on active duty or call to ac-

---

[38] *See* 29 C.F.R. §825.126(a).
[39] *See id.*, §825.126(b).

tive duty[40] for one or more of the following qualifying exigencies:

1. *Short-notice deployment:* To address any issues that arise from the fact that a covered military member is notified of an impending call or order to active duty seven or fewer calendar days prior to the date of the deployment. Leave taken for this purpose can be used for a period of seven calendar days beginning on the date a covered military member is notified of an impending call or order to active duty.

2. *Military events and related activities:* To attend any official ceremony, program, or event sponsored by the military that is related to the active duty or call to active duty status of a covered military member and to attend family support or assistance programs and informational briefings sponsored or promoted by the military, military service organizations, or the American Red Cross.

3. *Child care and school activities:* To arrange for child care, to provide child care to a covered military member's child on an urgent, immediate need basis, to enroll in or transfer to a new school or day care facility, or to attend meetings with staff at a school or a day care facility.

4. *Financial and legal arrangements:* To make or update financial or legal arrangements to address the covered military member's absence while on active duty or call to active duty status, and to act as the covered military member's representative before a federal, state, or local agency for purposes of obtaining, arranging, or appealing military service benefits while the covered military member is on active duty or call-to-active-duty status, and for a period of 90 days following the termination of the covered military members' active duty status.

---

[40]For definitions of *spouse, son, daughter,* and *parents, see* 29 C.F.R. §825.122.

5. *Counseling*: To attend counseling for oneself, the covered military member or his child, provided that the need for counseling arises from the active duty call or call-to-active-duty status of a covered military member.

6. *Rest and recuperation*: To spend time with a covered military member who is on short-term, temporary, rest and recuperation leave during the period of deployment. Eligible employees may take up to five days of leave for each instance of rest and recuperation. Some states, including California, have similar military family leave laws already in effect.

7. *Post-deployment activities*: To attend arrival ceremonies, reintegration briefings and events, and any other official ceremony or program sponsored by the military for a period of 90 days following the termination of the covered military member's active duty status and to address issues that arise from the death of a covered military member while on active duty status, such as meeting and recovering the body of the covered military member and making funeral arrangements.

8. *Additional activities*: To address other events that arise out of the covered military member's active duty or call-to-active-duty status provided that the employer and employee agree that such leave will qualify as an exigency and agree to both the timing and duration of such leave.[41]

Upon first requesting leave for a qualifying exigency, an employee may be required to furnish a copy of the covered military member's active duty orders or other documentation issued by the military indicating that he or she is on active duty or call-to-active-duty status, and the dates of active duty service.[42] An employee is only required to provide this information once. If the need to take such leave

---

[41]*See id.*, §825.126(a).
[42]*See id.*, §825.309(a).

arises out of a different period of active duty or call-to-active-duty status for the same covered servicemember, or for a different covered servicemember, the employer may request copies of any new orders or other military documentation. An employer may also require that leave for any qualifying exigency be supported by a certification from the employee.[43]

An employer must provide written notice of any certification requirements each time certification is required. In most cases, the employer should request that an employee furnish certification at the time the employee provides notice of the need for leave or within five business days thereafter, or in the case of unforeseen leave, within five business days after leave commences. If the employer later has reason to question the appropriateness of the leave or its duration, it may request certification at that time. The employee must return a completed certification form within 15 calendar days after the employer's request.

The Department of Labor (DOL) allows an employer to verify the employee's explanation only when the employee has failed to provide the required certification or the proffered exigency involves a third-party meeting.[44] If the latter case, the employer may contact the individual or entity with whom the employee was meeting for purposes of verifying that it took place. Employee permission is not required to verify meetings or appointments with third parties, but no additional information may be requested. An employer also may contact an appropriate unit of the Department of Defense to verify that a covered military member is on active duty or call-to-active-duty status without the employee's permission, but an employer may not seek additional information.

---

[43]*See id.*, §825.309(b).
[44]*See id.*, §825.309(d).

d. Duration and Timing of Leave

USERRA sets a five-year cumulative limit on the amount of military leave an employee can take while retaining reemployment rights.[45] If the employee subsequently obtains employment with a new employer, he or she receives a new five-year limit.

Under the FMLA, an otherwise eligible employee who has a serious health condition that renders him or her unable to perform the functions of the job is entitled to take a leave of absence of up to 12 weeks in a 12-month period.[46] As discussed above, the 12-week limit has been expanded under certain circumstances in connection with servicemember leave.

e. Health Benefits and Nature of Leave

During FMLA leave, an employer must maintain medical benefits on the same terms that the employee enjoyed prior to his departure.[47] The FMLA also permits an employee with a serious health condition to work intermittently or on a reduced work schedule if there is a medical need for leave that can best be accommodated through such a schedule.[48] Consequently, an employee with a serious health condition may be able to work part-time until the expiration of 12 weeks of FMLA leave, with health benefits maintained during this period.[49]

USERRA provides that employees on military leave are entitled to the same non-seniority-based benefits an employer provides to employees on other forms of extended leave or furlough.[50] There is debate, however, over the proper application of this provision. Some take the position

---

[45]See 38 U.S.C. §4312(a), (c); see also 20 C.F.R. §§1002.32, 1002.99–1002.104.
[46]See 29 U.S.C. §2612(a)(1)(D).
[47]See id., §2614(c)(1); 29 C.F.R. §825.209.
[48]See 29 U.S.C. §2612(b)(1).
[49]See 29 C.F.R. §825.702(c); see also EEOC FMLA, ADA, & Title VII Fact Sheet at No. 15, §9.II, found at http://www.eeoc.gov/policy/docs/fmlaada.html.
[50]See 38 U.S.C. §4316(b)(1)(B).

that this provision applies broadly, even to those benefits an employer is required to provide to its employees under another state or federal law.[51] Under this interpretation, if an employer provides employees on FMLA leave with continued health insurance because it is required to by law, then these same benefits would have to be provided to employees under USERRA.[52] Others take the view that this requirement applies only to those benefits voluntarily provided by an employer while an employee is on leave.[53] Under this view, the only applicable benefits would be those an employer chooses to provide (such as pay while on FMLA leave), not benefits it is forced to provide (such as health care payments under FMLA).[54] In considering this issue for purposes of USERRA's final regulations, the DOL refused to take a position, stating instead that the issue was to be decided on a "case-by-case" basis.[55]

Finally, the Veterans Benefits Improvement Act, which amended USERRA, requires that employers offer those on military leave and their dependents the right to continue in the employer's group health plan for up to 24 months of service.[55A]

f. Reemployment and Restoration

An employer's restoration obligations under the FMLA differ from those under USERRA. Under USERRA, an employer has an affirmative obligation to reemploy the employee subject only to limited exceptions. In addition, employees are entitled to reinstatement to the position they *would have attained* had they not taken military leave.[56] This obligation, also known as the "escalator provision," as well

---

[51] See 70 Fed. Reg. 75263 (December 19, 2005).

[52] See id.

[53] See id.

[54] See id.

[55] Id.

[55A] Veterans' Benefits Improvement Act of 2004, Pub. L. No. 108-454, §201(a), 118 Stat. 3598, 3606 (codified at 38 U.S.C. §4317(a)(1)(A).

[56] See 38 U.S.C. §4313(a).

as the obligation to make reasonable efforts to provide re-fresher training necessary to update a returning employee's skills, are plainly distinguishable from employers' obligations under the FMLA.

Under the FMLA, an employer must return the employee to the "same position the employee held when leave commenced, or to an equivalent position with equivalent benefits, pay, and other terms and conditions of employment."[57] There is no escalator counterpart under the FMLA. In addition, if the returning employee is unable to perform an essential function of the position because of a physical or mental condition, the employee has no right to restoration to another position under the FMLA.[58] Moreover, the FMLA does not require an employer to create a position for an employee who cannot perform the essential functions of his job.[59]

2. Americans With Disabilities Act

a. General Principles

The Americans with Disabilities Act (ADA)[60] prohibits covered employers from discriminating against a "qualified individual on the basis of disability" with regard to application, hiring, advancement, discharge, compensation, training, and other terms, conditions, and privileges of employment.[61] The ADA also generally requires covered employers to make reasonable accommodations—changes in the workplace or the way things are usually done—to individu-

---

[57]See 29 C.F.R. §825.214; 29 U.S.C. §2614(a)(1).

[58]See 29 C.F.R. §825.216(c).

[59]See WH Admin. Op. FMLA-47, Wage & Hour Manual 99:3043 (Oct. 17, 1994).

[60]42 U.S.C. §§12101–12213.

[61]42 U.S.C. §12112(a). For further discussion of disability discrimination and the ADA, see BARBARA T. LINDEMANN & PAUL GROSSMAN, ABA SECTION OF LABOR EMPLOYMENT LAW, EMPLOYMENT DISCRIMINATION LAW, Ch. 13 (C. Geoffrey Weirich et al. eds., 2007 & Deborah A. Millenson & Patrick O. Patterson et al. eds., BNA Books 2008 Supp.).

als with known disabilities, in furtherance of equal employment opportunities.

Both USERRA and the ADA obligate employers to provide reasonable accommodation to covered employees. However, not all employees who experience a medical condition in connection with military service qualify as individuals with a "disability" under the ADA, and an employer's obligations with respect to accommodating and reemploying disabled veterans can vary between the statutes.

b. Covered Employers and Eligible Employees

The ADA, which covers employers with 15 or more employees,[62] protects qualified individuals with a disability from discrimination as to all terms, conditions, and privileges of employment.[63] A covered employer is prohibited from discriminating against a qualified applicant or employee who has a disability, is regarded as having a disability, or has a record of having a disability.[64] To take on the status of a "qualified individual with a disability," the individual must be qualified to perform the essential functions of the job, with or without reasonable accommodation.[65]

The ADA defines a disabled individual as one with a physical or mental impairment that substantially limits one or more major life activities, a record of such an impair-

---

[62]See 42 U.S.C. §§12111, 12112; 29 U.S.C. §§2601, 2611(2), 2612.

[63]42 U.S.C. §12112(a)(5)(A). *Disability* is defined by the ADA to mean: (1) a physical or mental impairment that substantially limits one or more major life activities; (2) a record of such an impairment; or (3) being regarded as having such an impairment. 42 U.S.C. §12102(2). Major life activities include, but are not limited to, such tasks as caring for oneself, performing manual tasks, walking, seeing, hearing, speaking, breathing, learning, and working. *See* 29 C.F.R. at §1630.2(i). Factors used to determine whether an individual is substantially limited include the nature and severity of the impairment, the duration or expected duration of the impairment, and the expected long-term impact resulting from the impairment. 29 C.F.R. §1630.2(j)(2). The inability to perform a single, particular job, or even a narrow range of jobs, is not a substantial limitation on the major life activity of working. 29 C.F.R. §1630.2(j)(3).

[64]See 42 U.S.C. §§12102(1), 12112.

[65]See id., §12111(8).

ment, or one who is regarded as having such an impairment.[66]

Contrast that definition with one utilized by USERRA, which defines the term "disabled veteran" to mean an individual who has served on active duty in the armed forces, was honorably discharged, and has a service-connected disability, or is receiving compensation, disability retirement benefits, or pension because of a public statute administered by the Department of Veterans Affairs or a military department.[67]

Not every disabled veteran qualifies as an individual with a disability under the ADA. For example, the ADA definition of disability does not include transitory illnesses or temporary, non-chronic impairments of short duration, having little or no long-term or permanent impact.[68] There is no such limitation under USERRA. A returning servicemember may have rights under USERRA based on a service-related disability that is not permanent. Whereas the ADA covers only "disabilities" as defined within that statute, USERRA covers any disability incurred in or aggravated

---

[66]*See id.*, §12102(1). Whether a person is substantially impaired with respect to a major life activity is determined by the nature and severity of the impairment, the duration or expected duration of the impairment, and the actual or expected permanent or long-term impact of the impairment. *See* 29 C.F.R. §1630.2(j)(2).

[67]*See* 5 U.S.C.

[68]*See* 29 C.F.R. §1630 Appx. For example, appendicitis, concussions, sprains, broken limbs, and influenza are not ADA disabilities. 29 C.F.R. §1630.2(j). *See* Toyota Motor Mfg. Ky., Inc. v. Williams, 534 U.S. 184, 198, 12 AD Cases 993, 999 (2002) (holding that for an impairment to be a disability, its impact must be "permanent or long-term"); *see also* Hilburn v. Murata Elecs. N.A., Inc. 181 F.3d 1220 (11th Cir. 1999) (holding plaintiff's 38-day absence from work following her heart attack was an insufficient period of time to establish that she was substantially limited in the major life activity of working where she failed to establish that she had any substantially limiting residual effects from her heart problems); Ryan v. Grae & Rybicki, P.C., 135 F.3d 867 (2d Cir. 1998) (plaintiff's colitis not a disability where symptoms occurred only during summer months and years could pass without any symptoms); Sanders v. Arneson Prods., Inc., 91 F.3d 1351 (9th Cir. 1996) (psychological impairment that lasted for approximately 3½ months was a temporary impairment and not of sufficient duration to be an ADA disability), *cert. denied*, 520 U.S. 1116 (1997); McDonald v. Commonwealth of Pa. Dep't of Pub. Welfare, 62 F.3d 92 (3d Cir. 1995) (inability to work for almost two months following surgery is not a disability; court characterized condition as transitory and not for such an extended time as to fall within coverage of the ADA).

during service in the uniformed services.[69] Nevertheless, a veteran who was wounded on active duty may satisfy both the definition of a disabled veteran under USERRA and that of an individual with a disability under the ADA.

c. Duty to Accommodate Qualified Disabled Employees and Veterans

Under the ADA, employers are required to reasonably accommodate the known physical or mental limitations of a qualified disabled applicant or employee, unless the employer demonstrates that the accommodations would impose an undue hardship on the operation of the business.[70] The term "undue hardship" is defined as "an action requiring significant difficulty or expense."[71]

d. Leaves of Absence and Light Duty

Under the ADA, a reasonable accommodation may include extension of unpaid leave.[72] An employee who seeks such leave under the ADA would be required to accept any alternative reasonable accommodation that the employer

---

[69]See 20 C.F.R. §1002.226.

[70]See 42 U.S.C. §12112(b)(5)(A); US Airways, Inc. v. Barnett, 535 U.S. 391, 12 AD Cases 1729, 1734 (2002) (discussing "reasonable accommodation" and "undue hardship").

[71]42 U.S.C. §12111(10)(A). In determining whether the "undue hardship" standard is satisfied, the factors to be considered include the following:

(i) the nature and cost of the accommodation needed under this [chapter];

(ii) the overall financial resources of the facility or facilities involved in the provision of the reasonable accommodation; the number of persons employed at such facility; the effect on expenses and resources; or the impact otherwise of such an accommodation upon the operation of the facility;

(iii) the overall financial resources of the covered entity; the overall size of the business of a covered entity with respect to the number of its employees; the number, type, and location of its facilities; and

(iv) the type of operation or operations of the covered entity, including the composition, structure, and functions of the workforce of such entity; the geographic separateness, administrative, or fiscal relationship of the facility or facilities in question to the covered entity.

42 U.S.C. §12111(10)(B).

[72]See 42 U.S.C. §12111(9)(B).

may offer, so long as the proposed accommodation is an effective one.[73]

Although the ADA does not impose an affirmative obligation on the part of an employer to create a "light duty" position for a disabled employee, it does require an employer to provide a reasonable accommodation. Reasonable accommodation may include "job restructuring [and] part-time or modified work schedules."[74] If an employer already has a vacant "light duty" position for which a disabled worker is qualified, and no other reasonable accommodation will allow the employee to remain in his regular job, it may be required to reassign the worker to that light duty position.[75]

USERRA provides greater protections to temporarily disabled servicemembers than the ADA. Under USERRA, a servicemember with a temporary disability may be entitled to reemployment in an alternate position, provided he or she is qualified for the position and the disability will not affect his ability to perform the job. If no such alternative position exists, the disabled servicemember may be entitled to reinstatement under sick leave or light duty status until he or she recovers.[76]

e. Restoration

Under the ADA, an employee returning from leave is entitled to the position he or she held prior to the leave, unless that position is no longer vacant, either because holding the position open until the employee's return was not a reasonable accommodation or because it would have imposed an "undue hardship" to do so.[77] The ADA, how-

---

[73]See EEOC Enforcement Guidance: Reasonable Accommodation and Undue Hardship Under the Americans with Disabilities Act at No. 9 (2002), *available at* http://www.eeoc.gov/policy/docs/accommodation.html.
[74]42 U.S.C. §12111(9)(B).
[75]See EEOC Technical Assistance Manual for the ADA §9.4 (1992).
[76]See 20 C.F.R. §1002.226.
[77]See 42 U.S.C. §§12111(9)(B), 10(B); 29 C.F.R. §§1630.2(o)(2)(ii), (p)(2).

ever, may require the employer to make a reasonable accommodation by reassigning the employee to a vacant position, barring undue hardship.[78]

USERRA requires more than the ADA, to the extent that employers also have specific obligations to those returning from military leave with service-related disabilities or disabilities that were aggravated by military service.[79] Under USERRA, a disabled servicemember is entitled to the position he or she would have attained but for military service. If the disability limits the servicemember's ability to perform the job, the statute imposes an affirmative duty on the employer to make reasonable efforts to accommodate the disability.[80] This duty may include providing training or retraining for the position, or otherwise assisting a returning veteran to become qualified to perform the duties of his position, regardless of whether the individual has a service-connected disability requiring reasonable accommodation.[81]

If, despite reasonable accommodation efforts, the returning disabled servicemember cannot become qualified for his escalator position, he or she is entitled to "any other position which is equivalent in seniority, status, and pay."[82] If no such position exists, the servicemember is entitled to reemployment "in a position which is the nearest approximation ... in terms of seniority, status, and pay consistent with circumstances of such person's case."[83]

USERRA's disability provisions, however, do not appear to apply after the returning servicemember is reinstated. Section 4313(a) deals only with the position to which an employee must be "promptly reemployed" upon comple-

---

[78]See 29 C.F.R. §825.702(c)(4).
[79]See 20 C.F.R. §§1002.225–226.
[80]See 38 U.S.C. §4313(a)(3).
[81]See id., §4313; 20 C.F.R. §§1002.198, .225–26.
[82]See id., §4313(a)(3)(A).
[83]38 U.S.C. §4313(a)(3)(B); see Hembree v. Georgia Power Co., 637 F.2d 423 (5th Cir. 1981).

tion of military service.[84] This section does not apply to issues with respect to a servicemember's employment that arise after the employee is reinstated.[85] Thus, unlike the ADA, the provisions of Section 4313(a)(3) dealing with disabilities appear only applicable to the reinstatement process. Had Congress intended that USERRA's disability provisions apply beyond reinstatement, these provisions would be part of another section (such as the discrimination provisions found in 38 U.S.C. Section 4311) or encompassed in a separate section regarding disabilities. That they are not is evidence of Congress's intent to apply these disability requirements only to the reinstatement process.

f. Medical Inquiries and Records

The ADA prohibits employers from inquiring, through a medical examination, whether an individual has a disability unless the inquiry is "job related and consistent with business necessity."[86] The ADA also requires an employee's medical information to be maintained in a separate, confidential file.[87]

Nothing in the ADA or USERRA prohibits an employer from asking for medical information from applicants for affirmative action purposes.[88] Therefore, an employer may give applicants the option of identifying themselves as disabled veterans when the employer is doing so pursuant to a federal, state, or local law affirmative action program, or when the employer voluntarily uses the information to benefit individuals with disabilities, including veterans with service-related disabilities.

Specific rules and regulations exist that provide requirements for the hiring of veterans by federal employers.

---

[84]See 38 U.S.C. §4313(a).

[85]See id.

[86]29 C.F.R. §§1630.13, 1630.14(c).

[87]See 29 C.F.R. §§825.500(g), 1630.14(c).

[88]See generally EEOC ENFORCEMENT GUIDANCE: PREEMPLOYMENT DISABILITY-RELATED QUESTIONS AND MEDICAL EXAMINATIONS UNDER THE AMERICANS WITH DISABILITIES ACT OF 1990 (1995), at www.eeoc.gov/policy/docs/preemp.html.

Pursuant to these rules and regulations, federal agencies are permitted to utilize hiring authorities to seek out and hire—and consider for promotion and other employment decisions—individuals with disabilities, including disabled veterans.

3. COBRA

Under the Congressional Omnibus Budget Reconciliation Act of 1986 (COBRA),[89] employers with 20 or more employees must allow employees (and their covered dependents) who have lost their employer-provided group health coverage (medical, dental, vision, medical flexible spending, prescription, Employee Assistance Programs (EAP) coverage, and Health Reimbursement Arrangement (HRA)) due to certain qualifying events, including termination of the employee's employment (other than due to gross misconduct) and reduction in the employee's work hours, to continue such coverage for up to 18 months (29 months for disabled persons and related dependents who qualify for Social Security disability benefits).[90]

COBRA also provides coverage for up to 36 months to surviving spouses, divorced spouses, spouses of Medicare-entitled employees, and certain dependent children. Premiums for the continued health-plan coverage are paid by those who are covered. Plans are limited in the amount that they can charge, generally no more than 102 percent of regular group premium, and 150 percent in the case of an 11-month disability extension.

In 2004, Congress increased the time period for continuation of health benefits. USERRA now requires an employer to offer to individuals on military leave for a period of up to 24 months the option of continuing their health insurance coverage by self-paying the cost of such cover-

---

[89] 29 U.S.C. §1162 *et seq.*
[90] *Id.*, §1163.

age.[91] This provision is similar to the protections offered by COBRA, but it also applies to employers with fewer than 20 employees (who are otherwise exempt from COBRA). If the period of military leave is 31 days or less, the employee cannot be required to contribute more than his normal share of any premium. If military service exceeds 31 days, the employee may be required to contribute up to 102 percent of the full premium under the health plan; the extra two percent can be added to cover an employer's administrative costs.[92]

4. Fair Labor Standards Act

Among other things, the Fair Labor Standards Act[93] (FLSA) requires employers to pay minimum wages and overtime pay for employees who are covered and not otherwise exempt from these requirements. One of the conditions for satisfying the executive, administrative, and most professional overtime exemptions is that employees must be paid on a salary basis.[94] The FLSA salary basis regulation limits employer rights to reduce the pay of exempt employees for time missed from work, particularly for absences of less than one day.[95]

While nuanced interactions between USERRA and the FLSA are not extensive, employers must be mindful of the salary basis requirement when otherwise exempt employees miss part of a work week due to military service. Under the FLSA, an exempt employee cannot incur any reduction in weekly salary if the employee is absent for a portion of the work week due to military leave.[96] An employer is not obli-

---

[91]See 38 U.S.C. §4317; 20 C.F.R. §1002.164.
[92]See 38 U.S.C. §4317 (a)(2).
[93]29 U.S.C. §201 et seq. For complete coverage of the FLSA, see ABA SECTION OF LABOR EMPLOYMENT LAW, THE FAIR LABOR STANDARDS ACT (Ellen C. Kearns et al. eds., BNA Books 1999 & Amy P. Maloney ed., Cumulative Supp. BNA Books 2009).
[94]See 29 C.F.R. §§541.100(a)(1), .200(a)(1), .300(a)(1), .400(b), .602.
[95]See id., §541.602.
[96]See id., §541.118(a)(4).

gated to pay an employee's salary, however, if the employee is absent for a full work week due to such service.

5. Employee Retirement Income Security Act

Both the Internal Revenue Service (IRS) and the Department of the Treasury have indicated that a health or pension plan will be deemed not to be in conflict with applicable Internal Revenue Code (IRC) requirements relating to elections and re-enrollment in pension and health plans merely because of compliance with USERRA or its regulations.[97]

USERRA defines an employee pension benefit plan in a manner at least as broadly as the term is defined under the Employee Retirement Income Security Act (ERISA): any plan, fund, or program established or maintained by an employer or by an employee organization, or by both, that provides retirement income or results in the deferral of income for a period of time extending to or beyond the termination of employment covered by the plan.[98] USERRA provides that once the servicemember is reemployed, he or she is treated as not having had a break in service with the employer(s) maintaining the plan, even though the servicemember was away from work performing military service.

USERRA regulations describe the types of employee pension benefit plans that come within the scope of the Act and the pension benefits that must be provided to reemployed servicemembers. Although USERRA relies on the ERISA definition of an employee pension benefit plan, some plans excluded from ERISA coverage remain subject to USERRA. For example, USERRA, but not ERISA, extends coverage to plans sponsored by religious organiza-

---

[97]See 70 Fed. Reg. No. 242, at 75247 (December 19, 2005).
[98]See 29 U.S.C. §1002(2) ("employee pension benefit plan" and "pension plan" defined); 38 U.S.C. §4318(a).

tions and plans established under State or Federal law for government employees.[99]

Each period of uniformed service is treated as an uninterrupted period of employment with the employer maintaining the pension plan, for purposes of determining eligibility for plan participation, the non-forfeitability of accrued benefits, and the accrual of service credits, contributions, and elective deferrals.[100] For purposes of calculating these pension benefits, or for determining the amount of contributions or deferrals to the plan, the reemployed servicemember is treated as though he or she had remained continuously employed for pension purposes.[101]

C. State Laws

All 50 states have enacted legislation that provides some level of protection to servicemembers in the form of leaves of absence, reemployment, and/or job protection. The level of protection afforded to servicemembers varies from state to state. While some states have simply adopted USERRA as the governing law, other state legislatures have drafted more specific statutory provisions. These provisions vary substantially in the extent of coverage, from protecting only public sector employees, to protecting both public and private employees, and also in some cases, prohibiting employers from terminating returning servicemembers without cause for a full year.

For example, states such as Alabama, Maryland, Nebraska, Ohio, and Oklahoma, to name a few, have simply adopted some or all of USERRA's provisions, albeit with some minor modifications.[102] Other states have added protection to servicemembers by forbidding termination of

---

[99]*See* 20 C.F.R. §§1002.259–1002.267.
[100]*See* 38 U.S.C. §4318 (a)(2)(B).
[101]*See* 20 C.F.R. §§1002.259–.267.
[102]*See* Ala. Code §31-12-2; Md. Code Ann. Pub. Safety §13-705; Neb. Rev. Stat. Ann. §55-161; Ohio Rev. Code Ann. §5903.02.

reemployed persons without cause for a period of one year from the employee's date of reemployment. Georgia, Hawaii, Idaho, Illinois, Kansas, New Jersey, New York, North Dakota, and Oregon are examples of such states.[103]

III. Interrelationship With Employer Practices

A. Policies Providing Greater or Lesser Benefits Than Required by USERRA

USERRA contemplates its interrelationship with employment benefits. Indeed, the Act itself expressly states that an employer policy may provide greater benefits than USERRA, in which case the employee remains entitled to those benefits.[104] This analysis is often characterized in terms of USERRA creating a "floor" on benefits, rather than a "ceiling."[105] Consequently, employers retain the right to subsequently diminish employee benefits to minimum USERRA levels, as the Act creates no independent cause of action to enforce voluntary policies that exceed USERRA mandates.

Nonetheless, the Act supersedes any policy, practice, or provision purporting to reduce or eliminate USERRA benefits, or to impose additional conditions upon the receipt of such benefits.[106] Similarly, an employer voluntarily choosing to confer benefits that exceed USERRA requirements may not attempt to recoup its investment by reducing USERRA benefits in other areas.[107]

---

[103]See Ga. Code Ann. §38-2-280; Haw. Rev. Stat. §121-43; Idaho Code Ann. §46-407; 20 Ill. Comp. Stat. §1805/30-20(a); Kan. Stat. Ann. §48-517; N.J. Stat. Ann. §38:23C-20; N.Y. Mil. Law §317; N.D. Cent. Code §37-01-25.1; Or. Rev. Stat. §408.270.

[104]See 38 U.S.C. §4302(a); 20 C.F.R. §§1002.7(a), (c).

[105]20 C.F.R. §1002.7(a) ("USERRA establishes a floor, not a ceiling, for the employment and reemployment rights and benefits of those it protects").

[106]See 38 U.S.C. §4302(b); 20 C.F.R. §1002.7(b).

[107]See 20 C.F.R. §1002.7(d). Consequently, USERRA regulations suggest that an employer may choose to provide a fixed amount of paid military leave each year to members of the National Guard or Reserve. The fact that it voluntarily chooses to confer this benefit, however, does not allow the employer to refrain from providing unpaid military leave once the paid leave is exhausted. See id.

B. Employer Policy Considerations

Aside from its notice-posting obligations, USERRA (unlike the FMLA) does not impose any specific requirements with regard to the establishment and promulgation of a written policy. Nonetheless, a clearly stated military leave policy can facilitate employer compliance with USERRA obligations. Indeed, most employers choose to provide at least a brief explanation of employee rights and obligations in connection with military leave.

Long before USERRA's enactment, employers were administering a wide spectrum of military leave policies that ran the gamut in terms of pay, benefits, and reemployment. Although USERRA is essentially silent with regard to specific employment practices that may give rise to policy choices in this area, it stands to reason that a multitude of options are potentially available. Some of the more common areas that give rise to employer discretion in the military leave arena are set forth below.

1. Supplemental Paid Leave

Under USERRA, employees are entitled to *unpaid* time off from work without penalty to fulfill their uniformed service obligations. The Act imposes no requirement to grant paid leave.[108] Employers, however, are free to provide paid leave to employees on military leave. Some employers choose to make up the difference between an employee's standard wages and pay received for service in the uniformed services, while others choose to pay employees their full, unadjusted wages.[109] Still other employers pay one-time

---

[108]USERRA grants employees the right to use accrued vacation or annual paid leave to cover a period of military service. *See* 38 U.S.C. §4316(d). Thus, if a military leave is unpaid, an employee may seek to offset an overall pay loss with accrued vacation or annual paid leave.

[109]Employers who choose to supplement military pay retain the right to ask employees for a copy of their military pay voucher or similar pay records upon return from uniformed service. Some choose to withhold pay pending receipt of the voucher, while oth-

enlistment bonuses to employees who enter active service with a branch of the armed forces. Because USERRA does not require paid leave, eligibility for any and all such payments may be linked to the length or character of service or to such other, non-discriminatory factors as an employer may choose to adopt. For example, an employer may choose to confine supplemental pay to periods of active duty when such duty is involuntary, but not provide such pay for a voluntary enlistment.

Provided that they act on a consistent basis, employers tend to enjoy a degree of latitude with regard to regulating the means of pay continuation. For example, employers often require employees to exhaust accrued vacation or annual leave before they may qualify for paid military leave. While employers remain free to offer paid leave on an unlimited durational basis, most impose time limits that range from 6 to 12 months down to two weeks or less.[110]

2. Substitution of Paid Leave

Pursuant to USERRA, employees have the unilateral right to utilize accumulated holiday, vacation, annual, or similar leave to run concurrently with military leave. Employers, however, are precluded from requiring employees to use their accrued paid leave for these purposes.[111]

3. Medical Benefits

USERRA requires employees on military leave to be treated the same as employees on other leaves of absence.

---

ers continue regular pay, and treat the voucher as a deduction against future pay, thereby assuring continued cash flow to the employee's family.

[110]It is important to note that employer payments of supplemental wages during periods of temporary duty may be deemed wages subject to federal income tax (FIT) withholding, Federal Insurance Contributions Act (FICA) taxes, and Federal Unemployment Tax Act (FUTA) contributions. When employees are on indefinite active duty, however, the employment relationship is deemed severed for tax purposes and any civilian supplemental payments are exempt from FIT withholding, FICA, and FUTA. These amounts must then be reported to the individual using Form 1099-MISC.

[111]See 38 U.S.C. §4316(d).

Consequently, if an employer continues group health care coverage for furloughs or extended leaves of absence, it must do so for military leave as well.[112] If, on the other hand, the employer does not regularly continue group health coverage for extended leaves of absence, then it must offer (following the first 30 days of leave, which must be subsidized) "COBRA-like" continuation coverage.[113] The period of coverage is the lesser of 24 months[114] or the day after the date on which the employee fails to apply for or return to work.[115] As is the case with regular COBRA coverage, employees may be required to pay a maximum of 102 percent of the premium (i.e., the full premium plus a two percent administrative fee).[116]

When servicemembers are reemployed, their health coverage must be resumed as if no break in employment had occurred.[117] There should be no lapse in coverage, and employers may not impose waiting periods or exclusions on pre-existing conditions for returning employees or their dependents.

Employers may nonetheless choose to continue subsidized medical benefits and other coverage for uniformed servicemembers. Benefit continuation may be open-ended, but employers remain free to impose time limits as well. Subject to any constraints imposed by the applicable plan document, employers are free to go so far as to waive the employee's share of the medical premium, rather than establishing a mechanism for collecting it. At the same time, employers also remain free to discontinue short- and long-term disability benefits during uniformed service, subject again to plan language, and provided they are not singling out uniformed servicemembers for discriminatory treatment.

---

[112]See id., §4316(b)(1)(B).
[113]See id., §4317.
[114]See id., §4317(a)(1)(A).
[115]See id., §4317(a)(1)(B).
[116]See id., §4317(a)(2).
[117]See id., §4317(b)(1).

4. Expanded Eligibility

Although USERRA expressly excludes temporary[118] (as opposed to part-time) employees from coverage, there is nothing to preclude employers from voluntarily extending them leave benefits.

5. Accrual of Vacation and Other Forms of Paid Leave

USERRA does not mandate accrual of vacation, sick leave, or any other form of paid leave, so long as the employer counts military leave toward length of service for purposes of determining the rate at which employees earn vacation upon their return. Nonetheless, employers are free to voluntarily provide for continued accrual of vacation and other sick leave benefits during periods of uniformed service.

IV. Conclusion

Given USERRA's breadth, care must be taken in determining the overlap between USERRA and other federal laws. Additionally, practitioners must understand that inconsistent state and local laws, along with inconsistent employer policies, are explicitly superseded by USERRA. While understanding the scope of USERRA's "floor" of benefits is important, the effect of greater state or local rights cannot be overlooked. The thorough practitioner will start with a close review of USERRA and its regulations, and then expand to determine whether state or local laws, or employer policies, expand these requirements.

---

[118]This term is confined to those employees hired for a specific short-term project or for a limited term of employment that is scheduled to end in the foreseeable future. *See* 38 U.S.C. §4312(d)(1)(C).

CHAPTER 10

DISCRIMINATION, RETALIATION, AND HARASSMENT

I. DISCRIMINATION

A. Discrimination Based on Status

1. Protected Categories

The Uniformed Services Employment and Reemployment Rights Act (USERRA or the Act)[1] prohibits discrimination against individuals based on a specified status related to service in the uniformed services. There are six specified categories under which an individual is protected from discrimination:

- Persons who are members of a uniformed service;
- Persons who apply to be members of a uniformed service;
- Persons who perform uniformed service (presently);
- Persons who have (past) performed uniformed service;
- Persons who apply (future) to perform uniformed service; and
- Persons who have an obligation to perform uniformed service.[2]

USERRA's discrimination prohibitions apply to both positions of employment and offers of employment, which includes brief, nonrecurrent employment positions.[3]

---

[1]38 U.S.C. §§4301–4335.
[2]*See id.,* §4311(a).
[3]*See id.,* §4311(d); 20 C.F.R. §1002.18.

2. Scope of "Uniformed Services"

The term "uniformed services" applies to each of the six categories listed above. That term, as distinct from "armed forces" or "armed services," needs further clarification. The definition of "uniformed services" is broader than the term "'armed forces service" because "uniformed services" also includes service in the National Disaster Medical System and the U.S. Public Health Service.[4] Additionally, during a time of war or other national emergency, the President has the authority to designate any category of persons as a "uniformed service" for USERRA purposes.[5] At that point, each member of that new category would then be considered to be in "service in the uniformed services" under USERRA.[6]

Service as a cadet or midshipman at one of the service academies is also considered protected service, as is certain service in a Reserve Officer Training Corps (ROTC) program.[7] On the other hand, USERRA does not cover members of the Commissioned Corps of the National Oceanic and Atmospheric Administration (NOAA), the Civil Air Patrol, or the Coast Guard Auxiliary.[8] As the term "uniformed services" illustrates, some familiarity with service in the uniformed services is important to understand the nuances of the statute.

B. Discrimination Based on Membership in a Uniformed Service

1. General Rules

Membership in a uniformed service is a protected status under USERRA and applies to those who are currently

---

[4] See 38 U.S.C. §4303(16); 20 C.F.R. §§1002.56, 1002.58.
[5] See 20 C.F.R. §1002.59.
[6] See id.
[7] See id., §§1002.60, 1002.61.
[8] See id., §1002.62.

members, those who have been members in the past, and those who apply to be members for service at some future date. Most types of traditional military service are covered by USERRA. This includes service that is either voluntary or involuntary, during both peacetime and wartime, for both active and reserve components, and includes fitness-for-service examinations and service under the National Disaster Medical System.[9]

It is important to understand that USERRA does not apply to all types of National Guard duty. The National Guard has a dual status in that National Guard soldiers and air personnel are, typically, under the command and control of their respective states' governors, but also have a relationship with the reserve component of either the U.S. Army or Air Force. As such, National Guard duty that is under the control of a state is not covered by USERRA but, rather, is controlled by state law.[10] On the other hand, if National Guard personnel are called up by the President of the United States and serve under federal authority, USERRA applies to that portion of their service.[11] It must also be pointed out that, although purely state service is not protected service under USERRA, most states have statutes, many modeled after USERRA, that protect citizens who serve in their respective state Guard units.

Protection based on "membership" in a uniformed service does not require an individual to have actually served in a uniformed service. USERRA specifically applies to individuals who seek application in a uniformed service. The question arises, however, regarding what constitutes "seeking application" to join a uniformed service. While USERRA's protections clearly apply to those who have begun the affirmative recruiting process to join a uniformed service, application of these protections is less clear for

---

[9]*See* 20 C.F.R. §§1002.6, 1002.56.
[10]*See id.,* §1002.57.
[11]*See id.,* §1002.57(a).

those who only express an "intent" to join. A relatively recent case addressing this issue found that "potential" applicants for uniformed service lacked standing under USERRA to bring suit because only actual applicants are protected under the Act.[12] In that case, the plaintiff claimed that his employer effectively denied him permission to join the Navy Reserve.[13] The district court dismissed the plaintiff's USERRA discrimination claim because he had not alleged that he had suffered any adverse action with respect to his employment.[14] This decision is limited in its application, however, because a premise of the court's ruling is that the employee needed to seek permission from his employer to exercise his rights under USERRA in the first place.

It is important to note that employers are prohibited from discriminating against individuals based on *all* service in a uniformed service. Such service includes prior service, even if there is no current service-related obligation, current active or reserve component service, and future active or reserve component service.

2. *Performance of Service—Voluntary Versus Involuntary Service*

An issue subject to debate in this area is whether an employer's decision to provide paid leave for persons involuntarily called to uniformed service, but not to those who volunteer for uniformed service, can be considered discrimination on the basis of service. There are differing views on this issue.

Those who argue that USERRA protects against such distinctions point to the fact that one of USERRA's stated purposes is to "prohibit discrimination against persons because of their service in the uniformed services."[15] USERRA defines "service in the uniformed services" as "performance

---

[12]*See* Podszus v. City of Mt. Vernon, 2007 WL 2230106, at *3 (S.D.N.Y. July 12, 2007).
[13]*See id.* at *4.
[14]*See id.*
[15]38 U.S.C. §4301(a)(3).

of duty on a *voluntary or involuntary basis....*"[16] USERRA also provides that "[a] person who ... performs, has performed, applies to perform, or has an obligation to perform *service* in a uniformed service *shall not be denied ... any benefit* of employment by an employer on the basis of that ... performance of service, application for service, or obligation."[17] Finally, USERRA provides that employees are "entitled to such other rights and benefits not determined by seniority as are generally provided by the employer of the person to employees having similar seniority, status, and pay who are on furlough or leave of absence under a ... policy, practice, or plan in effect at the commencement of such service...."[18] A plain reading of these provisions, according to this argument, precludes employers from denying a benefit of employment, which includes a non-seniority-based pay differential benefit, to an individual because of either voluntary or involuntary military service.

Those who argue that USERRA permits a distinction in paid leave based on voluntary versus involuntary service point first to the fact that USERRA's definition of a "benefit of employment" specifically excludes "wages or salary for work performed."[19] Thus, USERRA's discrimination provision,[20] which prohibits an employer from denying "any benefit of employment" to a person who "performs" or "has an obligation to perform" service in a uniformed service, may not be read as applying to distinctions in pay an employer voluntarily chooses to provide certain employees on military leave, because pay is not a "benefit of employment." Similarly, USERRA Sections 4316(a) and (b) also reference "rights and benefits" of employment, which are subject to

---

[16]*Id.*, §4303(13) (emphasis added).
[17]*Id.*, §4311(a) (emphasis added).
[18]*Id.*, §4316(b)(1)(B).
[19]*See id.*, §4303(2), which defines "benefit," "benefit of employment," and/or "rights and benefits" to mean "any advantage, profit, privilege, gain, status, account for interest (*other than wages or salary from work performed*)" (emphasis added).
[20]*See id.*, §4311.

the same definition.[21] Further, the Department of Labor's comments to the final USERRA regulations regarding Section 4316(b) make clear that this section may only be interpreted "to mean that an employee who is absent from a position of employment by reason of service is not entitled to greater benefits than would be generally provided to a similarly situated employee on *non-military furlough or leave of absence*."[22] No mention is made in the DOL's comments or USERRA's regulations that pay distinctions based on a difference between voluntary and involuntary service are somehow violative of the Act.[23]

Unfortunately, at present this debate has not been addressed by any reported decision[24] or by the DOL's regulations.

3. Discriminatory Conduct

USERRA lists five types of adverse employment actions that are prohibited by the Act based on an individual's membership, application for membership, service, application for service, or obligation to serve, as noted previously. These prohibited employment actions are:

- Denial of initial employment,
- Denial of reemployment,
- Denial of retention in employment,
- Denial of promotion, or
- Denial of any benefit of employment.[25]

---

[21]*See id.*, §§4316(a), (b).

[22]*See* 70 Fed. Reg. No. 242, at 75262 (December 19, 2005) (emphasis added).

[23]A further argument in favor of permitting this distinction in paid benefits is that, were the distinction illegal under USERRA, employers would simply make all military leaves unpaid, thereby lessening benefits overall to persons eligible for military leave. Since USERRA leave is unpaid, employers who would be forced to provide pay for leaves of persons who volunteer for service would simply choose not to pay for any military leaves.

[24]Some support for the position that pay distinctions for employees based on differing types of military service are legal is found in the Seventh Circuit's recent decision in *Crews v. City of Mt. Vernon*, 567 F.3d 860, 866 (7th Cir. 2009), where the rescission of a work policy was considered non-discriminatory because the policy did not meet the definition of a "benefit of employment."

[25]*See* 38 U.S.C. §4311(a).

a. Discriminatory Refusal to Hire

Employers are prohibited from refusing to initially hire an individual because of that individual's protected status.[26] In *Beattie v. Trump Shuttle, Inc.*,[27] the defendant, after purchasing another company, offered employment to the previous company's employees, but only if those employees could be available for training prior to the start of new operations. One of the former company's employees had a conflict with the training dates set by the defendant because of scheduled military duty obligations. As a result, the defendant refused to hire him. The court held that the defendant's refusal to hire the employee violated the Veteran's Reemployment Rights Act, a predecessor to USERRA, based on the individual's protected status.[28]

In a more recent USERRA decision, *McLain v. City of Somerville*,[29] a municipality offered a law enforcement position to an applicant but conditioned the offer on the individual's ability to attend police academy training on a specific date. The applicant was to be on active duty during the academy training, however, and would not be released from active duty until some time thereafter. As in *Beattie*, the municipality withdrew its offer to the applicant. The court held that the municipality violated USERRA in withdrawing the employment offer because of the applicant's military duty requirements. The court also refused to consider the city's "undue hardship" defense, noting that the defense was only available for reemployment decisions, not initial hiring decisions.[30]

---

[26]*See* 20 C.F.R. §1002.40.

[27]758 F. Supp. 30 (D.D.C. 1991).

[28]*See id.* at 33–34. The VRRA is to be interpreted consistent with USERRA and "remain[s] in full force and effect, to the extent it is consistent with USERRA." 20 C.F.R. §1002.2; *see also* Rogers v. City of San Antonio, 392 F.3d 758, 762 n.8 (5th Cir. 2004).

[29]424 F. Supp. 2d 329 (D. Mass. 2006).

[30]*See id.* at 336.

b. Discriminatory Refusal to Reemploy

USERRA prohibits employers from refusing to reemploy an individual who has completed service in a uniformed service or who has returned from reserve component service.[31] Section 4312 outlines the specific reemployment rights of individuals covered by the Act. Section 4313 outlines the positions into which qualified individuals are to be reemployed. Finally, Sections 4314 and 4315 outline reemployment by the federal government and federal agencies.

In terms of discrimination, however, a purely technical violation of any of the provisions in Sections 4312–15 is not likely, in and of itself, to constitute discrimination under Section 4311. That is because proof of discriminatory intent is required under Section 4311, but not under Sections 4312–15.[32] Moreover, nothing in Section 4311 requires an employee, in order to establish an actionable claim for discriminatory refusal to reemploy, to have an actionable claim under either Section 4312 or Section 4313.[33]

c. Discriminatory Denial of Retention in Employment

Denying an employee retention in employment is a broad term that courts have construed to mean not only terminations of employment, but constructive discharges as well.[34] In *Wallace v. City of San Diego*,[35] Wallace, a police officer and an officer in the Navy Reserves, quit his job with the San Diego Police Department after receiving several disciplinary write-ups and transfers that he felt were related to

---

[31]38 U.S.C. §4311(a).

[32]*See id.*, §4311(c)(1); 20 C.F.R. §1002.23, both of which state that the employee must first prove that an employer's actions were "motivated" by certain actions based on the employee's service, etc.

[33]*See* 38 U.S.C. §4311.

[34]*See* Figueroa Reyes v. Hospital San Pablo del Este, 389 F. Supp. 2d 205 (D.P.R. 2005); Miller v. City of Indianapolis, 2001 WL 406346 (S.D. Ind. Apr. 13, 2001).

[35]479 F.3d 616 (9th Cir. 2007).

his military service. The Ninth Circuit found that the police department's "history of discriminatory conduct," its failure to take action against Wallace's supervisors and their retaliatory "unacceptable" performance rating and 90-day supplemental performance review given to Wallace after a transfer to another division, "permitted the jury to conclude that, despite the absence of discriminatory action in the events immediately precipitating Wallace's resignation, the totality of the circumstances surrounding his departure from the police department was such that a reasonable person in his position would have felt that he had no choice but to quit."[36] The court overturned a grant of judgment as a matter of law by the district court and ordered a new trial on a conditional basis.[37]

Similarly, in *Serricchio v. Wachovia Securities, LLC,*[38] the employee returned to work as a financial advisor after military duty. Upon returning to work, and during the one-year period in which he could only be terminated for cause, the employee claimed that his work conditions had changed from a "financially comfortable position" to one "in which he had no book of business and had to begin anew by cold-calling prospective customers in order to pay off the $2,000 monthly advance, which Wachovia offered him as compensation, leaving him incapable of supporting himself and his family."[39] As a result, the court denied summary judgment on the Section 4311 claim, noting that reasonable jurors could find the conditions under which the employee was offered reemployment "so intolerable that a reasonable person in the employee's position would have felt compelled to resign."[40]

---

[36] *Id.* at 626.
[37] *See id.* at 631.
[38] 556 F. Supp. 2d 99 (D. Conn. 2008).
[39] *Id.* at 109.
[40] *Id.* at 110 (quoting Pennsylvania State Police v. Suders, 542 U.S. 129, 141 (2004)).

By contrast, in *Wagner v. Novartis Pharmaceuticals Corp.*,[41] the court concluded that the employer's actions in failing to promote the employee and failing to provide him with timely access to a management training program, which led to the employee's frustration with his rate of advancement with the company and his assumption that he would never be promoted, did not rise to the level that would have forced a reasonable person to quit. And in *Figueroa Reyes v. Hospital San Pablo del Este*,[42] the court held that the employee failed to establish a constructive discharge claim despite alleging that he was unfairly accused of not giving advance notice of military absences, that he was transferred between hospital departments (noting that he did not suffer any change in responsibility, title, or benefit), that he was placed under the supervision of a strict disciplinarian, that his request to take leave while pursuing a graduate degree was not processed formally upon request (although informal permission was granted immediately), and that no one tried to persuade him not to leave when he offered his resignation. The court noted that the plaintiff's claims were "grossly insufficient" to support a claim of constructive discharge under USERRA, which requires allegations of a "tangible change in employment conditions."[43]

d. Discriminatory Denial of Promotion

In *Grosjean v. FirstEnergy*,[44] the plaintiff asserted a claim for discrimination based on the alleged denial of a promotion. The court held that there was no denial of promotion because the plaintiff applied for a position he already held. Although the employer admitted denying the plaintiff the opportunity to interview, if the plaintiff had received an interview he would have been interviewing for an "associate

---

[41]565 F. Supp. 2d 940, 946 (E.D. Tenn. 2008).
[42]389 F. Supp. 2d 205, 213–14 (D.P.R. 2005).
[43]*Id.* at 214.
[44]481 F. Supp. 2d 878 (N.D. Ohio 2007).

maintenance planner" position, the same position he already held. The court then noted that as an associate maintenance planner, the plaintiff "was already in the family of maintenance planners" and promotions within a job "family" are earned based upon the employee's performance and responsibilities, not through an application process. Consequently, according to the court, the denial of an interview is not a denial of a promotion because an interview would only have given the plaintiff an opportunity to apply for the same position he already held and, therefore, denying it could not be an adverse employment action.[45]

In *Maher v. City of Chicago*,[46] the plaintiff asserted a claim of discriminatory failure to promote. In denying the city's motion for summary judgment on that claim, the court noted that several of the plaintiff's supervisors had made comments over the years regarding why he was not being made a commissioner and that the reasons had to do with his service in Navy Reserves. These statements included one supervisor telling him he "really in good conscious [sic] couldn't recommend [him] for either a deputy commissionership or assistant commissionership [as]... it would not be fair to promote plaintiff because someone else had to do his job while he was 'off gallivanting in Bosnia.'"[47] The court held that it was up to a jury to determine whether the statements were actually made.[48]

In *Brandsasse v. City of Suffolk*,[49] the plaintiff was scheduled for military duty when a portion of a promotion examination was scheduled to take place. The plaintiff requested that he be allowed to take the portion of the examination he would miss due to military duty at another time, but the

---

[45]*See id.* at 885–86.
[46]406 F. Supp. 2d 1006 (N.D. Ill. 2006), *aff'd on other grounds, as amended,* 547 F.3d 817 (7th Cir. 2008).
[47]*Id.* at 1030.
[48]*Id.* Subsequently, this claim was tried to a jury, which found in the City's favor. *See* Maher v. City of Chicago, 547 F.3d 817, 821 (7th Cir. 2008). This jury verdict was upheld on appeal. *See id.* at 825–26.
[49]72 F. Supp. 2d 608 (E.D. Va. 1999).

City refused his request. As a result, the plaintiff did not sit for the promotion examination, and he asserted a discriminatory-denial-of-promotion claim. The court, in deciding the defendant's Rule 12 motion to dismiss, determined that the plaintiff had adequately pleaded a violation of Section 4311(a) for Rule 12 purposes by alleging a constructive denial of a promotion.[50]

Finally, in *Fink v. City of New York*,[51] a case similar to *Brandsasse*, the court noted that even though the employer may have a policy that applies to all employees in all circumstances to the effect that promotional examinations are to be administered only on particular dates, the employer's refusal to allow employees who would miss the examination because of military service to take a make-up exam may constitute discrimination under Section 4311.

e. Discriminatory Denial of Any Benefit of Employment

The term "benefit of employment" is defined by USERRA as any:

- advantage;
- profit;
- privilege;
- gain;
- status;
- account;
- interest that accrues by reason of an employment contract or agreement or employer policy, plan, or practice (other than wages or salary for work performed);
- rights and benefits under a pension plan;
- rights and benefits under a health plan;

---

[50]*See id.* at 614–15.
[51]129 F. Supp. 2d 511, 519 (E.D.N.Y. 2001).

- rights and benefits under an employee stock owner-ship plan;
- insurance coverage and awards;
- bonuses;
- severance pay;
- supplemental unemployment benefits;
- vacations; and
- the opportunity to select work hours or location of employment.[52]

As this list shows, the definition of a benefit of employ-ment is broadly defined.[53] To be actionable, the loss of a benefit of employment that has been discriminatorily de-nied by an employer must be a material loss.[54]

In a 2009 case, *Crews v. City of Mt. Vernon*,[55] the defen-dant's police department previously had permitted police officers who missed work due to military service in the Na-tional Guard to make up that work time after the service had ended. The department did not offer this opportunity to non-military officers. The department then rescinded this policy and the plaintiff sued, alleging that the rescission was a discriminatory denial of a benefit of employment. The Seventh Circuit disagreed, holding that rescission of a work-scheduling policy allowing police officers to make up weekend shifts missed while attending regular National Guard drill duties, which allowed officers to collect a full week of pay in addition to Guard pay, did not violate USERRA. The court held that the provision related to dis-criminatory denials of benefits of employment reached only discriminatory employment actions that provided military employees with fewer benefits and that the preferential work-scheduling policy was not a benefit of employment un-

---

[52]38 U.S.C. §4303(2).
[53]*See* S. REP. No. 103-158; Pub. L. No. 103-353, Uniformed Services Employment and Reemployment Rights Act, S. REP. No. 103-158 (Oct. 18, 1993).
[54]*See Grosjean*, 481 F. Supp. 2d at 883–84.
[55]2009 WL 1515449 (7th Cir., June 2, 2009).

der this provision since it was not available to all employees. The end result of the rescission of the policy, according to the court, was that it now provided equal work-scheduling benefits to all employees.

In *Maxfield v. Cintas Corp. No. 2*,[56] the Eighth Circuit held that transferring an employee after military leave to a position that previously had been eliminated constituted a denial of a benefit of employment. However, as noted in *Maher*,[57] the Seventh Circuit upheld a defense verdict in which an employee's transfer to a different division that did not result in a loss of status or seniority did not constitute a denial of a benefit of employment. The Eighth Circuit also found that although remaining at the same level in the employment hierarchy is not specifically listed as a benefit of employment in the Act, a demotion did, nevertheless, constitute a denial of a benefit of employment.[58]

In other decisions, the Federal Circuit has held that shift assignments and regular hours are considered benefits of employment under USERRA.[59] In *Clune v. Desmond's Formal Wear, Inc.*,[60] a district court found that reducing an employee's hours of work was a deprivation of a benefit of employment. Another district court held that changing an employee's job duties can also be a denial of a benefit of employment because the employee's status changes.[61] In addition, a poor performance evaluation that prevents an employee from receiving a raise may also be a denial of a benefit of employment.[62] The district court in *Wrigglesworth v. Brumbaugh* found that a plainclothes police detective's clothing allowance was a benefit of employment within the meaning of the Act.[63]

---

[56] 427 F.3d 544 (8th Cir. 2005).
[57] 547 F.3d at 825.
[58] *See* 427 F.3d at 551–52.
[59] *See* Smith v. U.S. Postal Serv., 540 F.3d 1364, 1366 (Fed. Cir. 2008).
[60] 2003 WL 21796388, at *6 (N.D. Ind. Feb. 4, 2003).
[61] *See* Harris v. City of Montgomery, 322 F. Supp. 2d 1319 (M.D. Ala. 2004).
[62] *See id.* at 1324.
[63] 129 F. Supp. 2d 1106, 1110 (W.D. Mich. 2001).

II. Retaliation

A. Retaliation in General

Under USERRA, an employer may not take adverse employment action against any person because he has engaged in certain protected conduct specified by the statute. There are four types of conduct protected under USERRA:

1. when an individual has taken an action to enforce a protection afforded any person under USERRA;
2. when an individual has testified or otherwise made a statement in or in connection with any proceeding under USERRA;
3. when an individual has assisted or otherwise participated in an investigation under USERRA; or
4. when an individual has exercised a right provided for in the USERRA statute.[64]

Significantly, USERRA's retaliation provision applies to all individuals—regardless of whether the person has ever performed service in the uniformed services (or even intends to do so).[65]

These protections apply to current and former employees as well as applicants for employment.[66] The retaliation provisions of USERRA also apply to those employees who are employed in brief, non-recurring positions that are excluded from USERRA's reemployment rights provisions.[67]

USERRA not only protects individuals who have never served in the uniformed services, but also protects individuals who are exercising someone else's rights under the Act, because it protects "any person" who engages in those rights listed above.[68]

---

[64]38 U.S.C. §4311(b).
[65]See id., §4311(b); 20 C.F.R. §1002.19.
[66]See 20 C.F.R. §1002.40.
[67]See 38 U.S.C. §§4311(b); 4312(d)(1)(C); 20 C.F.R. §1002.41; §4311(b).
[68]38 U.S.C. §4311(b).

Like most other retaliation statutes, USERRA's retaliation provision does not require that an underlying violation of USERRA has occurred, but only requires that an individual have a reasonable and good faith belief that a violation has occurred.[69]

B. Retaliatory Adverse Actions

USERRA lists several categories of adverse action employers are prohibited from taking because of an individual's membership, application for membership, service, applications to serve, or obligations to serve in a uniformed service. These are denials of: employment, reemployment, retention in employment, retraining, promotion, or any benefit of employment.[70] Section 4311(b), however, does not list specific prohibitions or adverse employment actions that are considered retaliatory under the Act. Rather, it states that employers "may not discriminate in employment" or "take any adverse employment action" against any person because of engaging in protected activity.[71] Consequently, the prohibited discriminatory acts listed in Section 4311(a) are also prohibited acts in retaliation for engaging in USERRA-protected activity. The list found in Section 4311(a) is not all-inclusive because Section 4311(b) protects individuals against "any" adverse employment actions.

III. BURDEN OF PROOF IN DISCRIMINATION AND RETALIATION CLAIMS

In both discrimination and retaliation suits, the individual plaintiff must show by a preponderance of the evidence that his protected status under USERRA was a motivating factor for the employer's adverse employment

---

[69]See Cook v. CTC Commc'ns Corp., 2007 WL 3284337, at *9 (D.N.H., Oct. 30, 2007).
[70]38 U.S.C. §4311(a).
[71]Id., §4311(b)

action.[72] To demonstrate *actionable discrimination* in violation of USERRA, a plaintiff must show, by a preponderance of the evidence, that: (a) the plaintiff was protected based upon membership, application for membership, current service, application for service, or obligation for service in a uniformed service; (b) that the employer took adverse action against the individual plaintiff by either denying the plaintiff initial employment, reemployment after service, retention in employment, promotion, or any benefit of employment; and (c) that the plaintiff's USERRA-protected status was a motivating factor in the employer taking an adverse employment action against the plaintiff.[73]

In order for a plaintiff to demonstrate *actionable retaliation* under USERRA, the plaintiff must show, by a preponderance of the evidence, that: (a) the individual plaintiff was engaged in protected activity by either taking action to enforce a USERRA protection, testifying or making a statement in connection with a proceeding designed to enforce USERRA rights, assisting or participating in a USERRA investigation, or exercising any right provided by the Act; (b) the defendant employer took some adverse employment action against the plaintiff; and (c) the individual plaintiff's USERRA-protected status or protected activity was a motivating factor for the employer taking the adverse employment action against the plaintiff.[74]

Once a plaintiff meets his burden for establishing either discrimination or retaliation, the burden of both production *and* persuasion switches to the employer to show that it would have taken the same action in the absence of the plaintiff's protected status or protected activity.[75]

---

[72]*See* 38 U.S.C. §§4311(c); 20 C.F.R. §§1002.23–.24.
[73]*See* 38 U.S.C. §4311(c)(1); 20 C.F.R. §§1002.22, .23(a).
[74]*See* 38 U.S.C. §4311(c)(2); 20 C.F.R. §§1002.22, .23(a).
[75]*See* 38 U.S.C. §4311(c); 20 C.F.R. §§1002.22, .23(b); Miller v. City of Indianapolis, 281 F.3d 648, 650 (7th Cir. 2002); Dean v. Consumer Prod. Safety Comm'n, 548 F.3d 1370, 1374 (Fed. Cir. 2008); Velazquez-Garcia v. Horizon Lines of P.R., Inc., 473 F.3d 11, 16–17 (1st Cir. 2007); Hill v. Michelin N. Am., Inc., 252 F.3d 307, 311–12 (4th Cir. 2001); Sheehan v. Department of Navy, 240 F.3d 1009, 1014–15 (Fed. Cir. 2001).

IV. "MOTIVATING FACTOR" REQUIREMENT

For both discrimination and retaliation claims under USERRA, plaintiffs must show that their military status or related obligation was a motivating factor in the employer's adverse action.[76] The "motivating factor" requirement represents a significant departure from a line of decisions interpreting USERRA's predecessor.

In *Monroe v. Standard Oil Co.*,[77] the U.S. Supreme Court held that the Vietnam Era Veterans' Readjustment Assistance Act of 1974[78] did not require employers to make certain work schedule accommodations for employee-reservists that it did not make for other employees.[79] In arriving at this holding, the Court stated, in dicta, that the Act protected an "employee-reservist against discriminations like discharge and demotion, motivated *solely* by reserve status."[80]

Following this pronouncement, some lower courts required plaintiffs to show that the adverse employment ac-

---

[76]*See* 38 U.S.C. §4311(c). USERRA's discrimination and retaliation prohibitions expressly reference "motivating factor":

(c) An employer shall be considered to have engaged in actions prohibited—

(1) under subsection (a), if the person's membership, application for membership, service, application for service, or obligation for service in the uniformed services is a *motivating factor* in the employer's action, unless the employer can prove that the action would have been taken in the absence of such membership, application for membership, service, application for service, or obligation for service; or

(2) under subsection (b), if the person's (A) action to enforce a protection afforded any person under this chapter, (B) testimony or making of a statement in or in connection with any proceeding under this chapter, (C) assistance or other participation in an investigation under this chapter, or (D) exercise of a right provided for in this chapter, is a *motivating factor* in the employer's action, unless the employer can prove that the action would have been taken in the absence of such person's enforcement action, testimony, statement, assistance, participation, or exercise of a right.

Id. (emphasis added).

[77]452 U.S. 549 (1981).

[78]Pub. L. No. 93-508, 88 Stat. 1594 (1974).

[79]*See* 452 U.S. at 565.

[80]*Id.* at 559 (emphasis added). At a later point in its opinion, the Court again references "sole" motivation as a requirement for successfully proving discrimination based upon an employee-reservist's obligations: "Yet Congress has provided in § 2021(b)(3) that employers may not rid themselves of such inconveniences and productivity losses by discharging or otherwise disadvantaging employee-reservists *solely* because of their military obligations." *Id.* at 565 (emphasis added).

tion was motivated solely by their military status or related obligations.[81]

In 1994, Congress specifically sought to supersede these holdings when it enacted USERRA:

> To the extent that courts have relied on dicta from the Supreme Court's decision in *Monroe v. Standard Oil Co.*, 452 U.S. 549, 559 (1981), that a violation of this section can occur only if the military obligation is the sole factor (*see Sawyer v. Swift &Co.*, 836 F.2d 1257, 1261 (10th Cir. 1988)), those decisions have misinterpreted the original legislative intent and history of 38 U.S.C. 2021(b)(3) and are rejected on that basis.[82]

In its place, Congress inserted into the text of USERRA the "motivating factor" requirement, which originated from the burden-of-proof analysis adopted by the National Labor Relations Board.[83]

Under the motivating-factor analysis, plaintiffs are no longer required to demonstrate that the protected conduct or status is the sole cause of the employment action.[84] In-

---

[81]*E.g.*, Burkhart v. Post-Browning, Inc., 859 F.2d 1245, 1247 (6th Cir. 1988); Sawyer v. Swift & Co., 836 F.2d 1257, 1262 (10th Cir. 1988); Clayton v. Blackhorse Truck Lines, Inc., 815 F.2d 1203, 1205 (8th Cir. 1987).

[82]H.R. Rep. No. 103-65(I), at 24 (1993), *reprinted in* 1994 U.S.C.C.A.N. 2449, 2457.

[83]In the House report accompanying passage of USERRA, Congress specifically mentioned this burden-of-proof analysis:

> Section 4311(b) would reaffirm that the standard of proof in a discrimination or retaliation case is the so-called "but for" test and that the burden of proof is on the employer, once a prima facie case is established. This provision is simply a reaffirmation of the original intent of Congress when it enacted current section 2021(b)(3) of title 38, in 1968. See Hearings on H.R. 11509 Before Subcommittee No. 3 of the House Committee on Armed Services, 89th Cong., 1st Sess. at 5320 (Feb. 23, 1966). In 1986, when Congress amended section 2021(b)(3) to prohibit initial hiring discrimination against Reserve and National Guard members, Congressman G.V. Montgomery (sponsor of the legislation and Chairman of the House Committee on Veterans Affairs) explained that, in accordance with the 1968 legislative intent cited above, the courts in these discrimination cases should use the burden of proof analysis adopted by the National Labor Relations Board and approved by the Supreme Court under the National Labor Relations Act. See 132 Cong. Rec. 29226 (Oct. 7, 1986) (statement of Cong. Montgomery) citing NLRB v. Transportation Management Corp., 462 U.S. 393 (1983).

Id.

[84]*See* Velazquez-Garcia v. Horizon Lines of P.R., Inc., 473 F.3d 11, 16 (1st Cir. 2007); Coffman v. Chugach Support Servs., Inc., 411 F.3d 1231, 1238 (11th Cir. 2005); Maxfield v. Cintas Corp. 2, 427 F.3d 544, 553 (8th Cir. 2005); Leisek v. Brightwood Corp., 278 F.3d 895, 898–99 (9th Cir. 2002); Hill v. Michelin N. Am., Inc., 252 F.3d 307, 312 (4th Cir. 2001); Sheehan v. Dep't of Navy, 240 F.3d 1009, 1013 (Fed. Cir. 2001); Curby v. Archon, 216 F.3d 549, 556 (6th Cir. 2000); Gummo v. Village of Depew, 75 F.3d 98, 106 (2d Cir. 1996).

stead, plaintiffs will meet this requirement if they can prove by the preponderance of evidence that military status or a related obligation is a factor that the defendant relied on, took into account, considered, or conditioned its decision on in making that consideration.[85] In other words, a motivating factor is one that a truthful employer would list as one of the factors if asked for the reasons for taking the adverse employment action.[86]

To prove an employer's motivation or intent, plaintiffs may use either direct or indirect evidence.[87] Direct evidence is evidence that establishes discriminatory intent without resorting to inferences raised from circumstantial evidence.[88] For example, direct evidence may take the form of negative references to military leave in a poor performance evaluation,[89] statements that promoting an employee would be unfair because "someone else had to do the job" while he attended to military obligations,[90] or remarks that an em-

---

[85] See Petty v. Metropolitan Gov't of Nashville-Davidson County, 538 F.3d 431, 446 (6th Cir. 2008); Lewis v. Rite of Passage, Inc., 217 Fed. Appx. 785, 786 (10th Cir. 2007); Coffman, 411 F.3d at 1238; Fink v. City of N.Y., 129 F. Supp. 2d 511, 520 (E.D.N.Y. 2001); Brandsasse v. City of Suffolk, 72 F. Supp. 2d 608, 617 (E.D.Va. 1999); Barreto v. ITT World Directories, Inc., 62 F. Supp. 2d 387, 391 (D.P.R. 1999); Robinson v. Morris Moore Chevrolet-Buick, Inc., 974 F. Supp. 571, 576 (E.D. Tex. 1997); Burgener v. Union Pac. Corp., 2009 WL 1082356, at *6 (N.D. Cal. Apr. 22, 2009); Sandoval v. City of Chicago, 2008 WL 2743750, at *4, aff'd, 560 F.3d 703 (7th Cir. 2009); McLaughlin v. Newark Paperboard Prods., 2006 WL 2571396, at *4 (W.D. Pa. 2006).

[86] See Petty, 538 F.3d at 446; Coffman, 411 F.3d at 1238; Fink, 129 F. Supp. 2d at 520; Brandsasse, 72 F. Supp. 2d at 617; Kelley v. Maine Eye Care Assocs., 37 F. Supp. 2d 47, 54 (D. Me. 1999); Robinson, 974 F. Supp. at 576; Burgener, 2009 WL 1082356, at *6; Sandoval, 2008 WL 2743750, at *4; Easton v. Continental Tire N. Am., Inc., 2006 WL 1004887, at *3 (S.D. Ill. 2006).

[87] See Coffman, 411 F.3d at 1238; Sheehan, 240 F.3d at 1014; Wagner v. Novartis Pharms. Corp., 565 F. Supp. 2d 940, 947 (E.D. Tenn. 2008); Woodard v. New York Health & Hosps. Corp., 554 F. Supp. 2d 329, 348 (E.D.N.Y. 2008); Gillie-Harp v. Cardinal Health, Inc., 249 F. Supp. 2d 1113, 1121 (W.D. Wis. 2003); Sandoval, 2008 WL 2743750, at *4; Bursese v. Paypal, Inc., 2007 WL 485984, at *6 (N.D. Cal. Feb. 12, 2007); McLaughlin, 2006 WL 2571396, at *4; Easton, 2006 WL 1004887, at *3; Hart v. Hillside Twp., 2006 WL 756000, at *5 (D.N.J. Mar. 17, 2006); Tagget v. Eaton Corp., 2001 WL 1397289, at *4 (E.D. Mich. Nov. 7, 2001).

[88] Gillie-Harp, 249 F. Supp. 2d at 1121.

[89] See Grosjean, 481 F. Supp. 2d at 883.

[90] See Maher, 406 F. Supp. 2d at 1030. While the Maher Court allowed evidence of comments regarding service obligations to survive summary judgment, those comments were of limited value at trial. See 547 F.3d 817.

ployee was selected for a reduction in force because of the fear that he "can be called up."[91]

Direct evidence, however, is not required.[92] Plaintiffs may use the circumstantial or indirect method of proof.[93] Using indirect evidence, motivation may be inferred from a variety of factors, including:

1. temporal proximity between the military obligation and the adverse employment action;

2. inconsistencies between the proffered reason and other actions of the employer;

3. an employer's expressed hostility toward protected members together with knowledge of the employee's military activity; and

4. disparate treatment between protected members and other employees with similar work records or offenses.[94]

Additionally, while certain negative comments or reactions concerning military obligations may not rise to the level of direct evidence, they nonetheless may be relevant in determining whether military status was a motivating factor in the adverse employment decision.[95]

---

[91]Brinkley v. Dialysis Clinic, Inc., 403 F. Supp. 2d 1090, 1093 (M.D. Ala. 2005); *see also* Diaz-Gandia v. Dapena-Thompson, 90 F.3d 609, 152 LRRM 2919 (1st Cir. 1996), 90 F.3d at 615 (interpreting USERRA's predecessor and finding direct evidence where supervisor stated that the reason the plaintiff had no telephone was that he was "on one of those damn military leaves" when the phones were installed).

[92]*See Wagner*, 565 F. Supp. 2d at 947; Tranter v. Crescent Township, 2007 WL 3274158, at *3, 183 LRRM (BNA) 2119 (W.D. Pa. Nov. 5, 2007); *Tagget*, 2001 WL 1397289, at *4.

[93]*See Coffman*, 411 F.3d at 1238; *Sheehan*, 240 F.3d at 1014; *Wagner*, 565 F. Supp. 2d at 947; *Tranter*, 2007 WL 3274158, at *3; *Hart*, 2006 WL 756000, at *5.

[94]*Coffman*, 411 F.3d at 1238; *Sheehan*, 240 F.3d at 1014; *Wagner*, 565 F. Supp. 2d at 947; *Woodard*, 554 F. Supp. 2d at 348; McDuffie v. Eli Lilly & Co., 2009 WL 857069, at *8; *Sandoval*, 2008 WL 2743750, at *4; *Bursese*, 2007 WL 485984, at *6; *Easton*, 2006 WL 1004887, at *4; *McLaughlin*, 2006 WL 2571396, at *4; *Hart*, 2006 WL 756000, at *5.

[95]*See Velazquez-Garcia*, 473 F.3d at 18; *Gillie-Harp*, 249 F. Supp. 2d at 1121; Johnson v. Village of Rockton, 2007 WL 5720626, at *3 (N.D. Ill. 2007).

V. AFFIRMATIVE DEFENSE: SAME ACTION ABSENT PROTECTED STATUS OR ACTIVITY

Unlike the framework applied in other federal antidiscrimination laws,[96] USERRA's procedural framework shifts the burden of production, as well as *persuasion*, to the employer once an employee demonstrates that military status or a related obligation was a motivating factor in the adverse employment action.[97] At that point, the employer must prove, by a preponderance of evidence, that it would have taken the same action absent USERRA-protected status or activity.[98]

Simply arguing that the same decision would have been justified is not the same as proving that the same deci-

---

[96]Originally developed in the Title VII context, the framework approved in *McDonnell Douglas Corp. v. Green*, 411 U.S. 792, 802–04 (1973), and *Texas Dep't of Community Affairs v. Burdine*, 450 U.S. 248, 253 (1981), has been expanded to a variety of different discrimination contexts. *E.g.*, Raytheon Co. v. Hernandez, 540 U.S. 44, 49–55 (2003) (applying *McDonnell Douglas* to an Americans with Disability Act of 1990 claim); O'Connor v. Consolidated Coin Caterers Corp., 517 U.S. 308, 311 (1996) (assuming that the *McDonnell Douglas* approach applies to an Age Discrimination in Employment Act claim); Crawford v. TRW Auto. U.S. LLC, 560 F.3d 607, 613 (6th Cir. 2009) (utilizing the *McDonnell Douglas* test in an ERISA claim); Metzler v. Federal Home Loan Bank of Topeka, 464 F.3d 1164, 1170 (10th Cir. 2006) ("Retaliation claims under the FMLA are subject to the burden-shifting analysis of *McDonnell Douglas Corp. v. Green* . . . ."). In fact, one court has described the framework and its pervasive use as "the ubiquitous burden-shifting framework that has, like some B-movie villain, devoured nearly every area of law with which it has come into contact." *Crawford*, 560 F.3d at 613 (utilizing the *McDonnell Douglas* test in the ERISA context).

[97]*See* 38 U.S.C. §4311(c); 20 C.F.R. §§1002.22; .23(b); Gagnon v. Sprint Corp., 284 F.3d 839, 854 (8th Cir. 2002), *abrogated on other grounds*, Desert Place, Inc. v. Costa, 539 U.S. 90 (2003).

[98]*See* 38 U.S.C. §4311(c); 20 C.F.R. §§1002.22; .23(b); *Gagnon*, 284 F.3d at 854; *Sheehan*, 240 F.3d at 1014; *Gummo*, 75 F.3d at 106. Again, consistent with Congress's intent, the affirmative defense mirrors the proof structure adopted by the National Labor Relations Board:

New section 4311(b) would provide, consistent with current law, that the employer would be considered to have committed a prohibited act of discrimination under the VRR law if the claimant's covered connection with service was a motivating factor in the employer's action, unless the employer showed that the action complained of would have been taken in the absence of service connection. This provision is a reaffirmation of the original intent of Congress when it enacted current section 4301(b)(3) of title 38 in 1968. The Committee intends, consistent with current section 4301(b)(3) and the approach followed by the National Labor Relations Board in and approved by the Supreme Court, NLRB v. Transportation Management Corp., 462 U.S. 393 (1983), that the burden of proof with respect to this affirmative defense would be on the employer.

S. REP. No. 103-158, at 45 (1993).

sion would have been taken.[99] Nor may an employer usually meet its burden by showing that the decision was motivated only in part by a legitimate reason.[100] Rather, the employer must show that its legitimate reason, standing alone, would have induced it to make the same decision.[101]

In contrast to the burden-shifting paradigm in *McDonnell Douglas v. Green*,[102] under USERRA, the employee does not have the burden of demonstrating that the employer's stated reason is a pretext.[103] Rather, as some courts have explained, the employer must show, by a preponderance of the evidence, that the stated reason was *not* pretext.[104]

In *Velázquez-Garcia v. Horizon Lines of Puerto Rico, Inc.*,[105] the First Circuit analyzed the proof needed for an employer to avail itself to this affirmative defense. The plaintiff, Carlos Velázquez-Garciá, was a reservist in the U.S. Marine Corps, which obligated him to report periodically for training sessions.[106] Velázquez-Garciá alleged that his employer complained about rescheduling his shifts to accommodate his military schedule.[107]

After enlisting as a reservist, Velázquez-Garciá began cashing checks for other employees in return for a fee.[108] Seven months later, one of Velázquez-Garciá's supervisors (who also purportedly complained about his military sched-

---

[99]*See Velazquez-Garcia*, 473 F.3d at 23 (noting that while a policy violation "may well be a fireable offense . . . but that is only the beginning of the analysis"); *Leisek*, 278 F.3d at 900 ("However, even though Leisek's unexcused absences would be a legitimate reason for terminating his employment, Brightwood has not established as an uncontroverted fact that it would have terminated Leisek even if he had not been active in the Guard's H.A.B.I.T. program"); *Woodard*, 554 F. Supp. 2d at 348; *Robinson*, 974 F. Supp. at 576 (quoting Givhan v. Western Line Consol. Sch. Dist., 439 U.S. 410, 416 (1979)).

[100]*See* Smith v. School Bd. of Polk County, 205 F. Supp. 2d 1308, 1315 (M.D. Fla. 2002); *Robinson*, 974 F. Supp. at 576 (quoting Price Waterhouse v. Hopkins, 490 U.S. 228, 250 (1989)).

[101]*See Coffman*, 411 F.3d at 1238-39 (quoting *Sheehan*, 240 F.3d at 1014); *Robinson*, 974 F. Supp. at 576.

[102]411 U.S. 792 (1973).

[103]*See* Reed v. Honeywell Int'l, Inc., 2009 WL 1125542, at *6 (D. Ariz. 2009).

[104]*See Velazquez-Garcia*, 473 F.3d at 17.

[105]*Id.*

[106]*Id.* at 14.

[107]*Id.*

[108]*Id.*

ule) reported this practice and terminated Velázquez-García for violating company policy.[109]

While the court acknowledged that the district court articulated the correct standard concerning the employer's affirmative defense, it found that the lower court implicitly and incorrectly kept the burden of persuasion on Velázquez-García at the summary judgment stage.[110] Specifically, the district court stated that the employer "was entitled to take the action it did," that the employer was "justified in dismissing" Velázquez-García, and that Velázquez-García "produced no evidence that would lead the Court to believe that [the employer's] stated reason for his termination was pretextual in nature."[111]

In reversing the district court's grant of summary judgment, the court explained why the lower court's analysis did not comport with USERRA's proof structure:

> The issue under USERRA is not whether an employer is "entitled" to dismiss an employee for a particular reason, but whether it would have done so if the employee were not in the military. Here, Velázquez's violation of the Code may well be a fireable offense under Horizon's policies, but that is only the beginning of the analysis. Horizon must go further and demonstrate, by a preponderance of the evidence, that it *would* indeed have fired Velázquez, regardless of his military status.[112]

Pointing to the ambiguities in the employer's policy—the employer's failure to provide any prior warnings, inconsistencies in punishment for similar violations, and the timing of Velázquez-García's termination—the Court found that the employer failed to meet its burden of proving that it would have taken the same action absent Velázquez-García's reservist status.[113]

---

[109]*Id.* at 14–15.
[110]*Id.* at 20.
[111]*Id.*
[112]*Id.*
[113]*Id.* at 20–21.

VI. HARASSMENT

Although the text of USERRA does not expressly prohibit harassment, a number of courts have considered whether the law nonetheless recognizes harassment claims.[114] Some of these courts assume for argument that USERRA does recognize a claim for harassment, but ultimately determine that the claim presented otherwise fails.[115] Others present the issue, but never directly answer whether USERRA alone permits a harassment claim.[116]

Courts that squarely address whether plaintiffs may raise USERRA harassment claims[117] often reference the Merit Systems Protection Board's (the Board) decision in *Petersen v. Department of the Interior.*[118] In that case, the Board reversed the administrative law judge's ruling that a veteran's harassment claim was not viable under USERRA.[119]

In its analysis, the Board first looked to the text and the history of USERRA. The text of USERRA prohibits employers from denying "any benefit of employment" because of

---

[114]*E.g.*, Miller v. City of Indianapolis, 281 F.3d 648 (7th Cir. 2002); Church v. City of Reno, No. 97-17097, 1999 WL 65205 (9th Cir. Feb. 9, 1999); Dees v. Hyundai Motor Mfg., Ala., *LLC*, 2009 WL 778700 (M.D. Ala. 2009); Steenken v. Campbell County, No. 04-224-DLB, 2007 WL 837173 (E.D. Ky. Mar. 15, 2007); Molina v. Rimco, Inc., No. 05-1181 (JAF), 2006 WL 2639297 (D.P.R. Sept. 13, 2006); *Maher*, 406 F. Supp. 2d 1006; *Figueroa Reyes*, 389 F. Supp. 2d 205; Vickers v. City of Memphis, 368 F. Supp. 2d 842 (W.D. Tenn. 2005); *see* Randall v. Department of Justice, 105 M.S.P.R. 524 (2007); Petersen v. Department of the Interior, 71 M.S.P.R. 227 (1996).

[115]*See Miller*, 281 F.3d at 653; *Molina*, 2006 WL 2639297, at *6; *Figueroa Reyes*, 389 F. Supp. 2d 205, 212.

[116]*See Church*, 1999 WL 65205, at *1 ("We need not reach the issue of whether a hostile work environment claim is cognizable under the statute, however, because to hold a party in contempt, the prohibitions of a consent decree must be clear enough that those who must obey them will know what the court intends to require and what it means to forbid"); *Vickers*, 368 F. Supp. 2d at 845 (holding that the USERRA harassment claim may proceed only if the plaintiff can produce an employment policy that prohibits the complained-of conduct).

[117]*Dees*, 2009 WL 778700, at *6 ("[I]n the absence of Eleventh Circuit precedent to the contrary, [the court] concludes that a claim for harassment on account of military service is cognizable under USERRA"); *Steenken*, 2007 WL 837173, at *3 ("Because the right to be free from a hostile work environment, broadly construed, is a benefit of employment, the Court, in the absence of Sixth Circuit authority to the contrary, concludes that Plaintiff's hostile work environment claim is cognizable under USERRA").

[118]*Petersen*, 71 M.S.P.R. 227.

[119]*Id.* at 239.

an employee's military status or related obligations.[120] The Board noted that the definition of "benefit of employment" is broad and includes "any advantage, profit, privilege, gain, status, account, or interest" that accrues by reason of any employer policy, plan or practice.[121] Looking next to the legislative history for guidance, the Board found that Congress expressly intended for the phrase "benefit of employment" to be interpreted expansively.[122]

The Board then referred to other antidiscrimination statutes that courts interpret to permit harassment claims.[123] Much as USERRA does not expressly prohibit harassment, these statutes likewise do not contain an explicit bar against harassment.[124] Given the broad interpretation Congress intended and the "well-established principle that discrimination encompasses hostile environment claims," the Board

---

[120]*Id.* at 235–36 (citing 38 U.S.C. §4311(a)).

[121]*Id.* at 236 (citing 38 U.S.C. §4302(2)).

[122]*Id.* Congress addressed the "benefit of employment" language in its legislative discussions and noted an intention for a broad interpretation:

I want to express the committee's strong disagreement with the recent decision in Rumsey v. N.Y. State Dept. of Corr. Services, 19 F.3d 83 (2nd Cir. 1994), which limited the protection given reservists on active duty for training only to "substantial rights" such as discharge, demotion, or failure to promote. While the amended act speaks in terms of "benefit, benefits of employment or rights and benefits," and no longer uses the term "incident or advantage of employment," the intent has always been to have an expansive interpretation, such as that expressed by the sixth circuit in Monroe v. Standard Oil Co., 613 F.2d 641, 645 (6th Cir. 1980), aff'd. 452 U.S. 549 (1981). "Incidents or advantages of employment * * * is intentionally framed in general terms to encompass the potential limitless variation in benefits of employment that are conferred by an untold number and variety of business concerns."

140 CONG. REC. H9177-05, H9133 (daily ed. Sept. 13, 1994) (statement of Rep. Montgomery).

Section 4303(2) would define "benefit, benefit of employment" and employment related "rights and benefits." These are the rights, incident to employment, which are protected under chapter 43. These rights are broadly defined to include all attributes of the employment relationship which are affected by the absence of a member of the uniformed services because of military service. The list of benefits is illustrative and not intended to be all inclusive.

H.R. REP. No. 103-65(I), at 24 (1993), *reprinted in* 1994 U.S.C.C.A.N. 2449, 2457; *see* Coffy v. Republic Steel Corp., 447 U.S. 191, 196 (1980) (interpreting USERRA's predecessor and stating that it should "be liberally construed for the benefit of the returning veteran").

[123]*Petersen,* 71 M.S.P.R. at 237–39.

[124]*Id.* (construing Title VII of the Civil Rights Act of 1964, Title VI of the Education Amendments of 1972, the Rehabilitation Act of 1973, and the Americans with Disabilities Act of 1990).

held that USERRA does allow for harassment claims based on prior service, provided that the conduct is sufficiently pervasive to alter the working conditions and create an abusive working environment.[125]

Since *Petersen*, courts have further articulated what a plaintiff must show to demonstrate actionable harassment. Courts consider a number of factors to determine whether the conduct is sufficiently severe or pervasive, including: the frequency of the conduct, its severity, whether it was physically threatening or humiliating, and whether it unreasonably interfered with the employee's work performance.[126] The conduct must be viewed objectively to assess whether a reasonable person would perceive the situation to be hostile.[127]

Assuming a plaintiff may succeed in proving harassment that is sufficiently severe and pervasive, some courts have noted an additional hurdle awaiting plaintiffs raising harassment claims. While USERRA does provide for lost wages and benefits (and potentially liquidated damages based upon that loss), the "remedial scheme conspicuously omits any recovery for mental anguish, pain and suffering, and punitive damages."[130] Thus, employees seeking a monetary remedy through USERRA harassment claims may risk a court dismissing their claims if they cannot prove that they suffered the type of harm remedied through the law.[131]

---

[125]*Id.* at 239.

[126]*See Miller*, 281 F.3d at 653; *Dees*, 2009 WL 778700, at *6; *Molina*, 2006 WL 2639297, at *6; *Maher*, 406 F. Supp. 2d 1023; *Figueroa Reyes*, 389 F. Supp. 2d at 213.

[127]Miller, 281 F.3d at 653.

[128][Reserved.]

[129][Reserved.]

[130]*Dees*, 2009 WL 778700, at *7; *see* Vander Wal v. Sykes Enters., Inc., 377 F. Supp. 2d 738, 746 (D.N.D. 2005) (same).

[131]*See Dees*, 2009 WL 778700, at *7 (holding that plaintiff had no standing to assert his USERRA harassment claim because "there is no relief the court can give [the plaintiff] for the harassment he may have suffered"). The court in *Dees* recognized that the plaintiff was not without any remedy under USERRA. *Id.* at 8. For example, if a plaintiff still works with the employer, he or she may be entitled to injunctive relief preventing any further harassment. *Id.* at *8 (citing 38 U.S.C. §4323(d)(1)(A)).

VII. DISPARATE IMPACT CLAIMS

A disparate impact claim arises when an employer implements practices that may be neutral on their face, and even neutral in intent, but in effect treat one group more harshly than another.[132] In contrast to a disparate treatment claim, the touchstone of a disparate impact claim is the consequences of employment practices, rather than the motivation of the employer.[133] In such cases, good faith will "not redeem employment procedures or testing mechanisms that operate as 'built-in headwinds' for [protected groups] and are unrelated to measuring job capability."[134]

To determine whether certain antidiscrimination laws lend themselves to disparate impact claims, courts have examined the legislative intent and the text of the laws.[135] Generally, where courts have recognized disparate impact claims, the text of the law focuses on the conduct's effects on the employee instead of the employer's motivation for the action.[136] Similarly, when Congress has weighed in on the issue, it too evidences an intent to prohibit neutral practices that create a disparate impact.[137]

Courts have expressed uncertainty as to whether a disparate impact claim exists under USERRA.[138] Specifically, the text of USERRA's antidiscrimination provision prohibits conduct where a "person's membership, application for

---

[132]See Ricci v. DeStefano, 129 S. Ct. 2658 (2009); Griggs v. Duke Power Co., 401 U.S. 424, 430 (1971); Miller v. City of Indianapolis, 281 F.3d 648, 651 (7th Cir. 2002).

[133]See Smith v. City of Jackson, 544 U.S. 228, 234 (2005).

[134]Id. (quoting Griggs, 401 U.S. at 432).

[135]E.g., id. at 239–40 (holding that the Age Discrimination in Employment Act permits disparate impact claims); Griggs, 401 U.S. at 431–32 (holding that Title VII of the Civil Rights Act of 1964 prohibits neutral employer practices that create a disparate impact).

[136]See Smith, 544 U.S. at 236 ("Thus the text [of the Age Discrimination in Employment Act] focuses on the *effects* of the action on the employee rather than the motivation for the action of the employer."); Griggs, 401 U.S. at 431 ("[Title VII] proscribes not only overt discrimination but also practices that are fair in form, but discriminatory in operation.").

[137]See Smith, 544 U.S. at 235 n.5; Griggs, 401 U.S. at 434–35.

[138]See Rosyln v. Northwest Airlines, Inc., No. 05-0441 (PAM/RLE), 2005 WL 1529937, at *4 (D. Minn., June 29, 2005) ("The Court also notes the uncertainty of whether USERRA provides a cause of action based on disparate impact").

membership, service, application for service, or obligation for service in the uniformed services is a *motivating factor* in the employer's action."[139] Additionally, Congress expressly adopted the "motivating factor" requirement from the test developed by the United States Supreme Court in *NLRB v. Transportation Management Corp.*,[140] which is a disparate treatment test.[141]

Few courts have discussed the viability of disparate impact claims in the context of USERRA. In *Miller v. City of Indianapolis*,[142] the Seventh Circuit avoided answering the question by holding that even if USERRA recognized the claim, the plaintiff could not succeed under a disparate impact theory.[143] The court left open whether a disparate impact claim may arise under USERRA, but noted that it does not always allow such claims and it previously declined to recognize disparate impact claims in other contexts.[144]

Another opportunity to address this issue arose in *Fink v. City of New York*.[145] Like the Seventh Circuit in *Miller*, the district court in *Fink* declined to affirmatively state that USERRA permits disparate impact claims because the plaintiff had already succeeded in his disparate treatment claim.[146] Unlike in *Miller*, however, the court in *Fink* seemingly was more receptive to USERRA disparate impact claims:

---

[139]38 U.S.C. §4311(c)(1) (emphasis added); *see* Fink v. City of N.Y., 129 F. Supp. 2d 511, 522 (E.D.N.Y. 2001) ("Discrimination, after all, requires motivation under the *NLRB* test").

[140]462 U.S. 393 (1983); H.R. Rep. No. 103-65(I), at 24 (1993), *reprinted in* 1994 U.S.C.C.A.N. 2449, 2457 (noting that "the courts in [USERRA] discrimination cases should use the burden of proof analysis adopted by the National Labor Relations Board and approved by the Supreme Court under the National Labor Relations Act").

[141]*See Fink*, 129 F. Supp. 2d at 522 ("The *NLRB* test, like the *McDonnell Douglas* test, is a disparate treatment test, demanding direct or circumstantial evidence of discriminatory intent").

[142]281 F.3d 648, 651 (7th Cir. 2002).

[143]*Id.* at 652 ("But whether a disparate impact claim can be prosecuted under USERRA will wait for another day. This case fails on the facts").

[144]*Id.*

[145]129 F. Supp. 2d 511 (E.D.N.Y. 2001).

[146]*Id.* at 523.

> While these kinds of inquiries are unnecessary in [the plaintiff's] case because the jury has enough evidence from which to infer discriminatory intent under the *NLRB* burden-shifting test, these modes of analysis may, in fact, be the more logically appropriate ways of handling cases like [the plaintiff's], some of which will certainly present fact patterns unamenable to the *NLRB* motivation test.[147]

But as both *Miller* and *Fink* acknowledged, the question of whether a disparate impact claim exists under USERRA remains unanswered and awaits another day.[148]

VIII. CONCLUSION

USERRA's discrimination, retaliation, and harassment provisions offer broad protections. Practitioners need to understand these protections and how they apply to the various claims that may be made under USERRA.

---

[147]*Id.; see id.* at 522 ("There seems to be no discriminatory intent on this [disparate impact] fact pattern, and yet, it simply cannot be the case that the injury suffered is not redressable under USERRA").

[148]*Miller*, 281 F.3d at 651; *Fink*, 129 F. Supp. 2d at 523. In *Ricci v. DeStefano*, 129 S. Ct. 2658 (2009), the Supreme Court discussed the burden of proof for disparate treatment claims.

Chapter 11

ENFORCEMENT, REMEDIES, AND OTHER ISSUES UNDER USERRA

I. Introduction

The Uniformed Services Employment and Reemployment Rights Act (USERRA or the Act)[1] provides significant enforcement rights and remedies for those who are entitled to claim its protections. This includes employees who take, or are entitled to take, military leave,[2] as well as employees who seek the protections of USERRA's discrimination, ha-

---

[1] *See* 38 U.S.C. §§4301–4335.
[2] *See id.*, §§4312–4319.

rassment, and retaliation provisions.[3] This chapter discusses the enforcement procedure, burden of proof, statute of limitations, declaratory judgments, and arbitration agreements under USERRA.

II. Enforcement Procedures

Employees seeking to claim USERRA's protections have two enforcement options: (1) pursue an administrative remedy provided through the United States Department of Labor (DOL), or (2) file a lawsuit seeking private enforcement of the person's claimed rights.[4] An employee claiming rights under USERRA may seek the assistance of the federal government by filing an administrative complaint with the DOL.[5] The Secretary of Labor (Secretary) has primary responsibility for executing and enforcing USERRA's rights and protections.[6] The Secretary's responsibilities are carried out through the DOL's Veterans Employment and Training Service (VETS).[7] The Secretary must investigate each complaint alleging USERRA violations and, in so doing, has the authority to examine and copy employer and employee documents relevant to the investigation, the right to reasonable access to interview persons, and the subpoena power to compel the attendance

---

[3]See id., 38 U.S.C. §4311. The provisions of Section 4311 apply not only to employees who take, or seek to take, military leave, but also to any person who in good faith complains about alleged discrimination prohibited by USERRA and any person who participates in the investigation of such a claim. Thus, like the protections afforded under Title VII of the Civil Rights Act of 1964, USERRA protects persons beyond the scope of the protected classes listed in the statute.

[4]See id., §§4322(a), 4323(a)(3).

[5]See id., §4322. Section 4322 refers only to "employment and reemployment rights or benefits with respect to employment by an employer." See id., §4322(a). While this section does not specifically reference the protections provided in Section 4311 against discrimination, harassment, and retaliation, these are presumably "employment . . . rights" under Section 4322 and subject to the DOL's administrative procedures. Nothing within USERRA or the DOL's regulations leads to a different conclusion.

[6]See id., §§4321, 4331.

[7]See id., §4321.

and testimony of witnesses and the production of documents.[8]

If a VETS investigation leads to the determination that a USERRA violation has occurred, the Secretary is obligated to make "reasonable efforts to ensure" that the employer complies with the law.[9] The Secretary, however, has no power to *force* compliance.[10] The Secretary, typically through representatives of VETS, may seek to resolve the complaint through informal means, such as mediation.[11] If the Secretary is unable to resolve the complaint, the complaining employee is notified and informed of the option to seek the assistance of the United States Attorney General in enforcing the rights at issue (or seek the assistance of the Office of the Special Counsel in the case of a federal employer) or to file a private lawsuit, as the case may be.[12]

Enforcement actions take different paths depending on whether the aggrieved individual is employed by the federal government, by a state governmental entity, or by a private employer. If the employer is a federal agency, the aggrieved employee may proceed with a complaint before the Merit Systems Protection Board (MSPB or Board).[13] If the aggrieved employee is employed by a state entity or private employer, the employee may commence an action in court at his or her own expense or seek representation from the United States Attorney General in a civil action against the employer.[14]

Unlike an action brought pursuant to Title VII, an employee is not required to first seek assistance from an administrative agency. Thus, an individual may file a complaint against his or her employer directly with the MSPB if the individual is employed by the federal government, or

---

[8] *See id.*, §§4322(d), 4326(a)–(b).
[9] *See id.*, §4322(d).
[10] *See* 20 C.F.R. §1002.290.
[11] *See* 38 U.S.C. §4321; 20 C.F.R. §1002.290.
[12] *See* 38 U.S.C. §§4322(e), 4323(a)(3), 4324(a).
[13] *See id.*, §4324(a).
[14] *See id.*, §4322(a); 20 C.F.R. §§1002.291–. 304.

with the appropriate court if the individual is employed by a state or private entity.[15]

A. Enforcement and Remedies Against the Federal Employer

The federal government is subject to USERRA.[16] Indeed, Congress declared in the Act that "the Federal Government should be a model employer in carrying out the provisions of this chapter."[17] The rights of a federal employee vary depending on the agency at issue.

Federal employees have no right to bring a private action in a federal or state court.[18] Instead, complaints brought by federal employees are litigated before the MSPB, unless the employee is employed by a federal agency with an intelligence mission.[19] A federal employee who is not part of an agency with an intelligence mission may submit a complaint, at his or her own expense, directly to the MSPB.[20] Alternatively, an employee may request that the Secretary refer a complaint filed with VETS to the Office of Special Counsel, which is authorized to act as counsel for the employee in an action on the complaint before the MSPB.[21] If the Office of Special Counsel is reasonably satisfied that the employee "is entitled to the rights or benefits sought," the Special Counsel may accept the referral and initiate an action before the MSPB.[22] If the Office of Special Counsel decides not to represent the employee, then the aggrieved military member may still commence his or her own action before the MSPB.[23]

---

[15]See 38 U.S.C. §§4323(a)(2)(A), 4324(b); 20 C.F.R. §§1002.291, .303.
[16]See 38 U.S.C. §4303(a)(4)(A)(ii).
[17]See id., §4301(b).
[18]See Lawrence v. Geren, No. JFM-07-3455, 2008 U.S. Dist. LEXIS 85099 (D. Md. Oct. 17, 2008) (USERRA does not provide federal employees a private right of action to bring suit in federal district court.).
[19]See 38 U.S.C. §§4324(b), 4325(a).
[20]See id., §4324(b).
[21]See id., §4324(a).
[22]See id., §4324(a)(2)(A).
[23]See id., §4324(b)(4).

If the MSPB determines that a federal agency has violated USERRA, the Board "shall" order the agency to comply with the statute and to compensate the employee for lost wages and benefits.[24] If the MSPB determines that the employer violated USERRA, and private counsel represented the employee, the Board may award attorneys' fees, expert witness fees, and other litigation costs.[25] An employee who receives an adverse decision from the MSPB may petition the Federal Circuit for review.[26] The Office of Special Counsel can represent an employee seeking appellate review if Special Counsel represented the person before the MSPB.[27]

USERRA's MSPB enforcement procedures do not apply to federal agencies with an intelligence mission.[28] Although these intelligence agencies are generally subject to USERRA's requirements, they follow their own enforcement rules, which eliminate the employee's right to seek relief through the MSPB. Instead, an aggrieved employee under these circumstances must submit a claim to the Inspector General of the agency in question for investigation and resolution.[29] There is no judicial review or public filings of complaints filed by employees of intelligence agencies. It is difficult, therefore, to determine USERRA compliance by these agencies.

B. Enforcement and Remedies Against the Private Employer

Individuals employed by private entities may file a civil action without first filing a complaint with VETS.[30] Al-

---

[24]*See id.*, §4324(c)(2).
[25]*See id.*, §4324(c)(4).
[26]*See id.*, §4324(d)(1); Johnson v. Secretary of Veterans Affairs, No. 07–12750, 2008 U.S. Dist. LEXIS 10546 (E.D. Mich. Feb. 13, 2008) (the MSPB has jurisdiction to hear USERRA claims but, under 38 U.S.C. Section 4324(d)(1), that decision may be appealed only to the Federal Circuit).
[27]*See* 38 U.S.C. §4324(d)(2).
[28]*See id.*, §4325.
[29]*See id.*, §4325(b).
[30]*See* 20 C.F.R. §1002.303.

though an employee need not request VETS' assistance prior to filing suit, if the employee seeks that assistance, he or she must wait for completion of VETS proceedings before proceeding with a private action.[31] If VETS finds a basis for a USERRA violation, the employee may request that VETS refer a complaint to the United States Department of Justice (DOJ) and request that the DOJ act as counsel for the employee.[32] If the DOJ is "reasonably satisfied" that the employee is entitled to the rights and benefits sought, it may accept the referral and initiate a civil action free of charge.[33] Such an action is initiated on behalf of the United States government.[34] If the DOJ refuses representation, the employee may still commence his or her own private action in federal court.[35] For private employers, venue will be proper in any federal district court where the employer maintains a place of business.[36]

A prevailing employee may be entitled to legal and equitable remedies.[37] Available remedies include compensation for lost wages/benefits, promotions, or placement into a position.[38] Prevailing employees who demonstrate that reinstatement is not a viable remedy may, in lieu of reinstatement, seek "front pay" damages.[39] If a "willful" violation is found, liquidated damages in an amount equal to the value of lost pay or benefits are available.[40] *Willful* is not defined in the Act, but courts have borrowed from the definition used by the United States Supreme Court in cases under the Age Discrimination in Employment Act,[41] which defines *willful* as the employer acting knowingly or recklessly in

---

[31]*See id.,* §4323(a).
[32]*See id.,* §4324(a).
[33]*See id.,* §4324(a)(2)(A).
[34]*See id.,* §4323(a).
[35]*See id.,* §4323(a)(1).
[36]*See id.,* §4323(c)(2).
[37]*See id.,* §4323(d)–(e).
[38]*See id.*
[39]*See* Graham v. Hall-McMillen Co., 925 F. Supp. 437, 443–47 (N.D. Miss. 1996).
[40]*See* 38 U.S.C. §4323(d)(1).
[41]*See* 29 U.S.C. §§621 *et seq.*

disregard of the law.[42] Although courts have disallowed emotional distress damages under USERRA, employees have successfully maintained separate claims for emotional distress.[43]

An employee who brings an enforcement action under USERRA cannot be assessed court costs or fees, even if the individual loses.[44] A jury trial may be authorized where there is evidence of willful employer noncompliance that could result in a liquidated damage award.[45]

C. Enforcement and Remedies Against the State Employer

Pursuant to its express terms, USERRA applies to state governments acting as employers.[46] Despite this express language, a question remains regarding the Eleventh Amendment's restriction on suing a state for damages.[47] As originally enacted in 1994, Section 4323 of USERRA permitted an individual to sue a state (as well as a political subdivision of a state or a private employer) in federal court, with private counsel or through the assistance of the DOL and DOJ.[48] Two years later, the United States Supreme Court's decision in *Seminole Tribe of Florida v. Florida*[49] clarified that Congress can abrogate Eleventh Amendment immunity only when it is acting under constitutional authority that

---

[42]*See* Fink v. City of New York, 129 F. Supp. 2d 511, 523 (E.D.N.Y. 2001) (quoting Trans World Airlines, Inc. v. Thurston, 469 U.S. 111, 126 (1985)).

[43]*See* Jordan v. Choa, No: 06-CV-0479 W (RBB) 2006 U.S. Dist. LEXIS 82561, at *2 (S.D. Cal. 2006); Murphree v. Communications Techs., Inc., 460 F. Supp. 2d 702, 711 (E.D. La. 2006); Lees v. Sea Breeze Health Care Ctr., Inc., 391 F. Supp. 2d 1103, 1104 (S.D. Ala. 2005).

[44]*See* 38 U.S.C. §4323(h)(1).

[45]*See* Spratt v. Guardian Auto. Prods. Inc., 997 F. Supp. 1138 (N.D. Ind. 1998).

[46]*See* 38 U.S.C. §4303(4)(A)(iii) (employer defined to include a state).

[47]*See* U.S. Const. amend XI. The Eleventh Amendment (ratified in 1795) reads: "The Judicial power of the United States shall not be construed to extend to any suit in law or equity, commenced or prosecuted against one of the United States by Citizens of another State or Citizens or Subjects of any Foreign State." Although the text of this amendment bars only suits against a state by a citizen of another state, the Supreme Court has held that Eleventh Amendment immunity also bars a suit against a state by a citizen of that same state. *See* Hans v. Louisiana, 134 U.S. 1 (1890).

[48]*See* 38 U.S.C. §4323 (1994).

[49]517 U.S. 44 (1996).

came after the states ratified the Eleventh Amendment in 1795.

USERRA is based on the War Powers clauses of the United States Constitution.[50] The Constitution predates the Eleventh Amendment by eight years. Thus, in *Velasquez v. Frapwell,* the Seventh Circuit applied *Seminole Tribe* and dismissed a USERRA claim brought by a private litigant against the state of Indiana, determining that USERRA was unconstitutional insofar as it authorized an individual to sue a state in federal court.[51]

Congress reacted to *Velasquez* by amending USERRA in 1998.[52] The 1998 amendment authorizes the United States Attorney General to bring a USERRA action against a state (as an employer) "in the name of the United States as plaintiff in the action."[53] The amendment was aimed at solving the Eleventh Amendment concern because the Eleventh Amendment precludes suits against states in federal court brought by *individuals.* The Eleventh Amendment does not preclude a lawsuit against a state brought by the Attorney General in the name of the United States.

The 1998 amendment also limited private USERRA claims brought by an employee against a state to a "State court of competent jurisdiction in accordance with the laws of the State."[54] Thus, an aggrieved employee bringing an action against a state employer must do so in accordance with the laws of that state. In *Turner v. Houk* , the Ohio Supreme Court dismissed a USERRA claim on the grounds that the aggrieved civil service employee had failed to proceed under Ohio's administrative appeal process in accordance with an Ohio regulation requiring civil service employees to proceed administratively.[55]

---

[50] *See* U.S. CONST. art. I, §8.
[51] *See* 160 F.3d 389 (7th Cir. 1998), *vacated in part,* 165 F.3d 593 (7th Cir. 1999).
[52] *See* Veterans Programs Enhancement Act of 1998, Pub. L. No. 105–368, 211(b), 112 Stat. 3315 (1998).
[53] 38 U.S.C. §4323(a)(1).
[54] *Id.,* §4323(b)(2).
[55] *See* 862 N.E.2d 104 (Ohio 2007).

Seven months after the 1998 amendments, the U.S. Supreme Court decided *Alden v. Maine.*[56] In *Alden,* employees of the state of Maine sued for relief under the Fair Labor Standards Act (FLSA). Like USERRA, the FLSA purportedly applies to state governments.[57] The action was brought in Maine state court and ultimately appealed to the United States Supreme Court, which held that "the powers delegated to Congress under Article I of the United States Constitution do not include the power to subject nonconsenting states to private suits for damages in state courts."[58] Thus, a state may not be sued by an *individual* asserting rights under USERRA in state court without the state's consent.[59] *Alden* does not impact USERRA actions filed against a state by the DOJ.

Individuals employed by a state are not completely without a USERRA remedy in either state or federal court. A state employee may pursue his or her USERRA claim through the Secretary and have it referred to the DOJ for litigation. However, if the employee chooses to file a private USERRA action against a state, either because the DOJ does not agree that the claim has merit or for other reasons, it may be difficult for the employee to prevail.[60]

Notably, Eleventh Amendment immunity does not apply to state officials sued in their official capacities if the remedy sought is injunctive relief.[61] In many cases, injunctive relief, such as reinstatement or promotion, is an important remedy to the aggrieved employee. In addition, Eleventh Amendment immunity does not apply to state officials

---

[56]527 U.S. 706 (1999).

[57]*See* 29 U.S.C. §203.

[58]*See Alden,* 527 U.S. at 712.

[59]*See id.*

[60]*See* Larkins v. Department of Mental Health & Mental Retardation, 806 So. 2d 358 (Ala. 2001). In *Larkins,* a reservist and employee of an Alabama state agency sued in federal court for denial of reemployment. His federal civil action was dismissed based on Eleventh Amendment immunity. He then sued in state court, but his case was dismissed based on sovereign immunity under the Alabama Constitution.

[61]*See* Alabama v. Pugh, 438 U.S. 781 (1978).

sued for damages in their individual capacities.[62] The crucial issue is whether the state official (as opposed to the state itself) is an employer within the meaning of USERRA.[63] The term "employer" is defined in the Act to include "a person ... to whom the employer has delegated the performance of employment-related responsibilities."[64]

It should also be noted that the Supreme Court has held that a state's political subdivisions, such as counties, cities, and school districts, do not have Eleventh Amendment immunity.[65] In fact, the Act defines "private employer" to include "a political subdivision of a State."[66] Therefore, if an aggrieved individual is employed by a political subdivision of a state, rather than the state itself, the person can bring a private civil action against the political subdivision in federal court.[67]

D. Mediation and Alternative Dispute Resolution

Although VETS has no ability to require employers to participate in mediation or other forms of alternative dispute resolution, it is charged by Congress with the obligation of providing assistance to any person with respect to "employment and reemployment rights and benefits" to which the person is entitled under USERRA.[68] VETS typically exercises this mediation role after it has completed the investigatory process.[69] Many employers take advantage of this program to seek to resolve issues under USERRA.[70]

Employers and employees may also take advantage of an informal ombudsman program offered by the United

---

[62]See id.
[63]See id.
[64]See 38 U.S.C. §4303(4)(A)(i).
[65]See Hopkins v. Clemson Agric. College, 221 U.S. 636, 645 (1911).
[66]38 U.S.C. §4323(i).
[67]See Sandoval v. City of Chicago, 560 F.3d 703, 704 (7th Cir. 2009); Maher v. City of Chicago, 182 LRRM (BNA) 3082 (N.D. Ill. 2007); but see Rimando v. Alum Rock Union Elementary Sch. Dist., No. 08–1874, 2008 U.S. Dist. LEXIS 73969 (N.D. Cal. Sept. 26, 2008).
[68]See 38 U.S.C. §4321; 20 C.F.R. §1002.290
[69]See VETS 2008 Annual Report to Congress, pgs. 1–2 (February 2008).
[70]See id., pg. 5.

States Department of Defense's Employer Support of the Guard and Reserve (ESGR).[71] ESGR uses volunteer ombudsmen to work with both employers and employees to resolve USERRA disputes.[72] This service may be employed prior to the filing of a complaint with VETS or at any time during the process.[73]

III. BURDEN OF PROOF

Courts analyze USERRA cases[74] under the "two-pronged burden-shifting"[75] evidentiary framework established under the National Labor Relations Act (NLRA).[76]

The first linchpin under the USERRA analyses is the "motivating factor" standard,[77] adopted by all circuits that have addressed burden shifting under USERRA.[78] To prove an employer has engaged in a prohibited activity, the employee bears the initial burden of demonstrating, by a preponderance of the evidence[79], that the employee's military service was simply "*a* motivating factor in the employer's [adverse] action,"[80] or, more specifically, just "*one* of the reasons that the employer took action against him or her."[81] "A motivating factor" means that the employee's military service was simply *a* factor, not the sole or most important factor, for the employer's adverse employment action.[82] Thus, the employee establishes a prima facie case under USERRA

---

[71] *See* www.esgr.org.

[72] *See* http://www.esgr.org/Site/Resources/EmployerResourceGuide/tabid/106/ Default.aspx.

[73] *See id.*

[74] *See* Velazquez-Garcia v. Horizon Lines of Puerto Rico, Inc., 473 F.3d 11, 16 (1st Cir. 2007).

[75] *Velazquez-Garcia,* 473 F.3d at 17.

[76] *See* NLRB v. Transportation Mgmt. Corp., 462 U.S. 393, 401 (1983).

[77] *See* Fink v. City of New York, 129 F. Supp. 2d 511, 520 (E.D.N.Y. 2001).

[78] *Velazquez-Garcia,* 473 F.3d at 16.

[79] *Velazquez-Garcia,* 473 F.3d at 17 (internal citations omitted).

[80] *See* 38 U.S.C. §4311(c)(1); 20 C.F.R. §1002.22; Gummo v. Village of Depew, 75 F.3d 98, 105 (2d Cir. 1996) (emphasis added); *accord Velazquez-Garcia,* 473 F.3d at 17.

[81] 20 C.F.R. §1002.22 (emphasis added).

[82] *See* Fink v. City of New York, 129 F. Supp. 2d 511, 520 (E.D.N.Y. 2001).

when the employee demonstrates: (1) performance of duty in a uniformed service; (2) loss of a benefit of employment; and (3) that the benefit was lost due to a previous military service.[83]

If the employee satisfies this initial showing, the second linchpin of the "two-pronged burden-shifting analysis" is that the burden of *persuasion* shifts to the employer.[84] An employer may avoid liability only if it demonstrates, by a preponderance of the evidence,[85] that it would have taken the adverse employment action, for a valid reason, despite the employee's military status.[86] This showing by the employer is considered an affirmative defense, since the employer has the burden of proof with respect to this element.[87]

Unlike the three-pronged *McDonnell Douglas* analysis utilized in Title VII actions, where the ultimate burden of proof rests with the employee to show that the employer's stated reason for termination was pretext, under USERRA, the employee *does not* have to prove that the employer's stated reason is a pretext.[88] Rather, once the employee establishes a prima facie case of discrimination (i.e., his or her protected military status was a substantial or motivating factor in the adverse employment action), the ultimate burden of proof then shifts to the employer to prove by a preponderance of evidence that the employer would have taken the adverse employment action despite the protected status.[89] This is a significant divergence from most employment law claims, and makes USERRA more likely to get to a

---

[83]Roll v. United States Postal Serv., 2003 WL 22344982, at *2 (Fed. Cir. Oct. 14, 2003); *see also* 20 C.F.R. §1002.22.

[84]20 C.F.R. §1002.22; *see also* Velazquez-Garcia v. Horizon Lines of Puerto Rico, Inc., 473 F.3d 11, 17 (1st Cir. 2007); Sheehan v. Dept. of Navy, 240 F.3d 1009, 1013 (Fed. Cir. 2001).

[85]*See id.,* §1002.139(d).

[86]*See id.,* §1002.22; *accord Velazquez-Garcia,* 473 F.3d at 17 (quoting *Sheehan,* 240 F.3d at 1014).

[87]*See* 20 C.F.R. §1002.22.

[88]*See Velazquez-Garcia,* 473 F.3d at 17.

[89]*See id.*

jury with the ultimate burden of persuasion placed squarely on the employer.

Accordingly, in a USERRA case, if the employer's showing persuades the court, then the employee will not be allowed to avoid summary judgment by proving pretext.[90] Thus, under USERRA, a service member cannot avoid summary judgment, and get to a jury, merely by showing that the presumed reason for the adverse action is not credible.[91]

In determining whether an employee has proven that military status was part of the discriminatory motivation for the adverse employment action, courts will typically review a variety of evidentiary factors, including:

1. proximity in time between the military activity and the adverse action;

2. inconsistencies between the proffered reasons and other actions of the employer;

3. an employer's express hostility toward protected employees along with knowledge of the employee's military activity; and

4. disparate treatment of protected employees as compared to nonprotected employees with similar work records or offenses.[92]

The employer's affirmative defense must prove a legitimate basis for the action at issue and that the action would

---

[90] *See* Reeves v. Sanderson Plumbing Prods., Inc., 530 U.S. 133 (2000). Although not a USERRA case, *Reeves* applies the same "motivating factor" analysis required under USERRA. It therefore provides proper guidance to the USERRA advisor regarding application of the elements of the "motivating factor" test.

[91] *See id.* at 148.

[92] *See* Sheehan v. Department of Navy, 240 F.3d 1009, 1014 (Fed. Cir. 2001), Hance v. Norfolk S. Ry. Co., 571 F.3d 511, 518 (6th Cir. 2009) (district court properly attributed decision-maker's "anti-military animus" to employer in support of USERRA violation); Barreto v. ITT World Directories, Inc., 62 F. Supp. 2d 387 (D.P.R. 1999) (mere awareness of military status and negative comments about details of sales event at military base were insufficient to create an inference of discrimination); Robinson v. Morris Moore Chevrolet-Buick, Inc., 974 F. Supp. 571, 572 (E.D. Tex. 1997) (military position and related obligations were a motivating factor if employer relied upon, took into account, considered, or conditioned its decision on employee's military-related absence).

have been taken regardless of the employee's military service.[93]

IV. STATUTE OF LIMITATIONS

Prior to October 10, 2008, USERRA precluded application of a state's statute of limitations, but did not include the same preclusion with respect to any federal statute of limitations.[94] Consequently, courts were split on what, if any, statute of limitations applied to USERRA claims. Several courts determined that the federal four-year statute of limitations applied to USERRA claims.[95] Those courts noted that the 1990 federal statute of limitations[96] specifically states that civil claims arising under federal laws that were enacted after 1990 are subject to a four-year limitations period, unless those laws specifically exclude the statute of limitations.[97]

Other courts concluded that because USERRA did not create a new cause of action, but instead merely expanded rights created by predecessor statutes, USERRA claims were not subject to the four-year statute of limitations.[98] In *Jones v. R.R. Donnelly & Sons*, the Supreme Court resolved the

---

[93]Lewis v. Rite of Passage, Inc., 217 Fed. Appx. 785 (10th Cir. 2007) (employer must establish both that it had a legitimate basis for taking the action and, as a matter of uncontroverted fact, that it would have taken the action regardless of the employee's military status); Madden v. Rolls-Royce Corp., 563 F.3d 636, 638 (7th Cir. 2009) ("All that is meant is that if the defendant has two reasons for taking an adverse action against the plaintiff, one of them forbidden by the statute and the other not, and the defendant can show that even if the forbidden one had been absent the adverse action would still have been taken, the plaintiff loses").

[94]See 38 U.S.C. §4243(i) (1998).

[95]See Wagner v. Novartis Pharm. Corp., 565 F. Supp. 2d 940, 945–46 (E.D. Tenn. 2008); Aull v. McKeon-Grano Assocs., No. 06–2752, 2007 WL 655484, at *4 (D.N.J. Feb. 26, 2007); O'Neill v. Putnam Retail Mgmt. LLP, 407 F. Supp. 2d 310, 316 (D. Mass. 2005); see also Middleton v. City of Chicago, 578 F. 3d 655, 2009 U.S. App. LEXIS 18979 (7th Cir., Aug. 24, 2009), in which the Seventh Circuit, in a case decided after the 2008 amendment of Section of USERRA, held that the federal four-year statute of limitations applies to claims under USERRA.

[96]See 28 U.S.C. §1658(a).

[97]See Wagner, 565 F. Supp. 2d at 945–46; Aull, 2007 WL 655484, at *4; O'Neill, 407 F. Supp. 2d at 316.

[98]See Akhdary v. City of Chattanooga, No. 01–0106, 2002 WL 32060140, at *6 (E.D. Tenn. May 22, 2002); Zubi v. AT&T Corp., 219 F.3d 220, 225 (3d Cir. 2000).

confusion regarding this issue when it determined that causes of action arise under legislation enacted after 1990 if the plaintiff's claims were made possible by a post–1990 enactment, even if the protected rights were accorded by previous statutes.[99] Several other courts relied on the equitable doctrine of laches to determine the timeliness of USERRA claims.[100]

On October 10, 2008, Congress provided a clear directive regarding the timeliness of USERRA claims when it amended Section 4327(b) to provide: "If any person seeks to file a complaint or claim with the Secretary, the Merit Systems Protection Board, or a Federal or State court under this chapter alleging a violation of this chapter, there shall be no limit on the period for filing the complaint or claim."[101] Under this amendment, *any* action filed after October 10, 2008, is not subject to a statute of limitations defense, regardless of when the relevant factual events occurred.[102] However, courts may apply their pre-amendment interpretation of the statute of limitations with respect to actions filed prior to the October 2008 amendment.

Prior to the October 2008 amendment, an employer and employee could contractually agree to a shorter statute of limitations for USERRA claims.[103] The Act only supersedes a contract or agreement if it "reduces, limits, or eliminates" a "right or benefit" provided for under USERRA.[104] The question now, post–October 2008, is whether expressly stating that there shall be no limit on the period for filing a

---

[99]541 U.S. 369 (2004).

[100]*See* McLain v. City of Somerville, 424 F. Supp. 2d 329, 336 (D. Mass. 2006); Garcia v. Department of State, 101 M.S.P.R. 172, 178 (M.S.P.B. 2006); Harper v. Department of Navy, 101 M.S.P.R. 166, 170 (M.S.P.B. 2006).

[101]38 U.S.C. §4327(b) (2008); *see* Veterans' Benefits Improvement Act, Pub. L. No. 110–389, 122 Stat. 4145, which codified the amended Section 4327(b).

[102]*See* Middleton v. City of Chicago, 2009 U.S. App. LEXIS 18979 *17–26 (7th Cir., August 24, 2009) (holding that 2008 amendment of USERRA's statute of limitations provision in Section 4327(b) cannot be applied retroactively); Hogan v. United Parcel Serv., No. 08-CV-4068, 2009 WL 2058803 (W.D. Mo. July 13, 2009).

[103]*See* Aull v. McKeon-Grano Assocs., 2007 U.S. Dist. LEXIS 13008 (D.N.J. Feb. 26, 2007) (six-month statute of limitations in the employment agreement applied and the employee's claim under USERRA was time-barred).

[104]*See* 38 U.S.C. §4302(b).

USERRA claim is a "right or benefit" provided for under USERRA. When enacting USERRA, Congress never declared that private contracts creating their own statutes of limitations were prohibited. Generally, private parties may contract for a shorter time period for the bringing of a claim than that allowed by the general statute of limitations.[105] Now, however, if the statute of limitations provision is considered a "right or benefit" provided by USERRA, the Act will supersede any contractual limitation on the time period for bringing USERRA causes of action.

V. Declaratory Judgments

Only persons claiming rights pursuant to USERRA may bring claims under the Act.[106] According to USERRA's legislative history, the purpose of this provision in the Act is to prevent employers, pension plans, or unions from filing actions for declaratory judgments to determine employees' potential claims.[107]

VI. Arbitration Agreements

Federal law generally favors the private arbitration of disputes. Although the United States Supreme Court has not expressly addressed the arbitrability of USERRA claims, federal appellate courts have addressed the issue and determined that claims asserting USERRA violations are subject to arbitration.

---

[105]*See, e.g.,* Western Filter Corp. v. Argan, Inc., 540 F.3d 947 (9th Cir. 2008); Maxcess, Inc. v Lucent Techs., Inc, 433 F.3d 1337 (11th Cir. 2005); In re Cotton Yarn Antitrust Litig., 505 F.3d 274 (4th Cir. 2007). *But see* Waterfowl Ltd. Liab. Co. v. United States, 473 F.3d 135 (5th Cir. 2006)(Louisiana law does not allow parties to modify statute of limitations).

[106]*See* 38 U.S.C. §4323(f).

[107]*See* H.R. Rep. No. 103–65, pt. I, at 39 (1993).

In *Garrett v. Circuit City Stores, Inc.*,[108] the Fifth Circuit reiterated the Supreme Court's pronouncements that an arbitration agreement is not a vehicle to waive substantive rights, but rather simply a mechanism to submit them for resolution to an arbitral rather than a judicial forum.[109] The Fifth Circuit also reviewed the USERRA provision stating that the Act supersedes any agreement that reduces, limits, or eliminates any USERRA right and concluded that this section applies only to the substantive rights afforded by USERRA, and not to the provision of the Act that permits an employee to bring his or her claims in federal court. Finally, the court found nothing in USERRA's legislative history or underlying structure or purpose that would conflict with Circuit City's arbitration policy and agreement.[110]

The Sixth Circuit in *Landis v. Pinnacle Eye Care, LLC*,[111] reached the same conclusion after reviewing the language of the arbitration agreement, which required arbitration of "any controversy, dispute or disagreement" related to the employment relationship that could not otherwise be amicably negotiated.[112] The employee had argued that USERRA preempted the arbitration agreement, but the court disagreed. The court determined that, although not every statutory claim may be appropriate for arbitration, parties who agree to arbitrate claims should be held to that agreement "unless Congress itself has evinced an intention to preclude waiver of judicial remedies for the statutory rights at issue."[113]

In sum, arbitration agreements including a provision that claims under USERRA must be arbitrated will, most likely, be enforceable.[114] Thus, parties to such arbitration

---

[108]Garrett v. Circuit City Stores, Inc., 449 F.3d 672 (5th Cir. 2006).

[109]*See id.* at 676 (quoting Mitsubishi Motors Corp. v. Soler Chrysler-Plymouth, Inc., 473 U.S. 614, 676 (1985)).

[110]*See id.* at 679–80.

[111]537 F.3d 559 (6th Cir. 2008).

[112]*See id.* at 560.

[113]*See id.* at 562.

[114]*See* Kitts v. Menards, Inc., 519 F. Supp. 2d 837 (N.D. Ind. 2007) (granting company's motion to compel arbitration and stay the lawsuit the employee filed in federal dis-

agreements should be aware of the specific dispute resolution requirements included in the agreement and be prepared to comply with the requirements.[115]

---

trict court); Ohlfs v. Charles Schwab & Co., 2008 U.S. Dist. LEXIS 82943 (D. Colo. Sept. 25, 2008).

[115]*See* Garrett v. Circuit City Stores, Inc., 449 F.3d 672 (5th Cir. 2006).

APPENDICES

APPENDIX A

UNIFORMED SERVICES EMPLOYMENT AND REEMPLOYMENT RIGHTS ACT
38 U.S.C. §§4301—4334

[*Editor's Note*: Enacted by Pub. Law 103-353, October 13, 1994, as amended]

CHAPTER 43—EMPLOYMENT AND REEMPLOYMENT RIGHTS OF MEMBERS OF THE UNIFORMED SERVICES

Subchapter I—General

Subchapter II—Employment and Reemployment Rights and Limitations; Prohibitions

Subchapter III—Procedures for Assistance, Enforcement, and Investigation

Subchapter IV—Miscellaneous Provisions

Subchapter I—General

§4301. Purposes; sense of Congress

(a) The purposes of this chapter are—

(1) to encourage noncareer service in the uniformed services by eliminating or minimizing the disadvantages to civilian careers and employment which can result from such service;

(2) to minimize the disruption to the lives of persons performing service in the uniformed services as well as to their employers, their fellow employees, and their communities, by providing for the prompt reemployment of such persons upon their completion of such service; and

(3) to prohibit discrimination against persons because of their service in the uniformed services.

(b) It is the sense of Congress that the Federal Government should be a model employer in carrying out the provisions of this chapter.

§4302. Relation to other law and plans and agreements

(a) Nothing in this chapter shall supersede, nullify or diminish any Federal or State law (including any local law or ordinance), contract, agreement, policy, plan, practice, or other matter that establishes a right or benefit that is more beneficial to, or is in addition to, a right or benefit provided for such person in this chapter.

(b) This chapter supersedes any State law (including any local law or ordinance), contract, agreement, policy, plan, practice, or other matter that reduces, limits, or eliminates in any manner any right or benefit provided by this chapter, including the establishment of additional prerequisites to the exercise of any such right or the receipt of any such benefit.

§4303. Definitions

For the purposes of this chapter—

(1) The term 'Attorney General' means the Attorney General of the United States or any person designated by the Attorney General to carry out a responsibility of the Attorney General under this chapter.

(2) The term "benefit", "benefit of employment", or "right and benefits" means any advantage, profit, privilege, gain, status, account, or interest (other than wages or salary for work performed) that accrues by reason of an employment contract or agreement or an employer policy, plan, or practice and includes rights and benefits under a pension plan, a health plan, an employee stock ownership plan, insurance coverage and awards, bonuses, severance pay, supplemental unemployment benefits, vacations, and the opportunity to select work hours or location of employment.

(3) The term 'employee' means any person employed by an employer. Such term includes any person who is a citizen, national, or permanent resident alien of the United States employed in a workplace in a foreign country by an employer that is an entity incorporated or otherwise organized in the United States or that is controlled by an entity organized in the United States, within the meaning of section 4319(c) of this title.

(4)(A) Except as provided in subparagraphs (B) and (C), the term "employer" means any person, institution, organization, or other entity that pays salary or wages for work performed or that has control over employment opportunities including—

(i) a person, institution, organization, or other entity to whom the employer has delegated the performance of employment-related responsibilities;

(ii) the Federal Government;

(iii) a State;

(iv) any successor in interest to a person, institution, organization, or other entity referred to in this subparagraph; and

(v) a person, institution, organization, or other entity that has denied initial employment in violation of section 4311.

(B) In the case of a National Guard technician employed under section 709 of title 32, the term "employer" means the adjutant general of the State in which the technician is employed.

(C) Except as an actual employer of employees, an employee pension benefit plan described in section 3(2) of the Employee Retirement Income Security Act of 1974 (29 U.S.C. 1002(2)) shall be deemed to be an employer only with respect to the obligation to provide benefits described in section 4318.

(5) The term "Federal executive agency" includes the United States Postal Service, the Postal Regulatory Commission, any nonappropriated fund instrumentality of the United States, any Executive agency (as that term is defined in section 105 of title 5) other than an agency referred to in section 2302(a)(2)(C)(ii) of title 5, and any military department (as that term is defined in section 102 of title 5) with respect to the civilian employees of title 5, and any military department (as that term is defined in section 102 of title 5) with respect to the civilian employees of that department.

(6) The term "Federal Government" includes any Federal executive agency, the legislative branch of the United States, and the judicial branch of the United States.

(7) The term "health plan" means an insurance policy or contract, medical or hospital service agreement, membership or subscription contract, or other arrangement under

which health services for individuals are provided or the expenses of such services are paid.

(8) The term "notice" means (with respect to subchapter II) any written or verbal notification of an obligation or intention to perform service in the uniformed services provided to an employer by the employee who will perform such service or by the uniformed service in which such service is to be performed.

(9) The term "qualified", with respect to an employment position, means having the ability to perform the essential tasks of the position.

(10) The term "reasonable efforts", in the case of actions required of an employer under this chapter, means actions, including training provided by an employer, that do not place an undue hardship on the employer.

(11) Notwithstanding section 101, the term "Secretary" means the Secretary of Labor or any person designated by such Secretary to carry out an activity under this chapter.

(12) The term "seniority" means longevity in employment together with any benefits of employment which accrue with, or are determined by, longevity in employment.

(13) The term "service in the uniformed services" means the performance of duty on a voluntary or involuntary basis in a uniformed service under competent authority and includes active duty, active duty for training, initial active duty for training, inactive duty training, full-time National Guard duty, a period for which a person is absent from a position of employment for the purpose of an examination to determine the fitness of the person to any such duty, and a period for which a person is absent from employment for the purpose of performing funeral honors duty as authorized by section 12503 of title 10 or section 115 of title 32.

(14) The term "State" means each of the several States of the United States, the District of Columbia, the Commonwealth of Puerto Rico, Guam, the Virgin Islands, and other territories of the United States (including the agencies and political subdivisions thereof.

(15) The term "undue hardship", in the case of actions taken by an employer, means actions requiring significant difficulty or expense, when considered in light of—

(A) the nature and cost of the action needed under this chapter;

(B) the overall financial resources of the facility or facilities involved in the provision of the action; the number of persons employed at such facility; the effect on expenses and resources, or the impact otherwise of such action upon the operation of the facility;

(C) the overall financial resources of the employer; the overall size of the business of an employer with respect to the number of its employees; the number, type, and location of its facilities; and

(D) the type of operation or operations of the employer, including the composition, structure, and functions of the work force of such employer; the geographic separateness, administrative, or fiscal relationship of the facility or facilities in question to the employer.

(16) The term "uniformed services" means the Armed Forces, the Army National Guard and the Air National Guard when engaged in active duty for training, inactive duty training, or full-time National Guard duty, the commissioned corps of the Public Health Service, and any other category of persons designated by the President in time of war or national emergency.

§4304. Character of service

A person's entitlement to the benefits of this chapter by reason of the service of such person in one of the uniformed services terminates upon the occurrence of any of the following events:

(1) A separation of such person from such uniformed service with a dishonorable or bad conduct discharge.

(2) A separation of such person from such uniformed service under other than honorable conditions, as characterized pursuant to regulations prescribed by the Secretary concerned.

(3) A dismissal of such person permitted under section 1161(a) of title 10.

(4) A dropping of such person from the rolls pursuant to section 1161(b) of title 10.

SUBCHAPTER II—EMPLOYMENT AND REEMPLOYMENT RIGHTS AND LIMITATIONS; PROHIBITIONS

§4311. Discrimination against persons who serve in the uniformed services and acts of reprisal prohibited

(a) A person who is a member of, applies to be a member of, performs, has performed, applies to perform, or has an obligation to perform service in a uniformed service shall not be denied initial employment, reemployment, retention in employment, promotion, or any benefit of employment by an employer on the basis of that membership, application for membership, performance of service, application for service, or obligation.

(b) An employer may not discriminate in employment against or take any adverse employment action against any person because such person (1) has taken an action to enforce a protection afforded any person under this chapter, (2) has testified or otherwise made a statement in or in connection with any proceeding under this chapter, (3) has assisted or otherwise participated in an investigation under this chapter, or (4) has exercised a right provided for in this chapter. The prohibition in this subsection shall apply with respect to a person regardless of whether that person has performed service in the uniformed services.

(c) An employer shall be considered to have engaged in actions prohibited—

(1) under subsection (a), if the person's membership, application for membership, service, application for service, or obligation for service in the uniformed services is a motivating factor in the employer's action, unless the employer can prove that the action would have been taken in the absence of such membership, application for membership, service, application for service, or obligation for service; or

(2) under subsection (b), if the person's (A) action to enforce a protection afforded any person under this chapter, (B) testimony or making of a statement in or in connection with any proceeding under this chapter, (C) assistance or other participation in an investigation under this chapter, or (D) exercise of a right provided for in this chapter, is a motivating factor in the employer's action, unless the employer can prove that the action would have been taken in the absence of such person's enforcement action, testimony, statement, assistance, participation, or exercise of a right.

(d) The prohibitions in subsections (a) and (b) shall apply to any position of employment, including a position that is described in section 4312(d)(1)(C) of this title.

§4312. Reemployment rights of persons who serve in the uniformed services

(a) Subject to subsections (b), (c), and (d) and to section 4304, any person whose absence from a position of employment is necessitated by reason of service in the uniformed services shall be entitled to the reemployment rights and benefits and other employment benefits of this chapter if—

(1) the person (or an appropriate officer of the uniformed service in which such service is performed) has given advance written or verbal notice of such service to such person's employer;

(2) the cumulative length of the absence and of all previous absences from a position of employment with that employer by reason of service in the uniformed services does not exceed five years; and

(3) except as provided in subsection (f), the person reports to, or submits an application for reemployment to, such employer in accordance with the provisions of subsection (e).

(b) No notice is required under subsection (a)(1) if the giving of such notice is precluded by military necessity or, under all of the relevant circumstances, the giving of such notice is otherwise impossible or unreasonable. A determination of military necessity for the purposes of this subsection shall be made pursuant to regulations prescribed by the Secretary of Defense and shall not be subject to judicial review.

(c) Subsection (a) shall apply to a person who is absent from a position of employment by reason of service in the uniformed services if such person's cumulative period of service in the uniformed services, with respect to the employer relationship for which a person seeks reemployment, does not exceed five years, except that any such period of service shall not include any service—

(1) that is required, beyond five years, to complete an initial period of obligated service;

(2) during which such person was unable to obtain orders releasing such person from a period of service in the uniformed services before the expiration of such five-year period and such inability was through no fault of such person;

(3) performed as required pursuant to section 10147 of title 10, under section 502(a) or 503 of title 32, or to fulfill additional training requirements determined and certified in writing by the Secretary concerned, to be necessary for professional development, or for completion of skill training or retraining; or

(4) performed by a member of a uniformed service who is—

(A) ordered to or retained on active duty under section 688, 12301(a), 12301(g), 12302, 12304, or 12305 of title 10 or under section 331, 332, 359, 360, 367, or 712 of title 14;

(B) ordered to or retained on active duty (other than for training) under any provision of law because of a war or national emergency declared by the President or the Congress. as determined by the Secretary concerned;

(C) ordered to active duty (other than for training) in support, as determined by the Secretary concerned, of an operational mission for which personnel have been ordered to active duty under section 12304 of title 10;

(D) ordered to active duty in support, as determined by the Secretary concerned, of a critical mission or requirement of the uniformed services; or

(E) called into Federal service as a member of the National Guard under chapter 15 of title 10 or under section 12406 of title 10.

(d)(1) An employer is not required to reemploy a person under this chapter if—

(A) the employer's circumstances have so changed as to make such reemployment impossible or unreasonable;

(B) in the case of a person entitled to reemployment under subsection (a)(3), (a)(4), or (b)(2)(B) of section 4313, such employment would impose an undue hardship on the employer; or

(C) the employment from which the person leaves to serve in the uniformed services is for a brief, nonrecurrent period and there is no reasonable expectation that such employment will continue indefinitely or for a significant period.

(2) In any proceeding involving an issue of whether—

(A) any reemployment referred to in paragraph (1) is impossible or unreasonable because of a change in an employer's circumstances,

(B) any accommodation, training, or effort referred to in subsection (a)(3), (a)(4), or (b)(2)(B) of section 4313 would impose an undue hardship on the employer, or

(C) the employment referred to in paragraph (1)(C) is for a brief, nonrecurrent period and there is no reasonable expectation that such employment will continue indefinitely or for a significant period, the employer shall have the burden of proving the impossibility or unreasonableness, undue hardship, or the brief or nonrecurrent nature of the employment without a reasonable expectation of continuing indefinitely or for a significant period.

(e)(1) Subject to paragraph (2), a person referred to in subsection (a) shall, upon the completion of a period of service in the uniformed services, notify the employer referred to in such subsection of the person's intent to return to a position of employment with such employer as follows:

(A) In the case of a person whose period of service in the uniformed services was less than 31 days, by reporting to the employer—

(I) not later than the beginning of the first full regularly scheduled work period on the first full calendar day following the completion of the period of service and the expiration of eight hours after a period allowing for the safe transportation of the person from the place of that service to the person's residence; or

(ii) as soon as possible after the expiration of the eight-hour period referred to in clause (i), if reporting within the period referred to in such clause is impossible or unreasonable through no fault of the person.

(B) In the case of a person who is absent from a position of employment for a period of any length for the purposes of an examination to determine the person's fitness to perform service in the uniformed services, by reporting in the manner and time referred to in subparagraph (A).

(C) In the case of a person whose period of service in the uniformed services was for more than 30 days but less than 181 days, by submitting an application for reemployment with the employer not later than 14 days after the completion of the period of service or if submitting such application within such period is impossible or unreasonable through no fault of the person, the next first full calendar day when submission of such application becomes possible.

(D) In the case of a person whose period of service in the uniformed services was for more than 180 days, by submitting an application for reemployment with the employer not later than 90 days after the completion of the period of service.

(2)(A) A person who is hospitalized for, or convalescing from, an illness or injury incurred in, or aggravated during, the performance of service in the uniformed services shall, at the end of the period that is necessary for the person to recover from such illness or injury, report to the person's employer (in the case of a person described in subparagraph (A) or (B) of paragraph (1)) or submit an application for reemployment with such employer (in the case of a person described in subparagraph (C) or (D) of such paragraph). Except as provided in subparagraph (B), such period of recovery may not exceed two years.

(B) Such two-year period shall be extended by the minimum time required to accommodate the circumstances beyond such person's control which make reporting within the period specified in subparagraph (A) impossible or unreasonable.

(3) A person who fails to report or apply for employment or reemployment within the appropriate period specified in this subsection shall not automatically forfeit such person's entitlement to the rights and benefits referred to in subsection (a) but shall be subject to the conduct rules, established policy, and general practices of the employer pertaining to explanations and discipline with respect to absence from scheduled work.

(f)(1) A person who submits an application for reemployment in accordance with subparagraph (C) or (D) of subsection (e)(1) or subsection (e)(2) shall provide to the person's employer (upon the request of such employer) documentation to establish that—

(A) the person's application is timely;

(B) the person has not exceeded the service limitations set forth in subsection (a)(2) (except as permitted under subsection (c)); and

(C) the person's entitlement to the benefits under this chapter has not been terminated pursuant to section 4304.

(2) Documentation of any matter referred to in paragraph (1) that satisfies regulations prescribed by the Secretary shall satisfy the documentation requirements in such paragraph.

(3)(A) Except as provided in subparagraph (B), the failure of a person to provide documentation that satisfies regulations prescribed pursuant to paragraph (2) shall not be a basis for denying reemployment in accordance with the provisions of this chapter if the failure occurs because such documentation does not exist or is not readily available at the time of the request of the employer. If, after such reemployment, documentation becomes available that establishes that such person does not meet one or more of the requirements referred to in subparagraphs (A), (B), and (C) of paragraph (1), the employer of such person may terminate the employment of the person and the provision of any rights or benefits afforded the person under this chapter.

(B) An employer who reemploys a person absent from a position of employment for more than 90 days may require that the person provide the employer with the documentation referred to in subparagraph (A) before beginning to treat the person as not having incurred a break in service for pension purposes under section 4318(a)(2)(A).

(4) An employer may not delay or attempt to defeat a reemployment obligation by demanding documentation that does not then exist or is not then readily available.

(g) The right of a person to reemployment under this section shall not entitle such person to retention, preference, or displacement rights over any person with a superior claim under the provisions of title 5, United States Code, relating to veterans and other preference eligibles.

(h) In any determination of a person's entitlement to protection under this chapter, the timing, frequency, and duration of the person's training or service, or the nature of such training or service (including voluntary service) in the uniformed services, shall not be a basis for denying protection of this chapter if the service does not exceed the limitations set forth in subsection (c) and the notice requirements established in subsection (a)(1) and the notification requirements established in subsection (e) are met.

§4313. Reemployment positions

(a) Subject to subsection (b) (in the case of any employee) and sections 4314 and 4315 (in the case of an employee of the Federal Government), a person entitled to reemployment under section 4312, upon completion of a period of service in the uniformed services, shall be promptly reemployed in a position of employment in accordance with the following order of priority:

(1) Except as provided in paragraphs (3) and (4), in the case of a person whose period of service in the uniformed services was for less than 91 days—

(A) in the position of employment in which the person would have been employed if the continuous employment of such person with the employer had not been interrupted by such service, the duties of which the person is qualified to perform; or

(B) in the position of employment in which the person was employed on the date of the commencement of the service in the uniformed services, only if the person is not qualified to perform the duties of the position referred to in subparagraph (A) after reasonable efforts by the employer to qualify the person.

(2) Except as provided in paragraphs (3) and (4), in the case of a person whose period of service in the uniformed services was for more than 90 days—

(A) in the position of employment in which the person would have been employed if the continuous employment of such person with the employer had not been interrupted by such service, or a position of like seniority, status and pay, the duties of which the person is qualified to perform; or

(B) in the position of employment in which the person was employed on the date of the commencement of the service in the uniformed services, or a position of like seniority, status and pay, the duties of which the person is qualified to perform, only if the person is not qualified to perform the duties of a position referred to in subparagraph (A) after reasonable efforts by the employer to qualify the person.

(3) In the case of a person who has a disability incurred in, or aggravated during, such service, and who (after reasonable efforts by the employer to accommodate the disability) is not qualified due to such disability to be employed in the position of employment in which the person would have been employed if the continuous employment of such person with the employer had not been interrupted by such service—

(A) in any other position which is equivalent in seniority, status, and pay, the duties of which the person is qualified to perform or would become qualified to perform with reasonable efforts by the employer; or

(B) if not employed under subparagraph (A), in a position which is the nearest approximation to a position referred to in subparagraph (A) in terms of seniority, status, and pay consistent with circumstances of such person's case.

(4) In the case of a person who (A) is not qualified to be employed in (i) the position of employment in which the person would have been employed if the continuous employment of such person with the employer had not been interrupted by such service, or (ii) in the position of employment in which such person was employed on the date of the commencement of the service in the uniformed services for any reason (other than disability incurred in, or aggravated during, service in the uniformed services), and (B) cannot become qualified with reasonable efforts by the employer, in any other position which is the nearest approximation to a position referred to first in clause (A)(i) and then in clause (A)(ii) which such person is qualified to perform, with full seniority.

(b)(1) If two or more persons are entitled to reemployment under section 4312 in the same position of employment and more than one of them has reported for such reemployment, the person who left the position first shall have the prior right to reemployment in that position.

(2) Any person entitled to reemployment under section 4312 who is not reemployed in a position of employment by reason of paragraph (1) shall be entitled to be reemployed as follows:

(A) Except as provided in subparagraph (B), in any other position of employment referred to in subsection (a)(1) or (a)(2), as the case may be (in the order of priority set out in the applicable subsection), that provides a similar status and pay to a position of employment referred to in paragraph (1) of this subsection, consistent with the circumstances of such person's case, with full seniority.

(B) In the case of a person who has a disability incurred in, or aggravated during, a period of service in the uniformed services that requires reasonable efforts by the employer for the person to be able to perform the duties of the position of employment, in any other position referred to in subsection (a)(3) (in the order of priority set out in that subsection) that provides a similar status and pay to a position referred to in paragraph (1) of this subsection, consistent with circumstances of such person's case, with full seniority.

§4314. Reemployment by the Federal Government

(a) Except as provided in subsections (b), (c), and (d), if a person is entitled to reemployment by the Federal Government under section 4312, such person shall be reemployed in a position of employment as described in section 4313.

(b)(1) If the Director of the Office of Personnel Management makes a determination described in paragraph (2) with respect to a person who was employed by a Federal executive agency at the time the person entered the service from which the person seeks reemployment under this section, the Director shall—

(A) identify a position of like seniority, status, and pay at another Federal executive agency that satisfies the requirements of section 4313 and for which the person is qualified; and

(B) ensure that the person is offered such position.

(2) The Director shall carry out the duties referred to in subparagraphs (A) and (B) of paragraph (1) if the Director determines that—

(A) the Federal executive agency that employed the person referred to in such paragraph no longer exists and the functions of such agency have not been transferred to another Federal executive agency; or

(B) it is impossible or unreasonable for the agency to reemploy the person.

(C) If the employer of a person described in subsection (a) was, at the time such person entered the service from which such person seeks reemployment under this section, a part of the judicial branch or the legislative branch of the Federal Government, and such employer determines that it is impossible or unreasonable for such employer to reemploy such person, such person shall, upon application to the Director of the Office of Personnel Management, be ensured an offer of employment in an alternative position in a Federal executive agency on the basis described in subsection (b).

(d) If the adjutant general of a State determines that it is impossible or unreasonable to reemploy a person who was a National Guard technician employed under section 709 of title 32, such person shall, upon application to the Director of the Office of Personnel Management, be ensured an offer of employment in an alternative position in a Federal executive agency on the basis described in subsection (b).

§4315. Reemployment by certain Federal agencies

(a) The head of each agency referred to in section 2302(a)(2)(C)(ii) of title 5 shall prescribe procedures for ensuring that the rights under this chapter apply to the employees of such agency.

(b) In prescribing procedures under subsection (a), the head of an agency referred to in that subsection shall ensure, to the maximum extent practicable, that the procedures of the agency for reemploying persons who serve in the uniformed services provide for the reemployment of such persons in the agency in a manner similar to the manner of reemployment described in section 4313.

(c)(1) The procedures prescribed under subsection (a) shall designate an official at the agency who shall determine whether or not the reemployment of a person referred to in subsection (b) by the agency is impossible or unreasonable.

(2) Upon making a determination that the reemployment by the agency of a person referred to in subsection (b) is impossible or unreasonable, the official referred to in paragraph (1) shall notify the person and the Director of the Office of Personnel Management of such determination.

(3) A determination pursuant to this subsection shall not be subject to judicial review.

(4) The head of each agency referred to in subsection (a) shall submit to the Select Committee on Intelligence and the Committee on Veterans' Affairs of the Senate and the Permanent Select Committee on Intelligence and the Committee on Veterans' Affairs of the House of Representatives on an annual basis a report on the number of persons whose reemployment with the agency was determined under this subsection to be impossible or unreasonable during the year preceding the report, including the reason for each such determination.

(d)(1) Except as provided in this section, nothing in this section, section 4313, or section 4325 shall be construed to exempt any agency referred to in subsection (a) from compliance with any other substantive provision of this chapter.

(2) This section may not be construed—

(A) as prohibiting an employee of an agency referred to in subsection (a) from seeking information from the Secretary regarding assistance in seeking reemployment from the agency under this chapter, alternative employment in the Federal Government under this chapter, or information relating to the rights and obligations of employee and Federal agencies under this chapter; or

(B) as prohibiting such an agency from voluntarily cooperating with or seeking assistance in or of clarification from the

Secretary or the Director of the Office of Personnel Management of any matter arising under this chapter.

(e) The Director of the Office of Personnel Management shall ensure the offer of employment to a person in a position in a Federal executive agency on the basis described in subsection (b) if—

(1) the person was an employee of an agency referred to in section 2302(a)(2)(C)(ii) of title 5 at the time the person entered the service from which the person seeks reemployment under this section;

(2) the appropriate officer of the agency determines under subsection (c) that reemployment of the person by the agency is impossible or unreasonable; and

(3) the person submits an application to the Director for an offer of employment under this subsection.

§4316. Rights, benefits, and obligations of persons absent from employment for service in a uniformed service

(a) A person who is reemployed under this chapter is entitled to the seniority and other rights and benefits determined by seniority that the person had on the date of the commencement of service in the uniformed services plus the additional seniority and rights and benefits that such person would have attained if the person had remained continuously employed.

(b)(1) Subject to paragraphs (2) through (6), a person who is absent from a position of employment by reason of service in the uniformed services shall be—

(A) deemed to be on furlough or leave of absence while performing such service; and

(B) entitled to such other rights and benefits not determined by seniority as are generally provided by the employer of the person to employees having similar seniority, status, and pay who are on furlough or leave of absence under a contract, agreement, policy, practice, or plan in effect at the commencement of such service or established while such person performs such service.

(2)(A) Subject to subparagraph (B), a person who—

(i) is absent from a position of employment by reason of service in the uniformed services, and

(ii) knowingly provides written notice of intent not to return to a position of employment after service in the uniformed service, is not entitled to rights and benefits under paragraph (1)(B).

(B) For the purposes of subparagraph (A), the employer shall have the burden of proving that a person knowingly provided clear written notice of intent not to return to a position of employment after service in the uniformed service and, in doing so, was aware of the specific rights and benefits to be lost under subparagraph (A).

(3) A person deemed to be on furlough or leave of absence under this subsection while serving in the uniformed services shall not be entitled under this subsection to any benefits to which the person would not otherwise be entitled if the person had remained continuously employed.

(4) Such person may be required to pay the employee cost, if any, of any funded benefit continued pursuant to paragraph (1) to the extent other employees on furlough or leave of absence are so required.

(5) The entitlement of a person to coverage under a health plan is provided for under section 4317.

(6) The entitlement of a person to a right or benefit under an employee pension benefit plan is provided for under section 4318.

(c) A person who is reemployed by an employer under this chapter shall not be discharged from such employment, except for cause—

(1) within one year after the date of such reemployment, if the person's period of service before the reemployment was more than 180 days; or

(2) within 180 days after the date of such reemployment, if the person's period of service before the reemployment was more than 30 days but less than 181 days.

(d) Any person whose employment with an employer is interrupted by a period of service in the uniformed services shall be permitted, upon request of that person, to use during such period of service any vacation, annual, or similar leave with pay accrued by the person before the commencement of such service. No employer may require any such person to use vacation, annual, or similar leave during such period of service.

(e)(1) An employer shall grant an employee who is a member of a reserve component an authorized leave of absence from a position of employment to allow that employee to perform funeral honors duty as authorized by section 12503 of title 10 or section 115 of title 32.

(e)(2) For purposes of section 4312(e)(1) of this title, an employee who takes an authorized leave of absence under paragraph (1) is deemed to have notified the employer of the employee's intent to return to such position of employment.

§4317. Health plans

(a)(1) In any case in which a person (or the person's dependents) has coverage under a health plan in connection with the person's position of employment, including a group health plan (as defined in section 607(1) of the Employee Retirement Income Security Act of 1974), and such person is absent from such position of employment by reason of service in the uniformed services, or such person becomes eligible for medical and dental care under chapter 55 of title 10 by reason of subsection (d) of section 1074 of that title, the plan shall provide that the person may elect to continue such coverage as provided in this subsection. The maximum period of coverage of a person and the person's dependents under such an election shall be the lesser of—

(A) the 24-month period beginning on the date on which the person's absence begins; or

(B) the day after the date on which the person fails to apply for or return to a position of employment, as determined under section 4312(e).

(2) A person who elects to continue health-plan coverage under this paragraph may be required to pay not more than 102 percent of the full premium under the plan (determined in the same manner as the applicable premium under section 4980B(f)(4) of the Internal Revenue Code of 1986) associated with such coverage for the employer's other employees, except that in the case of a person who performs service in the uniformed services for less than 31 days, such person may not be required to pay more than the employee share, if any, for such coverage.

(3) In the case of a health plan that is a multiemployer plan, as defined in section 3(37) of the Employee Retirement Income Security Act of 1974, any liability under the plan for employer contributions and benefits arising under this paragraph shall be allocated—

(A) by the plan in such manner as the plan sponsor shall provide; or

(B) if the sponsor does not provide—

(i) to the last employer employing the person before the period served by the person in the uniformed services, or

(ii) if such last employer is no longer functional, to the plan.

(b)(1) Except as provided in paragraph (2), in the case of a person whose coverage under a health plan was terminated by reason of service in the uniformed services, or by reason of the person's having become eligible for medical and dental care under chapter 55 of title 10 by reason of subsection (d) of section 1074 of that title, an exclusion or waiting period may not be imposed in connection with the reinstatement of such coverage upon reemployment under this chapter if an exclusion or waiting period would not have been imposed under a health plan had coverage of such person by such plan not been terminated as a result of such service or eligibility. This paragraph applies to the person who is reemployed and to any individual who is covered by such plan by reason of the reinstatement of the coverage of such person.

(2) Paragraph (1) shall not apply to the coverage of any illness or injury determined by the Secretary of Veterans Affairs to have been incurred in, or aggravated during, performance of service in the uniformed services.

(3) In the case of a person whose coverage under a health plan is terminated by reason of the person having become eligible for medical and dental care under chapter 55 of title 10 by reason of subsection (d) of section 1074 of that title but who subsequently does not commence a period of active duty under the order to active duty that established such eligibility because the order is canceled before such active duty commences, the provisions of paragraph (1) relating to any exclusion or waiting period in connection with the reinstatement of coverage under a health plan shall apply to such person's continued employment, upon the ter-

mination of such eligibility for medical and dental care under chapter 55 of title 10 that is incident to the cancellation of such order, in the same manner as if the person had become reemployed upon such termination of eligibility.

§4318. Employee pension benefit plans

(a)(1)(A) Except as provided in subparagraph (B), in the case of a right provided pursuant to an employee pension benefit plan (including those described in sections 3(2) and 3(33) of the Employee Retirement Income Security Act of 1974) or a right provided under any Federal or State law governing pension benefits for governmental employees, the right to pension benefits of a person reemployed under this chapter shall be determined under this section.

(B) In the case of benefits under the Thrift Savings Plan, the rights of a person reemployed under this chapter shall be those rights provided in section 8432b of title 5. The first sentence of this subparagraph shall not be construed to affect any other right or benefit under this chapter.

(2)(A) A person reemployed under this chapter shall be treated as not having incurred a break in service with the employer or employers maintaining the plan by reason of such person's period or periods of service in the uniformed services.

(B) Each period served by a person in the uniformed services shall, upon reemployment under this chapter, be deemed to constitute service with the employer or employers maintaining the plan for the purpose of determining the nonforfeitability of the person's accrued benefits and for the purpose of determining the accrual of benefits under the plan.

(b)(1) An employer reemploying a person under this chapter shall, with respect to a period of service described in subsection (a)(2)(B), be liable to an employee pension benefit plan for funding any obligation of the plan to provide the benefits described in subsection (a)(2) and shall allocate the amount of any employer contribution for the person in the same manner and to the same extent the allocation occurs for other employees during the period of service. For purposes of determining the amount of such liability and any obligation of the plan, earnings and forfeitures shall not be included. For purposes of determining the amount of such liability and for purposes of section 515 of the Employee Retirement Income Security Act of 1974 or any similar Federal or State law governing pension benefits for governmental employees, service in the uniformed services that is deemed under subsection (a) to be service with the employer shall be deemed to be service with the employer under the terms of the plan or any applicable collective bargaining agreement. In the case of a multiemployer plan, as defined in section 3(37) of the Employee Retirement Income Security Act of 1974, any liability of the plan described in this paragraph shall be allocated—

(A) by the plan in such manner as the sponsor maintaining the plan shall provide; or

(B) if the sponsor does not provide—

(i) to the last employer employing the person before the period served by the person in the uniformed services, or

(ii) if such last employer is no longer functional, to the plan.

(2) A person reemployed under this chapter shall be entitled to accrued benefits pursuant to subsection (a) that are contingent on the making of, or derived from, employee contributions or elective deferrals (as defined in section 402(g)(3) of the Internal Revenue Code of 1986) only to the extent the person makes payment to the plan with respect to such contributions or deferrals. No such payment may exceed the amount the person would have been per-

mitted or required to contribute had the person remained continuously employed by the employer throughout the period of service described in subsection (a)(2)(B). Any payment to the plan described in this paragraph shall be made during the period beginning with the date of reemployment and whose duration is three times the period of the person's service in the uniformed services, such payment period not to exceed five years.

(3) For purposes of computing an employer's liability under paragraph (1) or the employee's contributions under paragraph (2), the employee's compensation during the period of service described in subsection (a)(2)(B) shall be computed—

(A) at the rate the employee would have received but for the period of service described in subsection (a)(2)(B), or

(B) in the case that the determination of such rate is not reasonably certain, on the basis of the employee's average rate of compensation during the 12-month period immediately preceding such period (or, if shorter, the period of employment immediately preceding such period).

(c) Any employer who reemploys a person under this chapter and who is an employer contributing to a multiemployer plan, as defined in section 3(37) of the Employee Retirement Income Security Act of 1974, under which benefits are or may be payable to such person by reason of the obligations set forth in this chapter, shall, within 30 days after the date of such reemployment, provide information, in writing, of such reemployment to the administrator of such plan.

§4319. Employment and reemployment rights in foreign countries.

(a) Liability of Controlling United States Employer of Foreign Entity—If an employer controls an entity that is incorporated or otherwise organized in a foreign country, any denial of employment, reemployment, or benefit by such entity shall be presumed to be by such employer.

(b) Inapplicability to Foreign Employer—This subchapter does not apply to foreign operations of an employer that is a foreign person not controlled by a United States employer.

(c) Determination of Controlling Employer—For the purpose of this section, the determination of whether an employer controls an entity shall be based upon the interrelations of operations, common management, centralized control of labor relations, and common ownership or financial control of the employer and the entity.

(d) Exemption—Notwithstanding any other provision of this subchapter, an employer, or an entity controlled by an employer, shall be exempt from compliance with any of sections 4311 through 4318 of this title with respect to an employee in a workplace in a foreign country, if compliance with that section would cause such employer, or such entity controlled by an employer, to violate the law of the foreign country in which the workplace is located.

SUBCHAPTER III—PROCEDURES FOR ASSISTANCE, ENFORCEMENT, AND INVESTIGATION

§4321. *Assistance in obtaining reemployment or other employment rights or benefits*

The Secretary (through the Veterans' Employment and Training Service) shall provide assistance to any person with respect to the employment and reemployment rights and benefits to which such person is entitled under this chapter. In providing such assistance, the Secretary may request the assistance of existing Federal and State agencies engaged in similar or related activities and utilize the assistance of volunteers.

§4322. *Enforcement of employment or reemployment rights*

(a) A person who claims that—

(1) such person is entitled under this chapter to employment or reemployment rights or benefits with respect to employment by an employer; and

(2)(A) such employer has failed or refused, or is about to fail or refuse, to comply with the provisions of this chapter; or

(B) in the case that the employer is a Federal executive agency, such employer or the Office of Personnel Management has failed or refused, or is about to fail or refuse, to comply with the provisions of this chapter,

(C) may file a complaint with the Secretary in accordance with subsection (b), and the Secretary shall investigate such complaint.

(b) Such complaint shall be in writing, be in such form as the Secretary may prescribe, include the name and address of the employer against whom the complaint is filed, and contain a summary of the allegations that form the basis for the complaint.

(c) (1) Not later than five days after the Secretary receives a complaint submitted by a person under subsection (a), the Secretary shall notify such person in writing of his or her rights with respect to such complaint under this section and section 4323 or 4324, as the case may be.

(2) The Secretary shall, upon request, provide technical assistance to a potential claimant with respect to a complaint under this subsection, and when appropriate, to such claimant's employer.

(d) The Secretary shall investigate each complaint submitted pursuant to subsection (a). If the Secretary determines as a result of the investigation that the action alleged in such complaint occurred, the Secretary shall attempt to resolve the complaint by making reasonable efforts to ensure that the person or entity named in the complaint complies with the provisions of this chapter.

(e) If the efforts of the Secretary with respect to any complaint filed under subsection (a) do not resolve the complaint, the Secretary shall notify the person who submitted the complaint in writing of—

(1) the results of the Secretary's investigation; and

(2) the complainant's entitlement to proceed under the enforcement of rights provisions provided under section 4323 (in the case of a person submitting a complaint against a State or private employer) or section 4324 (in the case of a person submitting a complaint against a Federal executive agency or the Office of Personnel Management).

(f) Any action required by subsections (d) and (e) with respect to a complaint submitted by a person to the Secretary under subsection (a) shall be completed by the Secretary not later than 90 days after receipt of such complaint.

(g) This subchapter does not apply to any action relating to benefits to be provided under the Thrift Savings Plan under title 5.

§4323. *Enforcement of rights with respect to a State or private employer*

(a) Action for relief—(1) A person who receives from the Secretary a notification pursuant to section 4322(e) of this title of an unsuccessful effort to resolve a complaint relating to a State (as an employer) or a private employer may request that the Secretary refer the complaint to the Attorney

General. Not later than 60 days after the Secretary receives such a request with respect to a complaint, the Secretary shall refer the complaint to the Attorney General. If the Attorney General is [reasonably] satisfied that the person on whose behalf the complaint is referred is entitled to the rights or benefits sought, the Attorney General may appear on behalf of, and act as attorney for, the person on whose behalf the complaint is submitted and commence an action for relief under this chapter for such person. In the case of such an action against a State (as an employer), the action shall be brought in the name of the United States as the plaintiff in the action.

(2) Not later than 60 days after the date the Attorney General receives a referral under paragraph (1), the Attorney General shall—

(A) make a decision whether to appear on behalf of, and act as attorney for, the person on whose behalf the complaint is submitted; and

(B) notify such person in writing of such decision.

(3) A person may commence an action for relief with respect to a complaint against a State (as an employer) or a private employer if the person—

(A) has chosen not to apply to the Secretary for assistance under section 4322(a) of this title;

(B) has chosen not to request that the Secretary refer the complaint to the Attorney General under paragraph (1); or

(C) has been refused representation by the Attorney General with respect to the complaint under such paragraph.

(b) Jurisdiction—(1) In the case of an action against a State (as an employer) or a private employer commenced by the United States, the district courts of the United States shall have jurisdiction over the action.

(2) In the case of action against a State (as an employer) by a person, the action may be brought in a State court of competent jurisdiction in accordance with the laws of the State.

(3) In the case of an action against a private employer by a person, the district courts of the United States shall have jurisdiction of the action.

(c) Venue—(1) In the case of an action by the United States against a State (as an employer), the action may proceed in the United States district court for any district in which the State exercises any authority or carries out any function.

(2) In the case of an action against a private employer, the action may proceed in the United States district court for any district in which the private employer of the person maintains a place of business.

(d) Remedies—(1) In any action under this section, the court may award relief as follows:

(A) The court may require the employer to comply with the provisions of this chapter.

(B) The court may require the employer to compensate the person for any loss of wages or benefits suffered by reason of such employer's failure to comply with the provisions of this chapter.

(C) The court may require the employer to pay the person an amount equal to the amount referred to in subparagraph (B) as liquidated damages, if the court determines that the employer's failure to comply with the provisions of this chapter was willful.

(2)(A) Any compensation awarded under subparagraph (B) or (C) of paragraph (1) shall be in addition to, and shall not diminish, any of the other rights and benefits provided for under this chapter.

(B) In the case of an action commenced in the name of the United States for which the relief includes compensation awarded under subparagraph (B) or (C) of paragraph (1), such compensation shall be held in a special deposit account and shall be paid, on order of the Attorney General, directly to the person. If the compensation is not paid to the person because of inability to do so within a period of 3 years, the compensation shall be covered into the Treasury of the United States as miscellaneous receipts.

(3) A State shall be subject to the same remedies, including prejudgment interest, as may be imposed upon any private employer under this section.

(e) Equity powers—The court shall use, in any case in which the court determines it is appropriate, its full equity powers, including temporary or permanent injunctions, temporary restraining orders, and contempt orders, to vindicate fully the rights or benefits of persons under this chapter.

(f) Standing—An action under this chapter may be initiated only by a person claiming rights or benefits under this chapter under subsection (a) or by the United States under subsection (a)(1).

(g) Respondent—In any action under this chapter, only an employer or a potential employer, as the case may be, shall be a necessary party respondent.

(h) Fees, court costs—(1) No fees or court costs may be charged or taxed against any person claiming rights under this chapter.

(2) In any action or proceeding to enforce a provision of this chapter by a person under subsection (a)(2) who obtained private counsel for such action or proceeding, the

court may award any such person who prevails in such action or proceeding reasonable attorney fees, expert witness fees, and other litigation expenses.

(i) Definition—In this section, the term "private employer" includes a political subdivision of a State.

§4324. Enforcement of rights with respect to Federal executive agencies

(a)(1) A person who receives from the Secretary a notification pursuant to section 4322(e) may request that the Secretary refer the complaint for litigation before the Merit Systems Protection Board. Not later than 60 days after the date the Secretary receives such a request, the Secretary shall refer the complaint to the Office of Special Counsel established by section 1211 of title 5.

(2)(A) If the Special Counsel is reasonably satisfied that the person on whose behalf a complaint is referred under paragraph (1) is entitled to the rights or benefits sought, the Special Counsel (upon the request of the person submitting the complaint) may appear on behalf of, and act as attorney for, the person and initiate an action regarding such complaint before the Merit Systems Protection Board.

(B) Not later than 60 days after the date the Special Counsel receives a referral under paragraph (1), the Special Counsel shall—

(i) make a decision whether to represent a person before the Merit Systems Protection Board under subparagraph (A); and

(ii) notify such person in writing of such decision.

(b) A person may submit a complaint against a Federal executive agency or the Office of Personnel Management under this subchapter directly to the Merit Systems Protection Board if that person—

(1) has chosen not to apply to the Secretary for assistance under section 4322(a);

(2) has received a notification from the Secretary under section 4322(e);

(3) has chosen not to be represented before the Board by the Special Counsel pursuant to subsection (a)(2)(A); or

(4) has received a notification of a decision from the Special Counsel under subsection (a)(2)(B).

(c)(1) The Merit Systems Protection Board shall adjudicate any complaint brought before the Board pursuant to subsection (a)(2)(A) or (b), without regard as to whether the complaint accrued before, on, or after October 13, 1994. A person who seeks a hearing or adjudication by submitting such a complaint under this paragraph may be represented at such hearing or adjudication in accordance with the rules of the Board.

(2) If the Board determines that a Federal executive agency or the Office of Personnel Management has not complied with the provisions of this chapter relating to the employment or reemployment of a person by the agency, the Board shall enter an order requiring the agency or Office to comply with such provisions and to compensate such person for any loss of wages or benefits suffered by such person by reason of such lack of compliance.

(3) Any compensation received by a person pursuant to an order under paragraph (2) shall be in addition to any other right or benefit provided for by this chapter and shall not diminish any such right or benefit.

(4) If the Board determines as a result of a hearing or adjudication conducted pursuant to a complaint submitted by a person directly to the Board pursuant to subsection (b) that such person is entitled to an order referred to in paragraph (2), the Board may, in its discretion, award such person rea-

sonable attorney fees, expert witness fees, and other litigation expenses.

(d)(1) A person adversely affected or aggrieved by a final order or decision of the Merit Systems Protection Board under subsection (c) may petition the United States Court of Appeals for the Federal Circuit to review the final order or decision. Such petition and review shall be in accordance with the procedures set forth in section 7703 of title 5.

(2) Such person may be represented in the Federal Circuit proceeding by the Special Counsel unless the person was not represented by the Special Counsel before the Merit Systems Protection Board regarding such order or decision.

§4325. *Enforcement of rights with respect to certain Federal agencies*

(a) This section applies to any person who alleges that—

(1) the reemployment of such person by an agency referred to in subsection (a) of section 4315 was not in accordance with procedures for the reemployment of such person under subsection (b) of such section; or

(2) the failure of such agency to reemploy the person under such section was otherwise wrongful.

(b) Any person referred to in subsection (a) may submit a claim relating to an allegation referred to in that subsection to the inspector general of the agency which is the subject of the allegation. The inspector general shall investigate and resolve the allegation pursuant to procedures prescribed by the head of the agency.

(c) In prescribing procedures for the investigation and resolution of allegations under subsection (b), the head of an agency shall ensure, to the maximum extent practicable, that the procedures are similar to the procedures for investigating and resolving complaints utilized by the Secretary under section 4322(d).

(d) This section may not be construed—

(1) as prohibiting an employee of an agency referred to in subsection (a) from seeking information from the Secretary regarding assistance in seeking reemployment from the agency under this chapter or information relating to the rights and obligations of employees and Federal agencies under this chapter; or

(2) as prohibiting such an agency from voluntarily cooperating with or seeking assistance in or of clarification from the Secretary or the Director of the Office of Personnel Management of any matter arising under this chapter.

§4326. Conduct of investigation; subpoenas

(a) In carrying out any investigation under this chapter, the Secretary's duly authorized representatives shall, at all reasonable times, have reasonable access to and the right to interview persons with information relevant to the investigation and shall have reasonable access to, for purposes of examination, and the right to copy and receive, any documents of any person or employer that the Secretary considers relevant to the investigation.

(b) In carrying out any investigation under this chapter, the Secretary may require by subpoena the attendance and testimony of witnesses and the production of documents relating to any matter under investigation. In case of disobedience of the subpoena or contumacy and on request of the Secretary, the Attorney General may apply to any district court of the United States in whose jurisdiction such disobedience or contumacy occurs for an order enforcing the subpoena.

(c) Upon application, the district courts of the United States shall have jurisdiction to issue writs commanding any person or employer to comply with the subpoena of the Secretary or to comply with any order of the Secretary made pursuant to a lawful investigation under this chapter and the district courts shall have jurisdiction to punish failure to obey a subpoena or other lawful order of the Secretary as a contempt of court.

(d) Subsections (b) and (c) shall not apply to the legislative branch or the judicial branch of the United States.

§4327. Noncompliance of Federal officials with deadlines; inapplicability of statutes of limitations

(a) Effect of noncompliance of Federal officials with deadlines—(1) The inability of the Secretary, the Attorney General, or the Special Counsel to comply with a deadline applicable to such official under section 4322, 4323, or 4324 of this title—

(A) shall not affect the authority of the Attorney General or the Special Counsel to represent and file an action or submit a complaint on behalf of a person under Section 4323 or 4324 of this title;

(B) shall not affect the right of a person—

(i) to commence an action under Section 4323 of this title;

(ii) to submit a complaint under Section 4324 of this title; or

(iii) to obtain any type of assistance or relief authorized by this chapter;

(C) shall not deprive a Federal court, the Merit Systems Protection Board, or a State court of jurisdiction over an action or complaint filed by the Attorney General, the Special

Counsel, or a person under section 4323 or 4324 of this title; and

(D) shall not constitute a defense, including a statute of limitations period, that any employer (including a State, a private employer, or a Federal executive agency) or the Office of Personnel Management may raise in an action filed by the Attorney General, the Special Counsel, or a person under Section 4323 or 4324 of this title.

(2) If the Secretary, the Attorney General, or the Special Counsel is unable to meet a deadline applicable to such official in section 4322(f), 4323(a)(1), 4323(a)(2), 4324(a)(1), or 4324(a)(2)(B) of this title, and the person agrees to an extension of time, the Secretary, the Attorney General, or the Special Counsel, as the case may be, shall complete the required action within the additional period of time agreed to by the person.

(b) Inapplicability of statutes of limitations—If any person seeks to file a complaint or claim with the Secretary, the Merit Systems Protection Board, or a Federal or State court under this chapter alleging a violation of this chapter, there shall be no limit on the period for filing the complaint or claim.

Subchapter IV—Miscellaneous

§4331. Regulations

(a) The Secretary (in consultation with the Secretary of Defense) may prescribe regulations implementing the provisions of this chapter with regard to the application of this chapter to States, local governments, and private employers.

(b)(1) The Director of the Office of Personnel Management (in consultation with the Secretary and the Secretary of Defense) may prescribe regulations implementing the provisions of this chapter with regard to the application of this chapter to Federal executive agencies (other than the agencies referred to in paragraph (2)) as employers. Such regulations shall be consistent with the regulations pertaining to the States as employers and private employers, except that employees of the Federal Government may be given greater or additional rights.

(2) The following entities may prescribe regulations to carry out the activities of such entities under this chapter:

(A) The Merit Systems Protection Board.

(B) The Office of Special Counsel.

(C) The agencies referred to in section 2302(a)(2)(C)(ii) of title 5.

§4332. Reports

(a) Annual report by Secretary—The Secretary shall after consultation with the Attorney General and the Special Counsel referred to in section 4324(a)(1), transmit to Congress not later than July 1 each year a report on matters for the fiscal year ending in the year before the year in which such report is transmitted as follows:

(1) The number of cases reviewed by the Department of Labor under this chapter during the fiscal year for which the report is made.

(2) The number of cases reviewed by the Secretary of Defense under the National Committee for Employer Support of the Guard and Reserve of the Department of Defense during the fiscal year for which the report is made.

(3) The number of cases referred to the Attorney General or the Special Counsel pursuant to section 4323 or 4324, respectively, during each fiscal year and the number of ac-

tions initiated by the Office of Special Counsel before the Merit Systems Protection Board pursuant to section 4324 during such fiscal year.

(4) The number of complaints filed by the Attorney General pursuant to section 4323 during such fiscal year.

(5) The number of cases reviewed by the Secretary and the Secretary of Defense through the National Committee for Employer Support of the Guard and Reserve of the Department of Defense that involve the same person.

(6) With respect to the cases reported on pursuant to paragraphs (1), (2), (3), (4), and (5)-

(A) the number of such cases that involve a disability-related issue; and

(B) the number of such cases that involve a person who has a service-connected disability.

(7) The nature and status of each case reported on pursuant to paragraph (1), (2), (3), (4), or (5).

(8) With respect to the cases reported on pursuant to paragraphs (1), (2), (3), (4), and (5) the number of such cases that involve persons with different occupations or persons seeking different occupations, as designated by the Standard Occupational Classification System.

(9) An indication of whether there are any apparent patterns of violation of the provisions of this chapter, together with an explanation thereof.

(10) Recommendations for administrative or legislative action that the Secretary, the Attorney General, or the Special Counsel considers necessary for the effective implementation of this chapter, including any action that could be taken to encourage mediation, before claims are filed under this chapter, between employers and persons seeking employment or reemployment.

(b) Quarterly reports.—

(1) Quarterly report by the Secretary.—Not later than 30 days after the end of each fiscal quarter, the Secretary shall submit to Congress, the Secretary of Defense, the Attorney General, and the Special Counsel a report setting forth, for the previous full quarter, the following:

(A) The number of cases for which the Secretary did not meet the requirements of section 4322(f) of this title.

(B) The number of cases for which the Secretary received a request for a referral under paragraph (1) of section 4323(a) of this title but did not make such referral within the time period required by such paragraph.

(2) Quarterly report by Attorney General.—Not later than 30 days after the end of each fiscal quarter, the Attorney General shall submit to Congress, the Secretary, the Secretary of Defense, and the Special Counsel a report setting forth, for the previous full quarter, the number of cases for which the Attorney General received a referral under paragraph (1) of section 4323(a) of this title but did not meet the requirements of paragraph (2) of section 4323(a) of this title for such referral.

(3) Quarterly report by Special Counsel.—Not later than 30 days after the end of each fiscal quarter, the Special Counsel shall submit to Congress, the Secretary, the Secretary of Defense, and the Attorney General a report setting forth, for the previous full quarter, the number of cases for which the Special Counsel received a referral under paragraph (1) of section 4324(a) of this title but did not meet the requirements of paragraph (2)(B) of section 4324(a) of this title for such referral.

(c) Uniform categorization of data.—The Secretary shall coordinate with the Secretary of Defense, the Attorney General, and the Special Counsel to ensure that—

(1) the information in the reports required by this section is categorized in a uniform way; and

(2) the Secretary, the Secretary of Defense, the Attorney General, and the Special Counsel each have electronic access to the case files reviewed under this chapter by the Secretary, the Secretary of Defense, the Attorney General, and the Special Counsel with due regard for the provisions of section 552a of title 5.

§4333. Outreach

The Secretary, the Secretary of Defense, and the Secretary of Veterans Affairs shall take such actions as such Secretaries determine are appropriate to inform persons entitled to rights and benefits under this chapter and employers of the rights, benefits, and obligations of such persons and such employers under this chapter.

§4334. Notice of rights and duties

(a) Requirement to provide notice.—Each employer shall provide to persons entitled to rights and benefits under this chapter a notice of the rights, benefits, and obligations of such persons and such employers under this chapter. The requirement for the provision of notice under this section may be met by the posting of the notice where employers customarily place notices for employees.

(b) Content of notice.—The Secretary shall provide to employers the text of the notice to be provided under this section.

§4335. Training for Federal executive agency human resources personnel on employment and reemployment rights and limitations

(a) Training required.——The head of each Federal executive agency shall provide training for the human resources personnel of such agency on the following:

(1) The rights, benefits, and obligations of members of the uniformed services under this chapter.

(2) The application and administration of the requirements of this chapter by such agency with respect to such members.

(b) Consultation.——The training provided under subsection (a) shall be developed and provided in consultation with the Director of the Office of Personnel Management.

(c) Frequency.——The training under subsection (a) shall be provided with such frequency as the Director of the Office of Personnel Management shall specify in order to ensure that the human resources personnel of Federal executive agencies are kept fully and currently informed of the matters covered by the training.

(d) Human resources personnel defined.——In this section, the term "human resources personnel", in the case of a Federal executive agency, means any personnel of the agency who are authorized to recommend, take, or approve any personnel action that is subject to the requirements of this chapter with respect to employees of the agency.

DEPARTMENT OF LABOR REGULATIONS UNDER THE UNIFORMED SERVICES EMPLOYMENT AND REEMPLOYMENT RIGHTS ACT OF 1994
20 C.F.R. Part 1002

[Authority: Veterans Benefits Improvement Act of 2004 (VBIA) Pub. L. 108-454 (Dec. 10, 2004). *Available at* www.dol.gov/vets/regs/fedreg/final/2005023961.htm]

Subpart A—Introduction to the Regulations Under the Uniformed Services Employment and Reemployment Rights Act of 1994

General Provisions

Subpart B—Anti-Discrimination and Anti-Retaliation

Protection From Employer Discrimination and Retaliation

Subpart C—Eligibility for Reemployment

General Eligibility Requirements for Reemployment

Coverage of Employers and Positions

Coverage of Service in the Uniformed Services

Absence From a Position of Employment Necessitated by Reason of Service in the Uniformed Services

Requirement of Notice

Period of Service

Application for Reemployment

Character of Service

Employer Statutory Defenses

Subpart D—Rights, Benefits, and Obligations of Persons Absent from Employment Due to Service in the Uniformed Services

Furlough and Leave of Absence

Health Plan Coverage

Subpart E—Reemployment Rights and Benefits

Prompt Reemployment

Reemployment Position

Rate of Pay

Protection Against Discharge

Pension Plan Benefits

Subpart F—Compliance Assistance, Enforcement and Remedies

Compliance Assistance

Investigation and Referral

Enforcement of Rights and Benefits Against a State or Private Employer

SUBPART A–INTRODUCTION TO THE REGULATIONS UNDER THE UNIFORMED

Services Employment and Reemployment Rights Act of 1994

General Provisions

§1002.1 What is the purpose of this part?

This part implements the Uniformed Services Employment and Reemployment Rights Act of 1994 ("USERRA" or "the Act"). 38 U.S.C. 4301-4334. USERRA is a law that establishes certain rights and benefits for employees, and duties for employers. USERRA affects employment, reemployment, and retention in employment, when employees serve or have served in the uniformed services. There are five subparts to these regulations. Subpart A gives an introduction to the USERRA regulations. Subpart B describes USERRA's anti-discrimination and anti-retaliation provisions. Subpart C explains the steps that must be taken by a uniformed service member who wants to return to his or her previous civilian employment. Subpart D describes the rights, benefits, and obligations of persons absent from employment due to service in the uniformed services, including rights and obligations related to health plan coverage. Subpart E describes the rights, benefits, and obligations of the returning veteran or service member. Subpart F explains the role of the Department of Labor in enforcing and giving assistance under USERRA. These regulations implement USERRA as it applies to States, local governments, and private employers. Separate regulations published by the Federal Office of Personnel Management implement USERRA for Federal executive agency employers and employees.

§1002.2 Is USERRA a new law?

USERRA is the latest in a series of laws protecting veterans' employment and reemployment rights going back to the

Selective Training and Service Act of 1940. USERRA's immediate predecessor was commonly referred to as the Veterans' Reemployment Rights Act (VRRA), which was enacted as section 404 of the Vietnam Era Veterans' Readjustment Assistance Act of 1974. In enacting USERRA, Congress emphasized USERRA's continuity with the VRRA and its intention to clarify and strengthen that law. Congress also emphasized that Federal laws protecting veterans' employment and reemployment rights for the past fifty years had been successful and that the large body of case law that had developed under those statutes remained in full force and effect, to the extent it is consistent with USERRA. USERRA authorized the Department of Labor to publish regulations implementing the Act for State, local government, and private employers. USERRA also authorized the Office of Personnel Management to issue regulations implementing the Act for Federal executive agencies (other than some Federal intelligence agencies). USERRA established a separate program for employees of some Federal intelligence agencies.

§1002.3 When did USERRA become effective?

USERRA became law on October 13, 1994. USERRA's reemployment provisions apply to members of the uniformed services seeking civilian reemployment on or after December 12, 1994. USERRA's anti-discrimination and anti-retaliation provisions became effective on October 13, 1994.

§1002.4 What is the role of the Secretary of Labor under USERRA?

(a) USERRA charges the Secretary of Labor (through the Veterans' Employment and Training Service) with providing assistance to any person with respect to the employment and reemployment rights and benefits to which such person is entitled under the Act. More information about the

Secretary's role in providing this assistance is contained in Subpart F.

(b) USERRA also authorizes the Secretary of Labor to issue regulations implementing the Act with respect to States, local governments, and private employers. These regulations are issued under this authority.

(c) The Secretary of Labor delegated authority to the Assistant Secretary for Veterans' Employment and Training for administering the veterans' reemployment rights program by Secretary's Order 1-83 (February 3, 1983) and for carrying out the functions and authority vested in the Secretary pursuant to USERRA by memorandum of April 22, 2002 (67 FR 31827).

§1002.5 What definitions apply to USERRA?

(a) Attorney General means the Attorney General of the United States or any person designated by the Attorney General to carry out a responsibility of the Attorney General under USERRA.

(b) Benefit, benefit of employment, or rights and benefits means any advantage, profit, privilege, gain, status, account, or interest (other than wages or salary for work performed) that accrues to the employee because of an employment contract, employment agreement, or employer policy, plan, or practice. The term includes rights and benefits under a pension plan, health plan, or employee stock ownership plan, insurance coverage and awards, bonuses, severance pay, supplemental unemployment benefits, vacations, and the opportunity to select work hours or the location of employment.

(c) Employee means any person employed by an employer. The term also includes any person who is a citizen, national or permanent resident alien of the United States who is employed in a workplace in a foreign country by an employer that is an entity incorporated or organized in the United States, or that is controlled by an entity organized in the United States. "Employee" includes the former employees of an employer.

(d)(1) Employer, except as provided in paragraphs (d)(2) and (3) of this section, means any person, institution, organization, or other entity that pays salary or wages for work performed, or that has control over employment opportunities, including—

(i) A person, institution, organization, or other entity to whom the employer has delegated the performance of employment-related responsibilities, except in the case that such entity has been delegated functions that are purely ministerial in nature, such as maintenance of personnel files or the preparation of forms for submission to a government agency;

(ii) The Federal Government;

(iii) A State;

(iv) Any successor in interest to a person, institution, organization, or other entity referred to in this definition; and,

(v) A person, institution, organization, or other entity that has denied initial employment in violation of 38 U.S.C. 4311, USERRA's anti-discrimination and anti-retaliation provisions.

(2) In the case of a National Guard technician employed under 32 U.S.C. 709, the term "employer" means the adjutant general of the State in which the technician is employed.

(3) An employee pension benefit plan as described in section 3(2) of the Employee Retirement Income Security Act of 1974 (ERISA)(29 U.S.C. 1002(2)) is considered an employer for an individual that it does not actually employ

only with respect to the obligation to provide pension benefits.

(e) Health plan means an insurance policy, insurance contract, medical or hospital service agreement, membership or subscription contract, or other arrangement under which health services for individuals are provided or the expenses of such services are paid.

(f) National Disaster Medical System (NDMS) is an agency within the Federal Emergency Management Agency, Department of Homeland Security, established by the Public Health Security and Bioterrorism Preparedness and Response Act of 2002, Public Law 107-188. The NDMS provides medical-related assistance to respond to the needs of victims of public health emergencies. Participants in the NDMS are volunteers who serve as intermittent Federal employees when activated. For purposes of USERRA coverage only, these persons are treated as members of the uniformed services when they are activated to provide assistance in response to a public health emergency or to be present for a short period of time when there is a risk of a public health emergency, or when they are participating in authorized training. See 42 U.S.C. 300hh-11(e).

(g) Notice, when the employee is required to give advance notice of service, means any written or verbal notification of an obligation or intention to perform service in the uniformed services provided to an employer by the employee who will perform such service, or by the uniformed service in which the service is to be performed.

(h) Qualified, with respect to an employment position, means having the ability to perform the essential tasks of the position.

(i) Reasonable efforts, in the case of actions required of an employer, means actions, including training provided by an employer that do not place an undue hardship on the employer.

(j) Secretary means the Secretary of Labor or any person designated by the Secretary of Labor to carry out an activity under USERRA and these regulations, unless a different office is expressly indicated in the regulation.

(k) Seniority means longevity in employment together with any benefits of employment that accrue with, or are determined by, longevity in employment.

(l) Service in the uniformed services means the performance of duty on a voluntary or involuntary basis in a uniformed service under competent authority. Service in the uniformed services includes active duty, active and inactive duty for training, National Guard duty under Federal statute, and a period for which a person is absent from a position of employment for an examination to determine the fitness of the person to perform such duty. The term also includes a period for which a person is absent from employment to perform funeral honors duty as authorized by law (10 U.S.C. 12503 or 32 U.S.C. 115). The Public Health Security and Bioterrorism Preparedness and Response Act of 2002, Pub. L. 107-188, provides that service as an intermittent disaster-response appointee upon activation of the National Disaster Medical System (NDMS) or as a participant in an authorized training program is deemed "service in the uniformed services." 42 U.S.C. 300hh-11(e)(3).

(m) State means each of the several States of the United States, the District of Columbia, the Commonwealth of Puerto Rico, Guam, the Virgin Islands, and other territories of the United States (including the agencies and political subdivisions thereof); however, for purposes of enforcement of rights under 38 U.S.C. 4323, a political subdivision of a State is a private employer.

(n) Undue hardship, in the case of actions taken by an employer, means an action requiring significant difficulty or expense, when considered in light of—

(1) The nature and cost of the action needed under USERRA and these regulations;

(2) The overall financial resources of the facility or facilities involved in the provision of the action; the number of persons employed at such facility; the effect on expenses and resources, or the impact otherwise of such action upon the operation of the facility;

(3) The overall financial resources of the employer; the overall size of the business of an employer with respect to the number of its employees; the number, type, and location of its facilities; and,

(4) The type of operation or operations of the employer, including the composition, structure, and functions of the work force of such employer; the geographic separateness, administrative, or fiscal relationship of the facility or facilities in question to the employer.

(o) Uniformed services means the Armed Forces; the Army National Guard and the Air National Guard when engaged in active duty for training, inactive duty training, or full-time National Guard duty; the commissioned corps of the Public Health Service; and any other category of persons designated by the President in time of war or national emergency. For purposes of USERRA coverage only, service as an intermittent disaster response appointee of the NDMS when federally activated or attending authorized training in support of their Federal mission is deemed "service in the uniformed services," although such appointee is not a member of the "uniformed services" as defined by USERRA.

§1002.6 What types of service in the uniformed services are covered by USERRA?

USERRA's definition of "service in the uniformed services" covers all categories of military training and service, including duty performed on a voluntary or involuntary basis, in time of peace or war. Although most often understood as applying to National Guard and reserve military personnel, USERRA also applies to persons serving in the active components of the Armed Forces. Certain types of service specified in 42 U.S.C. 300hh-11 by members of the National Disaster Medical System are covered by USERRA.

§1002.7 How does USERRA relate to other laws, public and private contracts, and employer practices?

(a) USERRA establishes a floor, not a ceiling, for the employment and reemployment rights and benefits of those it protects. In other words, an employer may provide greater rights and benefits than USERRA requires, but no employer can refuse to provide any right or benefit guaranteed by USERRA.

(b) USERRA supersedes any State law (including any local law or ordinance), contract, agreement, policy, plan, practice, or other matter that reduces, limits, or eliminates in any manner any right or benefit provided by USERRA, including the establishment of additional prerequisites to the exercise of any USERRA right or the receipt of any USERRA benefit. For example, an employment contract that determines seniority based only on actual days of work in the place of employment would be superseded by USERRA, which requires that seniority credit be given for periods of absence from work due to service in the uniformed services.

(c) USERRA does not supersede, nullify or diminish any Federal or State law (including any local law or ordinance), contract, agreement, policy, plan, practice, or other matter that establishes an employment right or benefit that is more beneficial than, or is in addition to, a right or benefit provided under the Act. For example, although USERRA does not require an employer to pay an employee for time away from work performing service, an employer policy, plan, or practice that provides such a benefit is permissible under USERRA.

(d) If an employer provides a benefit that exceeds USERRA's requirements in one area, it cannot reduce or limit other rights or benefits provided by USERRA. For example, even though USERRA does not require it, an employer may provide a fixed number of days of paid military leave per year to employees who are members of the National Guard or Reserve. The fact that it provides such a benefit, however, does not permit an employer to refuse to provide an unpaid leave of absence to an employee to perform service in the uniformed services in excess of the number of days of paid military leave.

Subpart B—Anti-Discrimination and Anti-Retaliation

Protection From Employer Discrimination and Retaliation

§1002.18 What status or activity is protected from employer discrimination by USERRA?

An employer must not deny initial employment, reemployment, retention in employment, promotion, or any benefit of employment to an individual on the basis of his or her membership, application for membership, performance of service, application for service, or obligation for service in the uniformed services.

§1002.19 What activity is protected from employer retaliation by USERRA?

An employer must not retaliate against an individual by taking any adverse employment action against him or her because the individual has taken an action to enforce a protection afforded any person under USERRA; testified or otherwise made a statement in or in connection with a proceeding under USERRA; assisted or participated in a USERRA investigation: or, exercised a right provided for by USERRA.

§1002.20 Does USERRA protect an individual who does not actually perform service in the uniformed services?

Yes. Employers are prohibited from taking actions against an individual for any of the activities protected by the Act, whether or not he or she has performed service in the uniformed services.

§1002.21 Do the Act's prohibitions against discrimination and retaliation apply to all employment positions?

The prohibitions against discrimination and retaliation apply to all covered employers (including hiring halls and potential employers, see sections 1002.36 and .38) and employment positions, including those that are for a brief, nonrecurrent period, and for which there is no reasonable expectation that the employment position will continue indefinitely or for a significant period. However, USERRA's reemployment rights and benefits do not apply to such brief, nonrecurrent positions of employment.

§1002.22 Who has the burden of proving discrimination or retaliation in violation of USERRA?

The individual has the burden of proving that a status or activity protected by USERRA was one of the reasons that the employer took action against him or her, in order to establish that the action was discrimination or retaliation in violation of USERRA. If the individual succeeds in proving that the status or activity protected by USERRA was one of the reasons the employer took action against him or her, the employer has the burden to prove the affirmative defense that it would have taken the action anyway.

§1002.23 What must the individual show to carry the burden of proving that the employer discriminated or retaliated against him or her?

(a) In order to prove that the employer discriminated or retaliated against the individual, he or she must first show that the employer's action was motivated by one or more of the following:

(1) Membership or application for membership in a uniformed service;

(2) Performance of service, application for service, or obligation for service in a uniformed service;

(3) Action taken to enforce a protection afforded any person under USERRA;

(4) Testimony or statement made in or in connection with a USERRA proceeding;

(5) Assistance or participation in a USERRA investigation; or,

(6) Exercise of a right provided for by USERRA.

(b) If the individual proves that the employer's action was based on one of the prohibited motives listed in paragraph (a) of this section, the employer has the burden to prove the affirmative defense that the action would have been taken anyway absent the USERRA-protected status or activity.

Subpart C–Eligibility For Reemployment

General Eligibility Requirements for Reemployment

§1002.32 What criteria must the employee meet to be eligible under USERRA for reemployment after service in the uniformed services?

(a) In general, if the employee has been absent from a position of civilian employment by reason of service in the uniformed services, he or she will be eligible for reemployment under USERRA by meeting the following criteria:

(1) The employer had advance notice of the employee's service;

(2) The employee has five years or less of cumulative service in the uniformed services in his or her employment relationship with a particular employer;

(3) The employee timely returns to work or applies for reemployment; and,

(4) The employee has not been separated from service with a disqualifying discharge or under other than honorable conditions.

(b) These general eligibility requirements have important qualifications and exceptions, which are described in detail in §§1002.73 through 1002.138. If the employee meets these eligibility criteria, then he or she is eligible for reemployment unless the employer establishes one of the defenses described in Sec. 1002.139. The employment position to which the employee is entitled is described in Sec. Sec. 1002.191 through 1002.199.

§1002.33 Does the employee have to prove that the employer discriminated against him or her in order to be eligible for reemployment?

No. The employee is not required to prove that the employer discriminated against him or her because of the employee's uniformed service in order to be eligible for reemployment.

Coverage of Employers and Positions

§1002.34 Which employers are covered by USERRA?

(a) USERRA applies to all public and private employers in the United States, regardless of size. For example, an employer with only one employee is covered for purposes of the Act.

(b) USERRA applies to foreign employers doing business in the United States. A foreign employer that has a physical location or branch in the United States (including U.S. territories and possessions) must comply with USERRA for any of its employees who are employed in the United States.

(c) An American company operating either directly or through an entity under its control in a foreign country must also comply with USERRA for all its foreign operations, unless compliance would violate the law of the foreign country in which the workplace is located.

§1002.35 Is a successor in interest an employer covered by USERRA?

USERRA's definition of "employer" includes a successor in interest. In general, an employer is a successor in interest where there is a substantial continuity in operations, facilities, and workforce from the former employer. The determination whether an employer is a successor in interest must be made on a case-by-case basis using a multi-factor test that considers the following:

(a) Whether there has been a substantial continuity of business operations from the former to the current employer;

(b) Whether the current employer uses the same or similar facilities, machinery, equipment, and methods of production;

(c) Whether there has been a substantial continuity of employees;

(d) Whether there is a similarity of jobs and working conditions;

(e) Whether there is a similarity of supervisors or managers; and,

(f) Whether there is a similarity of products or services.

§1002.36　Can an employer be liable as a successor in interest if it was unaware that an employee may claim reemployment rights when the employer acquired the business?

Yes. In order to be a successor in interest, it is not necessary for an employer to have notice of a potential reemployment claim at the time of merger, acquisition, or other form of succession.

§1002.37　Can one employee be employed in one job by more than one employer?

Yes. Under USERRA, an employer includes not only the person or entity that pays an employee's salary or wages, but also includes a person or entity that has control over his or her employment opportunities, including a person or entity to whom an employer has delegated the performance of employment-related responsibilities. For example, if the employee is a security guard hired by a security company and he or she is assigned to a work site, the employee may report both to the security company and to the site owner.

In such an instance, both employers share responsibility for compliance with USERRA. If the security company declines to assign the employee to a job because of a uniformed service obligation (for example, National Guard duties), then the security company could be in violation of the reemployment requirements and the anti-discrimination provisions of USERRA. Similarly, if the employer at the work site causes the employee's removal from the job position because of his or her uniformed service obligations, then the work site employer could be in violation of the reemployment requirements and the anti-discrimination provisions of USERRA.

§1002.38 Can a hiring hall be an employer?

Yes. In certain occupations (for example, longshoreman, stagehand, construction worker), the employee may frequently work for many different employers. A hiring hall operated by a union or an employer association typically assigns the employee to the jobs. In these industries, it may not be unusual for the employee to work his or her entire career in a series of short-term job assignments. The definition of "employer" includes a person, institution, organization, or other entity to which the employer has delegated the performance of employment-related responsibilities. A hiring hall therefore is considered the employee's employer if the hiring and job assignment functions have been delegated by an employer to the hiring hall. As the employer, a hiring hall has reemployment responsibilities to its employees. USERRA's anti-discrimination and anti-retaliation provisions also apply to the hiring hall.

§1002.39 Are States (and their political subdivisions), the District of Columbia, the Commonwealth of Puerto Rico, and United States territories, considered employers?

Yes. States and their political subdivisions, such as counties, parishes, cities, towns, villages, and school districts, are considered employers under USERRA. The District of Columbia, the Commonwealth of Puerto Rico, Guam, the Virgin Islands, and territories of the United States, are also considered employers under the Act.

§1002.40 Does USERRA protect against discrimination in initial hiring decisions?

Yes. The Act's definition of employer includes a person, institution, organization, or other entity that has denied initial employment to an individual in violation of USERRA's anti-discrimination provisions. An employer need not actually employ an individual to be his or her "employer" under the Act, if it has denied initial employment on the basis of the individual's membership, application for membership, performance of service, application for service, or obligation for service in the uniformed services. Similarly, the employer would be liable if it denied initial employment on the basis of the individual's action taken to enforce a protection afforded to any person under USERRA, his or her testimony or statement in connection with any USERRA proceeding, assistance or other participation in a USERRA investigation, or the exercise of any other right provided by the Act. For example, if the individual has been denied initial employment because of his or her obligations as a member of the National Guard or Reserves, the company or entity denying employment is an employer for purposes of USERRA. Similarly, if an entity withdraws an offer of employment because the individual is called upon to fulfill an obligation in the uniformed services, the entity withdrawing the employment offer is an employer for purposes of USERRA.

§1002.41 Does an employee have rights under USERRA even though he or she holds a temporary, part-time, probationary, or seasonal employment position?

USERRA rights are not diminished because an employee holds a temporary, part-time, probationary, or seasonal employment position. However, an employer is not required to reemploy an employee if the employment he or she left to serve in the uniformed services was for a brief, nonrecurrent period and there is no reasonable expectation that the employment would have continued indefinitely or for a significant period. The employer bears the burden of proving this affirmative defense.

§1002.42 What rights does an employee have under USERRA if he or she is on layoff, on strike, or on a leave of absence?

(a) If an employee is laid off with recall rights, on strike, or on a leave of absence, he or she is an employee for purposes of USERRA. If the employee is on layoff and begins service in the uniformed services, or is laid off while performing service, he or she may be entitled to reemployment on return if the employer would have recalled the employee to employment during the period of service. Similar principles apply if the employee is on strike or on a leave of absence from work when he or she begins a period of service in the uniformed services.

(b) If the employee is sent a recall notice during a period of service in the uniformed services and cannot resume the position of employment because of the service, he or she still remains an employee for purposes of the Act. Therefore, if the employee is otherwise eligible, he or she is entitled to reemployment following the conclusion of the period of service even if he or she did not respond to the recall notice.

(c) If the employee is laid off before or during service in the uniformed services, and the employer would not have recalled him or her during that period of service, the employee is not entitled to reemployment following the period of service simply because he or she is a covered employee. Reemployment rights under USERRA cannot put the employee in a better position than if he or she had remained in the civilian employment position.

§1002.43 Does an individual have rights under USERRA even if he or she is an executive, managerial, or professional employee?

Yes. USERRA applies to all employees. There is no exclusion for executive, managerial, or professional employees.

§1002.44 Does USERRA cover an independent contractor?

(a) No. USERRA does not provide protections for an independent contractor.

(b) In deciding whether an individual is an independent contractor, the following factors need to be considered:

(1) The extent of the employer's right to control the manner in which the individual's work is to be performed;

(2) The opportunity for profit or loss that depends upon the individual's managerial skill;

(3) Any investment in equipment or materials required for the individual's tasks, or his or her employment of helpers;

(4) Whether the service the individual performs requires a special skill;

(5) The degree of permanence of the individual's working relationship; and,

(6) Whether the service the individual performs is an integral part of the employer's business.

(c) No single one of these factors is controlling, but all are relevant to determining whether an individual is an employee or an independent contractor.

Coverage of Service in the Uniformed Services

§1002.54 Are all military fitness examinations considered "service in the uniformed services?"

Yes. USERRA's definition of "service in the uniformed services" includes a period for which an employee is absent from a position of employment for the purpose of an examination to determine his or her fitness to perform duty in the uniformed services. Military fitness examinations can address more than physical or medical fitness, and include evaluations for mental, educational, and other types of fitness. Any examination to determine an employee's fitness for service is covered, whether it is an initial or recurring examination. For example, a periodic medical examination required of a Reserve component member to determine fitness for continued service is covered.

§1002.55 Is all funeral honors duty considered "service in the uniformed services?"

(a) USERRA's definition of "service in the uniformed services" includes a period for which an employee is absent from employment for the purpose of performing authorized funeral honors duty under 10 U.S.C. 12503 (members of Reserve ordered to perform funeral honors duty) or 32 U.S.C. 115 (Member of Air or Army National Guard ordered to perform funeral honors duty).

(b) Funeral honors duty performed by persons who are not members of the uniformed services, such as members of veterans' service organizations, is not "service in the uniformed services."

§1002.56 What types of service in the National Disaster Medical System are considered "service in the uniformed services?"

Under a provision of the Public Health Security and Bioterrorism Preparedness and Response Act of 2002, 42 U.S.C. 300hh 11(e)(3), "service in the uniformed services" includes service performed as an intermittent disaster-response appointee upon activation of the National Disaster Medical System or participation in an authorized training program, even if the individual is not a member of the uniformed services.

§1002.57 Is all service as a member of the National Guard considered "service in the uniformed services?"

The National Guard has a dual status. It is a Reserve component of the Army, or, in the case of the Air National Guard, of the Air Force. Simultaneously, it is a State military force subject to call-up by the State Governor for duty not subject to Federal control, such as emergency duty in cases of floods or riots. National Guard members may perform service under either Federal or State authority, but only Federal National Guard service is covered by USERRA.

(a) National Guard service under Federal authority is protected by USERRA. Service under Federal authority includes active duty performed under Title 10 of the United States Code. Service under Federal authority also includes duty under Title 32 of the United States Code, such as active duty for training, inactive duty training, or full-time National Guard duty.

(b) National Guard service under authority of State law is not protected by USERRA. However, many States have laws protecting the civilian job rights of National Guard members who serve under State orders. Enforcement of those State laws is not covered by USERRA or these regulations.

§1002.58 Is service in the commissioned corps of the Public Health Service considered "service in the uniformed services?"

Yes. Service in the commissioned corps of the Public Health Service (PHS) is "service in the uniformed services" under USERRA.

§1002.59 Are there any circumstances in which special categories of persons are considered to perform "service in the uniformed services?"

Yes. In time of war or national emergency the President has authority to designate any category of persons as a "uniformed service" for purposes of USERRA. If the President exercises this authority, service as a member of that category of persons would be "service in the uniformed services" under USERRA.

§1002.60 Does USERRA cover an individual attending a military service academy?

Yes. Attending a military service academy is considered uniformed service for purposes of USERRA. There are four service academies: The United States Military Academy (West Point, New York), the United States Naval Academy (Annapolis, Maryland), the United States Air Force Academy (Colorado Springs, Colorado), and the United States Coast Guard Academy (New London, Connecticut).

§1002.61 Does USERRA cover a member of the Reserve Officers Training Corps?

Yes, under certain conditions.

(a) Membership in the Reserve Officers Training Corps (ROTC) or the Junior ROTC is not "service in the uniformed services." However, some Reserve and National Guard enlisted members use a college ROTC program as a means of qualifying for commissioned officer status. National Guard and Reserve members in an ROTC program may at times, while participating in that program, be receiving active duty and inactive duty training service credit with their unit. In these cases, participating in ROTC training sessions is considered "service in the uniformed services," and qualifies a person for protection under USERRA's reemployment and anti-discrimination provisions.

(b) Typically, an individual in a College ROTC program enters into an agreement with a particular military service that obligates such individual to either complete the ROTC program and accept a commission or, in case he or she does not successfully complete the ROTC program, to serve as an enlisted member. Although an individual does not qualify for reemployment protection, except as specified in (a) above, he or she is protected under USERRA's anti-discrimination provisions because, as a result of the agreement, he or she has applied to become a member of the uniformed services and has incurred an obligation to perform future service.

§1002.62 Does USERRA cover a member of the Commissioned Corps of the National Oceanic and Atmospheric Administration, the Civil Air Patrol, or the Coast Guard Auxiliary?

No. Although the Commissioned Corps of the National Oceanic and Atmospheric Administration (NOAA) is a "uniformed service" for some purposes, it is not included in USERRA's definition of this term. Service in the Civil Air Patrol and the Coast Guard Auxiliary similarly is not considered "service in the uniformed services" for purposes of USERRA. Consequently, service performed in the Commissioned Corps of the National Oceanic and Atmospheric Administration (NOAA), the Civil Air Patrol, and the Coast Guard Auxiliary is not protected by USERRA.

Absence From a Position of Employment Necessitated by Reason of Service in the Uniformed Services

§1002.73 Does service in the uniformed services have to be an employee's sole reason for leaving an employment position in order to have USERRA reemployment rights?

No. If absence from a position of employment is necessitated by service in the uniformed services, and the employee otherwise meets the Act's eligibility requirements, he or she has reemployment rights under USERRA, even if the employee uses the absence for other purposes as well. An employee is not required to leave the employment position for the sole purpose of performing service in the uniformed services. For example, if the employee is required to report to an out of State location for military training and he or she spends off-duty time during that assignment moonlighting as a security guard or visiting relatives who live in that State, the employee will not lose reemployment rights simply because he or she used some of the time away from the job to do something other than attend the military training. Also, if an employee receives advance notification of a mobilization order, and leaves his or her employment position in order to prepare for duty, but the mobilization is cancelled, the employee will not lose any reemployment rights.

§1002.74 Must the employee begin service in the uniformed services immediately after leaving his or her employment position in order to have USERRA reemployment rights?

No. At a minimum, an employee must have enough time after leaving the employment position to travel safely to the uniformed service site and arrive fit to perform the service. Depending on the specific circumstances, including the duration of service, the amount of notice received, and the location of the service, additional time to rest, or to arrange affairs and report to duty, may be necessitated by reason of service in the uniformed services. The following examples help to explain the issue of the period of time between leaving civilian employment and beginning of service in the uniformed services:

(a) If the employee performs a full overnight shift for the civilian employer and travels directly from the work site to perform a full day of uniformed service, the employee would not be considered fit to perform the uniformed service. An absence from that work shift is necessitated so that the employee can report for uniformed service fit for duty.

(b) If the employee is ordered to perform an extended period of service in the uniformed services, he or she may require a reasonable period of time off from the civilian job to put his or her personal affairs in order, before beginning the service. Taking such time off is also necessitated by the uniformed service.

(c) If the employee leaves a position of employment in order to enlist or otherwise perform service in the uniformed services and, through no fault of his or her own, the beginning date of the service is delayed, this delay does not terminate any reemployment rights.

Requirement of Notice

§1002.85 Must the employee give advance notice to the employer of his or her service in the uniformed services?

(a) Yes. The employee, or an appropriate officer of the uniformed service in which his or her service is to be performed, must notify the employer that the employee intends to leave the employment position to perform service in the uniformed services, with certain exceptions described below. In cases in which an employee is employed by more than one employer, the employee, or an appropriate office of the uniformed service in which his or her service is to be performed, must notify each employer that the employee intends to leave the employment position to perform service in the uniformed services, with certain exceptions described below.

(b) The Department of Defense USERRA regulations at 32 CFR 104.3 provide that an "appropriate officer" can give notice on the employee's behalf. An "appropriate officer" is a commissioned, warrant, or non-commissioned officer authorized to give such notice by the military service concerned.

(c) The employee's notice to the employer may be either verbal or written. The notice may be informal and does not need to follow any particular format.

(d) Although USERRA does not specify how far in advance notice must be given to the employer, an employee should provide notice as far in advance as is reasonable under the circumstances. In regulations promulgated by the Department of Defense under USERRA, 32 CFR 104.6(a)(2)(i)(B), the Defense Department "strongly recommends that advance notice to civilian employers be provided at least 30 days prior to departure for uniformed service when it is feasible to do so."

§1002.86 When is the employee excused from giving advance notice of service in the uniformed services?

The employee is required to give advance notice of pending service unless giving such notice is prevented by military necessity, or is otherwise impossible or unreasonable under all the circumstances.

(a) Only a designated authority can make a determination of "military necessity," and such a determination is not subject to judicial review. Guidelines for defining "military necessity" appear in regulations issued by the Department of Defense at 32 CFR 104.3. In general, these regulations cover situations where a mission, operation, exercise or requirement is classified, or could be compromised or otherwise adversely affected by public knowledge. In certain cases, the Secretary of Homeland Security, in consultation with the Secretary of Defense, can make a determination that giving of notice by intermittent disaster-response appointees of the National Disaster Medical System is precluded by "military necessity." See 42 U.S.C. 300hh-11(e)(3)(B).

(b) It may be impossible or unreasonable to give advance notice under certain circumstances. Such circumstances may include the unavailability of the employee's employer or the employer's representative, or a requirement that the employee report for uniformed service in an extremely short period of time.

§1002.87 Is the employee required to get permission from his or her employer before leaving to perform service in the uniformed services?

No. The employee is not required to ask for or get his or her employer's permission to leave to perform service in the uniformed services. The employee is only required to give the employer notice of pending service.

§1002.88 Is the employee required to tell his or her civilian employer that he or she intends to seek reemployment after completing uniformed service before the employee leaves to perform service in the uniformed services?

No. When the employee leaves the employment position to begin a period of service, he or she is not required to tell the civilian employer that he or she intends to seek reemployment after completing uniformed service. Even if the employee tells the employer before entering or completing uniformed service that he or she does not intend to seek reemployment after completing the uniformed service, the employee does not forfeit the right to reemployment after completing service. The employee is not required to decide in advance of leaving the civilian employment position whether he or she will seek reemployment after completing uniformed service.

Period of Service

§1002.99 Is there a limit on the total amount of service in the uniformed services that an employee may perform and still retain reemployment rights with the employer?

Yes. In general, the employee may perform service in the uniformed services for a cumulative period of up to five (5) years and retain reemployment rights with the employer. The exceptions to this rule are described below.

§1002.100 Does the five-year service limit include all absences from an employment position that are related to service in the uniformed services?

No. The five-year period includes only the time the employee spends actually performing service in the uniformed services. A period of absence from employment before or after performing service in the uniformed services does not count against the five-year limit. For example, after the employee completes a period of service in the uniformed services, he or she is provided a certain amount of time, depending upon the length of service, to report back to work or submit an application for reemployment. The period between completing the uniformed service and reporting back to work or seeking reemployment does not count against the five-year limit.

§1002.101 Does the five-year service limit include periods of service that the employee performed when he or she worked for a previous employer?

No. An employee is entitled to a leave of absence for uniformed service for up to five years with each employer for whom he or she works. When the employee takes a position with a new employer, the five-year period begins again regardless of how much service he or she performed while working in any previous employment relationship. If an employee is employed by more than one employer, a separate five-year period runs as to each employer independently, even if those employers share or co-determine the employee's terms and conditions of employment.

§1002.102 Does the five-year service limit include periods of service that the employee performed before USERRA was enacted?

It depends. USERRA provides reemployment rights to which an employee may become entitled beginning on or after December 12, 1994, but any uniformed service performed before December 12, 1994, that was counted against the service limitations of the previous law (the Veterans Reemployment Rights Act), also counts against USERRA's five-year limit.

§1002.103 Are there any types of service in the uniformed services that an employee can perform that do not count against USERRA's five-year service limit?

(a) USERRA creates the following exceptions to the five-year limit on service in the uniformed services:

(1) Service that is required beyond five years to complete an initial period of obligated service. Some military specialties require an individual to serve more than five years because of the amount of time or expense involved in training. If the employee works in one of those specialties, he or she has reemployment rights when the initial period of obligated service is completed;

(2) If the employee was unable to obtain orders releasing him or her from service in the uniformed services before

the expiration of the five-year period, and the inability was not the employee's fault;

(3) (i) Service performed to fulfill periodic National Guard and Reserve training requirements as prescribed by 10 U.S.C. 10147 and 32 U.S.C. 502(a) and 503; and,

(ii) Service performed to fulfill additional training requirements determined and certified by a proper military authority as necessary for the employee's professional development, or to complete skill training or retraining;

(4) Service performed in a uniformed service if he or she was ordered to or retained on active duty under:

(i) 10 U.S.C. 688 (involuntary active duty by a military retiree);

(ii) 10 U.S.C. 12301(a) (involuntary active duty in wartime);

(iii) 10 U.S.C. 12301(g) (retention on active duty while in captive status);

(iv) 10 U.S.C. 12302 (involuntary active duty during a national emergency for up to 24 months);

(v) 10 U.S.C. 12304 (involuntary active duty for an operational mission for up to 270 days);

(vi) 10 U.S.C. 12305 (involuntary retention on active duty of a critical person during time of crisis or other specific conditions);

(vii) 14 U.S.C. 331 (involuntary active duty by retired Coast Guard officer);

(viii) 14 U.S.C. 332 (voluntary active duty by retired Coast Guard officer);

(ix) 14 U.S.C. 359 (involuntary active duty by retired Coast Guard enlisted member);

(x) 14 U.S.C. 360 (voluntary active duty by retired Coast Guard enlisted member);

(xi) 14 U.S.C. 367 (involuntary retention of Coast Guard enlisted member on active duty); and

(xii) 14 U.S.C. 712 (involuntary active duty by Coast Guard Reserve member for natural or man-made disasters).

(5) Service performed in a uniformed service if the employee was ordered to or retained on active duty (other than for training) under any provision of law because of a war or national emergency declared by the President or the Congress, as determined by the Secretary concerned;

(6) Service performed in a uniformed service if the employee was ordered to active duty (other than for training) in support of an operational mission for which personnel have been ordered to active duty under 10 U.S.C. 12304, as determined by a proper military authority;

(7) Service performed in a uniformed service if the employee was ordered to active duty in support of a critical mission or requirement of the uniformed services as determined by the Secretary concerned; and,

(8) Service performed as a member of the National Guard if the employee was called to respond to an invasion, danger of invasion, rebellion, danger of rebellion, insurrection, or the inability of the President with regular forces to execute the laws of the United States.

(b) Service performed to mitigate economic harm where the employee's employer is in violation of its employment or reemployment obligations to him or her.

§1002.104 Is the employee required to accommodate his or her employer's needs as to the timing, frequency or duration of service?

No. The employee is not required to accommodate his or her employer's interests or concerns regarding the timing, frequency, or duration of uniformed service. The employer cannot refuse to reemploy the employee because it believes that the timing, frequency or duration of the service is unreasonable. However, the employer is permitted to bring its concerns over the timing, frequency, or duration of the employee's service to the attention of the appropriate military authority. Regulations issued by the Department of Defense at 32 CFR 104.4 direct military authorities to provide assistance to an employer in addressing these types of employment issues. The military authorities are required to consider requests from employers of National Guard and Reserve members to adjust scheduled absences from civilian employment to perform service.

Application for Reemployment

§1002.115 Is the employee required to report to or submit a timely application for reemployment to his or her pre-service employer upon completing the period of service in the uniformed services?

Yes. Upon completing service in the uniformed services, the employee must notify the pre-service employer of his or her intent to return to the employment position by either reporting to work or submitting a timely application for reemployment. Whether the employee is required to report to work or submit a timely application for reemployment depends upon the length of service, as follows:

(a) Period of service less than 31 days or for a period of any length for the purpose of a fitness examination. If the period of service in the uniformed services was less than 31 days, or the employee was absent from a position of employment for a period of any length for the purpose of an examination to determine his or her fitness to perform service, the employee must report back to the employer not later than the beginning of the first full regularly-scheduled work period on the first full calendar day following the completion of the period of service, and the expiration of eight hours after a period allowing for safe transportation from the place of that service to the employee's residence. For example, if the employee completes a period of service and travel home, arriving at ten o'clock in the evening, he or she cannot be required to report to the employer until the beginning of the next full regularly-scheduled work period that begins at least eight hours after arriving home, i.e., no earlier than six o'clock the next morning. If it is impossible or unreasonable for the employee to report within such time period through no fault of his or her own, he or she must report to the employer as soon as possible after the expiration of the eight-hour period.

(b) Period of service more than 30 days but less than 181 days. If the employee's period of service in the uniformed services was for more than 30 days but less than 181 days, he or she must submit an application for reemployment (written or verbal) with the employer not later than 14 days after completing service. If it is impossible or unreasonable for the employee to apply within 14 days through no fault of his or her own, he or she must submit the application not later than the next full calendar day after it becomes possible to do so.

(c) Period of service more than 180 days. If the employee's period of service in the uniformed services was for more than 180 days, he or she must submit an application for reemployment (written or verbal) not later than 90 days after completing service.

§1002.116 Is the time period for reporting back to an employer extended if the employee is hospitalized for, or convalescing from, an illness or injury incurred in, or aggravated during, the performance of service?

Yes. If the employee is hospitalized for, or convalescing from, an illness or injury incurred in, or aggravated during, the performance of service, he or she must report to or submit an application for reemployment to the employer at the end of the period necessary for recovering from the illness or injury. This period may not exceed two years from the date of the completion of service, except that it must be extended by the minimum time necessary to accommodate circumstances beyond the employee's control that make reporting within the period impossible or unreasonable. This period for recuperation and recovery extends the time period for reporting to or submitting an application for reemployment to the employer, and is not applicable following reemployment.

§1002.117 Are there any consequences if the employee fails to report for or submit a timely application for reemployment?

(a) If the employee fails to timely report for or apply for reemployment, he or she does not automatically forfeit entitlement to USERRA's reemployment and other rights and benefits. Rather, the employee becomes subject to the conduct rules, established policy, and general practices of the employer pertaining to an absence from scheduled work.

(b) If reporting or submitting an employment application to the employer is impossible or unreasonable through no fault of the employee, he or she may report to the employer as soon as possible (in the case of a period of service less than 31 days) or submit an application for reemployment to the employer by the next full calendar day after it becomes possible to do so (in the case of a period of service from 31 to 180 days), and the employee will be considered to have timely reported or applied for reemployment.

§1002.118 Is an application for reemployment required to be in any particular form?

An application for reemployment need not follow any particular format. The employee may apply orally or in writing. The application should indicate that the employee is a former employee returning from service in the uniformed services and that he or she seeks reemployment with the pre-service employer. The employee is permitted but not required to identify a particular reemployment position in which he or she is interested.

§1002.119 To whom must the employee submit the application for reemployment?

The application must be submitted to the pre-service employer or to an agent or representative of the employer who has apparent responsibility for receiving employment applications. Depending upon the circumstances, such a person could be a personnel or human resources officer, or a first-line supervisor. If there has been a change in ownership of the employer, the application should be submitted to the employer's successor-in-interest.

§1002.120 If the employee seeks or obtains employment with an employer other than the pre-service employer before the end of the period within which a reemployment application must be filed, will that jeopardize reemployment rights with the pre-service employer?

No. The employee has reemployment rights with the pre-service employer provided that he or she makes a timely reemployment application to that employer. The employee may seek or obtain employment with an employer other than the pre-service employer during the period of time within which a reemployment application must be made, without giving up reemployment rights with the pre-service employer. However, such alternative employment during the application period should not be of a type that would constitute cause for the employer to discipline or terminate the employee following reemployment. For instance, if the employer forbids employees from working concurrently for a direct competitor during employment, violation of such a policy may constitute cause for discipline or even termination.

§1002.121 Is the employee required to submit documentation to the employer in connection with the application for reemployment?

Yes, if the period of service exceeded 30 days and if requested by the employer to do so. If the employee submits an application for reemployment after a period of service of more than 30 days, he or she must, upon the request of the employer, provide documentation to establish that:

(a) The reemployment application is timely;

(b) The employee has not exceeded the five-year limit on the duration of service (subject to the exceptions listed at Sec. 1002.103); and,

(c) The employee's separation or dismissal from service was not disqualifying.

§ 1002.122 Is the employer required to reemploy the employee if documentation establishing the employee's eligibility does not exist or is not readily available?

Yes. The employer is not permitted to delay or deny reemployment by demanding documentation that does not exist or is not readily available. The employee is not liable for administrative delays in the issuance of military documentation. If the employee is reemployed after an absence from employment for more than 90 days, the employer may require that he or she submit the documentation establishing entitlement to reemployment before treating the employee as not having had a break in service for pension purposes. If the documentation is received after reemployment and it shows that the employee is not entitled to reemployment, the employer may terminate employment and any rights or benefits that the employee may have been granted.

§1002.123 What documents satisfy the requirement that the employee establish eligibility for reemployment after a period of service of more than thirty days?

(a) Documents that satisfy the requirements of USERRA include the following:

(1) DD (Department of Defense) 214 Certificate of Release or Discharge from Active Duty;

(2) Copy of duty orders prepared by the facility where the orders were fulfilled carrying an endorsement indicating completion of the described service;

(3) Letter from the commanding officer of a Personnel Support Activity or someone of comparable authority;

(4) Certificate of completion from military training school;

(5) Discharge certificate showing character of service; and,

(6) Copy of extracts from payroll documents showing periods of service;

(7) Letter from National Disaster Medical System (NDMS) Team Leader or Administrative Officer verifying dates and times of NDMS training or Federal activation.

(b) The types of documents that are necessary to establish eligibility for reemployment will vary from case to case. Not all of these documents are available or necessary in every instance to establish reemployment eligibility.

Character of Service

§1002.134 What type of discharge or separation from service is required for an employee to be entitled to reemployment under USERRA?

USERRA does not require any particular form of discharge or separation from service. However, even if the employee is otherwise eligible for reemployment, he or she will be disqualified if the characterization of service falls within one of four categories. USERRA requires that the employee not have received one of these types of discharge.

§1002.135 What types of discharge or separation from uniformed service will make the employee ineligible for reemployment under USERRA?

Reemployment rights are terminated if the employee is:

(a) Separated from uniformed service with a dishonorable or bad conduct discharge;

(b) Separated from uniformed service under other than honorable conditions, as characterized by regulations of the uniformed service;

(c) A commissioned officer dismissed as permitted under 10 U.S.C. 1161(a) by sentence of a general court-martial; in commutation of a sentence of a general court-martial; or, in time of war, by order of the President; or,

(d) A commissioned officer dropped from the rolls under 10 U.S.C. 1161(b) due to absence without authority for at least three months; separation by reason of a sentence to confinement adjudged by a court-martial; or, a sentence to confinement in a Federal or State penitentiary or correctional institution.

§1002.136 Who determines the characterization of service?

The branch of service in which the employee performs the tour of duty determines the characterization of service.

§1002.137 If the employee receives a disqualifying discharge or release from uniformed service and it is later upgraded, will reemployment rights be restored?

Yes. A military review board has the authority to prospectively or retroactively upgrade a disqualifying discharge or release. A retroactive upgrade would restore reemployment rights providing the employee otherwise meets the Act's eligibility criteria.

§1002.138 If the employee receives a retroactive upgrade in the characterization of service, will that entitle him or her to claim back wages and benefits lost as of the date of separation from service?

No. A retroactive upgrade allows the employee to obtain reinstatement with the former employer, provided the employee otherwise meets the Act's eligibility criteria. Back pay and other benefits such as pension plan credits attributable to the time period between discharge and the retroactive upgrade are not required to be restored by the employer in this situation.

Employer Statutory Defenses

§1002.139 Are there any circumstances in which the preservice employer is excused from its obligation to reemploy the employee following a period of uniformed service? What statutory defenses are available to the employer in an action or proceeding for reemployment benefits?

(a) Even if the employee is otherwise eligible for reemployment benefits, the employer is not required to reemploy him or her if the employer establishes that its circumstances have so changed as to make reemployment impossible or unreasonable. For example, an employer may be excused from reemploying the employee where there has been an intervening reduction in force that would have included that employee. The employer may not, however, refuse to reemploy the employee on the basis that another employee was hired to fill the reemployment position during the employee's absence, even if reemployment might require the termination of that replacement employee;

(b) Even if the employee is otherwise eligible for reemployment benefits, the employer is not required to reemploy him or her if it establishes that assisting the employee in becoming qualified for reemployment would impose an undue hardship, as defined in Sec. 1002.5(n) and discussed in Sec. 1002.198, on the employer; or,

(c) Even if the employee is otherwise eligible for reemployment benefits, the employer is not required to reemploy him or her if it establishes that the employment position vacated by the employee in order to perform service in the uniformed services was for a brief, nonrecurrent period and there was no reasonable expectation that the employment would continue indefinitely or for a significant period.

(d) The employer defenses included in this section are affirmative ones, and the employer carries the burden to prove by a preponderance of the evidence that any one or more of these defenses is applicable.

Subpart D—Rights, Benefits, and Obligations of Persons Absent from Employment Due to Service in the Uniformed Services

Furlough and Leave of Absence

§1002.149 What is the employee's status with his or her civilian employer while performing service in the uniformed services?

During a period of service in the uniformed services, the employee is deemed to be on furlough or leave of absence from the civilian employer. In this status, the employee is entitled to the non-seniority rights and benefits generally provided by the employer to other employees with similar seniority, status, and pay that are on furlough or leave of absence. Entitlement to these non-seniority rights and benefits is not dependent on how the employer characterizes the employee's status during a period of service. For example, if the employer characterizes the employee as "terminated" during the period of uniformed service, this characterization cannot be used to avoid USERRA's requirement that the employee be deemed on furlough or leave of absence, and therefore entitled to the non-seniority rights and benefits generally provided to employees on furlough or leave of absence.

§1002.150 Which non-seniority rights and benefits is the employee entitled to during a period of service?

(a) The non-seniority rights and benefits to which an employee is entitled during a period of service are those that the employer provides to similarly situated employees by an employment contract, agreement, policy, practice, or plan in effect at the employee's workplace. These rights and benefits include those in effect at the beginning of the employee's employment and those established after employment began. They also include those rights and benefits that become effective during the employee's period of service and that are provided to similarly situated employees on furlough or leave of absence.

(b) If the non-seniority benefits to which employees on furlough or leave of absence are entitled vary according to the type of leave, the employee must be given the most favorable treatment accorded to any comparable form of leave when he or she performs service in the uniformed services. In order to determine whether any two types of leave are comparable, the duration of the leave may be the most significant factor to compare. For instance, a two-day funeral leave will not be "comparable" to an extended leave for service in the uniformed service. In addition to comparing the duration of the absences, other factors such as the purpose of the leave and the ability of the employee to choose when to take the leave should also be considered.

(c) As a general matter, accrual of vacation leave is considered to be a non-seniority benefit that must be provided by an employer to an employee on a military leave of absence only if the employer provides that benefit to similarly situated employees on comparable leaves of absence.

§1002.151 If the employer provides full or partial pay to the employee while he or she is on military leave, is the employer required to also provide the non-seniority rights and benefits ordinarily granted to similarly situated employees on furlough or leave of absence?

Yes. If the employer provides additional benefits such as full or partial pay when the employee performs service, the employer is not excused from providing other rights and benefits to which the employee is entitled under the Act.

§1002.152 If employment is interrupted by a period of service in the uniformed services, are there any circumstances under which the employee is not entitled to the non-seniority rights and benefits ordinarily granted to similarly situated employees on furlough or leave of absence?

If employment is interrupted by a period of service in the uniformed services and the employee knowingly provides written notice of intent not to return to the position of employment after service in the uniformed services, he or she is not entitled to those non-seniority rights and benefits. The employee's written notice does not waive entitlement to any other rights to which he or she is entitled under the Act, including the right to reemployment after service.

§1002.153 If employment is interrupted by a period of service in the uniformed services, is the employee permitted upon request to use accrued vacation, annual or similar leave with pay during the service? Can the employer require the employee to use accrued leave during a period of service?

(a) If employment is interrupted by a period of service, the employee must be permitted upon request to use any accrued vacation, annual, or similar leave with pay during the period of service, in order to continue his or her civilian pay. However, the employee is not entitled to use sick leave that accrued with the civilian employer during a period of service in the uniformed services, unless the employer allows employees to use sick leave for any reason, or allows other similarly situated employees on comparable furlough or leave of absence to use accrued paid sick leave. Sick leave is usually not comparable to annual or vacation leave; it is generally intended to provide income when the employee or a family member is ill and the employee is unable to work.

(b) The employer may not require the employee to use accrued vacation, annual, or similar leave during a period of service in the uniformed services.

Health Plan Coverage

§1002.163 What types of health plans are covered by USERRA?

(a) USERRA defines a health plan to include an insurance policy or contract, medical or hospital service agreement, membership or subscription contract, or arrangement under which the employee's health services are provided or the expenses of those services are paid.

(b) USERRA covers group health plans as defined in the Employee Retirement Income Security Act of 1974 (ERISA) at 29 U.S.C. 1191b(a). USERRA applies to group health plans that are subject to ERISA, and plans that are not subject to ERISA, such as those sponsored by State or local governments or religious organizations for their employees.

(c) USERRA covers multiemployer plans maintained pursuant to one or more collective bargaining agreements between employers and employee organizations. USERRA applies to multiemployer plans as they are defined in ERISA at 29 U.S.C. 1002(37). USERRA contains provisions that apply specifically to multiemployer plans in certain situations.

§1002.164 What health plan coverage must the employer provide for the employee under USERRA?

If the employee has coverage under a health plan in connection with his or her employment, the plan must permit the employee to elect to continue the coverage for a certain period of time as described below:

(a) When the employee is performing service in the uniformed services, he or she is entitled to continuing coverage for himself or herself (and dependents if the plan offers dependent coverage) under a health plan provided in connection with the employment. The plan must allow the employee to elect to continue coverage for a period of time that is the lesser of:

(1) The 24-month period beginning on the date on which the employee's absence for the purpose of performing service begins; or,

(2) The period beginning on the date on which the employee's absence for the purpose of performing service begins, and ending on the date on which he or she fails to return from service or apply for a position of employment as provided under sections 1002.115-123 of these regulations.

(b) USERRA does not require the employer to establish a health plan if there is no health plan coverage in connection with the employment, or, where there is a plan, to provide any particular type of coverage.

(c) USERRA does not require the employer to permit the employee to initiate new health plan coverage at the beginning of a period of service if he or she did not previously have such coverage.

§1002.165 How does the employee elect continuing health plan coverage?

USERRA does not specify requirements for electing continuing coverage. Health plan administrators may develop reasonable requirements addressing how continuing coverage may be elected, consistent with the terms of the plan and the Act's exceptions to the requirement that the employee give advance notice of service in the uniformed services. For example, the employee cannot be precluded from electing continuing health plan coverage under circumstances where it is impossible or unreasonable for him or her to make a timely election of coverage.

§1002.166 How much must the employee pay in order to continue health plan coverage?

(a) If the employee performs service in the uniformed service for fewer than 31 days, he or she cannot be required to pay more than the regular employee share, if any, for health plan coverage.

(b) If the employee performs service in the uniformed service for 31 or more days, he or she may be required to pay no more than 102% of the full premium under the plan, which represents the employer's share plus the employee's share, plus 2% for administrative costs.

(c) USERRA does not specify requirements for methods of paying for continuing coverage. Health plan administrators may develop reasonable procedures for payment, consistent with the terms of the plan.

§1002.167 What actions may a plan administrator take if the employee does not elect or pay for continuing coverage in a timely manner?

The actions a plan administrator may take regarding the provision or cancellation of an employee's continuing coverage depend on whether the employee is excused from the requirement to give advance notice, whether the plan has established reasonable rules for election of continuation coverage, and whether the plan has established reasonable rules for the payment for continuation coverage.

(a) No notice of service and no election of continuation coverage: If an employer provides employment-based health coverage to an employee who leaves employment for uniformed service without giving advance notice of service, the plan administrator may cancel the employee's health plan coverage upon the employee's departure from employment for uniformed service. However, in cases in which an employee's failure to give advance notice of service was excused under the statute because it was impossible, unreasonable, or precluded by military necessity, the plan administrator must reinstate the employee's health coverage retroactively upon his or her election to continue coverage and payment of all unpaid amounts due, and the employee must incur no administrative reinstatement costs. In order to qualify for an exception to the requirement of timely election of continuing health care, an employee must first be excused from giving notice of service under the statute.

(b) Notice of service but no election of continuing coverage: Plan administrators may develop reasonable requirements addressing how continuing coverage may be elected. Where health plans are also covered under the Consolidated Omnibus Budget Reconciliation Act of 1985, 26 U.S.C. 4980B (COBRA), it may be reasonable for a health plan administrator to adopt COBRA-compliant rules regarding election of continuing coverage, as long as those rules do not conflict with any provision of USERRA or this rule. If an employer provides employment-based health coverage to an employee who leaves employment for uniformed service for a period of service in excess of 30 days after having given advance notice of service but without making an election regarding continuing coverage, the plan administrator may cancel the employee's health plan coverage upon the employee's departure from employment for uniformed service, but must reinstate coverage without the imposition of administrative reinstatement costs under the following conditions:

(1) Plan administrators who have developed reasonable rules regarding the period within which an employee may elect continuing coverage must permit retroactive reinstatement of uninterrupted coverage to the date of departure if the employee elects continuing coverage and pays all unpaid amounts due within the periods established by the plan;

(2) In cases in which plan administrators have not developed rules regarding the period within which an employee may elect continuing coverage, the plan must permit retroactive reinstatement of uninterrupted coverage to the date of departure upon the employee's election and payment of all unpaid amounts at any time during the period established in section 1002.164(a).

(c) Election of continuation coverage without timely payment: Health plan administrators may adopt reasonable rules allowing cancellation of coverage if timely payment is not made. Where health plans are covered under COBRA, it may be reasonable for a health plan administrator to adopt COBRA-compliant rules regarding payment for continuing coverage, as long as those rules do not conflict with any provision of USERRA or this rule.

§1002.168 If the employee's coverage was terminated at the beginning of or during service, does his or her coverage have to be reinstated upon reemployment?

(a) If health plan coverage for the employee or a dependent was terminated by reason of service in the uniformed services, that coverage must be reinstated upon reemployment. An exclusion or waiting period may not be imposed in connection with the reinstatement of coverage upon reemployment, if an exclusion or waiting period would not have been imposed had coverage not been terminated by reason of such service.

(b) USERRA permits a health plan to impose an exclusion or waiting period as to illnesses or injuries determined by the Secretary of Veterans Affairs to have been incurred in, or aggravated during, performance of service in the uniformed services. The determination that the employee's illness or injury was incurred in, or aggravated during, the performance of service may only be made by the Secretary of Veterans Affairs or his or her representative. Other coverage, for injuries or illnesses that are not service-related (or for the employee's dependents, if he or she has dependent coverage), must be reinstated subject to paragraph (a) of this section.

§1002.169 Can the employee elect to delay reinstatement of health plan coverage until a date after the date he or she is reemployed?

USERRA requires the employer to reinstate health plan coverage upon request at reemployment. USERRA permits but does not require the employer to allow the employee to delay reinstatement of health plan coverage until a date that is later than the date of reemployment.

§1002.170 In a multiemployer health plan, how is liability allocated for employer contributions and benefits arising under USERRA's health plan provisions?

Liability under a multiemployer plan for employer contributions and benefits in connection with USERRA's health plan provisions must be allocated either as the plan sponsor provides, or, if the sponsor does not provide, to the employee's last employer before his or her service. If the last employer is no longer functional, liability for continuing coverage is allocated to the health plan.

§1002.171 How does the continuation of health plan benefits apply to a multiemployer plan that provides health plan coverage through a health benefits account system?

(a) Some employees receive health plan benefits provided pursuant to a multiemployer plan that utilizes a health benefits account system in which an employee accumulates prospective health benefit eligibility, also commonly referred to as "dollar bank," "credit bank," and "hour bank" plans. In such cases, where an employee with a positive health benefits account balance elects to continue the coverage, the employee may further elect either option below:

(1) The employee may expend his or her health account balance during an absence from employment due to service in the uniformed services in lieu of paying for the continuation of coverage as set out in Sec. 1002.166. If an employee's health account balance becomes depleted during the applicable period provided for in Sec. 1002.164(a), the employee must be permitted, at his or her option, to continue coverage pursuant to Sec. 1002.166. Upon reemployment, the plan must provide for immediate reinstatement of the employee as required by Sec. 1002.168, but may require the employee to pay the cost of the coverage until the employee earns the credits necessary to sustain continued coverage in the plan.

(2) The employee may pay for continuation coverage as set out in Sec. 1002.166, in order to maintain intact his or her account balance as of the beginning date of the absence from employment due to service in the uniformed services. This option permits the employee to resume usage of the account balance upon reemployment.

(b) Employers or plan administrators providing such plans should counsel employees of their options set out in this subsection.

SUBPART E—REEMPLOYMENT RIGHTS AND BENEFITS

Prompt Reemployment

§1002.180 When is an employee entitled to be reemployed by his or her civilian employer?

The employer must promptly reemploy the employee when he or she returns from a period of service if the employee meets the Act's eligibility criteria as described in Subpart C of these regulations.

§1002.181 How is "prompt reemployment" defined?

"Prompt reemployment" means as soon as practicable under the circumstances of each case. Absent unusual circumstances, reemployment must occur within two weeks of the employee's application for reemployment. For example, prompt reinstatement after a weekend National Guard duty generally means the next regularly scheduled working day. On the other hand, prompt reinstatement following several years of active duty may require more time, because the employer may have to reassign or give notice to another employee who occupied the returning employee's position.

Reemployment Position

§1002.191 What position is the employee entitled to upon reemployment?

As a general rule, the employee is entitled to reemployment in the job position that he or she would have attained with reasonable certainty if not for the absence due to uniformed service. This position is known as the escalator position. The principle behind the escalator position is that, if not for the period of uniformed service, the employee could have been promoted (or, alternatively, demoted, transferred, or laid off) due to intervening events. The escalator principle requires that the employee be reemployed in a position that reflects with reasonable certainty the pay, benefits, seniority, and other job perquisites, that he or she would have attained if not for the period of service. Depending upon the specific circumstances, the employer may have the option, or be required, to reemploy the employee in a position other than the escalator position.

§1002.192 How is the specific reemployment position determined?

In all cases, the starting point for determining the proper reemployment position is the escalator position, which is the job position that the employee would have attained if his or her continuous employment had not been interrupted due to uniformed service. Once this position is determined, the employer may have to consider several factors before determining the appropriate reemployment position in any particular case. Such factors may include the employee's length of service, qualifications, and disability, if any. The reemployment position may be either the escalator position; the pre-service position; a position comparable to the escalator or pre-service position; or, the nearest approximation to one of these positions.

§1002.193 Does the reemployment position include elements such as seniority, status, and rate of pay?

(a) Yes. The reemployment position includes the seniority, status, and rate of pay that an employee would ordinarily have attained in that position given his or her job history, including prospects for future earnings and advancement. The employer must determine the seniority rights, status, and rate of pay as though the employee had been continuously employed during the period of service. The seniority rights, status, and pay of an employment position include those established (or changed) by a collective bargaining agreement, employer policy, or employment practice. The sources of seniority rights, status, and pay include agreements, policies, and practices in effect at the beginning of the employee's service, and any changes that may have occurred during the period of service. In particular, the employee's status in the reemployment position could include opportunities for advancement, general working conditions, job location, shift assignment, rank, responsibility, and geographical location.

(b) If an opportunity for promotion, or eligibility for promotion, that the employee missed during service is based on a skills test or examination, then the employer should give him or her a reasonable amount of time to adjust to the employment position and then give a skills test or examination. No fixed amount of time for permitting adjustment to reemployment will be deemed reasonable in all cases. However, in determining a reasonable amount of time to permit an employee to adjust to reemployment before scheduling a makeup test or examination, an employer may take into account a variety of factors, including but not limited to the length of time the returning employee was absent from work, the level of difficulty of the test itself, the typical time necessary to prepare or study for the test, the duties and responsibilities of the reemployment position and the promotional position, and the nature and responsibilities of the service member while serving in the uniformed service. If the employee is successful on the makeup exam and, based on the results of that exam, there is a reasonable certainty that he or she would have been promoted, or made eligible for promotion, during the time that the employee served in the uniformed service, then the promotion or eligibility for promotion must be made effective as of the date it would have occurred had employment not been interrupted by uniformed service.

§1002.194 Can the application of the escalator principle result in adverse consequences when the employee is reemployed?

Yes. The Act does not prohibit lawful adverse job consequences that result from the employee's restoration on the seniority ladder. Depending on the circumstances, the escalator principle may cause an employee to be reemployed in a higher or lower position, laid off, or even terminated. For example, if an employee's seniority or job classification would have resulted in the employee being laid off during the period of service, and the layoff continued after the date of reemployment, reemployment would reinstate the employee to layoff status. Similarly, the status of the reemployment position requires the employer to assess what would have happened to such factors as the employee's opportunities for advancement, working conditions, job location, shift assignment, rank, responsibility, and geographical location, if he or she had remained continuously employed. The reemployment position may involve transfer to another shift or location, more or less strenuous working conditions, or changed opportunities for advancement, depending upon the application of the escalator principle.

§1002.195 What other factors can determine the reemployment position?

Once the employee's escalator position is determined, other factors may allow, or require, the employer to reemploy the employee in a position other than the escalator position. These factors, which are explained in Sec. Sec. 1002.196 through 1002.199, are:

(a) The length of the employee's most recent period of uniformed service;

(b) The employee's qualifications; and,

(c) Whether the employee has a disability incurred or aggravated during uniformed service.

§1002.196 What is the employee's reemployment position if the period of service was less than 91 days?

Following a period of service in the uniformed services of less than 91 days, the employee must be reemployed according to the following priority:

(a) The employee must be reemployed in the escalator position. He or she must be qualified to perform the duties of this position. The employer must make reasonable efforts to help the employee become qualified to perform the duties of this position.

(b) If the employee is not qualified to perform the duties of the escalator position after reasonable efforts by the employer, the employee must be reemployed in the position in which he or she was employed on the date that the period of service began. The employee must be qualified to perform the duties of this position. The employer must make reasonable efforts to help the employee become qualified to perform the duties of this position.

(c) If the employee is not qualified to perform the duties of the escalator position or the pre-service position, after reasonable efforts by the employer, he or she must be reemployed in any other position that is the nearest approximation first to the escalator position and then to the pre-service position. The employee must be qualified to perform the duties of this position. The employer must make reasonable efforts to help the employee become qualified to perform the duties of this position.

§1002.197 What is the reemployment position if the employee's period of service in the uniformed services was more than 90 days?

Following a period of service of more than 90 days, the employee must be reemployed according to the following priority:

(a) The employee must be reemployed in the escalator position or a position of like seniority, status, and pay. He or she must be qualified to perform the duties of this position. The employer must make reasonable efforts to help the employee become qualified to perform the duties of this position.

(b) If the employee is not qualified to perform the duties of the escalator position or a like position after reasonable efforts by the employer, the employee must be reemployed in the position in which he or she was employed on the date that the period of service began or in a position of like seniority, status, and pay. The employee must be qualified to perform the duties of this position. The employer must make reasonable efforts to help the employee become qualified to perform the duties of this position.

(c) If the employee is not qualified to perform the duties of the escalator position, the pre-service position, or a like position, after reasonable efforts by the employer, he or she must be reemployed in any other position that is the nearest approximation first to the escalator position and then to the pre-service position. The employee must be qualified to perform the duties of this position. The employer must make reasonable efforts to help the employee become qualified to perform the duties of this position.

§1002.198 What efforts must the employer make to help the employee become qualified for the reemployment position?

The employee must be qualified for the reemployment position. The employer must make reasonable efforts to help the employee become qualified to perform the duties of this position. The employer is not required to reemploy the employee on his or her return from service if he or she cannot, after reasonable efforts by the employer, qualify for the appropriate reemployment position.

(a)(1) "Qualified" means that the employee has the ability to perform the essential tasks of the position. The employee's inability to perform one or more non-essential tasks of a position does not make him or her unqualified.

(2) Whether a task is essential depends on several factors, and these factors include but are not limited to:

(i) The employer's judgment as to which functions are essential;

(ii) Written job descriptions developed before the hiring process begins;

(iii) The amount of time on the job spent performing the function;

(iv) The consequences of not requiring the individual to perform the function;

(v) The terms of a collective bargaining agreement;

(vi) The work experience of past incumbents in the job; and/or

(vii) The current work experience of incumbents in similar jobs.

(b) Only after the employer makes reasonable efforts, as defined in Sec. 1002.5(i), may it determine that the employee is not qualified for the reemployment position. These reasonable efforts must be made at no cost to the employee.

§1002.199 What priority must the employer follow if two or more returning employees are entitled to reemployment in the same position?

If two or more employees are entitled to reemployment in the same position and more than one employee has reported or applied for employment in that position, the employee who first left the position for uniformed service has the first priority on reemployment in that position. The remaining employee (or employees) is entitled to be reemployed in a position similar to that in which the employee would have been reemployed according to the rules that normally determine a reemployment position, as set out in Sec. 1002.196 and 1002.197.

Seniority Rights and Benefits

§1002.210 What seniority rights does an employee have when reemployed following a period of uniformed service?

The employee is entitled to the seniority and seniority-based rights and benefits that he or she had on the date the uniformed service began, plus any seniority and seniority-based rights and benefits that the employee would have attained if he or she had remained continuously employed. In determining entitlement to seniority and seniority-based rights and benefits, the period of absence from employment due to or necessitated by uniformed service is not considered a break in employment. The rights and benefits protected by USERRA upon reemployment include those provided by the employer and those required by statute. For example, under USERRA, a reemployed service member would be eligible for leave under the Family and Medical Leave Act of 1993, 29 U.S.C. 2601-2654 (FMLA), if the number of months and the number of hours of work for which the service member was employed by the civilian employer, together with the number of months and the number of hours of work for which the service member would have been employed by the civilian employer during the period of uniformed service, meet FMLA's eligibility requirements. In the event that a service member is denied FMLA leave for failing to satisfy the FMLA's hours of work requirement due to absence from employment necessitated by uniformed service, the service member may have a cause of action under USERRA but not under the FMLA.

§1002.211 Does USERRA require the employer to use a seniority system?

No. USERRA does not require the employer to adopt a formal seniority system. USERRA defines seniority as longevity in employment together with any employment benefits that accrue with, or are determined by, longevity in employment. In the absence of a formal seniority system, such as one established through collective bargaining, USERRA looks to the custom and practice in the place of employment to determine the employee's entitlement to any employment benefits that accrue with, or are determined by, longevity in employment.

§1002.212 How does a person know whether a particular right or benefit is a seniority-based right or benefit?

A seniority-based right or benefit is one that accrues with, or is determined by, longevity in employment. Generally, whether a right or benefit is seniority-based depends on three factors:

(a) Whether the right or benefit is a reward for length of service rather than a form of short-term compensation for work performed;

(b) Whether it is reasonably certain that the employee would have received the right or benefit if he or she had remained continuously employed during the period of service; and,

(c) Whether it is the employer's actual custom or practice to provide or withhold the right or benefit as a reward for length of service. Provisions of an employment contract or policies in the employee handbook are not controlling if the employer's actual custom or practice is different from what is written in the contract or handbook.

§1002.213 How can the employee demonstrate a reasonable certainty that he or she would have received the seniority right or benefit if he or she had remained continuously employed during the period of service?

A reasonable certainty is a high probability that the employee would have received the seniority or seniority-based right or benefit if he or she had been continuously employed. The employee does not have to establish that he or she would have received the benefit as an absolute certainty. The employee can demonstrate a reasonable certainty that he or she would have received the seniority right or benefit by showing that other employees with seniority similar to that which the employee would have had if he or she had remained continuously employed received the right or benefit. The employer cannot withhold the right or benefit based on an assumption that a series of unlikely events could have prevented the employee from gaining the right or benefit.

Disabled Employees

§1002.225 Is the employee entitled to any specific reemployment benefits if he or she has a disability that was incurred in, or aggravated during, the period of service?

Yes. A disabled service member is entitled, to the same extent as any other individual, to the escalator position he or she would have attained but for uniformed service. If the employee has a disability incurred in, or aggravated during, the period of service in the uniformed services, the employer must make reasonable efforts to accommodate that disability and to help the employee become qualified to perform the duties of his or her reemployment position. If the employee is not qualified for reemployment in the escalator position because of a disability after reasonable efforts by the employer to accommodate the disability and to help the employee to become qualified, the employee must be reemployed in a position according to the following priority. The employer must make reasonable efforts to accommodate the employee's disability and to help him or her to become qualified to perform the duties of one of these positions:

(a) A position that is equivalent in seniority, status, and pay to the escalator position; or,

(b) A position that is the nearest approximation to the equivalent position, consistent with the circumstances of the employee's case, in terms of seniority, status, and pay. A position that is the nearest approximation to the equivalent position may be a higher or lower position, depending on the circumstances.

§1002.226 If the employee has a disability that was incurred in, or aggravated during, the period of service, what efforts must the employer make to help him or her become qualified for the reemployment position?

(a) USERRA requires that the employee be qualified for the reemployment position regardless of any disability. The employer must make reasonable efforts to help the employee to become qualified to perform the duties of this position. The employer is not required to reemploy the employee on his or her return from service if he or she cannot, after reasonable efforts by the employer, qualify for the appropriate reemployment position.

(b) "Qualified" has the same meaning here as in §1002.198.

Rate of Pay

§1002.236 How is the employee's rate of pay determined when he or she returns from a period of service?

The employee's rate of pay is determined by applying the same escalator principles that are used to determine the reemployment position, as follows:

(a) If the employee is reemployed in the escalator position, the employer must compensate him or her at the rate of pay associated with the escalator position. The rate of pay must be determined by taking into account any pay increases, differentials, step increases, merit increases, or periodic increases that the employee would have attained with reasonable certainty had he or she remained continuously employed during the period of service. In addition, when considering whether merit or performance increases would have been attained with reasonable certainty, an employer may examine the returning employee's own work history, his or her history of merit increases, and the work and pay history of employees in the same or similar position. For example, if the employee missed a merit pay increase while performing service, but qualified for previous merit pay increases, then the rate of pay should include the merit pay increase that was missed. If the merit pay increase that the employee missed during service is based on a skills test or examination, then the employer should give the employee a reasonable amount of time to adjust to the reemployment position and then give him or her the skills test or examination. No fixed amount of time for permitting adjustment to reemployment will be deemed reasonable in all cases. However, in determining a reasonable amount of time to permit an employee to adjust to reemployment before scheduling a makeup test or examination, an employer may take into account a variety of factors, including but not limited to the length of time the returning employee was absent from work, the level of difficulty of the test itself, the typical time necessary to prepare or study for the test, the duties and responsibilities of the reemployment position and the promotional position, and the nature and responsibilities of the service member while serving in the uniformed service. The escalator principle also applies in the event a pay reduction occurred in the reemployment position during the period of service. Any pay adjustment must be made effective as of the date it would have occurred had the employee's employment not been interrupted by uniformed service.

(b) If the employee is reemployed in the pre-service position or another position, the employer must compensate him or her at the rate of pay associated with the position in which he or she is reemployed. As with the escalator position, the rate of pay must be determined by taking into account any pay increases, differentials, step increases, merit increases, or periodic increases that the employee would have attained with reasonable certainty had he or she remained continuously employed during the period of service.

Protection Against Discharge

§1002.247 Does USERRA provide the employee with protection against discharge?

Yes. If the employee's most recent period of service in the uniformed services was more than 30 days, he or she must not be discharged except for cause—

(a) For 180 days after the employee's date of reemployment if his or her most recent period of uniformed service was more than 30 days but less than 181 days; or,

(b) For one year after the date of reemployment if the employee's most recent period of uniformed service was more than 180 days.

§1002.248 What constitutes cause for discharge under USERRA?

The employee may be discharged for cause based either on conduct or, in some circumstances, because of the application of other legitimate nondiscriminatory reasons.

(a) In a discharge action based on conduct, the employer bears the burden of proving that it is reasonable to discharge the employee for the conduct in question, and that he or she had notice, which was express or can be fairly implied, that the conduct would constitute cause for discharge.

(b) If, based on the application of other legitimate nondiscriminatory reasons, the employee's job position is eliminated, or the employee is placed on layoff status, either of these situations would constitute cause for purposes of USERRA. The employer bears the burden of proving that the employee's job would have been eliminated or that he or she would have been laid off.

Pension Plan Benefits

§1002.259 How does USERRA protect an employee's pension benefits?

On reemployment, the employee is treated as not having a break in service with the employer or employers maintaining a pension plan, for purposes of participation, vesting and accrual of benefits, by reason of the period of absence from employment due to or necessitated by service in the uniformed services.

(a) Depending on the length of the employee's period of service, he or she is entitled to take from one to ninety days following service before reporting back to work or applying for reemployment (See § 1002.115). This period of time must be treated as continuous service with the employer for purposes of determining participation, vesting and accrual of pension benefits under the plan.

(b) If the employee is hospitalized for, or convalescing from, an illness or injury incurred in, or aggravated during, service, he or she is entitled to report to or submit an application for reemployment at the end of the time period necessary for him or her to recover from the illness or injury. This period, which may not exceed two years from the date the employee completed service, except in circumstances beyond his or her control, must be treated as continuous service with the employer for purposes of determining the participation, vesting and accrual of pension benefits under the plan.

§1002.260 What pension benefit plans are covered under USERRA?

(a) The Employee Retirement Income Security Act of 1974 (ERISA) defines an employee pension benefit plan as a plan that provides retirement income to employees, or defers employee income to a period extending to or beyond the termination of employment. Any such plan maintained by the employer or employers is covered under USERRA. USERRA also covers certain pension plans not covered by ERISA, such as those sponsored by a State, government entity, or church for its employees.

(b) USERRA does not cover pension benefits under the Federal Thrift Savings Plan; those benefits are covered under 5 U.S.C. 8432b.

§1002.261 Who is responsible for funding any plan obligation to provide the employee with pension benefits?

With the exception of multiemployer plans, which have separate rules discussed below, the employer is liable to the pension benefit plan to fund any obligation of the plan to provide benefits that are attributable to the employee's period of service. In the case of a defined contribution plan, once the employee is reemployed, the employer must allocate the amount of its make-up contribution for the employee, if any; his or her make-up employee contributions, if any; and his or her elective deferrals, if any; in the same manner and to the same extent that it allocates the amounts for other employees during the period of service. In the case of a defined benefit plan, the employee's accrued benefit will be increased for the period of service once he or she is reemployed and, if applicable, has repaid any amounts previously paid to him or her from the plan and made any employee contributions that may be required to be made under the plan.

§1002.262 When is the employer required to make the plan contribution that is attributable to the employee's period of uniformed service?

(a) The employer is not required to make its contribution until the employee is reemployed. For employer contributions to a plan in which the employee is not required or permitted to contribute, the employer must make the contribution attributable to the employee's period of service no later than ninety days after the date of reemployment, or when plan contributions are normally due for the year in which the service in the uniformed services was performed, whichever is later. If it is impossible or unreasonable for the employer to make the contribution within this time period, the employer must make the contribution as soon as practicable.

(b) If the employee is enrolled in a contributory plan he or she is allowed (but not required) to make up his or her missed contributions or elective deferrals. These makeup contributions or elective deferrals must be made during a time period starting with the date of reemployment and continuing for up to three times the length of the employee's immediate past period of uniformed service, with the repayment period not to exceed five years. Makeup contributions or elective deferrals may only be made during this period and while the employee is employed with the post-service employer.

(c) If the employee's plan is contributory and he or she does not make up his or her contributions or elective deferrals, he or she will not receive the employer match or the accrued benefit attributable to his or her contribution because the employer is required to make contributions that are contingent on or attributable to the employee's contributions or elective deferrals only to the extent that the employee makes up his or her payments to the plan. Any employer contributions that are contingent on or attributable to the employee's make-up contributions or elective deferrals must be made according to the plan's requirements for employer matching contributions.

(d) The employee is not required to make up the full amount of employee contributions or elective deferrals that he or she missed making during the period of service. If the employee does not make up all of the missed contributions or elective deferrals, his or her pension may be less than if he or she had done so.

(e) Any vested accrued benefit in the pension plan that the employee was entitled to prior to the period of uniformed service remains intact whether or not he or she chooses to be reemployed under the Act after leaving the uniformed service.

(f) An adjustment will be made to the amount of employee contributions or elective deferrals the employee will be able to make to the pension plan for any employee contributions or elective deferrals he or she actually made to the plan during the period of service.

§1002.263 Does the employee pay interest when he or she makes up missed contributions or elective deferrals?

No. The employee is not required or permitted to make up a missed contribution in an amount that exceeds the amount he or she would have been permitted or required to contribute had he or she remained continuously employed during the period of service.

§1002.264 Is the employee allowed to repay a previous distribution from a pension benefits plan upon being reemployed?

Yes. provided the plan is a defined benefit plan. If the employee received a distribution of all or part of the accrued benefit from a defined benefit plan in connection with his or her service in the uniformed services before he or she became reemployed, he or she must be allowed to repay the withdrawn amounts when he or she is reemployed. The amount the employee must repay includes any interest that would have accrued had the monies not been withdrawn. The employee must be allowed to repay these amounts during a time period starting with the date of reemployment and continuing for up to three times the length of the employee's immediate past period of uniformed service, with the repayment period not to exceed five years (or such longer time as may be agreed to between the employer and the employee), provided the employee is employed with the post-service employer during this period.

§1002.265 If the employee is reemployed with his or her pre-service employer, is the employee's pension benefit the same as if he or she had remained continuously employed?

The amount of the employee's pension benefit depends on the type of pension plan.

(a) In a non-contributory defined benefit plan, where the amount of the pension benefit is determined according to a specific formula, the employee's benefit will be the same as though he or she had remained continuously employed during the period of service.

(b) In a contributory defined benefit plan, the employee will need to make up contributions in order to have the same benefit as if he or she had remained continuously employed during the period of service.

(c) In a defined contribution plan, the benefit may not be the same as if the employee had remained continuously employed, even though the employee and the employer make up any contributions or elective deferrals attributable to the period of service, because the employee is not entitled to forfeitures and earnings or required to experience losses that accrued during the period or periods of service.

§1002.266 What are the obligations of a multiemployer pension benefit plan under USERRA?

A multiemployer pension benefit plan is one to which more than one employer is required to contribute, and which is maintained pursuant to one or more collective bargaining agreements between one or more employee organizations and more than one employer. The Act uses ERISA's definition of a multiemployer plan. In addition to the provisions of USERRA that apply to all pension benefit plans, there are provisions that apply specifically to multiemployer plans, as follows:

(a) The last employer that employed the employee before the period of service is responsible for making the employer contribution to the multiemployer plan, if the plan sponsor does not provide otherwise. If the last employer is no longer functional, the plan must nevertheless provide coverage to the employee.

(b) An employer that contributes to a multiemployer plan and that reemploys the employee pursuant to USERRA must provide written notice of reemployment to the plan administrator within 30 days after the date of reemployment. The returning service member should notify the reemploying employer that he or she has been reemployed pursuant to USERRA. The 30-day period within which the reemploying employer must provide written notice to the multiemployer plan pursuant to this subsection does not begin until the employer has knowledge that the employee was reemployed pursuant to USERRA.

(c) The employee is entitled to the same employer contribution whether he or she is reemployed by the pre-service employer or by a different employer contributing to the same multiemployer plan, provided that the pre-service employer and the post-service employer share a common means or practice of hiring the employee, such as common participation in a union hiring hall.

§1002.267 How is compensation during the period of service calculated in order to determine the employee's pension benefits, if benefits are based on compensation?

In many pension benefit plans, the employee's compensation determines the amount of his or her contribution or the retirement benefit to which he or she is entitled.

(a) Where the employee's rate of compensation must be calculated to determine pension entitlement, the calculation must be made using the rate of pay that the employee would have received but for the period of uniformed service.

(b)(1) Where the rate of pay the employee would have received is not reasonably certain, such as where compensation is based on commissions earned, the average rate of compensation during the 12-month period prior to the period of uniformed service must be used.

(2) Where the rate of pay the employee would have received is not reasonably certain and he or she was employed for less than 12 months prior to the period of uniformed service, the average rate of compensation must be derived from this shorter period of employment that preceded service.

Subpart F—Compliance Assistance, Enforcement and Remedies

Compliance Assistance

§1002.277 What assistance does the Department of Labor provide to employees and employers concerning employment, reemployment, or other rights and benefits under USERRA?

The Secretary, through the Veterans' Employment and Training Service (VETS), provides assistance to any person or entity with respect to employment and reemployment rights and benefits under USERRA. This assistance includes a wide range of compliance assistance outreach activities, such as responding to inquiries; conducting USERRA briefings and Webcasts; issuing news releases; and, maintaining the elaws USERRA Advisor (located athttp://www.dol.gov/elaws/userra.htm), the e-VETS Resource Advisor and other web-based materials (located at http://www.dol.gov/vets), which are designed to increase awareness of the Act among affected persons, the media, and the general public. In providing such assistance, VETS may request the assistance of other Federal and State agencies, and utilize the assistance of volunteers.

Investigation and Referral

§1002.288 How does an individual file a USERRA complaint?

If an individual is claiming entitlement to employment rights or benefits or reemployment rights or benefits and alleges that an employer has failed or refused, or is about to fail or refuse, to comply with the Act, the individual may file a complaint with VETS or initiate a private legal action in a court of law (see Sec. 1002.303). A complaint may be filed with VETS either in writing, using VETS Form 1010, or electronically, using VETS Form e1010 (instructions and the forms can be accessed at http://www.dol.gov/elaws/vets/userra/1010.asp). A complaint must include the name and address of the employer, a summary of the basis for the complaint, and a request for relief.

§1002.289 How will VETS investigate a USERRA complaint?

(a) In carrying out any investigation, VETS has, at all reasonable times, reasonable access to and the right to interview persons with information relevant to the investigation.

VETS also has reasonable access to, for purposes of examination, the right to copy and receive any documents of any person or employer that VETS considers relevant to the investigation.

(b) VETS may require by subpoena the attendance and testimony of witnesses and the production of documents relating to any matter under investigation. In case of disobedience of or resistance to the subpoena, the Attorney General may, at VETS' request, apply to any district court of the United States in whose jurisdiction such disobedience or resistance occurs for an order enforcing the subpoena. The district courts of the United States have jurisdiction to order compliance with the subpoena, and to punish failure to obey a subpoena as a contempt of court. This paragraph does not authorize VETS to seek issuance of a subpoena to the legislative or judicial branches of the United States.

§1002.290 Does VETS have the authority to order compliance with USERRA?

No.

If VETS determines as a result of an investigation that the complaint is meritorious, VETS attempts to resolve the complaint by making reasonable efforts to ensure that any persons or entities named in the complaint comply with the Act. If VETS' efforts do not resolve the complaint, VETS notifies the person who submitted the complaint of:

(a) The results of the investigation; and,

(b) The person's right to proceed under the enforcement of rights provisions in 38 U.S.C. 4323 (against a State or private employer), or 38 U.S.C. 4324 (against a Federal executive agency or the Office of Personnel Management (OPM)).

§1002.291 What actions may an individual take if the complaint is not resolved by VETS?

If an individual receives a notification from VETS of an unsuccessful effort to resolve his or her complaint relating to a State or private employer, the individual may request that VETS refer the complaint to the Attorney General.

§1002.292 What can the Attorney General do about the complaint?

(a) If the Attorney General is reasonably satisfied that an individual's complaint is meritorious, meaning that he or she is entitled to the rights or benefits sought, the Attorney General may appear on his or her behalf and act as the individual's attorney, and initiate a legal action to obtain appropriate relief.

(b) If the Attorney General determines that the individual's complaint does not have merit, the Attorney General may decline to represent him or her.

Enforcement of Rights and Benefits Against a State or Private Employer

§1002.303 Is an individual required to file his or her complaint with VETS?

No. The individual may initiate a private action for relief against a State or private employer if he or she decides not to apply to VETS for assistance.

§1002.304 If an individual files a complaint with VETS and VETS' efforts do not resolve the complaint, can the individual pursue the claim on his or her own?

Yes. If VETS notifies an individual that it is unable to resolve the complaint, the individual may pursue the claim on his or her own. The individual may choose to be represented by private counsel whether or not the Attorney General decides to represent him or her as to the complaint.

§1002.305 What court has jurisdiction in an action against a State or private employer?

(a) If an action is brought against a State or private employer by the Attorney General, the district courts of the United States have jurisdiction over the action. If the action is brought against a State by the Attorney General, it must be brought in the name of the United States as the plaintiff in the action.

(b) If an action is brought against a State by a person, the action may be brought in a State court of competent jurisdiction according to the laws of the State.

(c) If an action is brought against a private employer or a political subdivision of a State by a person, the district courts of the United States have jurisdiction over the action.

(d) An action brought against a State Adjutant General, as an employer of a civilian National Guard technician, is considered an action against a State for purposes of determining which court has jurisdiction.

§1002.306 Is a National Guard civilian technician considered a State or Federal employee for purposes of USERRA?

A National Guard civilian technician is considered a State employee for USERRA purposes, although he or she is considered a Federal employee for most other purposes.

§1002.307 What is the proper venue in an action against a State or private employer?

(a) If an action is brought by the Attorney General against a State, the action may proceed in the United States district court for any district in which the State exercises any authority or carries out any function.

(b) If an action is brought against a private employer, or a political subdivision of a State, the action may proceed in the United States district court for any district in which the employer maintains a place of business.

§1002.308 Who has legal standing to bring an action under USERRA?

An action may be brought only by the United States or by the person, or representative of a person, claiming rights or benefits under the Act. An employer, prospective employer or other similar entity may not bring an action under the Act.

§1002.309 Who is a necessary party in an action under USERRA?

In an action under USERRA only an employer or a potential employer, as the case may be, is a necessary party respondent. In some circumstances, such as where terms in a collective bargaining agreement need to be interpreted, the court may allow an interested party to intervene in the action.

§1002.310 How are fees and court costs charged or taxed in an action under USERRA?

No.fees or court costs may be charged or taxed against an individual if he or she is claiming rights under the Act. If the individual obtains private counsel for any action or proceeding to enforce a provision of the Act, and prevails, the court may award reasonable attorney fees, expert witness fees, and other litigation expenses.

§1002.311 Is there a statute of limitations in an action under USERRA?

USERRA does not have a statute of limitations, and it expressly precludes the application of any State statute of limitations. At least one court, however, has held that the four-year general Federal statute of limitations, 28 U.S.C. 1658, applies to actions under USERRA. Rogers v. City of San Antonio, 2003 WL 1566502 (W.D. Texas), reversed on other grounds, 392 F.3d 758 (5th Cir. 2004). But see Akhdary v. City of Chattanooga, 2002 WL 32060140 (E.D. Tenn.). In addition, if an individual unreasonably delays asserting his or her rights, and that unreasonable delay causes prejudice to the employer, the courts have recognized the availability of the equitable doctrine of laches to bar a claim under USERRA. Accordingly, individuals asserting rights under USERRA should determine whether the issue of the applicability of the Federal statute of limitations has been resolved and, in any event, act promptly to preserve their rights under USERRA.

§1002.312 What remedies may be awarded for a violation of USERRA?

In any action or proceeding the court may award relief as follows:

(a) The court may require the employer to comply with the provisions of the Act;

(b) The court may require the employer to compensate the individual for any loss of wages or benefits suffered by reason of the employer's failure to comply with the Act;

(c) The court may require the employer to pay the individual an amount equal to the amount of lost wages and benefits as liquidated damages, if the court determines that the employer's failure to comply with the Act was willful. A violation shall be considered to be willful if the employer either knew or showed reckless disregard for whether its conduct was prohibited by the Act.

(d) Any wages, benefits, or liquidated damages awarded under paragraphs (b) and (c) of this section are in addition to, and must not diminish, any of the other rights and benefits provided by USERRA (such as, for example, the right to be employed or reemployed by the employer).

§1002.313 Are there special damages provisions that apply to actions initiated in the name of the United States?

Yes. In an action brought in the name of the United States, for which the relief includes compensation for lost wages, benefits, or liquidated damages, the compensation must be held in a special deposit account and must be paid, on order of the Attorney General, directly to the person. If the compensation is not paid to the individual because of the Federal Government's inability to do so within a period of three years, the compensation must be converted into the Treasury of the United States as miscellaneous receipts.

§1002.314 May a court use its equity powers in an action or proceeding under the Act?

Yes. A court may use its full equity powers, including the issuance of temporary or permanent injunctions, temporary restraining orders, and contempt orders, to vindicate the rights or benefits guaranteed under the Act.

[Editor's Note: The following does not appear on the DOL Web site but was added to the regulations by 73 Fed. Reg. 63632 (Oct. 27, 2008), updating 70 FR 75316 (Dec. 19, 2005).

Appendix to Part 1002—Notice of Your Rights Under USERRA

Pursuant to 38 U.S.C. 4334(a), each employer shall provide to persons entitled to rights and benefits under USERRA a notice of the rights, benefits, and obligations of such persons and such employers under USERRA. The requirement for the provision of notice under this section may be met by posting the following notice where employers customarily place notices for employees. Posting one of the original notices published in 70 FR 75316 (Dec. 19, 2005) will also satisfy this requirement. The following text is provided by the Secretary of Labor to employers pursuant to 38 U.S.C. 4334(b). Text A is appropriate for use by employers in the private sector and for State government employers. Text B is appropriate for use by Federal Executive Agencies.

Text for Use by All Employers

Your Rights Under USERRA

A. *The Uniformed Services Employment and Reemployment Rights Act*

USERRA protects the job rights of individuals who voluntarily or involuntarily leave employment positions to undertake military service or certain types of service in the National Disaster Medical System. USERRA also prohibits employers from discriminating against past and present members of the uniformed services, and applicants to the uniformed services.

B. *Reemployment Rights*

You have the right to be reemployed in your civilian job if you leave that job to perform service in the uniformed service and:

- You ensure that your employer receives advance written or verbal notice of your service;
- You have five years or less of cumulative service in the uniformed services while with that particular employer;

- You return to work or apply for reemployment in a timely manner after conclusion of service; and

- You have not been separated from service with a disqualifying discharge or under other than honorable conditions.

If you are eligible to be reemployed, you must be restored to the job and benefits you would have attained if you had not been absent due to military service or, in some cases, a comparable job.

C. Right To Be Free From Discrimination and Retaliation

If you:

- Are a past or present member of the uniformed service;

- Have applied for membership in the uniformed service; or

- Are obligated to serve in the uniformed service;

then an employer may not deny you

- Initial employment;

- Reemployment;

- Retention in employment;

- Promotion; or

- Any benefit of employment.

because of this status.

In addition, an employer may not retaliate against anyone assisting in the enforcement of USERRA rights, including testifying or making a statement in connection with a proceeding under USERRA, even if that person has no service connection.

D. Health Insurance Protection

- If you leave your job to perform military service, you have the right to elect to continue your existing employer-based health plan coverage for you and your dependents for up to 24 months while in the military.
- Even if you don't elect to continue coverage during your military service, you have the right to be reinstated in your employer's health plan when you are reemployed, generally without any waiting periods or exclusions (e.g., pre-existing condition exclusions) except for service-connected illnesses or injuries.

E. Enforcement

- The U.S. Department of Labor, Veterans' Employment and Training Service (VETS) is authorized to investigate and resolve complaints of USERRA violations.

For assistance in filing a complaint, or for any other information on USERRA, contact VETS at 1-866-4-USA-DOL or visit its Web site at http://www.dol.gov/vets. An interactive online USERRA Advisor can be viewed at http://www.dol.gov/elaws/userra.htm.

- If you file a complaint with VETS and VETS is unable to resolve it, you may request that your case be referred to the Department of Justice or the Office of Special Counsel, as applicable, for representation.
- You may also bypass the VETS process and bring a civil action against an employer for violations of USERRA.

The rights listed here may vary depending on the circumstances. The text of this notice was prepared by VETS, and may be viewed on the Internet at this address: http://www.dol.gov/vets/programs/userra/poster.htm.

Federal law requires employers to notify employees of their rights under USERRA, and employers may meet this requirement by displaying the text of this notice where they customarily place notices for employees. U.S. Department of Labor, Veterans' Employment and Training Service, 1-866-487-2365.

EEOC EMPLOYERS GUIDE

[Editor's Note: This document is posted on the EEOC Web site at http://eeoc.gov/facts/veterans-disabilities-employers.html.]

VETERANS WITH SERVICE-CONNECTED DISABILITIES AND THE AMERICANS WITH DISABILITIES ACT (ADA): A GUIDE FOR EMPLOYERS

NOTICE CONCERNING THE AMERICANS WITH DISABILITIES ACT AMENDMENTS ACT OF 2008

The Americans with Disabilities Act (ADA) Amendments Act of 2008 was signed into law on September 25, 2008 and becomes effective January 1, 2009. Because this law makes several significant changes, including changes to the definition of the term "disability," the EEOC will be evaluating the impact of these changes on this document and other publications. See the *list of specific changes to the ADA* made by the ADA Amendments Act.

INTRODUCTION

Each year, thousands of military personnel stationed around the world leave active duty and seek to return to jobs they held before entering the service or look to find their first, or new, civilian jobs. According to government statistics, between October 2001 and February, 2008, more

than 30,000[1] veterans returned home with service-connected disabilities (e.g., amputations, burns, post traumatic
stress disorder (PTSD), and traumatic brain injuries).[2]

At least two federal laws provide important protections
for veterans with disabilities. The Uniformed Services Employment and Reemployment Rights Act (USERRA), which
is enforced by the U.S. Department of Labor (DOL), sets
forth the requirements for reemploying veterans with and
without service-connected disabilities. Title I of the Americans with Disabilities Act (ADA), which the U.S. Equal Employment Opportunity Commission (EEOC) enforces, prohibits private and state and local government employers
with 15 or more employees from discriminating against individuals on the basis of disability. Title I of the ADA also
generally requires covered employers to make reasonable
accommodations—changes in the workplace or in the way
things are usually done that provide individuals with disabilities equal employment opportunities. Section 501 of the
Rehabilitation Act applies the same standards of non-discrimination and reasonable accommodation as the ADA to
Federal Executive Branch agencies and the United States
Postal Service.

This guide briefly explains how protections for veterans with service-connected disabilities differ under
USERRA and the ADA, and then describes how the ADA in
particular applies to recruiting, hiring, and accommodating
veterans with service-connected disabilities.[3]

1.　How does USERRA differ from the ADA?

USERRA prohibits employers from discriminating
against employees or applicants for employment on the basis of their military status or military obligations. It also protects the reemployment rights of those who leave their civilian jobs (whether voluntarily or involuntarily) to serve in
the uniformed services, including the U.S. Reserve forces

and state, District of Columbia, and territory (e.g., Guam) National Guards.

Both USERRA and the ADA include reasonable accommodation obligations; however, USERRA requires employers to go further than the ADA by making reasonable efforts to assist a veteran who is returning to employment **in becoming qualified for a job.** The employer must help the veteran become qualified to perform the duties of the position whether or not the veteran has a service-connected disability requiring reasonable accommodation. This could include providing training or retraining for the position. *See* 38 U.S. Code §4313; 20 C.F.R. §§ 1002.198, 1002.225 -.226. Additionally, reasonable accommodations may be available under USERRA for individuals whose service-connected disabilities may not necessarily meet the ADA's definition of "disability." USERRA also applies to all employers, regardless of size. Information on the reemployment rights of uniformed service personnel can be found on DOL's website at www.dol.gov/vets.

Title I of the ADA prohibits employers from discriminating against qualified individuals with disabilities with respect to hiring, promotion, termination, and other terms, conditions, and privileges of employment. The ADA also prohibits disability-based harassment and provides that, absent undue hardship ("significant difficulty or expense"), applicants and employees with disabilities are entitled to reasonable accommodation. Reasonable accommodations under the ADA range from job-restructuring (e.g., shifting marginal—or minor—functions that an employee is unable to perform because of a disability to other employees) to reassignment of an employee with a disability to a vacant position, where the employee's disability prevents performance of the current position or where providing reasonable accommodation in the current position would result in undue hardship. (*See* Question 7.) Where providing a particular accommodation would result in undue hardship, an employer must consider whether another accommodation would not. Under the ADA, an individual may request a reasonable accommodation any time during the application process or during employment. Additionally, the obligation under the ADA to make a reasonable accommodation is ongoing, meaning that an employer may need to provide an additional or different accommodation from one that it is already providing (e.g., when the nature of a disability or a job changes). Documents explaining Title I of the ADA can be found on EEOC's website at www.eeoc.gov.

2. Is a veteran with a service-connected disability automatically protected by the ADA?

No. A veteran must meet the ADA's definition of disability. The ADA defines an "individual with a disability" as a person who (1) has a physical or mental impairment that substantially limits one or more major life activities; (2) has a record of such an impairment; or (3) is regarded as having such an impairment. This definition of disability may differ from the definition used in other laws. For example, the term "disabled veteran" means an individual who has served on active duty in the armed forces, was honorably discharged, and has a service-connected disability, or is receiving compensation, disability retirement benefits, or pension because of a public statute administered by the Department of Veterans Affairs or a military department. *See* 5 U.S.C.A. § 2108. Nevertheless, many veterans who were wounded or became ill while on active duty meet both the definition of "disabled veteran" and the ADA's definition of "individual with a disability."

Under the ADA, an individual with a disability also must be "qualified" for the job the individual has or wants. To be qualified, an individual with a disability must meet the employer's requirements for the job (such as education, training, skills, or licenses) and must be able to perform the job's essential or fundamental duties, with or without reasonable accommodation.

3. *May an employer ask if an applicant is a "disabled veteran" if it is seeking to hire someone with a service-connected disability?*

Yes. Although employers generally may not ask for medical information from applicants prior to making a job offer, they may do so for affirmative action purposes. *See* EEOC Enforcement Guidance: Preeemployment Disability-Related Questions and Medical Examinations Under the Americans with Disabilities Act of 1990 (1995) at www.eeoc.gov/policy/docs/preemp.html. An employer, therefore, may ask applicants to voluntarily self-identify as individuals with disabilities or "disabled veterans" when the employer is:

- undertaking affirmative action because of a federal, state, or local law (including a veterans' preference law) that requires affirmative action for individuals with disabilities; or,

- voluntarily using the information to benefit individuals with disabilities, including veterans with service-connected disabilities.

An employer also may ask organizations that help find employment for veterans with service-connected disabilities whether they have suitable applicants for particular jobs and may access websites on which veterans with service-connected disabilities post resumes or otherwise express interest in employment.

4. *What steps should an employer take if it asks an applicant to self-identify as a "disabled veteran" for affirmative action purposes?*

If an employer invites applicants to voluntarily self-identify, the employer must indicate clearly and conspicuously on any written questionnaire used for this purpose, or state clearly (if no written questionnaire is used), that:

- the information requested is intended for use solely in connection with its affirmative action obligations or its voluntary affirmative action efforts; and

- the specific information is being requested on a voluntary basis, it will be kept confidential in accordance with the ADA, that refusal to provide it will not subject the employee to any adverse treatment, and that it will be used only in accordance with the ADA.

Information collected for affirmative action purposes must be kept separate from the application to ensure that confidentiality is maintained.

5. *May an employer give preference in hiring to a veteran with a service-connected disability over other applicants?*

Yes. The ADA prohibits discrimination "against a qualified individual with a disability because of the disability of such individual." However, the law neither prohibits nor requires affirmative action on behalf of individuals with disabilities. An employer, therefore, may–but is not required to–hire a qualified individual with a disability (including a veteran with a service-connected disability) over a qualified applicant without a disability.

Specific rules and regulations govern the hiring of veterans by federal employers. Federal agencies are allowed to use "special hiring authorities" to hire individuals with disabilities outside the normal competitive hiring process, and sometimes are even required to give preferential treatment to veterans, including disabled veterans, in making hiring, promotion, or other employment decisions. *See* the U.S. Office of Personnel Management's question-and-answer guide on "Excepted Service—Appointment of Persons with Disabilities and Career and Career-Conditional Appointments" at www.opm.gov/disability/appointment_disabilities.asp and OPM's "Vet Guide" at www.opm.gov/veterans/html/

vetguide.asp; *see also* OPM's Disabled Veterans Affirmative Action Program at www.opm.gov/veterans/dvaap.asp.

Even where employers do not specifically recruit veterans with service-connected disabilities, they should make sure that there is nothing in a job announcement or on an application form that would discourage anyone with a disability from applying. For example, employers should not state in vacancy announcements that applicants must be in "excellent health" or describe how a function must be performed (e.g., "requires extended standing") but, instead, should describe the actual function to be performed (e.g., "requires frequent lifting of objects that weigh more than 50 pounds"). Often, reasonable accommodations are available that will allow a veteran with a service-connected disability to perform a function in a way that is different from the way it is typically done.

6. *What are some specific steps employers may take to recruit and hire veterans with service-connected disabilities?*

In addition to measures specifically applicable to federal employers (see Question 5), there are a number of steps that any employer may take to recruit and hire veterans with service-connected disabilities, such as:

- stating on a job advertisement or vacancy announcement that it is an equal opportunity employer and that individuals with disabilities, including "disabled veterans" or veterans with service-connected disabilities, are encouraged to apply"

- ensuring that on-line job announcements, recruiting information, and application processes are accessible to individuals with disabilities, including applicants who have service-connected disabilities

- making written recruiting materials, such as application forms and brochures, available in alternate formats (e.g., Braille, large print, etc.), or assisting veterans with disabilities in completing application materials when necessary

- sending vacancy announcements to, and asking for referrals from, government, community, military organizations, and One Stop Career Centers that train and/or support veterans with service-connected disabilities

- posting advertisements and vacancy announcements in publications for veterans

- attending job fairs and using online resume databases that connect job-seeking veterans with civilian employers

- surveying other employers to learn about their successful outreach efforts

7. *What types of reasonable accommodations may veterans with service-connected disabilities need for the application process or during employment?*

While not all veterans with service-connected disabilities will need an accommodation or require the same accommodation, some may need one or more of the following to apply for or perform a job:

- written materials in accessible formats, such as large print, Braille, or on computer disk

- recruitment fairs, interviews, tests, and training held in accessible locations

- modified equipment or devices (e.g., assistive technology that would allow a blind person to use a computer or someone who is deaf or hard of hearing to use a telephone; a glare guard for a computer monitor used by a person with a traumatic brain injury; a one-handed keyboard for a person missing an arm or hand)

- physical modifications to the workplace (e.g., recon-figuring a workspace, including adjusting the height of a desk or shelves for a person in a wheelchair)
- permission to work from home
- leave for treatment, recuperation, or training related to their disability
- modified or part-time work schedules
- a job coach who could assist an employee who initially has some difficulty learning or remembering job tasks
- reassignment to a vacant position where a disability prevents performance of the employee's current job, or where accommodating the employee in the current job would result in undue hardship

8. *How does an employer know when a veteran with a service-connected disability needs an accommodation?*

Usually, the process of providing a reasonable accommodation will begin with a request from the individual with a service-connected disability. A family member, friend, health professional, rehabilitation counselor, or other representative also may request a reasonable accommodation on the veteran's behalf. The request does not have to mention the ADA or use the term "reasonable accommodation" and simply can be an oral or written statement indicating that the individual needs an adjustment or change in the application process or at work for a reason related to a medical condition. A request for reasonable accommodation is the first step in an informal interactive process between the individual and the employer.

The process will involve determining whether the veteran requesting a reasonable accommodation has a disability (where this is not obvious or already known) and identifying accommodation solutions. Employers should ask the particular veteran requesting accommodation because of disability what is needed to do the job. There also are extensive public and private resources to help employers identify reasonable accommodations for employees with particular disabilities. For example, the website for the Job Accommodation Network (JAN) provides a practical guide for employers on reasonable accommodation, as well as information about accommodations for specific disabilities, including one on "Accommodating Service Members and Veterans with PTSD." *See* JAN's website at www.jan.wvu.edu.

9. *May an employer ask a veteran with a service-connected disability whether a reasonable accommodation is needed if none has been requested?*

Sometimes. During the application process, an employer may explain what the hiring process involves (e.g., an interview, timed written test, or job demonstration) and ask all applicants whether they will need a reasonable accommodation to participate in any part of the process. In addition, if an employer reasonably believes that a veteran with an obvious service-connected disability (e.g., a veteran who is blind or missing a limb) who is applying for a particular job will need a reasonable accommodation to do that job, the employer may ask whether an accommodation is needed and, if so, what type. Once a veteran with a service-connected disability has started working, an employer may ask whether an accommodation is needed when it reasonably appears that the person is experiencing workplace problems because of a medical condition.

Because many veterans may not view their service-related injuries as disabilities, they may not ask, or know that they are entitled to ask, for a reasonable accommodation. As a result, it may be critical for the employer to initiate a conversation with a veteran who is experiencing problems to determine an appropriate accommodation. Working together, the employer and veteran should identify what the veteran cannot do and then discuss ways to address any identified performance issue(s).

10. Where can employers find out more about employing veterans with service-connected disabilities?

This guide includes a list of public and private organizations that can assist employers who want to recruit and hire veterans with service-connected disabilities, or who have more questions about their obligations under USERRA and the ADA. It also includes resources on reasonable accommodation.

RESOURCES

Laws Protecting Veterans with Service-Connected Disabilities

*ADA
Equal Employment Opportunity Commission (EEOC)
www.eeoc.gov/ada/adadocs.html

EEOC's website provides enforcement guidances and other policy documents on the ADA.

USERRA
The Department of Labor (DOL)
www.dol.gov/vets

DOL, through the Veterans' Employment and Training Service, provides information for employers on USERRA, including a resource guide and fact sheet.

Recruiting

President's National Hire Veterans Committee—Hire Vets First
www.hirevetsfirst.gov

This comprehensive career website is designed to help employers find qualified veterans, as well as help veterans to make the most of a national network of employment resources.

One Stop Career Centers
www.hirevetsfirst.gov/onestop_emp.asp; Careeronestop, www.servicelocator.org

The One Stop Career Centers serve the needs of those looking for jobs and employers seeking employees. They assist businesses with recruitment, training, and retention of skilled workers. There are nearly 2,000 One Stop Career Centers nationwide.

Employer Assistance and Recruiting Network (EARN)
www.earnworks.com, 1-866-EARN NOW (327-6669)

Funded by the U.S. Department of Labor's Office of Disability Employment Policy (ODEP), EARN is a national toll-free and electronic information referral service to assist employers in locating and recruiting qualified individuals with disabilities who are seeking jobs.

*Occupational Information Network (O*NET) Online*
www.online.onetcenter.org

Through the Department of Labor, employers may access a comprehensive database that helps align military skills, knowledge, and training with workplace needs. Information on reasonable accommodation also is available.

Vocational Rehabilitation

www.va.gov

The U.S. Department of Veterans Affairs supports a nation-wide employment training program for veterans with service-related injuries. There are 56 regional offices which administer this program.

State Veteran Employment Services

www.dol.gov/vets/aboutvets/contacts/main.htm

The U.S. Department of Labor (DOL), through its Veterans Employment Training Service (VETS), helps support a network of local employment service professionals dedicated to assisting veterans with service-related injuries in locating and securing employment.

Veteran Service Organizations (VSOs)

www1.va.gov/vso/

Many of the national VSOs, such as Disabled American Veterans, AMVETS, Paralyzed Veterans Association, and Blinded Veterans Association, offer employment-related services to veterans with service-related injuries in various localities and can be an excellent resource for locating job seekers.

Reasonable Accommodation

EEOC Enforcement Guidance: Reasonable Accommodation and Undue Hardship Under the ADA (2002)

www.eeoc.gov/policy/docs/accommodation.html

This extensive guidance clarifies the rights and responsibilities of employers and individuals with disabilities regarding reasonable accommodation and undue hardship and provides practical examples of the types of accommodations that may be needed to enable a person with a disability to be considered for a position, perform the essential functions of a job, or enjoy the equal benefits and privileges of employment.

Job Accommodation Network (JAN)
www.jan.wvu.edu

JAN provides a variety of resources for employers seeking to hire employees with disabilities. JAN also provides lists of possible accommodations based on specific disabilities as well as links to various other accommodation providers.

Department of Defense Computer/Electronic Accommodations Program (CAP)
www.tricare.mil/cap

CAP provides assistive technology and services to individuals with disabilities, federal managers, supervisors, and IT professionals.

EEOC Veterans Guide

[*Editor's Note:* This document is intended for use by veterans. It is posted on the EEOC website at http://eeoc.gov/facts/veterans-disabilities.html.]

VETERANS WITH SERVICE-CONNECTED DISABILITIES IN THE WORKPLACE AND THE AMERICANS WITH DISABILITIES ACT (ADA)

NOTICE CONCERNING THE AMERICANS WITH DISABILITIES ACT AMENDMENTS ACT OF 2008

The Americans with Disabilities Act (ADA) Amendments Act of 2008 was signed into law on September 25, 2008 and becomes effective January 1, 2009. Because this law makes several significant changes, including changes to the definition of the term "disability," the EEOC will be evaluating the impact of these changes on this document and other publications. See the *list of specific changes to the ADA* made by the ADA Amendments Act.

INTRODUCTION

According to government statistics, between October 2001 and February, 2008, more than 30,000veterans serving in Iraq, Afghanistan, and surrounding duty stations have been wounded in action.[1] Many of them have lost a hand or limb or been severely burned or blinded. Others have been diagnosed with hearing loss, post traumatic stress disorder (PTSD), traumatic brain injuries (TBIs), and other service-connected disabilities.[2] Despite their injuries, many veterans who leave active duty are able to work.

This guide answers questions that veterans with service-connected disabilities may have about the protections they are entitled to when they seek to return to their former jobs or look to find their first, or new, civilian jobs. It also explains changes or adjustments that veterans may need, because of their injuries, to apply for, or perform, a job, or to enjoy equal access to the workplace. Finally, this guide includes resources on where veterans can find more information about the employment rights of individuals with disabilities.

1. *Are there any laws that protect veterans with service-connected disabilities?*

Yes. At least two federal laws provide important protections for veterans with disabilities. **The Uniformed Services Employment and Reemployment Rights Act (USERRA) has requirements for reemploying veterans with and without service-connected disabilities. The U.S. Department of Labor (DOL) enforces USERRA**. In addition, Title I of the **Americans with Disabilities Act (ADA)** prohibits private and state and local government employers with 15 or more employees from discriminating against individuals on the basis of disability. Title I of the ADA also generally requires covered employers to make reasonable accommodations— changes in the workplace or in the way things are usually done that provide individuals with disabilities equal employment opportunities. The U.S. Equal Employment Opportunity Commission (EEOC) enforces Title I of the ADA. Finally, Section 501 of the Rehabilitation Act applies the same standards of non-discrimination and reasonable accommodation as the ADA to Federal Executive Branch agencies and the United States Postal Service.

2. How does USERRA differ from the ADA?

USERRA prohibits employers from discriminating against employees or applicants for employment on the basis of their military status or military obligations. It also protects the reemployment rights of those who leave their civilian jobs (whether voluntarily or involuntarily) to serve in the uniformed services, including the U.S. Reserve forces and state, District of Columbia, and territory (e.g., Guam) National Guards.

Both USERRA and the ADA include reasonable accommodation obligations; however, USERRA requires employers to go further than the ADA by making reasonable efforts to assist a veteran who is returning to employment **in becoming qualified for a job**. The employer must help the veteran become qualified to perform the duties of the position whether or not the veteran has a service-connected disability requiring reasonable accommodation. This could include providing training or retraining for the position. See 38 U.S. Code §4313; 20 C.F.R. §§ 1002.198, 1002.225 -.226. Additionally, reasonable accommodations may be available under USERRA for individuals whose service-connected disabilities may not necessarily meet the ADA's definition of "disability." USERRA also applies to all employers, regardless of size. Information on the reemployment rights of uniformed service personnel can be found on DOL's website at www.dol.gov/vets.

Title I of the ADA prohibits employers from discriminating against qualified individuals with disabilities with respect to hiring, promotion, termination, and other terms, conditions, and privileges of employment. The ADA also prohibits disability-based harassment and provides that, absent undue hardship (significant difficulty or expense to the employer), applicants and employees with disabilities are entitled to reasonable accommodation to apply for jobs, to perform their jobs, and to enjoy equal benefits and privileges of employment (e.g., access to the parts of an employer's facility available to all employees and access to employer-sponsored training and social events). Under the ADA, an individual may ask for a reasonable accommodation at any time during the application process or during employment. It is best to request a reasonable accommodation as soon as possible after recognizing that one is needed. Additionally, an employer may have to provide someone who has been given one type of reasonable accommodation with a different or additional one (e.g., if the nature of the disability or the job changes, or if another type of accommodation becomes available). Documents explaining Title I of the ADA can be found on EEOC's website at www.eeoc.gov.

3. *I was severely injured during active duty but don't think of myself as "disabled." How do I know if I am protected by the ADA?*

You are protected if you meet the ADA's definition of disability. The ADA defines an **"individual with a disability"** as a person who (1) has a physical or mental impairment that substantially limits one or more major life activities (e.g., hearing, seeing, speaking, sitting, standing, walking, concentrating, or performing manual tasks); (2) has a record of such an impairment (i.e. was substantially limited in the past, such as prior to undergoing rehabilitation); or (3) is regarded, or treated by an employer, as having a substantially limiting impairment, even if no substantial limitation exists.

The ADA covers more than just individuals who were born with disabilities. It also covers individuals who use wheelchairs, were blinded, or became deaf because of an accident or injury and individuals who are diagnosed with medical conditions such as traumatic brain injury, major depression, and PTSD at any point in their lives.

The ADA does not require that someone be completely unable to work or perform other major life activities. In fact, the law recognizes that many people with physical or mental impairments are capable of working and protects them from discrimination that results from employer misperceptions or from the failure to make what are often simple workplace modifications.

4. *I have been found to have a service-connected disability for purposes of receiving benefits related to my military service. Does this mean I am covered by the ADA?*

It depends. The definition of "disability" under the ADA may differ from the definition used in other laws. For example, you may be considered a "disabled veteran" if you served on active duty in the armed forces, were honorably discharged, and have a service-connected disability, or are receiving compensation, disability retirement benefits, or pension because of a public statute administered by the Department of Veterans Affairs or a military department. See 5 U.S.C.A. § 2108. It is possible that you may be a "disabled veteran" but not covered under the ADA. For example, if you receive benefits based on a 10% disability rating for service-connected tinnitus (which causes ringing in the ear), but are not substantially limited in hearing or some other major life activity, do not have a record of a substantial limitation, and are not treated by an employer as if you are substantially limited, then you do not have a disability under the ADA. However, it is certainly possible that you will meet both the definition of "disabled veteran" and the ADA's definition of "individual with a disability." For example, if you have a complete loss of vision due to a combat-related injury, you are a "disabled veteran" entitled to military benefits and also an individual with a disability under the ADA.

5. *Is an employer required to hire me over other applicants because I have a service-connected disability?*

In most cases, no. The ADA prohibits discrimination "against a qualified individual with a disability because of the disability of such individual." This means that if you are qualified for a job, an employer cannot refuse to hire you because you have a disability or because you may need a reasonable accommodation to perform the job. You are considered qualified under the ADA if you are able to meet the employer's requirements for the job, such as education, training, employment experience, skills, or licenses and are able to perform the job's essential or fundamental duties with or without reasonable accommodation. Even if you are qualified for a job, however, an employer may choose another applicant without a disability because that individual is better qualified.

Though it is not **required** to do so, an employer may **decide** to give a veteran with a service-connected disability a preference in hiring. In fact, federal agencies may use specific rules and regulations, called "special hiring authorities," to hire individuals with disabilities outside the normal competitive hiring process, and sometimes may even be required to give preferential treatment to veterans, including disabled veterans, in making hiring, promotion, or other employment decisions. See the U.S. Office of Personnel Management's question-and-answer guide on "Excepted Service—Appointment of Persons with Disabilities and Career and Career-Conditional Appointments" at www.opm.gov/disability/appointment_disabilities.asp and OPM's "Vet Guide" at www.opm.gov/veterans/html/vetguide.asp; see also OPM's Disabled Veterans Affirmative Action Program at www.opm.gov/veterans/dvaap.asp. :hf

6. *During a job interview, may an employer ask about my missing arm, why I am in a wheelchair, or how I sustained any other injury I may have?*

No. Even if your disability is obvious, an employer cannot ask questions about when, where, or how you were injured. However, where it seems likely that you will need a reasonable accommodation to do the job, an employer may ask you if an accommodation is needed and, if so, what type. In addition, an employer may ask you to describe or demonstrate how you would perform the job with or without an accommodation. For example, if the job requires that you lift objects weighing up to 50 pounds, the employer can ask whether you will need assistance or ask you to demonstrate how you will perform this task. Similarly, if you voluntarily reveal that you have an injury or illness and an employer reasonably believes that you will need an accommodation, it may ask what accommodation you need to do the job.

7. *Do I have to disclose an injury or illness that is not obvious during an interview or indicate on a job application that I have a disability?*

No. The ADA does not require you to disclose that you have any medical condition on a job application or during an interview, unless you will need a reasonable accommodation to participate in the application process, such as more time to take a test or permission to provide oral instead of written responses. Some veterans with service-connected disabilities, however, may choose to disclose that they have medical conditions, such as PTSD or a TBI, because of symptoms they experience or because they will need a reasonable accommodation at work. Once an employer makes a job offer, it may ask you questions about your medical conditions, and perhaps even require you to take a medical examination, as long as it requires everyone else in the same job to answer the same questions and/or take the same medical examination before starting work.

8. *Some applications ask me to indicate whether I am a "disabled veteran." Is this legal?*

Yes. if the information is being requested for **affirmative action purposes**. See EEOC Enforcement Guidance: Preemployment Disability-Related Questions and Medical Examinations Under the Americans with Disabilities Act of 1990 (1995) at www.eeoc.gov/policy/docs/preemp.html. An employer may ask applicants to voluntarily self-identify as individuals with disabilities or "disabled veterans" when the employer is: (1) undertaking affirmative action because of a federal, state, or local law (including a veterans' preference law) that requires affirmative action for individuals with disabilities; or (2) voluntarily using the information to benefit individuals with disabilities, including veterans with service-connected disabilities.

If an employer invites you to voluntarily self-identify as a disabled veteran, it must clearly inform you in writing (or orally, if no written questionnaire is used) that: (1) the information is being requested as part of the employer's affirmative action program; (2) providing the information is voluntary; (3) failure to provide it will not subject you to any adverse treatment; and (4) the information will be kept confidential and only used in a way that complies with the ADA.

9. *What types of reasonable accommodations may I want to request for the application process or on the job?*

The following are examples of types of accommodations that may be needed for the application process or while on the job:

- written materials in accessible formats, such as large print, Braille, or on computer disk

- extra time to complete a test for a person who has difficulty concentrating or has a learning disability or traumatic brain injury
- recruitment fairs, interviews, tests, and training held in accessible locations
- modified equipment or devices (e.g., assistive technology that would allow a blind person to use a computer or someone who is deaf or hard of hearing to use a telephone; a glare guard for a computer monitor used by a person with a TBI; a one-handed keyboard for a person missing an arm or hand)
- physical modifications to the workplace (e.g., reconfiguring a workspace, including adjusting the height of a desk or shelves for a person in a wheelchair)
- permission to work from home
- leave for treatment, recuperation, or training related to the disability
- modified or part-time work schedules
- a job coach who could assist an employee who initially has some difficulty learning or remembering job tasks
- reassignment to a vacant position where a disability prevents performance of an employee's current position or where any reasonable accommodation in the current position would result in undue hardship (i.e., significant difficulty or expense)

10. How do I ask for a reasonable accommodation?

You simply have to indicate—orally or in writing—that you need an adjustment or change in the application process or at work for a reason related to a medical condition. For example, if you have a vision loss and cannot read standard print, you would need to inform the employer that you need the application materials in some other format (e.g., large print or on computer disk) or read to you. You do not have to mention the ADA or use the term "reasonable accommodation." The request also can be made by someone acting on your behalf, such as a family member, rehabilitation counselor, health professional, or other representative.

11. What happens after I request a reasonable accommodation?

A request for reasonable accommodation is the first step in an informal interactive process between you and the employer.

The process will involve determining whether you have a disability as defined by the ADA (where this is not obvious or already known) and identifying accommodation solutions. An employer also may ask if you know what accommodation you need that will help you apply for or do the job. There are extensive public and private resources to help identify reasonable accommodations for applicants and employees with particular disabilities. For example, the website for the Job Accommodation Network (JAN) provides a practical guide for individuals with disabilities on requesting and discussing reasonable accommodations and on finding the right job. See JAN's website at www.jan.wvu.edu/portals/individuals.htm.

12. I am not sure whether I will need a reasonable accommodation. If I don't ask for one before I start working, can I still ask for one later?

Yes. You can request an accommodation at any time during the application process or when you start working even if you did not ask for one when applying for a job or after receiving a job offer. Generally, you should request an accommodation when you know that there is a workplace barrier that is preventing you from competing for or performing a job or having equal access to the benefits of employment. As a practical matter, it is better to request a reasonable accommodation before your job performance suffers.

13. Where can I find more information on USERRA and the ADA?

This guide includes resources on where to find information on your employment rights under both laws and provides a list of public and private organizations that can assist veterans with service-connected disabilities who are seeking employment. It also includes resources on reasonable accommodation.

RESOURCES

Laws Protecting Veterans with Service-Connected Disabilities

ADA
Equal Employment Opportunity Commission (EEOC)

www.eeoc.gov/ada/adadocs.html
EEOC's website provides enforcement guidances and other policy documents on the ADA, as well as information on how to file a charge of discrimination under any of the statutes EEOC enforces.

USERRA
The Department of Labor (DOL)
www.dol.gov/vets

DOL, through the Veterans' Employment and Training Service, provides information on USERRA, including a resource guide and fact sheet.

Employer Support of the Guard and Reserve (ESGR)
www.esgr.net

ESGR is a unit in the Department of the Defense, established to promote cooperation and understanding between Reserve component members and their civilian employers. ESGR has more than 900 volunteers who help employers and employees understand what USERRA requires.

Locating and Securing Employment

President's National Hire Veterans Committee—Hire Vets First
www.hirevetsfirst.gov

This comprehensive career website is designed to help employers find qualified veterans, as well as help veterans to make the most of a national network of employment resources.

One Stop Career Centers
www.hirevetsfirst.gov/onestop_emp.asp; Careeronestop, www.servicelocator.org

The One Stop Career Centers serve the needs of those looking for jobs and employers seeking employees. They assist businesses with recruitment, training, and retention of skilled workers. There are nearly 2,000 One Stop Career Centers nationwide.

Vocational Rehabilitation
www.vba.va.gov/bln/vre
www.vetsuccess.gov/cominghome

The U.S. Department of Veterans Affairs, through its regional offices, supports nationwide employment training programs for veterans with service-related injuries.

State Veteran Employment Services
www.dol.gov/vets/aboutvets/contacts/main.htm

The U.S. Department of Labor (DOL), through its Veterans Employment Training Service (VETS), helps support a network of local employment service representatives dedicated to assisting veterans with service-related injuries in locating and securing employment.

Veteran Service Organizations (VSOs)
www1.va.gov/vso/

Many of the national VSOs, such as Disabled American Veterans, AMVETS, Paralyzed Veterans Association, and Blinded Veterans Association, offer employment-related services to veterans with service-related injuries in various localities.

Reasonable Accommodation

EEOC Enforcement Guidance: Reasonable Accommodation and Undue Hardship Under the ADA (2002)
www.eeoc.gov/policy/docs/accommodation.html

This extensive guidance clarifies the rights and responsibilities of employers and individuals with disabilities regarding reasonable accommodation and undue hardship and provides practical examples of the types of accommodations that may be needed to enable a person with a disability to be considered for a position, perform the essential functions of a job, or enjoy the equal benefits and privileges of employment.

Job Accommodation Network (JAN)
www.jan.wvu.edu

JAN provides a variety of resources for employers and individuals with disabilities. JAN also provides lists of possible accommodations based on specific disabilities as well as links to various other accommodation providers.

Department of Defense Computer/Electronic Accommodations Program (CAP)
www.tricare.mil/cap

CAP provides assistive technology and services to individuals with disabilities, federal managers, supervisors, and IT professionals.

SUMMARY OF STATE LAWS CONCERNING MILITARY LEAVE/REEMPLOYMENT RIGHTS[1]

---

[1]Reprinted by permission from BNA's *Individual Employment Rights (State Laws)*, copyright © 2009 The Bureau of National Affairs, Inc., Arlington, VA.

ALABAMA

The state statute provides leave rights for active members of the Alabama National Guard and reserve components of the U.S. Armed Forces, regardless of who employs them. Coverage is extended to members of the state guard or naval militia who are called, drafted, or ordered into the service of the U.S. (*Ala. Code § 31–2–13, as amended by 1995 Ala. Acts 256*)

[*Note:* The law specifies that officers and employees of private businesses or industries are covered, but this application has been declared unconstitutional (*White v. Assoc. Indus.*, 373 So. 2d 616 (Ala. 1979)). In upholding the constitutionality of jury duty leave, the court distinguished the *White* decision (see *Juneman Elec. Inc. v. Cross*, 414 So. 2d 108 (*Ala. Civ. App. 1982*))].

Alaska

Summary: Alaska employers must grant leave to employees called to active state military service and must re-instate them following discharge.

Coverage: Private employees who are members of the organized militia called to active state service are covered.

Reemployment Rights: Private employees must be reinstated to the former position or a comparable position, at the pay, seniority, and benefit level the employee would have had without the leave of absence. The employee must report for work at the beginning of the work day following the last calendar day necessary for travel from the site of service to the employee's worksite. Failure to report subjects employee to discipline for unexcused absence from work.

If the employee is disabled because of active state military service and cannot perform the duties of the former position, the employer must offer another available, vacant position which most closely approximates the pay and benefits of the employee's former position for which the employee is qualified. Reemployment rights are lost if not requested within 30 days of receiving a physician's release to return to work.

Remedies/Penalties: An employer that tries to deter employees from enlisting in the National Guard or Naval Militia is guilty of a misdemeanor and subject to a fine of up to $100.

Employees who are not re-instated may bring an action in Superior Court within two years after the claim arises.
(*Alaska Stat. § 26.05.075, as enacted by 1990 Alaska Sess. Laws 77*)

ARIZONA

Coverage: Employers must permit employees who are National Guard members to take leave for active service or for attending military camps, maneuvers, formations, or armory drills.

National Guard members are entitled to military leave without loss of time or efficiency rating. Leave is available for all days on which employees are on training duty, or attend camps, maneuvers, formations, or drills under orders with any branch, reserve, or auxiliary of the U.S. armed forces. They shall not be charged for military leave on days that they are not scheduled to work. Leave may not exceed 30 days in two consecutive years.

Effect of Leave on Benefits: Seniority is not lost while an employee is on National Guard duty.

Employees do not lose time or efficiency rating for any day spent on military leave. Time spent on military leave is not deducted from the employee's paid vacation time. However, employers need not consider the period of absence as a period of work performed in determining eligibility for vacation and vacation pay.

Re-Employment Rights: National Guard members have the right to be restored to their former position upon return from leave. If an employee would be entitled by virtue of seniority to a higher position, the employee must be given that position.

Penalties: Violations of the military leave law constitute a Class 3 misdemeanor.
(*Ariz. Rev. Stat. § 26–168, as amended by 2002 Ariz. Sess. Laws 219*)

ARKANSAS

Summary: Private-sector employees have a right to obtain and hold employment without discrimination on the basis of military service.

Coverage: Full-time and part-time employees of private-sector employers who employ five or more employees in the state in each of 20 or more calendar weeks in the current or preceding year before a cause of action arises. Exceptions—Employees of religious organizations and entities.

Retaliation Prohibited: It is unlawful to coerce, intimidate, threaten, or interfere with employees who are exercising rights granted to them on the basis of military service. It is unlawful to retaliate or discriminate against a person who in good faith opposes any unlawful act based on an employee's military service, or who made a claim, testified, assisted, or participated in any investigation or hearing regarding any such alleged unlawful act.

Definitions: Military service means current honorable service or honorably discharged from service within six months from the date of the alleged discrimination in any active or reserve component of the U.S. armed forces.

Interpretation: In construing the rights provided by this law, courts may look for guidance from the federal Uniformed Services Employment and Reemployment Rights Act, 38 U.S.C. § 4301 et seq.

Defenses: An employer may avoid liability if it can establish that the adverse employment action was taken on the basis of legitimate, nondiscriminatory factors and not reasons related to military service.

Penalties/Remedies: An employee who suffers discrimination or retaliation from an employer may bring a civil action in a circuit court of competent jurisdiction. *Statute of limitations:* An action must be brought within one year after the alleged violation, except that if the service member is deployed for active duty at any time during the one-year period, then an action may be brought within one year after the end of the mobilization.

The employee may seek back pay and interest in addition to an injunction against the discriminatory practice, re-employment, reasonable attorneys' fees, and court costs.

Total compensatory and punitive damage awards can range from $15,000 to $300,000 depending on the number of employees in each of 20 or more calendar weeks in the current or preceding calendar year before the cause of action arises.

(*Ark. Code Ann. §§ 12–62–801 to 12–62–808, as enacted by 2005 Ark. Acts 920*)

CALIFORNIA

Summary: California employers must grant employees leave to participate in National Guard and military reserve training and must re-employ workers called up for military duty.

Coverage: Employers of employees who are members of the National Guard, the U.S. reserve corps, the naval militia, and the state military reserve are covered.

Amount of Leave: Employers are required to provide employees who are members of the National Guard, the U.S. reserve corps, and the naval militia up to 17 days per year of unpaid leave for training.

Employers must grant members of the state military reserve up to 15 days per year of unpaid leave for training.

Pay and Benefits: Employers cannot restrict or terminate "collateral" benefits of employees who are temporarily incapacitated following military service. An incapacity is temporary if it lasts 52 weeks or less. Collateral benefits include health insurance continued at employee's expense, life insurance, disability insurance, and seniority status.

Re-Employment Rights: Employers must reinstate full-time employees to their former position or to a position of similar seniority, status, and pay if the employees have been honorably discharged and have applied for reinstatement within 40 days of discharge. They cannot discharge these employees without cause within one year of reinstatement.

Employers must reinstate part-time employees who are honorably discharged and apply for reinstatement within five days of discharge from military service.

Discrimination Prohibition: Employers cannot discriminate against any officer, warrant officer, or enlisted member of the military or naval forces because of that membership. No member of the military forces can be prejudiced or injured by any employer with respect to that member's employment, position, or status, or be denied or disqualified for employment because of that membership.

Employers cannot discharge employees because of their performance of any ordered military duty or training, or because they are officers, warrant officers, or enlisted members of the military or naval forces. Employers also cannot hinder or prevent employees from performing any military service or from attending any military training.

Employers cannot dissuade, prevent or stop employees from enlisting or accepting a warrant or commission in the California National Guard or Naval Militia.

Spousal Leave Rights: Covered employers must grant up to 10 days of unpaid leave to employees whose spouses are members of the armed forces (including the national guard and reserves) and on leave during a period of military conflict. Only employers who have at least 25 employees are covered. To be eligible, an employee must work an average of 20 or more hours per week.

An employee must notify his or her employer within two business days of receiving official notice of a spouse's leave from deployment of the intent to take spousal leave. Documentation certifying that the employee's spouse will be on leave during the time of the leave of absence is required.

Employers cannot retaliate against employees for requesting or taking a spousal leave of absence.

Enforcement: The Superior Court in the county where an employer resides enforces the law. The employee may be represented by the district attorney of the county, or city prosecutor of the city, in which the employer maintains a business. No fees or court costs are required to be paid by the employee seeking benefits.

Penalties/Remedies: Employers that fail to re-employ workers following military service can be compelled to comply by court order and can be required to compensate employees for any loss of wages or benefits.

Employers that violate the discrimination prohibition are guilty of a misdemeanor and are liable for actual damages plus reasonable attorneys' fees.

(*Cal. Mil. & Vet. Code §§ 394, as amended by 2007 Cal. Stat. 358, effective Oct. 9, 2007; 394.5, as enacted by 1957 Cal. Stat. 469; 395.06, as amended by 2008 Cal. Stat. 243; 395.10, as enacted by 2007 Cal. Stat. 361, effective Oct. 9, 2007*)

COLORADO

Summary: Colorado employers must grant employees leave to participate in National Guard and military reserve training, and must re-employ workers called up for military duty.

Coverage: Employers of members of the National Guard, the U.S. reserve corps, and civil air patrol are covered.

Amount of Leave: Employers must grant 15 days of leave per year for military training for National Guard or Reserve members. Civil air patrol members are entitled to up to 15 days of leave annually. There is no time limit on leave for state active duty.

Pay and Benefits: Employers are not required to pay employees on military leave.

Employees do not lose vacation and sick leave, and keep any bonuses, advancement, or other benefits while on military leave.

Retaliation Prohibited: Employers are prohibited from retaliating against any member of the civil air patrol because of such membership and shall not hinder or prevent a member from performing during any civil air patrol mission for which a member is entitled to leave.

Re-Employment Rights: Employees must be reinstated to the position they left, or a similar job with the same status, pay, and seniority.

Penalties/Remedies: Employers are subject to civil suits for failure to grant military leave and re-employment rights.

Employers that violate any provisions of the military leave law are guilty of a misdemeanor and can be fined up to $5,000.

A civil air patrol member may bring a civil action for damages and equitable relief. The court will award reasonable attorneys' fees and costs to the prevailing party.
(*Colo. Rev. Stat. §§ 28–1–103, 28–1–105, and 28–1–106, as enacted by 2008 Colo. Sess. Laws 174, effective Aug. 8, 2008; §§ 28–3–506, 28–3–609, 28–3–610, 28–3–610.5, 28–3–611, as amended by 2002 Colo. Sess. Laws 588, 589, 600, and 693*)

CONNECTICUT

All employees are entitled to a leave of absence from employment if necessary to attend military reserve or National Guard meetings or drills.

All employees are covered if engaged in civil preparedness activity or eligible for induction.

An employee on leave of absence to attend military reserve or National Guard meetings or drills is not subject to loss of vacation or holiday privileges. An employee may not be prejudiced by reason of absence to military service in promotion or continuation in employment, or in reemployment.

No employee may be discharged because of membership in any organization engaged in civil preparedness or because the individual is eligible for induction into the U.S. armed forces.

Any National Guard member ordered into active state service by the governor has all of the protections afforded to service members on federal active service by the Uniformed Services Employment and Reemployment Rights Act, 38 U.S.C. § 4301 et seq. and by the Servicemembers Civil Relief Act (except for the provisions pertaining to life insurance).
(*Conn. Gen. Stat. §§ 27–33a, as amended by 1999 Conn. Acts 139; 27–34a, as enacted by 2006 Conn. Acts 62; and § 28–17, as amended by 1973 Conn. Acts. 544*)

Delaware

Summary: Delaware employers must grant employees the same leave to participate in National Guard duty as required under federal law (see e.g., 38 U.S.C. § 4301 et seq.).

Amount of Leave: Employers must extend the same leave under state law as is required under federal law.

Pay and Benefits: Employers do not have to pay employees while the employees are on military leave.

Re-Employment Rights: Employers must extend the same re-employment rights under state law as under federal law.

Penalties/Remedies: Employers can be sued by employees in the Superior Court.

(*Del. Code Ann. tit. 20, § 905, as amended by 70 Del. Laws 186*)

District of Columbia

For active duty, inactive-duty training (as defined in 37 U.S.C. § 101), or to engage in field coast defense training (under 32 U.S.C. §§ 502 through 505) as reserve members of the armed forces or members of the National Guard, employees of the District of Columbia government are entitled to leave without loss of, or reduction in, pay, leave to which he or she would be otherwise entitled, and credit for service or a performance rating.

Military leave for those reasons must not exceed 15 calendar days per fiscal year and, to the extent that it is not used in a fiscal year, accumulates for use in the succeeding fiscal year until it totals 15 days at the beginning of a fiscal year. In the case of part-time employment, the rate at which leave accrues is a percentage of the rate prescribed above which is determined by dividing 40 into the number of hours in the regularly scheduled workweek of that employee during that fiscal year. The minimum charge for leave is one hour, and additional charges are in multiples thereof.

An employee who is a member of a reserve component of the armed forces (as described in 10 U.S.C. § 10101) or the National Guard (as described in 32 U.S.C. § 101) is entitled to leave without loss of, or reduction in, pay, leave to which he or she would be otherwise entitled, and credit for service or a performance rating, while providing military aid to enforce the law or for the purpose of providing assistance to civil authorities in the protection or saving of life or property, or the prevention of injury, under the following:

- federal service under 10 U.S.C. §§ 331, 332, 333, or 12406 or other provision of law, as applicable, or
- full-time military service for his or her state, the District of Columbia, the Commonwealth of Puerto Rico, or a territory of the United States.

Leave for these purposes must not exceed 22 workdays in a calendar year.

Upon the request of an employee, the period for which an employee is absent to perform service may be charged to the employee's accrued annual leave or to compensatory time available to the employee instead of being charged as leave to which the employee is entitled under the military leave law. The period of absence may not be charged to sick leave. An employee who is a member of the National Guard of the District of Columbia is entitled to leave without limitation and without loss in pay or time for each day of a parade or encampment ordered or authorized under title 49 of the District of Columbia Official Code. This provision covers each day of service in the National Guard, or a portion thereof, that an employee is ordered to perform by the Commanding General.

An amount (other than travel, transportation, or per diem allowance) received by an employee for military service as a member of the reserve or National Guard for a period for which he or she is entitled to military leave will be credited against the pay payable to the employee for the same period.

Family leave: In addition, an employee is entitled to not more than 3 days of leave without loss of or reduction in pay, leave, or service to make arrangements for or attend the funeral or memorial service for an immediate relative who died as a result of wound, disease or injury incurred while serving as a member of the armed forces in a combat zone.

(*D.C. Code § 1–612.03, as amended by D.C. Law 15-105 (Mar. 13, 2004)*)

FLORIDA

Summary: Employers are prohibited from discharging, reprimanding, or in any way penalizing members of the National Guard who are required to report for state active duty.

Discrimination Prohibited: Any person who seeks or holds an employment position may not be denied employment or retention in employment, or any promotion or advantage of employment, because of any obligation as a member of the military reserves.

Notification: After completing National Guard service, the employee must promptly notify the employer of the intent to return to work.

Re-Employment Rights: After returning from active state service, the employee is entitled to the seniority held at the time of departure, any additional seniority that the member would have attained if he or she had remained continuously employed, and the rights and benefits applicable to an employee with such seniority.

The employer is prohibited from requiring that the returning service member use accrued vacation, annual, compensatory, or similar leave to cover the time missed while on active duty. The employee is permitted to use voluntarily those types of leave hours accrued prior to leaving for active service.

Exceptions to Re-Employment: The employer is not required to re-employ a National Guard member if the employer's circumstances have so changed as to make re-employment impossible or unreasonable; re-employment would impose an undue hardship on the employer; the National Guard member's previous position was for a brief nonrecurrent period and was not reasonably expected to continue indefinitely or for a significant period of time; or the employer had legally sufficient cause to terminate the employee at the time he or she left for active state duty.

At-Will Employment Exception: The employee cannot be discharged from employment without cause for one year after the date of return to work.

Penalties: A National Guard member may bring a civil action against the employer. The adjutant general must certify the cause of action prior to the suit. If the employee prevails, the employer is liable for the greater of actual damages or $500, reasonable attorneys' fees, and costs.

The Florida state courts have concurrent jurisdiction for enforcement of federal laws protecting returning service members. The courts may levy a civil penalty of not more than $1,000 per violation against a person who violates the rights of members of the U.S. Armed Forces, the U.S. Reserve Forces, or the National Guard.

(*Fla. Stat. §§ 250.82, as amended by 2009 Fla. Laws ch. 122, effective July 1, 2009; 250.84, as amended by 2007 Fla. Laws ch. 5; 250.481, as amended by 2003 Fla. Laws ch. 68; and 250.482, as amended by 2009 Fla. Laws ch. 122, effective July 1, 2009*)

GEORGIA

Summary: An employee who has left a position, other than a temporary position, with an employer to perform military service must be restored to the same position or a position of like seniority, status, and pay, provided the individual:

- has received a certificate of completion of military duty;
- is still qualified to perform the duties of the job; and
- applies for re-employment within 90 days after the end of the military service (if employer is a private employer).

An individual who is discharged or suspended by an employer because of service in the organized militia, reserve component of the U.S. armed forces, or any state's national guard is entitled to reinstatement if the individual applies within 10 days of receiving the notice of discharge or suspension, or within 10 days of the end of active duty, if later.

Re-Employment Rights: A re-employed individual is considered to have been on furlough or leave of absence. re-employment must be without loss of seniority.

The employee is entitled to participate in insurance and other benefits in the same way as other employees returning from furlough or a leave of absence.

Re-employment rights also apply to any person who leaves employment temporarily to participate in assemblies or annual training, or to attend service schools. Application for re-employment must be made within 10 days of the end of the temporary performance of service. Only six months of service is permitted in any four-year period.

A re-employed individual may not be discharged without cause for one year after re-employment.

Remedies/Penalties: An employer who fails to comply with these re-employment provisions is subject to a court order to reinstate the employee, and pay for any loss of wages or benefits. The state attorney general may represent the claimant.
(*Ga. Code Ann. §§ 38–2–280, as last amended by 1995 Ga. Laws p. 730; 38–2–284, as enacted by 1993 Ga. Laws p. 1774*)

Relevant Cases: *Britt v. Ga. Power Co.*, 677 F. Supp. 1169, 127 LRRM 3192 (N.D. Ga. 1987).

HAWAII

Summary: National Guard members employed in the private sector are entitled to leave to fulfill National Guard duties.

Re-Employment Rights: Employees returning from National Guard service, if still qualified to perform their duties, must be restored to their original position or to a position of like seniority, status, and pay. If the returning employee is no longer qualified by reason of disability sustained during military service, but is still able to perform the duties of any other position, such person must be offered employment in that other position most similar to the original job unless the employer's circumstances have so changed as to make it impossible or unreasonable to do so.

Reinstated employees shall be treated as having been on furlough or leave of absence and must be re-employed:

- without loss of seniority;
- in such a manner as to provide the same status as they would have had but for taking the leave; and
- able to participate in insurance or other benefits programs in accordance with the employer's established rules and practices relating to employees on furlough or leave.

Reinstated employees may not be discharged without cause within one year after being re-employed.

Discrimination Prohibited: An employee may not be denied retention in employment or any promotion or other incident of advantage of employment because of National Guard obligations.

Remedies/Penalties: Violation of National Guard provisions is an unlawful discriminatory practice. The Civil Rights Commission may order appropriate affirmative action, such as reinstatement, or upgrading of employees, with or without back pay, or other remedies, including a requirement for reporting on the manner of compliance.

In any civil action brought under these provisions, the court may enjoin the employer from engaging in the discriminatory practice and order affirmative action as may be appropriate, including reinstatement, hiring, or upgrading of employees, with or without back pay, or any other equitable relief the court deems appropriate. Back pay liability does not accrue from a date more than two years prior to the filing of the complaint with the commission. In addition to any judgment awarded to the plaintiff or plaintiffs, the court may also order costs of fees of any nature and reasonable attorneys' fees to be paid by the defendant.

(*Haw. Rev. Stat. § 121–43, as amended by 1984 Haw. Sess. Laws 90;*

§§ 378–2, as amended by 2009 H.B. 31, effective July 1, 2009; and 378–5, as amended by 1989 Haw. Sess. Laws 386)

IDAHO

Employees who are members of the Idaho National Guard or national reserves may take up to 15 days in a calendar year to train with the U.S. armed forces. Such leave is considered as an absence without leave and within the discretion of the employer. The leave may be with or without pay.

The employees must be reinstated to their previous or similar positions with the same status, pay, and seniority if:

- the employee was not in a temporary position;
- the employee provided notice to the employer of the date of departure and date of return 90 days prior to date of departure;
- the employee provided evidence of satisfactory completion of the training immediately after it ended; and
- the employee is still qualified to perform the duties of the position.

The absence for military training does not affect the employee's right to receive normal vacation, sick leave, bonus, advancement, and other normal advantages of employment. Seniority continues to accrue during the absence.

Employers may be subject to an action at law for damages or equitable relief in district court by affected employees for failing to comply with military training leave provisions.

(Idaho Code §§ 46–224 to 46–226, as amended by 2006 Idaho Sess. Laws 172)

ILLINOIS

Coverage: Private employees who are enlisted or drafted into the U.S. Armed Forces or state militia training or service or ordered to state active duty are considered to be on furlough or leave of absence during military service.

Effect of Leave on Benefits: Employees do not lose seniority if they are reinstated or are seeking to be reinstated.

Employees are entitled to participate in insurance and other benefits offered by the employer for employees on furlough or leave of absence in effect at the time that the employees entered into military service. Employers who provide such employees with health insurance may not impose an exclusion or waiting period in connection with the coverage of a health or physical condition of these employees or other persons covered by these employees' insurance if the condition arose before or during the employees' time of military service, if the exclusion or waiting period would not have been imposed for the condition during the period of the employees' coverage, and if the condition has not been determined to be service-related.

Re-Employment Rights: An employee who is honorably discharged or has evidence or a certificate of satisfactory completion from the U.S. Armed Forces or state militia training or service is entitled to be restored to his or her former position or to a position of like seniority, status, and pay if still qualified to perform the duties of the position. The employee must be given the same status, seniority, and wage increases as if he or she had been continuously employed during the military service. The employee must apply for **re-employment** within 90 days after being relieved from military service, or not more than one year after hospitalization continuing from military discharge. If the employee is not qualified to perform the duties of the prior position because of a service-related disability, but is qualified to perform the duties of another position, the employee must be restored to that position and be granted the same seniority, status, and pay as the prior position, or the nearest approximation consistent with the employee's circumstances. An employee may not be removed from such a position without cause within one year of reinstatement.

Employees who leave employment to enter the U.S. Armed Forces or state militia service or by order to state active duty and are rejected due to a lack of qualification must be restored to the same position that the employee left to enter the military without loss of seniority status and wage increases as if he or she were continuously employed during his or her attempt to enlist in the military or a position of like seniority, status, and pay if the employee remains qualified for the former position and upon application for re-employment within 90 days of receiving official notice of military rejection.

Exceptions to Re-Employment Rights: Employees may not be reinstated if implementation is impossible or unreasonable because of an employer's changed circumstances. Private employees who are unable to perform duties of their prior position because of a service-related disability may not be reinstated if implementation is impossible or unreasonable because of an employer's changed circumstances.

When an employee who entered the U.S. Armed Forces or state militia service or was ordered to state active duty is replaced by one or more employees who then enter such military service, all of the employees must be given preference in reinstatement in the order in which they entered service, and the employer is not required to retain more than one of those employees.

Remedies/Penalties: Employees may bring a suit in the circuit court against private employers failing or refusing to comply with military leave or re-employment rights provisions to require employer compliance with such provisions and to recover lost wages or benefits together with reasonable attorneys' fees and costs.

Employers are subject to a fine of not less than $5,000 and not more than $10,000 for a knowing violation of the law.
(*330 Ill. Comp. Stat. 60/1 to 60/4 and 60/5 to 60/7, as amended by 2004 Ill. Laws 93-822 and 93-828*)

It is a petty offense to willfully deprive or prevent employment of Illinois State Guard members, obstruct or annoy Illinois State Guard members or their employers with respect to trade, business, or employment because of Guard membership, or dissuade any person, if that person enlists, from enlisting in the Illinois State Guard by threat of injury with respect to employment,

trade, or business.
(*20 Ill. Comp. Stat. 1815/79, as enacted by Ill. Laws 77-2830*)

Copy of Employment Offer Required: If an employer has given a new employee a date when full-time permanent employment is to commence, but the new employee is called to active military duty prior to the start date pursuant to an act of Congress, or order of the U.S. President or governor of Illinois, the employer must provide, upon request of the new employee, a written copy of the employment offer. The written copy must include at least the following: statement repeating the employment offer and the date work was to commence, a description of the job and title, compensation offered, and the employer's signature.
(*330 Ill. Comp. Stat. 60/4.5, as enacted by 2005 Ill. Laws 94-162*)

Civil Air Patrol Leave

Covered employers must provide unpaid leave to eligible employees who are members of the Civil Air Patrol (i.e., the civilian auxiliary of the U.S. Air Force) to perform civil air patrol missions. Eligible employees must have worked for a covered employer for at least 12 months and have performed at least 1,250 hours of service in that 12-month period. Employers with between 15 and 50 employees must provide up to 15 days of unpaid civil air patrol leave. Employers with more than 50 employees must provide up to 30 days of unpaid leave.

Employees must give the employer at least 14 days' notice of the intended date on which the civil air patrol leave will commence if leave will be five or more consecutive work days. The employee should consult with the employer to schedule leave so as to not unduly disrupt operations. Employees taking less than five consecutive days must give the employer reasonable advance notice.

The employer may require certification from the civil air patrol authorities to verify the employee's eligibility for the leave.

Employers are prohibited from requiring that employees exhaust all other accrued leaves (vacation, personal, compensatory, sick, disability, etc.).

Re-Employment Rights: An employee who exercises the right to leave, upon expiration of the leave, is entitled to be restored by the employer to the position held when the leave commenced or to a position with equivalent seniority status, employee benefits, pay and other terms and conditions.

Employers may prove that the employee was not restored because of conditions unrelated to the employee's exercise of leave rights.

Benefits: Taking civil air patrol leave must not result in the loss of any employee benefit accrued before the date on which the leave commenced. During leave, the employer must allow an employee to continue benefits at the employee's expense.

Retaliation Prohibited: An employer is prohibited from interfering with, restraining, or denying the exercise—or the attempt to exercise—any right under the leave law. Employers are prohibited from taking adverse employment actions against an employee who exercises rights under the law, or who opposes any practice made unlawful under the leave law.

Enforcement: A civil action may be brought in the circuit court having jurisdiction by an employee to enforce the law. The circuit court may enjoin any act or practice that is a violation or may be a violation and may order any other equitable relief that is necessary and appropriate to redress the violation or to enforce the law.

(820 Ill. Comp. Stat. 148/1 to 148/30, as enacted by 2008 Ill. Laws 95-763, effective Jan. 1, 2009)

Family Military Leave

Leave Rights: During the time federal or state deployment orders are in effect for a family member of an employee, the employee is eligible for unpaid family military leave. The maximum amount of leave is dependent on the size of the employer:

- up to 15 days for employers with between 15 and 50 employees;
- up to 30 days for employers with more than 50 employees.

Eligibility: Employees must have worked for the same employer for 12 consecutive months prior to the leave, and have been employed at least 1,250 hours of service during the 12-month period.

Family military leave means leave requested by an employee who is the spouse or parent of a person called to military service lasting longer than 30 days with the state or United States pursuant to the orders of the governor or the president.

Before an employee can take family military leave, the employee must exhaust all accrued vacation leave, personal leave, compensatory leave, and any other leave that may be granted to the employee, except sick leave and disability leave.

The employer may require certification from the proper military authorities to verify the employee's eligibility.

Notice: The employee must give at least 14 days notice of the intended date upon which the family military leave will commence if leave will consist of five or more consecutive work days. Employees taking less than five days leave must give the employer notice as soon as is possible.

Re-Employment Rights: An employee who exercises the right to family military leave, upon expiration of the leave, is entitled to be restored by the employer to the position held when the leave commenced or to a position with equivalent seniority status, employee benefits, pay and other terms and conditions.

Employers may prove that the employee was not restored because of conditions unrelated to the employee's exercise of leave rights.

Benefits: Taking family military leave must not result in the loss of any employee benefit accrued before the date on which the leave commenced. During family military leave, the employer must allow an employee to continue benefits at the employee's expense.

Retaliation Prohibited: An employer is prohibited from interfering with, restraining, or denying the exercise—or the attempt to exercise—any right under the leave law. Employers are prohibited from taking adverse employment actions against an employee who exercises rights under the law.

Enforcement: A civil action may be brought in the circuit court having jurisdiction by an employee to enforce the law. The circuit court may enjoin any act or practice that is a violation or may be a violation and may order any other equitable relief that is necessary and appropriate to redress the violation or to enforce the law.

(*820 Ill. Comp. Stat. 151/1 to 151/30, as enacted by 2005 Ill. Laws 94-589*)

INDIANA

Summary: Indiana employers must grant employees leave to participate in National Guard and military reserve training, and must re-employ workers called up for military duty. Employers of members of the National Guard, the U.S. reserve corps, and the state military reserve are covered.

Amount of Leave: Employers must provide members of the reserves up to 15 days of leave in any calendar year. Employers must grant National Guard members leave for the total number of days the employees are on active state duty.

Pay and Benefits: Employers can, but are not required to, pay employees during leave to serve in the National Guard and reserves. Employers must provide the same vacation, sick leave, bonuses, advancement, and other benefits to employees on military leave as they provide to other employees.

Re-Employment Rights: Employers must reinstate a member of the National Guard or the reserves if the employee in order to receive military training with the armed forces of the United States (not to exceed 15 days in one calendar year):

- leaves a position other than a temporary position;
- gives notice of dates of departure and return 90 days before leaving;
- provides evidence of satisfactory completion of the training; and

- remains qualified to perform the job.

Remedies/Penalties: The Circuit Court enforces the military leave law.

Employers of members of the Indiana National Guard must allow them to attend meetings of the Guard. Failure to do so is a Class B misdemeanor.

Employers that do not comply with the leave and re-employment requirements can be sued for damages in the circuit court.
(*Ind. Code §§ 10–16–7–1, 10–16–7–2, 10–16–7–4, 10–16–7–6, as enacted by 2003 Ind. Acts 2; and 10–17–4–1, as amended by 2003 Ind. Acts 260; and 10–17–4–3, as enacted by 2003 Ind. Acts 2*)

Relevant Cases: *Koppin v. Strode,* 761 N.E.2d 455 (Ind. Ct. App. 2002); *Downing v. City of Columbus,* 505 N.E.2d 841 (Ind. Ct. App. 1987).

Family Military Leave

Employers with 50 or more employees for at least 20 calendar workweeks must provide employees who are the spouse, parent, grandparent, child, or sibling of an individual ordered to active duty up to 10 working days of leave per calendar year either before, during, or after the individual's deployment. Employees must have worked for at least 12 months and 1,500 hours during that period.

Leave can be unpaid. Employees can substitute any available paid leave, except medical or sick leave, for any part of the 10-day leave period.

Employers must make it possible for employees to continue health care benefits at the employees' expense during family military leave.

Employees must provide written notice of the date leave will begin, including a copy of the active duty orders if available, at least 30 days prior, unless the orders are issued less than 30 days before the leave date.

Employers can be enjoined by the circuit court from acts or practices that violate the rights of employees to take family military leave.

Employees who take family military leave must be restored to the same or equivalent position they held before leave, with equivalent seniority, pay, and benefits, unless employers can prove that nonreinstatement is unrelated to employees' exercise of leave rights.
(*Ind. Code §§ 22–2–13–1 to 22–2–13–16, as amended by 2009 Ind. Acts 45, effective July 1, 2009*)

Iowa

Summary: Members of the National Guard, organized national reserves, or civil air patrol who are in other than temporary positions and who are ordered to temporary active duty for training or state military service are entitled to leave for the period of such service.

Effect of Leave on Benefits: Private employees' rights to vacation, sick leave, bonus, or other employment benefits are not affected by military leave.

Re-Employment Rights: An employee is entitled to be restored to the former position or a position of like seniority, status, and pay, if the employee can perform the duties of the position and provide evidence of satisfactory completion of military duty or service.

Penalties: It is a simple misdemeanor to engage in the following:

- to discriminate against any officer or enlisted member of the National Guard, organized national reserves, or civil air patrol because of such membership;
- for an employer or agent of employer to discharge an employee because of being an officer or enlisted member of state military forces or to hinder or prevent such officer or enlisted member from performing any authorized military service; or

- for a private employer to violate military leave and re-employment provisions for employees, in other than temporary positions, who are members of the National Guard, U.S. organized reserves, or civil air patrol.

(*Iowa Code §§ 29A.1, as amended by 2005 Iowa Acts 119; and 29A.43, as amended by 2008 Iowa Acts 1003, effective Feb. 14, 2008*)

Relevant Cases: *Bewley v. Villisca, Iowa Cmty. Sch. Dist.*, 299 N.W.2d 904 (Iowa 1980).

KANSAS

Coverage: All employers, public and private are covered.

Effect of Leave on Employment Status: Employees restored to a position must have the same status in employment as they would have enjoyed if they had remained in their employment continuously from the time they were called to state duty until the time of restoration to such employment.

Reinstatement: Any person called to active duty by the state, whether by the Kansas National Guard, Kansas Air National Guard, Kansas State Guard, or other state military force, who gave notice to the employer of the call-up, is entitled to reinstatement upon satisfactory performance of military duty and release from such duty.

Reinstatement is to the same position of employment, except a temporary position. The individual must report to the place of employment within 72 hours of release from duty or recovery from disease or injury resulting from the duty.

If the person is no longer qualified to perform the duties of the position because of disability sustained during the period of state duty, but is qualified to perform another job offered by the employer, the person shall be reemployed in a position that will provide like seniority status and pay, or the nearest approximation thereof consistent with the circumstances.

A person restored to employment following state duty is considered to have been on temporary leave of absence, and shall be restored without loss of seniority. The person also shall be entitled to participate in any benefits offered by the employer pursuant to established rules and practices relating to employees on leave of absence.

An individual restored to employment cannot be discharged without cause within one year after restoration to the position.

Penalties: It is a misdemeanor for an employer to refuse permission to a guard member to attend drill or annual muster or to perform active service when ordered. An employer that refuses leave or discharges or disciplines an employee for being absent in order to perform military duty is subject to a fine of $5 to $50 for each offense.

An individual claiming to be entitled to reemployment following state service may make an application to the state attorney general. If the attorney general is convinced the individual is in fact entitled to the benefits claimed, he or she may act as attorney for the applicant, and may bring suit in the appropriate district court. If the court determines that the employer failed to comply with the law regarding reinstatement, it may order the employer to comply with the law and to compensate the claimant for any loss of wages or benefits, plus interest. If the court determines that the failure was willful, damages in an amount equal to the amount of loss may be assessed.

(Kan. Stat. Ann. §§ 48–222 and 48–517, as enacted by 1996 Kan. Sess. Laws 137)

KENTUCKY

Summary: All employers must grant employees leave for the period required to perform active duty or training in the National Guard. An employer is not required to pay an employee who is on leave for National Guard service.

State law prohibits any person from depriving or preventing employment of a member of the Kentucky National Guard or state active militia, or obstructing the employee in the conduct of his or her trade or profession. It is also unlawful for a business, trade, or employment association or corporation through its constitution, rules, bylaws, resolutions, or regulations to discriminate against any member because of the membership, eligibility for membership, or right to retain membership in the state militia.

Re-Employment Rights: Employees on leave for National Guard service must be reinstated to their former position without loss of seniority, status, pay, or any other rights or benefits.

Remedies/Penalties: Discrimination against employees because of membership in the Kentucky National Guard or Kentucky active militia is punishable by a fine of $100 to $500, imprisonment for up to six months, or both.

Violation of the military leave provision is a Class A misdemeanor.

(Ky. Rev. Stat. Ann. §§ 38.238, and 38.990, as amended by 1980 Ky. Acts 249; and § 38.460, as amended by 1954 Ky. Acts 98)

LOUISIANA

Coverage: Private employees who are members of uniformed services are covered. Uniformed services include the following:

- U.S. armed forces;
- Army and Air National Guard;
- Public Health Service commissioned corps; and
- any other category designated by the president in time of war or emergency.

Notice Requirement: The employee is entitled to military service leave provided that the employee notifies the employer in writing of the intent to return to a position of employment.

Salary Continuation: Employers may, at their discretion, give paid military leave to uniformed service members while in service. If employer chooses to pay employee while in service, employer must pay all employees uniformly.

Effect of Leave on Benefits: Uniformed service members may use any amount or combination of accrued vacation or annual, paid military, or compensatory leave, at their discretion, while on military leave. While on military leave, these employees continue to accrue sick, annual, vacation, military leave, holiday pay, and any paid leave offered by the employer, pursuant to the employer's stated leave of absence policy. No employer may deduct from compensation of these employees any cost of replacing employee while on military leave.

Re-Employment Rights: Private employees who are called or ordered to state active duty are entitled to be reinstated to former position at same pay and seniority or position of like seniority, status, and pay. They must be restored if discharged under honorable conditions, satisfactorily completed service, and they report to former employment within 72 hours of release from duty or recovery from disease or injury resulting from duty. If employee cannot perform duties of former position because of service-related disability but can perform another position, employee is entitled to be restored to such position providing like seniority, status, and pay. These employees must be restored to employment status as if continuously employed and may not be discharged from positions within one year of being restored without cause. If two or more of these employees are entitled to be reinstated and left the same position to enter state duty, the employee who left the position first shall have the prior right to be restored without prejudice to the re-employment Rights of other employee(s) to be restored.

Uniformed service members are entitled to be reinstated within 10 days of providing written notice to the employer of the intent to return to a position of employment, if prior service absences do not exceed five years, and the following requirements are followed:

- If service was for more than 30 days but less than 180 days, written notice of intent to return to employment is due no later than 14 days after the completion of service; if written notice is impossible or unreasonable through no fault of the person, then notice is due the next first full calendar day when submission of the written notice becomes possible.

- If service was for more than 180 days, written notice of intent to return to employment is due no later than 90 days after completion of service.
- If employee was injured during service, written notice of intent to return to employment is due at the end of the recovery period, which may not exceed two years.

However, employers are not required to reinstate these employees if it is impossible or unreasonable because of changed circumstances, if it would impose an undue hardship upon employer, or employee's position was for a brief, nonrecurrent period with no reasonable expectation for continued employment.

Uniformed service members are entitled to be restored to the same seniority and other rights and benefits as if continuously employed. These employees are entitled to complete any training program that was applicable to their former position while in military service, and they may not be discharged from positions without cause within one year.

An employee who fails to submit written notice of the intent to return to a position of employment within the prescribed time limits does not automatically forfeit these rights and benefits but shall be subject to employer explanations and discipline concerning absence from work.

Discrimination Prohibited: It is illegal to deny a member or applicant of uniformed services initial employment, retention in employment, promotion, or any other benefit of employment by an employer because of military service.

National reservists and Louisiana National Guard members shall not be discriminated against in employment by being denied employment, retention in employment, or any promotion or other advantage of employment because of any reserve or Guard obligation.

Mandatory Poster: Employers must post the notice available from the Louisiana Workforce Commission regarding military leave rights.

Remedies/Penalties: A uniformed service member may seek enforcement of military leave and re-employment provisions in district court to require employer to comply with military leave and re-employment provisions and to compensate employee for any loss of wages or benefits and pay of an amount equal to the amount of lost wages or benefits as liquidated damages if employer's failure to comply was willful.

National reservists and Louisiana National Guard members may bring mandamus proceedings in district court to require employer to comply with nondiscrimination provisions and to compensate for any lost wages or benefits.

Private employees called or ordered to state active duty may bring mandamus proceedings in district court to require employer to comply with reinstatement provisions and to compensate for any lost wages or benefits.

The secretary of the Louisiana Workforce Commission or director of state department of civil service shall aid employees, in other than temporary positions, who are state militia, state National Guard, or any other state military force members called or ordered to state active duty, to be reinstated.

(*La. Rev. Stat. Ann. §§ 29:38, as amended by 2002 La. Acts 1st ex. sess. 57; 29:38.1, as enacted by 1987 La. Acts 918; §§ 29:403 to 29:406, and 29:410, as amended by 2005 La. Acts 144*)

MAINE

Summary: Employees who are state military members, state Army and Air National Guard members, or national reservists and employed in other than a temporary position may receive military leave.

Salary and Benefits: Employees, who are state military members, state Army and Air National Guard members, or national reservists, may receive paid or unpaid military leave at employer's discretion.

Time spent for state military and guard or national reserve military training shall not affect the employee's right to receive regular vacation, sick leave, bonus, advancement and other advantages of the employee's position.

Re-Employment Rights: Employees who are state military and guard members or national reservists are entitled to reinstatement without loss of pay, seniority, benefits, status, or other advantages of employment, if they previously notified the employer of military leave. The employer has the right to first confirm authorized satisfactory completion of military duty.

The amount of time an employee has to report back to employment varies with the length of the military service. In all cases, the time period begins to run after the employees have had enough time to safely return to their residence.

Employees serving for three days or less must report to employment after 24 hours. Employees serving more than three days but no more than 15 days must report after 48 hours. Employees serving more than 15 days but no more than 30 days must report after 72 hours. Employees serving more than 30 days but no more than 180 days must report after 14 days. Employees serving more than 180 days must report after 90 days.

Remedies/Penalties: It is a class E crime for employers:

- to penalize any member of state military forces and state Army and Air National Guard with regard to compensation, hiring, tenure, terms, conditions, or privileges of employment or to deny any other incident or advantage of employment because of membership in state military forces;
- to willfully deprive or prevent employment of any member of state military forces and state Army and Air National Guard, obstruct such member in respect to occupation or business because of state military or guard membership, or dissuade any person from enlisting in state military forces by threat of injury to occupation or business;
- to intentionally molest, abuse, or interfere with any member of state military forces in performance of duty; and

- as an association or corporation organized to promote trade, occupation, or business of members to discriminate by rule or act against any state military force member with respect to the member's eligibility or right to retain association or corporation membership or aid in enforcing a rule or action, with an intent to discriminate, against a state military force member.

Employees may bring a civil suit for damages or seek equitable relief in court against any employer failing to comply with state military and guard or national reservist provisions. (*Me. Rev. Stat. Ann. tit. 26, §§ 811 to 813, as amended by 2005 Me. Laws 524; and tit. 37-B, § 342, as amended by 2003 Me. Laws 583*)

Family Military Leave

Summary: Employers with 15 or more employees must provide 15 days per year of leave to the spouse, domestic partner, or parent of a member of the military called to active duty lasting more than 180 days.

Family military leave may be taken only during the 15 days immediately prior to deployment or the 15 days immediately following the period of deployment, or both. Leave also can be taken during a leave period granted to an already deployed military member.

Family military leave can be unpaid. Employees can take family military leave only if they have exhausted all accrued vacation leave, personal leave, compensatory leave, or other leave, except sick leave and disability leave.

Serious Health Condition/Death of Military Member: In addition, under the state's family medical leave law, any employer with 15 or more employees must allow an eligible employee to take up to 10 workweeks of unpaid leave in a two-year period in the event of the serious health condition or death of a spouse, domestic partner, parent, or child while on active duty with Maine military forces or U.S. Armed Forces, including the National Guard and Reserves.

Employees who are employed by the same employer for 12 consecutive months are eligible for such family medical leave.

Definitions: Employee means any person who may be permitted, required or directed by an employer in consideration of direct or indirect gain or profit to engage in any employment and who has been employed by the same employer for at least 12 months and has been employed for at least 1,250 hours of service during the 12-month period immediately preceding the commencement of the employee's family military leave.

Family military leave means leave requested by an employee who is the spouse, domestic partner, or parent of a person who is a resident of the state and is deployed for military service for a period lasting longer than 180 days with the state or United States pursuant to the orders of the governor or the president.

Prohibited Actions: An employer may not:

- interfere with, restrain, or deny the exercise or the attempt to exercise any right provided under the family military leave law;
- discharge, fine, suspend, expel, discipline, or in any other manner discriminate against any employee who exercises any right provided under the family military leave law; nor
- discharge, fine, suspend, expel, discipline, or in any other manner discriminate against any employee for opposing any practice made unlawful by the family military leave law.

Taking family military leave does not result in the loss of benefits accrued prior to the leave. The leave provisions of the law do not affect employers' obligations to abide by a collective bargaining agreement or employee benefit plan that provides greater leave rights to employees. Family military leave benefits cannot be diminished by any collective bargaining agreement or employee benefit plan.

Prior Notice: Employees must give at least 14 days' notice of family military leave that will last five or more consecutive work days.

Employees taking leave for less than five consecutive work days must give their employer as much advance notice as is practicable.

The employee shall consult with the employer to attempt to schedule the leave so as to not unduly disrupt the operations of the employer.

Reinstatement Rights: Employers must reinstate employees, upon expiration of family military leave, to the position held by the employee at the beginning of the leave, or to a position with equivalent seniority, benefits, pay, and other terms and conditions of employment. Employers do not have to reinstate employees if they can prove that the failure to reinstate them was because of conditions unrelated to the exercise of their right to family military leave.

Certification: An employer may require certification from the proper military authority to verify an employee's eligibility for the family military leave requested.

Remedies/Penalties: Employees can bring civil suits to enforce the family military leave law. The court may enjoin any act or practice that violates or may violate the law and may order any other equitable relief that is necessary and appropriate to redress the violation or to enforce the law.

Employers that violate the right of an employee to take leave for the serious health condition or death of a spouse, domestic partner, parent, or child while on active duty can be sued by the employee. Employers that are sued can be ordered to:

- stop violating the family medical leave provisions;
- pay employees' lost wages, salary, employment benefits, or other compensation and an additional amount equal to the lost wages, salary, benefits, or other compensation for willful violations;
- pay liquidated damages of $100 per day for each day of violation, reasonable attorneys' fees, and costs; and
- comply with any other court orders.

(Me. Rev. Stat. Ann. tit. 26, §§ 814 and 843, both as amended by 2007 Me. Laws 388)

Maryland

The federal Uniformed Services Employment and Reemployment Rights Act of 1994 (USERRA) applies to members of the Maryland Army National Guard and Maryland Defense Force when ordered to military duty, regardless of length of service. *(Md. Code Ann., Pub. Safety § 13–705, as amended by 2006 Md. Laws 88)*

Massachusetts

Employment Rights: Employers and employment agencies are prohibited from denying initial employment, re-employment, retention, promotion, or any benefit of employment because a person is a member of, applies to perform, or has an obligation to perform service in a uniformed military service of the U.S. or the National Guard.

Leave Rights: All employees are allowed up to 17 days of military leave per calendar year.

Salary Continuation: Leave may be granted with or without pay, at the discretion of the employer.

Effect of Leave on Benefits: Employers may not deny vacation, sick leave, bonuses, advancements, or other advantages of employment to workers on military leave.

Re-Employment Rights: Upon returning from military duty, employees are entitled to be restored to the former position or to a similar position with the same status, pay, and seniority.

Penalties: Employers who violate these provisions may be sued in civil court.

(Mass. Gen. Laws ch. 149, § 52A, as enacted by 1956 Mass. Acts 385; ch. 151B, § 4(1D), as enacted by 2004 Mass. Acts 355, effective Dec. 22, 2004)

Michigan

Summary: If an employee provides advance notice of the need for leave to participate in military service or to report for induction or pre-induction physical examinations, the employer must permit the employee to take leave. Employers must re-employ workers called up for military duty.

Coverage: The law applies to employers of members of the National Guard, the U.S. reserve corps, the naval militia, and the state military reserve. An employee is not entitled to re-employment Rights if he or she is terminated from the service with other than an honorable discharge.

Amount of Leave: The law does not specify a limit to the amount of military leave.

Re-Employment Rights: Employers must re-employ employees who report or apply to the employer within 45 days—within 90 days if the service was for more than 180 days—following release from service, release from duty, or rejection.

For employees who take leave for one to 90 days, on return from military leave, the employee must be placed in the position in which he or she would have been employed but for the interruption for military leave as long as the employee is qualified to perform the duties. The employer must make reasonable efforts to help the employee qualify for the duties. If the employee continues to be unqualified to perform the duties, then the employer must give the employee the position that the person had at commencement of military leave.

If the employee was on leave for 91 days or more, and reasonable efforts to help the employee qualify for the position have failed, the employer has the option of placing the employee in a job that is the nearest approximation in status and pay to:

- the one that the employee would have had but for the interruption for military leave, or
- the position the employee held prior to commencement of military leave if the employee is not qualified for the different position.

If the employee is on military leave for more than five years, the employer is not obligated to re-employ the person. However, in calculating the five-year period, the following periods of time are not included:

- any service that is required beyond five years to complete an initial period of obligated service;
- any service during which the person was unable to obtain release orders and the inability was through no fault of the employee;
- any service performed as required pursuant to 10 U.S.C. § 10147, under 32 U.S.C. §§ 502(a) or 503, or to fulfill additional training requirements determined and certified by the appropriate service secretary to be necessary for professional development or for completion of skill training or retraining;
- any service performed under orders to remain in active service pursuant to specified federal laws.

Enforcement: Employees can sue employers that wrongfully deny re-employment.

Remedies/Penalties: Employers that violate the military leave laws can be fined up to $500, imprisoned for up to 90 days, or both fined and imprisoned (see *Mich. Comp. Laws § 750.504*).

Employers that are sued by employees who qualify for reinstatement after military service can be ordered to reinstate employees and pay reasonable attorneys' fees.
(*Mich. Comp. Laws §§ 32.272 to 32.274, as amended by 2008 Mich. Pub. Acts 106, effective April 25, 2008; § 750.398, as amended by 1931 Mich. Pub. Acts 328*)

MINNESOTA

Summary: Minnesota employers must grant employees unpaid leave to participate in active military service, and must re-employ workers called up for military duty.

The law does not specify an amount of leave.

Coverage: Employers of any workers called to active military service in time of emergency are covered.

Job Applicants: Employers are prohibited from asking job applicants whether they are members of the national guard or reserve component of the U.S. armed forces. Job applicants cannot be required to make any oral or written statements concerning their military service status as a condition of employment.

Civil Air Patrol: Unless the leave would unduly disrupt operations, the employer will grant a leave of absence without pay to an employee for time rendering service as a member of the civil air patrol on the request of the state or any of its subdivisions.

Re-Employment Rights: Following periods of active military service, employers must re-employ workers to the positions they left if those positions still exist and the employees can still perform the job duties; otherwise, they must be offered positions of similar seniority, status, and pay.

Employees must apply for reinstatement within 90 days of leaving military service, and must have an honorable discharge or equivalent.

Re-employed workers cannot be discharged within one year of reinstatement, except for cause.

Enforcement: The courts enforce the state military leave law.

Penalties/Remedies: Employers that discharge workers because they belong to the military or naval forces of the United States, the state of Minnesota, or any other state commit a gross misdemeanor.

Employers that prevent any person from performing military service or dissuade any person from enlisting in military service by threat or injury are guilty of a gross misdemeanor.

(Minn. Stat. §§ 181.535, as enacted by 2004 Minn. Laws 256; 181.946, as enacted by 1997 Minn. Laws 20; 192.34, as amended by 1986 Minn. Laws 444; 192.261, as amended by 2005 Minn. Laws 35 and 156; and 192.502, as amended by 2006 Minn. Laws 273)

Military Family Rights

Summary: Employers must provide unpaid leave to the families of military personnel injured or killed in action. Employers also must provide unpaid leave to the family members of military personnel to attend specified events and programs.

Leave Amounts: Employees and independent contractors are entitled to 10 days of unpaid leave if an immediate family member has been injured or killed while in active military service.

Employers must provide a reasonable amount of nonpaid time off —not to exceed two consecutive days or six days in a calendar year— for the employee to attend the following events related to the employee's spouse, parent, or child and to which the employee is invited or otherwise called upon to attend by military authorities: departure or return ceremonies for deploying or returning military personnel or units; family training or readiness events sponsored or conducted by the military; and events held as part of official military reintegration programs. Employers are prohibited from taking adverse employment action against, or otherwise hindering an employee from attending the events.

The employer must not compel the employee to use accumulated but unused vacation for these events.

[*Note:* Minn. Stat. § 181.948 provides that covered employees, but not independent contractors, are entitled to up to one day of unpaid leave to attend a send-off or homecoming ceremony for an immediate family member. Immediate family member means a person's parent, child, grandparents, siblings, or spouse.]

Notice Requirements: Employees must give their employers as much notice as practicable of the need to use family leave.

Retaliation Prohibited: Employers are prohibited from taking adverse employment action against any employee because of the membership of that employee's spouse, parent, or child in the military forces of the United States or any state.

(*Minn. Stat. §§ 181.947 and 181.948, as enacted by 2006 Minn. Laws 273; 192.325, as enacted by 2008 Minn. Laws 297, effective Aug. 1, 2008*)

MISSISSIPPI

Summary: Any person who is a member of any reserve component of the armed forces of the U.S., or honorably discharged former member of the service of the U.S. who, in order to perform duties or receive training, leaves employment, and who satisfactorily completes the duty or training, and remains qualified to perform the duties of the position, is entitled to be restored to the previous or a similar position. The period of absence for military duty or training shall be construed as an absence with leave but may be without pay. Members of the Mississippi National Guard are entitled to the same leave for purposes of active state duty, state training duty, or any other authorized military duty.

Private employers may not deprive a member of any reserve component or any honorably discharged former member of the U.S. armed forces, of employment, or prevent employment, or discriminate in any of the conditions of employment.

Coverage: Private and public employees.

Salary Continuation: Private employers need not pay employees on leave of absence for military training or service, but must restore them to their previous positions.

Remedies/Penalties: A private employer who discriminates against an employee because of military service, or who attempts to dissuade an employee from enlistment or acceptance of a warrant or commission in any reserve or active component of the U.S. armed forces is guilty of a misdemeanor and subject to a fine of up to $1,000, six months imprisonment, or both.
(*Miss. Code Ann. §§ 33–1–15, as amended by 1991 Miss. Laws 492; and 33–1–19, as amended by 1991 Miss. Laws 432*)

MONTANA

Summary: Montana employers must grant employees leave to participate in National Guard and military reserve training, and must re-employ workers called up for military duty. The law does not specify the amount of leave.

Federal Rights: A person ordered to federally funded military duty is entitled to all of the employment and re-employment rights and benefits provided pursuant to the federal Uniformed Services Employment and Reemployment Rights Act of 1994, 38 U.S.C. 4301, et seq., and other applicable federal laws.

Retaliation Prohibited: Employers cannot deny employment, re-employment, reinstatement, retention, promotion, or any benefit of employment or obstruct, injure, discriminate against, or threaten consequences against employees because of their membership, application for membership, or potential application for membership in the state organized militia or because employees exercise or have exercised their right to military leave.

Effect of Leave on Benefits: Employers cannot deduct time spent on military leave from sick leave, vacation leave, or other leave. Employers can, but do not have to, permit accrual of vacation leave and other benefits while employees are on military leave; however, employees must accrue the same leave provided to other employees in a similar but nonmilitary leave status.

Employees on military leave can voluntarily use accrued vacation or other benefits during leave.

Re-Employment Rights: Employers must reinstate workers following military service if they are still capable of performing their jobs. Employees must be reinstated with the same seniority, status, pay, health insurance, pension, and other benefits as they would have accrued if they had not been absent for state active duty.

If employees were on probationary status when ordered to active duty, employers can require them to resume the probationary period from the date the leave of absence for state active duty began.

If employees cannot be re-employed in their former jobs, they must be re-employed in a position of similar seniority, status, and pay, unless this is impossible because of employers' changed circumstances.

Exceptions to Re-Employment Rights: Employers are not obligated to allow employees to return to employment under any of the following conditions:

- An employee is no longer qualified to perform the duties of the position because of a physical or mental disability.
- An employee's position was temporary and the temporary employment period has expired.
- An employee's request to return to work was not done in a timely manner.
- An employer's circumstances have changed so significantly that the employee's continued employment cannot reasonably be expected.
- An employee's return would cause the employer undue hardship.

Definitions: Federally funded military duty means duty, including training, performed pursuant to orders issued under Title 10 or 32 of the U.S. Code and the time period, if any, required pursuant to a licensed physician's certification to recover from an illness or injury incurred while performing the duty.

State active duty means duty performed by a member when a disaster or an emergency has been declared by the proper authority of the state pursuant to Art. VI, § 13, of the state constitution to include the time period, if any, required pursuant to a licensed physician's certification to recover from an illness or injury incurred while performing the active duty.

Timely manner is dependent on the length of duty. An employee has returned in a timely manner if after active duty of:

- up to 30 days, the employee returned to work on the next regular work shift following safe travel time plus eight hours; 30 to 180 days, the employee returned to work within 14 days of the end of active duty;
- more than 180 days, the employee returned to work within 90 days of the end of active duty.

Enforcement Powers: The Department of Labor and Industry has the power to:

- enter and inspect the places of business, question employees, and investigate facts, conditions, or matters that the department considers appropriate to determine whether an employer has violated the military leave provisions; and
- administer oaths, examine witnesses, issue subpoenas; compel the attendance of witnesses; inspect papers, books, accounts, records, payrolls, documents, and testimony; and take depositions and affidavits.

Remedies/Penalties: Employees who claim their employers have failed to comply with the military leave provisions can file a complaint with the department. Complaints must be submitted in writing within 15 days after an employee discovered the employer's failure to comply. Within 60 days of receiving a complaint, the department will make a finding about whether a violation has occurred and will notify the employee and the employer. The department will attempt to resolve the matter; however, if the department fails to resolve the matter in 90 days, the employee can request that the department refer the complaint to the state attorney general. The state attorney general can file a lawsuit and act as the employee's attorney.

If the state attorney general is satisfied that the complaint has merit, the state attorney general may file a lawsuit on behalf of and act as an attorney for the complainant in seeking relief. If the state attorney general sues on behalf of the person, fees or court costs may not be assessed against the complainant.

Employees retain the right to file independent lawsuits. However, if a person files a complaint with the department, the person must have exhausted the administrative remedies available under the law before having standing to initiate an independent lawsuit.

The lawsuit must be brought in the district court in the county in which the claimant's employer maintains a place of business. The lawsuit must be commenced within three years of when the claimant can reasonably be expected to have discovered the facts constituting a violation of the claimant's rights or benefits.

The court can require employers to comply with the military leave provisions, require employers to compensate employees for losses suffered because of violations, or require employers to pay damages if violations were willful.

If the complainant is the prevailing party, the court may award reasonable attorneys' fees to the complainant. The court may use its full equity powers, including temporary or permanent injunctions, temporary restraining orders, and contempt orders, to vindicate fully the rights or benefits of a person.
(Mont. Code Ann. §§ 10–1–1001 to 10–1–1007, and 10–1–1015 to 10–1–1021, as enacted by 2005 Mont. Laws 381)

Nebraska

Employers must grant employees who work 120 hours or more in three consecutive weeks up to 120 hours of leave each year. They must grant employees working less than 120 hours in three consecutive weeks leave that is equal to the number of hours they work or are scheduled to work, whichever is greater, in three consecutive weeks.

The state has adopted the following sections of the Uniformed Services Employment and Reemployment Rights Act of 1994, 38 U.S.C. ch. 43: §§ 4301(a) [purpose]; 4302 [relation to other law and plans or agreements]; 4303(2), (4), (7) through (13), (15), and (16) and those portions of subparagraph (3) not relating to employment in a foreign country [definitions]; 4304 [character of service]; 4311 [discrimination and acts of reprisal prohibited]; 4312 [re-employment rights]; 4313 [re-employment positions], with the exception of that portion of subparagraph (a) dealing with re-employment of federal employees; 4316 [rights, benefits, and obligations of persons absent from employment for military service]; 4317 [health plans]; and 4318 [pension benefit plans].

Re-Employment Rights: An employee who has been on military leave must be reinstated to his or her former position, or to a position with equivalent seniority, status, and pay.

Remedies/Penalties: If any employer fails to comply with any of the military leave provisions, the employee may bring a lawsuit for damages for such noncompliance. The employee may also apply to the courts for equitable relief as may be just and proper under the circumstances.

Any person, firm, or organization violating the military leave provisions shall be guilty of a Class IV misdemeanor, and, in addition, must restore to the employee all rights of which the employee was illegally deprived.
(*Neb. Rev. Stat. §§ 55–102, as amended by 1953 Neb. Laws 188; 55–161, 55–164 and 55–165, all as amended by 2002 Neb. Laws 722; and 55–166, as amended by 1977 Neb. Laws 39*)

Relevant Cases: *Ferguson v. Union Pac. R.R.*, 601 N.W.2d 907, 165 LRRM 2495 (Neb. 1999).

Family Military Leave

Summary: Employers with between 15 and 50 employees must provide up to 15 days of unpaid family military leave to eligible employees, while employers of more than 50 employees must provide up to 30 days.

Eligible Employees: An employee is entitled to family military leave if the employee:

- has been employed by the same employer for at least 12 months;
- has been employed for at least 1,250 hours of service during the 12-month period immediately preceding the commencement of the leave; and
- is the spouse or parent of a person called to military service lasting 179 days or longer.

Notification: An employee taking family military leave that will consist of five or more consecutive work days must provide the employer at least 14 days' notice of the intended date upon which the leave will commence. Employees taking family military leave for less than five consecutive days must give the employer advance notice as is practicable. Where possible, the employee should consult with the employer to schedule the leave to avoid undue disruption of the employer's operations.

Certification: An employer may require certification from the proper military authority to verify an employee's eligibility for family military leave.

Job Restoration: An employee returning from covered family military leave is entitled to be restored to his or her previous position or to a position with equivalent seniority status, benefits, pay, and other terms and conditions of employment. This provision does not apply if the employer proves that failure to restore the employee's employment was unrelated to the employee's exercise of rights under the law.

Retaliation Prohibited: An employer is prohibited from:

- interfering with, restraining, or denying the exercise of or the attempt to exercise any right provided under the Family Military Leave Act;
- discharging, fining, suspending, expelling, disciplining, or otherwise discriminating against an employee who exercises any right provided under the act; or
- discharging, fining, suspending, expelling, disciplining, or otherwise discriminating against an employee for opposing any practice made unlawful by the act.

Remedies/Penalties: An employee alleging a violation of the Family Military Leave Act may file a civil action to enforce the provisions of the law. The court may enjoin any act or practice that violates or may violate the act and order any other equitable relief it deems necessary and appropriate to redress the violation or to enforce the act.

(Neb. Rev. Stat. §§ 55–501 to 55–507, as enacted by 2007 Neb. Laws 497)

NEVADA

Employers may not discriminate against any member of the Nevada National Guard because of Guard membership. Willfully aiding in discriminatory action against a Guard member is a misdemeanor.

An employer may not terminate an employee member of the National Guard because the employee is called to active service. Violation is a misdemeanor. The commissioner of labor may levy an administrative penalty of up to $5,000 for each violation.

Statute of limitations: A member of the Nevada National Guard who believes his or her employment was terminated in violation of the law may, within 60 days of receiving notice of termination, request a hearing before the labor commissioner.

If a hearing determines that the employee was improperly terminated, the employee is entitled to immediate reinstatement without loss of seniority or benefits, and to receive all wages and benefits lost because of the termination.

(*Nev. Rev. Stat. §§ 412.139, as amended by 2003 Nev. Stat. 800; 412.606, as amended by 1985 Nev. Stat. 758; 412.1393, as amended by 1993 Nev. Stat. 1605; and 412.1395, as enacted by 1985 Nev. Stat. 753*)

NEW HAMPSHIRE

New Hampshire employers must grant employees called to state active duty the same rights as are granted to those called to federal duty. Employers of members of any state military unit are covered.

Employers cannot refuse to hire, discharge, or deny promotion or other advantages of employment because of an employee's obligation as a member of the national guard or state militia.

The law does not specify an amount of leave, but private employers are encouraged to grant employees the same military leave as the state grants to public employees (up to 15 days of paid leave per year to attend drills, training, or other temporary duty (see *N.H. Rev. Stat. Ann. §§ 112:8 and 112:9*)).

Employers must grant the same re-employment rights to employees absent for state military duty as are required for employees absent for federal military duty.

National Guard members who feel their rights have been violated must first attempt to have the issue mediated by the Employer Support of the Guard and Reserve organization. If that fails, the Department of Labor enforces the law. The department may order the employer to correct the violation and compensate the employee (limited to pay, time credit, health benefits, or other areas over which the employer has control).

If the Department of Labor cannot resolve a complaint, the employee may request that the complaint be referred to the state attorney general. If the attorney general declines to proceed, or if the employee does not seek the attorney general's help, the employee may file a petition in superior court for relief.

The prevailing party may be awarded attorneys' fees.

(N.H. Rev. Stat. Ann. §§ 110-C:1 and 110-C:2, both as enacted by 2002 N.H. Laws 82; and 112:12, as enacted by 1951 N.H. Laws 121)

NEW JERSEY

Summary: Employers that have employees who take leave to serve in the National Guard, the U.S. reserve corps, the naval militia, or the state military reserve must re-employ those employees after the military service is completed.

Re-Employment Rights: Employers must re-employ workers who leave their jobs in order to perform military service if the employees remain qualified to do the jobs, present a certificate of completion of military service, and apply for re-employment within 90 days of leaving service.

Employers must re-employ workers in the same job or in a position of similar seniority, status, and pay, unless the employer's circumstances have changed so as to make a direct reinstatement impossible. If circumstances changed to make a direct reinstatement impossible in time of war or in an emergency, employers must re-employ individuals in any position available, upon their request, provided that they are able or qualified to perform the duties of the position.

Employers must re-employ workers who leave to participate in assemblies or annual training, or to attend service schools for up to three months in any four-year period. The employee must apply for re-employment within 10 days after completion of the temporary service.

Retaliation Prohibited: Employers cannot discharge members of the organized militia or prevent their employment.

Employers cannot refuse to hire applicants, discharge employees, or require employees to retire, because of an obligation to service in the U.S. Armed Forces, unless justified by lawful considerations other than age.

Within one year of re-employment, employers are prohibited from discharging without cause a military service member.

Remedies/Penalties: Employers that discharge members of the organized militia, or prevent their employment, are guilty of a misdemeanor, punishable either by a fine of up to $500, imprisonment for up to one year, or both.

Employers that fail to comply with the re-employment provisions can be sued in the Superior Court. The court can require re-employment and compensation for any loss of wages or benefits. The attorney general can represent the employee.
(*N.J. Stat. Ann. § 10:5-12, as amended by 2007 N.J. Laws 325, effective Jan. 13, 2008; § 38:23C-20, as amended by 2007 N.J. Laws 239, effective Jan. 3, 2008*)

New Mexico

Summary: It is illegal for an employer to refuse to hire, penalize, or discharge from employment any person on the basis of the person's membership in the state defense force or the national guard, or to prevent the person from performing any military service he or she is called upon to perform.

Re-Employment Rights: Employees returning from active duty service or training may apply for reinstatement within 90 days after being released from service or training.

To be eligible for reinstatement, the employee must have left a non-temporary position, have been honorably discharged or released from service, and still be qualified to perform the duties of the job.

An employer must reinstate an employee in his or her former position or a position of like seniority, status, and pay, unless circumstances have so changed as to make it impossible or unreasonable to do so. Employees returning from active military duty cannot be discharged for one year.

National Guard Service: Members of the state's National Guard ordered to federal or state active duty for a period of 30 or more consecutive days have the rights, benefits, and protections of the federal Uniformed Services Employment and Reemployment Rights Act and Servicemember's Civil Relief Act.

Remedies/Penalties: Violation of the provisions prohibiting discrimination in employment on the basis of military service is a misdemeanor.

An employee who is refused reinstatement may file suit in the district court for injunctive relief and damages, including lost wages and benefits.

(*N.M. Stat. § 20–4–6, as enacted by 1987 N.M. Laws 318; § 20–4–7.1, as enacted by 2004 N.M. Laws 37; § 20–5–13 and § 20–11–6, both as enacted by 1987 N.M. Laws 318; and § 28–15–1 to 28–15–3, as amended by 1971 N.M. Laws 163*)

NEW YORK

Summary: Employers must reinstate individuals to their former positions or to positions of like pay, seniority, and status following military service, unless circumstances have so changed as to make it unreasonable or impossible to do so.

To qualify for re-employment, the employee must:

- have a certificate of completion of military service;
- still be qualified to perform the duties of the position; and
- apply for re-employment within 90 days after being released from military service.

Coverage: Private employers.

Remedies/Penalties: Employers who fail or refuse to comply with these provisions may be ordered by a state court to comply and to compensate such person for lost wages or benefits.

Any person who willfully deprives a member of the organized militia of employment, or prevents the militia member from being employed because he or she is a member of the militia, is guilty of a misdemeanor.
(*N.Y. Mil. Law § 251, as amended by 1967 N.Y. Laws 680; and § 317, as amended by 1993 N.Y. Laws 312*)

Military Spouse Leave

Summary: A spouse of a member of the U.S. armed forces, national guard, or reserves who has been deployed during a period of military conflict is entitled to 10 days unpaid leave when that employee's spouse is on leave from military duty.

Coverage: The law applies to employers with 20 or more employees on any site.

Definition: Employee means a person who performs service for hire for an employer for an average of 20 or more hours per week, but does not include an independent contractor.

Retaliation Prohibited: Employers are prohibited from retaliating against an employee for requesting or taking unpaid military spouse leave.
(*N.Y. Lab. Law § 202-i, as amended by 2007 N.Y. Laws 516, effective Aug. 16, 2007*)

NORTH CAROLINA

Coverage: No employer may discharge any person from employment because of the performance of any military duty by reason of being an officer, warrant officer, or enlisted person of the military or naval forces of North Carolina or the United States. (*N.C. Gen. Stat. § 127B-14, as enacted 1985 N.C. Sess. Laws 522*)

A member of the North Carolina National Guard called into service has the right to take leave without pay from his or her civilian employment. (*N.C. Gen. Stat. § 127A-111, as amended by 1997 N.C. Sess. Laws 153*)

All employers are subject to the nondiscrimination requirement. (*N.C. Gen. Stat. § 127B-11, as enacted by 1985 N.C. Sess. Laws 522*)

National Guard Leave: An employer may not deny initial employment, re-employment, retention in employment, promotion, or any benefit of employment to an individual because of that individual's membership in the North Carolina National Guard and because that individual performs, applies to perform, or has an obligation to perform service in the National Guard, including performing active duty at the direction of the President, Governor, or any other competent authority. (*N.C. Gen. Stat. § 127A-202.1, as amended by 2004 N.C. Sess. Laws 130*)

A member of the National Guard called into service shall have the right to take leave without pay from civilian employment. The National Guard member cannot be forced to use or exhaust vacation or other accrued leave from civilian employment for a period of active service. Choice of leave is solely at the discretion of the National Guard member. (*N.C. Gen. Stat. § 127A-111, as amended by 1997 N.C. Sess. Laws 153*)

Re-Employment Rights: Any member of the North Carolina National Guard is entitled, upon honorable release from state duty, to all re-employment rights.

An employee shall make written application for re-employment within five days of release from duty. If still qualified, the employee shall be reinstated to the previous employment or a position of like seniority, status, and salary, unless the employer's circumstances make such reinstatement unreasonable. If the employee is no longer qualified for the previously occupied position, the employee shall be placed in another position for which the employee is qualified, with appropriate seniority, status, and salary. (*N.C. Gen. Stat. § 127A-202, as enacted by 1979 N.C. Sess. Laws 155*)

Penalties: If an employer fails to reinstate an employee following military leave, the employee may petition the superior court, and the court may require the employer to reinstate the employee and compensate the employee for any lost wages or benefits. (*N.C. Gen. Stat. § 127A-203, as enacted by 1979 N.C. Sess. Laws 155*)

Violations are Class 2 misdemeanors. (*N.C. Gen. Stat. § 127B-15, as amended by 1994 (1st ex. s.) N.C. Sess. Laws 24*)

[*Note:* For violations of National Guard members' re-employment rights, the enforcement and penalty provisions are codified as part of the state's Retaliatory Employment Discrimination Act (*N.C. Gen. Stat. §§ 95-240 to 95-245*)]

Relevant Cases: *Jones v. Philip Morris USA Inc.*, 2004 U.S. Dist. LEXIS 6224 (M.D.N.C. 2004); *Lederer v. Hargraves Tech. Corp.*, 256 F. Supp. 2d 467 (W.D.N.C. 2003).

NORTH DAKOTA

Employers must grant to employees called to active service for 30 consecutive days or longer the same rights as members of the U.S. armed forces under the Soldiers and Sailors Civil Relief Act of 1940, 50 U.S.C. § 501 et seq. (*N.D. Cent. Code § 37–01–43, as enacted by 2003 N.D. Laws 296*)

OHIO

Summary: State law grants employees who serve in the uniformed services or in the Ohio organized militia the same reinstatement and re-employment rights as under the federal Uniformed Services Employment and Reemployment Rights Act (38 U.S.C. § 4301 et seq.).

Service in the uniformed services means duty performed on a voluntary or involuntary basis in a uniformed service, including active duty, inactive and active duty training, full-time National Guard duty, and any time spent undergoing fitness-for-duty ex-

aminations. Uniformed services include the armed forces and reserves, the Army National Guard and Air National Guard, the
Commissioned Corps of the Public Health Service, and any other
category of persons designated by the president in time of war or
emergency.

Remedies/Penalties: Violation of an employee's reinstatement
or re-employment rights may be punished by a fine of up to
$1,000, imprisonment for up to six months, or both.

Employers can be sued in Ohio Common Pleas courts for denying re-employment or reinstatement to employees who are absent from work due to service in the uniformed services or Ohio
organized militia. As an alternative, the employee may also bring
a claim under 38 U.S.C. § 4323. However, effective April 7, 2009,
an employee cannot receive a remedy under both the state and
federal laws on the same set of facts. If a remedy is received under state law, and the employee subsequently receives a federal
remedy under the same set of facts, the employee must reimburse the state for any state remedy he or she received.

If the employee prevails, the court will require the defendant to
pay the court costs. If the employee does not prevail, the court
may allocate the costs among the parties. Attorneys' fees and other litigation expenses may be awarded to a prevailing plaintiff. If
the employee is unsuccessful, the court shall not require the employee to reimburse the state or the defendant for attorneys'
fees.

(*Ohio Rev. Code Ann. §§ 5903.02, as amended by 2008 Ohio S248, effective April 7, 2009; and 5903.99, as amended by 2008 Ohio S289, effective Aug. 22, 2008; and 5919.29, as amended by 1997 Ohio Laws
S130*)

OKLAHOMA

Summary: Oklahoma employers must grant employees leave to
participate in federal military service, and National Guard and
military reserve training, and must re-employ workers called up
for military duty.

Coverage: Employers of members of the U.S. military or reserve corps or the National Guard are covered.

For the benefit of National Guard members, the state has adopted the federal Servicemembers Civil Relief Act of 2003 (codified at 50 U.S.C. App., § 501 et seq.) and Uniformed Services Employment and Reemployment Rights Act (38 U.S.C. §§ 4301 through 4333).

Amount of Leave: The law does not provide a specific time for military leave.

Pay and Benefits: Employers can, at their own discretion, pay employees the difference between civilian and military pay.

Employees on military leave do not lose status or seniority.

Re-Employment Rights: Employers must re-employ workers in their prior jobs or jobs of similar seniority, status, and pay, following military leave.

Administration/Enforcement: The district court enforces the military leave law.

Penalties/Remedies: Employers that refuse to permit state National Guard members to attend drills, exercises, or other duties commit a misdemeanor punishable by a fine of $50 to $200, imprisonment for 10 to 60 days, or both.

Employers that discriminate against National Guard members, discharge them, or hinder them from performing military services because of their membership in the Guard are subject to a fine of up to $100, imprisonment for up to 30 days, or both.
(*Okla. Stat. tit. 44, §§ 71, as enacted by 1951 Okla. Sess. Laws p. 117; 208, as enacted by 1935 Okla. Sess. Laws p. 91; 208.1, as amended by 2005 Okla. Sess. Laws 130; tit. 72 §§ 47, as amended by 2002 Okla. Sess. Laws 396; and 48.1, enacted by 1994 Okla. Sess. Laws 94*)

OREGON

State Militia
Coverage: Employees who are members of the Oregon state militia or of any other state's organized militia, are entitled to a leave

of absence when called for state active service by the governor of Oregon or the governor of the state where the employee will serve.

Exceptions: Employees who are members of the state organized militia, who work as a copartner of employers, independent contractor, or for the federal government are not entitled to a leave of absence when called for state active service by the governor.

Salary Continuation: Employers are not required to pay wages or other monetary compensation to employees who are members of the state militia while on leave of absence when called for state active service.

Re-Employment Rights: Employees who are members of the state militia may not be removed or discharged from their positions because of leave of absence when called for state active service. Their regular positions are to be considered vacant only while these employees are on leave of absence when they are called for state active service.

Employees who are members of the state militia are entitled to be restored to their former position or to an equivalent position without loss of seniority, vacation credits, sick leave credits, service credits under a pension plan, or any other employee benefit or right that had been earned at the time of leave.

Remedies/Penalties: The commissioner of the Bureau of Labor and Industries enforces state organized militia leave and reemployment provisions similar to enforcement of unlawful employment practices.

An applicant or employee may bring a civil action in circuit court. The court may order equitable relief, including the reinstatement or hiring of the person; back pay; court costs; reasonable attorneys' fees; compensatory damages or $200, whichever is greater; and punitive damages.

(*Or. Rev. Stat. §§ 399.230, as amended by 2005 Or. Laws 78; and 399.235, as amended by 2003 Or. Laws 387; and 659A.885, as amended by 2009 Or. Laws 378 and 478, both effective Jan. 1, 2010*)

Uniformed Services

Summary: Employers are prohibited from denying any of the following because the person is a member of, applies to be a member of, performs, has performed, applies to perform, or has an obligation to perform service in a uniformed service:

- initial employment;
- re-employment following return from leave taken to perform service;
- retention in employment;
- promotion; or
- any other term, condition, or privilege of employment.

Exception: Employers may lawfully base their actions on a bona fide occupational requirement reasonably necessary to the normal operation of the business, if the actions could not be avoided by making a reasonable accommodation for the person's service.

Coverage: The protections apply to the uniformed services: U.S. Army, Navy, Air Force, Marine Corps, Coast Guard, National Guard, or military reserve forces.

Remedies/Penalties: An applicant or employee may bring a civil action in circuit court. The court may order equitable relief, including the reinstatement or hiring of the person; back pay; court costs; reasonable attorneys' fees; compensatory damages or $200, whichever is greater; and punitive damages.
(*Or. Rev. Stat. §§ 659A.885, as amended by 2009 Or. Laws 378 and 478, and § 1 of 2009 Or. Laws 378 (H.B. 3256), all effective Jan. 1, 2010*)

Military Family Leave

Summary: During a period of military conflict, an employee who is a spouse of a member of the U.S. Armed Forces, the National Guard, or the U.S. military reserve forces is entitled to a total of 14 days of unpaid leave when the servicemember has been notified of an impending call or order to active duty or has been deployed. The 14 days of leave is available for each deployment but must be taken either before the deployment or during the servicemember's leave from deployment.

Use of Accrued Leave: An employee who takes military family leave may elect to substitute any accrued leave to which the employee is entitled for any part of the military family leave.

Military family leave taken is included in the total amount of leave authorized as family leave (see *Or. Rev. Stat. § 659A.162*).

Re-Employment Rights: After returning to work after taking military family leave, an eligible employee is entitled to be restored to the position held when the leave commenced if that position still exists, without regard to whether the employer filled the position with a replacement worker during the period of military family leave.

If the position held by the employee at the time leave commenced no longer exists, the employee is entitled to be restored to any available equivalent position with equivalent employment benefits, pay, and other terms and conditions of employment. If an equivalent position is not available at the job site of the employee's former position, the employee may be offered an equivalent position at a job site located within 20 miles of the job site of the employee's former position.

Except for employee benefits used during the period of leave, the taking of military family leave shall not result in the loss of any employment benefit accrued before the date on which the leave commenced.

The employee is not entitled to any accrual of seniority or employment benefits during a period of military family leave; or any right, benefit, or position of employment other than the rights, benefits, and position that the employee would have been entitled to had the employee not taken the family leave.

Benefits are not required to continue to accrue during a military family leave unless continuation or accrual is required under an agreement of the employer and the employee, a collective bargaining agreement, or an employer policy.

Definitions: Employee means an individual who performs services for compensation for an employer for an average of at least 20 hours per week. The term includes all individuals employed at any site owned or operated by an employer, but does not include independent contractors.

Employer means a person, firm, corporation, partnership, legal representative, or other business entity that engages in any business, industry, profession or activity in the state and that employs 25 or more persons in the state for each working day during each of 20 or more calendar workweeks in the year in which leave is taken or the year immediately preceding the year in which the leave is to be taken.

Retaliation Prohibited: It is an unlawful practice for an employer to deny military family leave to an employee who is entitled to such leave, or to retaliate or in any way discriminate against an individual with respect to hire or tenure or any other term or condition of employment because:

- the individual has inquired about military family leave rights;
- submitted a request for military family leave; or
- invoked any military family leave right.

Notification Requirement: An employee who intends to take military family leave must provide the employer with notice of the intention within five business days of receiving official notice of an impending call or order to active duty, or of a leave from deployment.

(*Or. Rev. Stat. § 659A.171; and 2009 Or. Laws 559, effective June 25, 2009*)

Pennsylvania

Summary: Employees who enlist or are drafted into active national or state military service are automatically granted a military leave of absence.

Re-Employment Rights: As long as a private or public employee is on a military leave of absence, the employee cannot be removed from employment, and the employee's duties are to be performed by other employees or by a temporary substitute.

Military leave expires 90 days after the completion of the military duty.

Upon completion of military leave, the employee must be reinstated by the employer in the former position or a position of like seniority, status, and pay.

Salary Continuation: Employees, who enlist or are drafted into active national or state military service, are not entitled to paid leave.

Penalties: Discrimination against, or discharge of, an employee because of employee's membership in any reserve component is prohibited.

(51 Pa. Cons. Stat. §§ 7302, as amended by 2000 Pa. Laws 90; 7303, as amended by 1990 Pa. Laws 174; and 7309, as amended by 2005 Pa. Laws 83)

Relevant Cases: *Witter v. Pa. Nat'l Guard,* 462 F. Supp. 299, 100 LRRM 2834 (E.D. Pa. 1978).

PUERTO RICO

Coverage: Public and private officers and employees who are members of the Military Forces of Puerto Rico, State Guard of Puerto Rico, or national reserves. Public employees requesting military leave must, in addition to the request for leave, submit official evidence accrediting the order of such military service or any other evidence required by the Labor Relations Board.

Effect of Leave on Benefits: Private officers and employees, who are members of the Military Forces of Puerto Rico, are entitled to military leave without loss of time or efficiency rating for annual training or when called to commonwealth active duty.

Re-Employment Rights: Officers and employees who are members of the Puerto Rico National Guard or State Guard of Puerto Rico and on military leave for commonwealth active service or training shall be reinstated to their former positions if they were honorably discharged from such military service or training, are still qualified to perform the duties of such positions, and make applications for re-employment within 40 days of being relieved from such service and training. The officers and employees may be restored to positions of like seniority, status, and pay, unless the employers' circumstances have so changed as to make it impossible or unreasonable to do so, if former positions are unavailable.

The Puerto Rico Veteran's Bill of Rights grants a veteran the right to be reinstated in the same position he or she held at the time called into the armed forces, if the veteran requests reinstatement within six months following discharge from the military and the same position or office still exists or if there is another similar position.

Penalties: Public and private employers are guilty of a felony if they prevent, obstruct, or do not allow members of the Military Forces of Puerto Rico, to be absent from employment or office in order to report to military duty, either for training or when called into active commonwealth duty, or if they dismiss or otherwise discriminate against employees because of the employees' absences in performance of military duty or because of being a member of the Military Forces of Puerto Rico. Upon conviction, these employers shall be fined up to $5,000 or imprisoned for up to 3 years or both.

Public and private employers, who dismiss or discriminate against employees because of military leave of absence for performance of military duty in the Military Forces of Puerto Rico or because of being a member of the Military Forces of Puerto Rico, must reinstate employees without any loss of pay and retroactive to the date of dismissal, and/or reinstate employees in all rights, privileges, and/or benefits retroactive to the date of dismissal or discrimination, as applicable. Public and private employees have up to six months from the day of dismissal or discrimination to demand that these employers comply with this provision.

Public and private employers who by themselves or with another person deprive a member of the Military Forces of Puerto Rico from employment or obstruct or impair such member from obtaining such employment because of belonging to the Military Forces of Puerto Rico, or dissuade a person from enlisting in the Military Forces of Puerto Rico under threat of bodily injury or another form of intimidation shall be guilty of a misdemeanor. Upon conviction, these employers shall be fined not less than $500 or imprisoned for up to six months or both.
(*25 P.R. Laws Ann. §§ 2083, 2089, and 2203, as enacted by 1969 P.R. Laws 62; and 2084, as amended by 1976 P.R. Laws 44; 29 P.R. Laws Ann. § 814, as amended by 2004 P.R. Laws 423*)

RHODE ISLAND

Summary: Rhode Island employers must grant employees leave to participate in National Guard and military reserve service, and must re-employ workers called up for military duty.

Coverage: Leave and re-employment Rights apply to members of the National Guard and the U.S. reserve corps. Members of the federal armed forces are entitled to job reinstatement.

Amount of Leave: The law does not specify an amount of time of military leave.

Pay and Benefits: Employers do not have to pay employees while on military leave.

For employees absent to serve in the U.S. reserve forces or state's national guard, employers must grant them normal vacation, sick leave, bonus, advancement, and other advantages of employment as if the employee were not absent.

Re-Employment Rights: Employers must restore workers to their previous jobs following military leave, or to jobs of equivalent status, pay, and seniority. The employee may be required to provide evidence of satisfactory completion of military duty.

Members of the federal armed forces must request reinstatement to their former jobs within 40 days of an honorable discharge. The employer must re-employ the veteran if he or she is still qualified to perform the duties in the same job, or in a job with similar seniority, status, and pay. An exception exists if the employer's circumstances have so changed as to make reinstatement impossible or unreasonable.

Administration/Enforcement: The superior court enforces the military leave law.

Penalties/Remedies: Employers that discharge employees because of membership in state military forces or national reserves commit a misdemeanor punishable by a fine of up to $500 or imprisonment for up to one year or both.

For state military forces or national reserves, employers that violate the leave, benefits, or re-employment provisions of the law are subject to a civil suit for damages in superior court.

For federal armed forces, the penalty for failure to reinstate is a fine of not less than $50 and not more than $500.
(*R.I. Gen. Laws §§ 30–11–2 to 30–11–9, as amended by 2001 R.I. Pub. Laws 164; and § 30–21–1, as enacted by 1943 R.I. Pub. Laws 1351*)

Relevant Cases: *Pomom v. Gen. Dynamics Corp.*, 574 F. Supp. 147, 115 LRRM 2494 (D.R.I. 1983).

Family Military Leave

Summary: Employers with at least 15 employees must provide unpaid family military leave to employees who have a spouse or parent called to military service for longer than 30 days.

Definitions: Employee includes an individual who has been employed by a covered employer for at least 12 months, and has been employed for at least 1,250 hours of service during a 12-month period immediately preceding the commencement of leave. Independent contractors are considered employees for purposes of the leave act.

Family military leave means leave requested by an employee who is the spouse or parent of a person called to military service lasting longer than 30 days with the state or the United States pursuant to the orders of the governor or the president.

Leave Amounts: Employers that employ between 15 and 50 employees shall provide up to 15 days of unpaid family military leave to an employee during the time federal or state orders are in effect.

Employers with more than 50 employees shall provide up to 30 days of unpaid family military leave to an employee during the time federal or state orders are in effect.

An employee shall not take unpaid family military leave unless he or she has exhausted all accrued vacation leave, personal leave, compensatory leave or time, and any other leave that may be granted to the employee, with the exception of sick leave and disability leave.

Notification: If the leave will consist of five or more consecutive workdays, the employee must give notice at least 14 days prior to the intended date upon which family military leave will commence. Where possible, the employee shall consult with the employer to schedule the leave to not unduly disrupt the employer's operations.

Employees taking family military leave for less than five consecutive days shall give the employer advance notice as is practicable.

Certification: The employer may require certification from the proper military authority to verify the employee's eligibility to take the requested family military leave.

Job Restoration: Any employee who exercises the right to family military leave is entitled to restoration, by the employer, to the position held by the employee when the leave commenced or to a position with equivalent seniority status, employee benefits, pay and other terms and conditions of employment. The employer is not required to restore the employee if the employer proves that the job restoration was not possible because of conditions unrelated to the employee's exercise of rights under the family military leave act.

Prohibited Actions: An employer shall not:

- interfere with, restrain, or deny the exercise or the attempt to exercise any right provided by the family military
  leave law; nor
- discharge, fine, suspend, expel, discipline, or in any other
  manner discriminate against any employee who exercises
  any right provided under the law, or who opposes any unlawful practice.

Remedies/Penalties: An employee may bring a civil action in the
state court having jurisdiction to enforce the law. The court may
enjoin any act or practice that violates or may violate the military
family leave law and may order any other equitable relief that is
necessary and appropriate to redress the violation or to enforce
the law.
(*R.I. Gen. Laws §§ 30–33–2 to 30–33–6, as enacted by 2008 R.I. Pub.
Laws 61 and 65, effective June 23, 2008*)

South Carolina

Leave Rights: It is a misdemeanor to willfully deprive or prevent
South Carolina National Guard members of employment, obstruct or annoy such members in trade, business, or employment
because of National Guard membership, or dissuade or attempt
to dissuade any person from enlisting in the National Guard by
threat of injury to employment, trade, or business and is punishable by a fine of not more than $100 or imprisonment in the
county jail for not more than 30 days.

Re-Employment Rights: Upon honorable discharge, South Carolina National Guard and State Guard members who entered authorized state duty are entitled to be restored to their former positions, if they are still qualified and upon written application
within five days of being released from duty or hospitalization. If
they are not restored to their former positions, they will be reinstated to positions of like seniority, status, and salary, unless it is
unreasonable because of an employer's changed circumstances.
However, if they are no longer qualified for former positions,
they will be placed in other positions, for which they are quali-

fied, and which provide appropriate seniority, status, and salary, unless it is unreasonable because of an employer's changed circumstances.

Enforcement: Any South Carolina National Guard or South Carolina State Guard member may bring suit in circuit court to require an employer to comply with the **Re-Employment** provisions and to compensate the employee for any lost wages or benefits. (*S.C. Code Ann. § 25–1–10, as amended by 2001 S.C. Acts 85; § 25–1–2190, as last amended in 1964; §§ 25–1–2310 to 25–1–2340, as enacted by 1982 S.C. Acts 322*)

South Dakota

Employees who are members of the state's National Guard, when ordered to active duty service by the governor or the president of the United States, have all the protections afforded to persons serving on federal active duty by the Soldiers and Sailors Civil Relief Act (50 U.S.C. app. §§ 501 to 548 and 560 to 591) and by the Uniformed Services Employment and Reemployment Rights Act (38 U.S.C. §§ 4301 to 4333). (*S.D. Codified Laws § 33–17–15.1, as enacted by 2002 S.D. Laws 164*)

Tennessee

Employers are prohibited from terminating an employee for being a member of the national guard or because of absence from work while attending any prescribed drill, including annual field training. Violation of the law is a class E felony. (*Tenn. Code Ann. § 58–1–604, as amended by 1989 Tenn. Pub. Acts 591*)

Relevant Cases: *Mills v. Earthgrains Baking Cos.*, 175 LRRM 2811 (E.D. Tenn. 2004).

Texas

Summary: A private employer may not terminate the employment of a permanent employee who is a member of any state's military force because the employee is ordered to attend training or duty by a proper authority. The employee is entitled to return to the same employment held when ordered to training or duty and may not be subjected to loss of time, efficiency rating, vacation time, or any benefit of employment during or because of the absence.

Definitions: Reserve militia means the persons liable to serve, but not serving, in the state military forces

State militia means the state military forces and the reserve militia.

State military forces means the Texas National Guard, the Texas State Guard, and any other active militia or military force organized under state law.

Texas National Guard means the Texas Army National Guard and the Texas Air National Guard.

Notification Requirement: The employee, as soon as practicable after release from duty, must give written or actual notice of intent to return to employment.

An employer may not delay or attempt to defeat a re-employment obligation by demanding documentation that does not exist or is not readily available at the time the notice of intent is given.

Employer Defenses: It is a defense to an action if the employer's circumstances changed while the employee was in training or on duty to an extent that makes re-employment impossible or unreasonable. The employer has the burden of proving the impossibility or unreasonableness of re-employing the employee under the employer's changed circumstances.

Remedies/Penalties: A person injured by a violation is entitled to damages in an amount not exceeding six months' compensation at the rate at which the person was compensated when ordered to training or duty and reasonable attorneys' fees.

(*Tex. Gov't Code Ann. §§ 431.001, as amended by 2007 Tex. Gen. Laws 1381; and 431.006, as amended by 2007 Tex. Gen. Laws 365*)

UTAH

Summary: Utah employers must grant employees leave to participate in National Guard and military reserve training, and must re-employ workers at the end of the military duty.

Coverage: Employers of members of the National Guard and the state military reserve are covered.

Amount of Leave: Military leave can last up to five years.

Pay and Benefits: Employers do not have to pay employees who are on military leave.

Re-Employment Rights: Employers must reinstate employees following military leave. Employees must have a satisfactory release. Employers must allow employees to return to their former jobs with the same seniority, status, pay, and vacation, as if they had been continuously employed.

Administration/Enforcement: The courts enforce the military leave law.

Remedies/Penalties: Employers that fail to re-employ workers following active duty or that discriminate in hiring based on national reserves membership commit a class B misdemeanor.
(*Utah Code Ann. § 39–1–36, as amended by 1989 Utah Laws 15*)

VERMONT

Summary: Vermont employers must grant employees leave to participate in National Guard and military reserve training, and must re-employ workers called up for military duty.

Coverage: Employers of members of the National Guard, the U.S. reserve corps, and the ready reserve are covered.

Amount of Leave: Covered employees are eligible for a total of 15 days in a calendar year.

Pay and Benefits: Employers do not have to pay employees who are on military leave. Employers cannot deduct military leave time from employees' vacation or sick leave. Employers cannot deduct any bonus, advance, or other advantage of employment from employees on leave for training or active duty.

Re-Employment Rights: On return from the leave, employers must reinstate permanent employees to the same job with the same status, pay, and seniority, including seniority that accrued during the military leave.

Administration/Enforcement: The courts enforce the military leave law. The state attorney general or state's attorney can investigate violations and bring suit to enforce the law.

Remedies/Penalties: Employers cannot deny employment, retention in employment, promotion, or any benefit of employment because of employees' military obligations. Employers that fail to comply with the leave and re-employment laws can be sued in superior court.
(*Vt. Stat. Ann. tit. 21, §§ 491, 492, 493, as amended by 2007 Vt. Acts & Resolves 44, effective July 1, 2007*)

Virginia

Summary: Virginia employers must grant employees leave if called to active duty in the National Guard, state defense force, or naval militia, and must re-employ workers called up for military duty.

Retaliation Prohibited: State law prohibits persons from obstructing employees from becoming members of the armed forces or discriminating against an employee or applicant for employment on the basis of military service.

Coverage: Employers of members of the Virginia National Guard, the state defense force, or the naval militia are covered.

Amount of Leave: The law does not specify an amount of military leave.

Pay and Benefits: Employers cannot require employees to use or exhaust vacation or other accrued leave when on active military service.

Re-Employment Rights: Employers must re-employ workers following military leave in the samc jobs they held before the leave.

If the job no longer exists the worker must be reinstated to a position of similar seniority, status, and pay.

Workers must apply for re-employment within 14 days of release from duty.

Re-instatement is not required if the employee has been absent for more than five years for all military absences, whether or not consecutive.

Remedies/Penalties: Employers that discriminate against or fail to re-employ employees who are members of the military can be sued in circuit court. The state attorney general can represent the employee in court.

The court can require the employer to comply with the re-employment and nondiscrimination requirements, and to compensate the employee for any loss of wages or benefits, and for reasonable attorneys' fees and costs.

Employers that fail to re-employ members of the Virginia National Guard, Virginia State Defense Force, or naval militia commit a misdemeanor punishable by a fine up to $500, imprisonment for up to 30 days, or both.

Employers that deprive a member of the Virginia National Guard, Virginia State Defense Force, or naval militia of employment, or dissuade employees from enlisting, are guilty of a misdemeanor, punishable by a fine of up to $500, imprisonment for up to 30 days, or both.

(*Va. Code Ann. §§ 44–93.2 through 44–93.5, as amended by 2007 Va. Acts ch. 167 and 214, both effective July 1, 2007 ; 44–98, as amended by 1984 Va. Acts ch. 765; and 44–102.1, as enacted by 2003 Va. Acts ch. 769*)

WASHINGTON

Summary: Washington employers cannot discharge employees because of participation in the National Guard and military reserve training or service and must re-employ workers called up for military duty. Employers of members of the National Guard, the U.S. armed forces, the commissioned corps of the public health service, and the coast guard are covered. Employers do not have to pay employees during military leave.

Re-Employment Rights: Employers must reinstate workers following military leave in the job they left or a job similar in seniority, status, or pay, unless the employers' circumstances have changed so that reinstatement is impossible or unreasonable.

Employees must furnish employers with proof of an honorable discharge (or equivalent) and must apply for reinstatement as follows:

- if service was less than 31 days, on the first full calendar day following completion of service plus eight hours transportation time;
- if service was for 30 to 180 days, within 14 days of completion of service;
- if service was for more than 180 days, within 90 days of completion of service.

If circumstances beyond an employee's control make application for re-employment impracticable in the time specified, time must be extended to accommodate the circumstances.

Employees who fail to apply for re-employment within the time period do not forfeit their rights, but re-employment is governed by the employer's established policy and practices relating to absence from scheduled work.

Remedies/Penalties: Employers that fail to re-employ workers following military service can be sued in superior court. Employers can be ordered to reinstate the employees and compensate them for any lost wages or benefits.

The state attorney general can represent an employee.

Employers that willfully deprive members of the organized militia of Washington of employment are guilty of a gross misdemeanor, punishable by a fine of up to $500, imprisonment for up to six months, or both.

Employers that discriminate against, refuse to hire, or refuse to re-employ any member of the Washington organization militia because of that membership are guilty of a misdemeanor punishable by a fine of up to $100, forfeit the right to do business for 30 days, and can be sued by the employee.

(*Wash. Rev. Code §§ 38.40.040 and 38.40.050, as amended by 1989 Wash. Laws 19; 38.40.110, as amended by 1991 Wash. Laws 43; and §§ 73.16.031 to 73.16.035 and 73.16.051 to 73.16.100, as amended by 2001 Wash. Laws 133*)

Relevant Cases: *Nichols v. Snohomish County,* 746 P.2d 1208 (Wash. 1987); *State ex rel. Ford v. King County,* 290 P.2d 465 (Wash. 1955); *Gossage v. State,* 49 P.3d 927 (Wash. Ct. App. 2002); *Mitchell v. Bd. of Indus. Ins. Appeals,* 34 P.3d 267 (Wash. Ct. App. 2001); *Wash. Fed'n of State Employees v. State Pers. Bd.,* 773 P.2d 421 (Wash. Ct. App. 1989).

Family Military Leave

Summary: Employees who are spouses of members of the U.S. armed forces, National Guard, or reserves called to active duty or on leave from deployment during a time of war or national emergency are entitled to 15 days of leave per deployment. Spouse is defined to mean husband or wife (see *Wash. Rev. Code § 49.78.020*).

To be eligible, the employee must have worked for the employer on an average of 20 or more hours per week. Independent contractors are not covered.

Family military leave can be unpaid. Employees can elect to substitute any accrued leave for unpaid family military leave.

Notice to Employers: Within five business days of receiving official notice of an impending call or order to active duty or of a leave from deployment, an employee must provide notice to the employer of his or her intent to take leave.

Re-Employment Rights: Employers must restore employees who return from family military leave to their prior positions or equivalent jobs and permit the continuation of benefits (see *Wash. Rev. Code § 49.78.280*).

Retaliation Prohibited: Employers cannot interfere with, restrain, or deny any rights provided by the family military leave provisions. They also cannot discharge employees or otherwise discriminate against anyone who seeks to take or takes family military leave, files a proceeding or a lawsuit under the family military leave provisions, or testifies or otherwise participates in family military leave-related proceedings (see *Wash. Rev. Code § 49.78.300*).

Administration/Enforcement: The Washington Department of Labor and Industries administers and enforces the family military leave provisions. [*Note:* The family military leave act refers to *Wash. Rev. Code ch. 49.78* (family medical leave) for the specifics of enforcement and penalties.]

The department also investigates family military leave complaints filed by employees. If the department's investigations of employee complaints indicate possible employer violations of the family military leave provisions, a hearing is held and the department issues a written determination of the complaint. Employers and employees can appeal the department's determination according to state administrative law (see *Wash. Rev. Code § 49.78.310*).

Remedies/Penalties: An employer found to have violated family military leave provisions may be assessed a penalty of not less than $1,000 per violation (see *Wash. Rev. Code § 49.78.320*).

Employees may sue for violations of the family military leave law. An employer is liable for damages equal to the amount of wages, salary, employment benefits, or other compensation denied or lost to such employee, including interest on those amounts; any actual monetary losses sustained by the employee as a direct result of the violation; liquidated damages equal to the sum of the amount of lost compensation plus interest; equitable relief, including employment, reinstatement, and promotion; reasonable attorneys' and witness fees; and other court costs.

The court has the discretion to reduce the amount of the liability to the amount of lost compensation and interest owed on that amount if the employer can prove that the act or omission was in good faith and that the employer had reasonable grounds for be-

lieving that no violation occurred.
(*Enacted by 2008 Wash. Laws 71, effective June 12, 2008*)

WEST VIRGINIA

Members of the state military forces ordered to active state duty are entitled to the same re-employment rights granted to members of the federal armed forces. (*W. Va. Code § 15–1E–135 and § 15–1F–8, as amended by 1992 W. Va. Acts 129*)

WISCONSIN

Federal Service

Summary: An employee who is ordered into active duty with the U.S. armed forces for a period of 90 days or more, or whose services have been requested by the federal government for national defense work as a civilian during an officially-proclaimed national emergency, is entitled to be re-employed upon completion of duty/service in the position he or she left, or to a position of like seniority, status, pay and salary advancement as though his or her employment had not been interrupted.

Coverage: All employers.

Eligibility: To be restored to employment, the individual must:

- present the employer evidence that the military duty or federal service has been completed, or the individual has been discharged under conditions other than dishonorable;
- still be qualified to perform the duties of such position; and
- apply for **Re-Employment** and resume work within 90 days after completing duty/service or being discharged, or within six months after release from hospitalization for duty-connected or service-connected injury or disease.

The employer is not required to re-employ the employee if the employer's circumstances have changed so as to make reinstatement impossible or unreasonable, or if the military service was for more than five years, unless such time limit is extended by law.

Re-Employment Rights: The service of any person restored to a position under these circumstances is not considered an interruption of service, except for compensation purposes for the period of absence. The individual is entitled to participate in insurance, pensions, retirement plans, or other benefits offered by the employer under rules and practices relating to employees on furlough or leave of absence that existed at the time the employee entered military service.

An individual re-employed after military duty or federal service cannot be discharged without cause within one year of restoration.

Remedies/Penalties: If an employer fails or refuses to comply with these provisions, an employee may petition a court to order the employer's compliance. In addition, the court may award the employee wages and benefits lost as a result of the employer's unlawful action.
(*Wis. Stat. § 321.64, as amended by 2007 Wis. Laws 200, effective March 29, 2008*)

Employees in Active State Service

Summary: Employees who are ordered to active service in the national guard of any state or active service with the Wisconsin Laboratory of Hygiene to assist during a state of emergency are entitled to re-employment if:

- advance notice of the period of active service was given to the employer (unless military necessity precluded giving such notice);
- the cumulative length of the absence and of all previous absences from employment for state and federal active duty does not exceed five years;

- the individual reports to the employer or submits a petition for re-employment within the time limits provided (see below); and
- the employee's service was not terminated in other than honorable conditions.

Time Limits: To receive the re-employment benefits, a person who has been absent from employment:

- for less than 31 days because of active state service, been absent for any period of time for the purpose of examination to determine the person's fitness to perform active state service, or who is hospitalized for or convalescing from an illness or injury incurred in active state service, must report to the employer no later than the beginning of the first full regularly-scheduled work period on the first full calendar day following the completion of the active service or period of hospitalization, plus any time required for return to the employee's home, plus an eight-hour rest period. If through no fault of the employee, it is unreasonable or impossible to report within the designated time, the employee should report to the employer as soon as possible after the eight-hour rest period.
- for more than 30 days but less than 181 days, or who is hospitalized for or convalescing from an illness or injury incurred in active state service, must submit a petition for re-employment by no later than 14 days following the completion of the active service or period of hospitalization.
- for more than 180 days, or who is hospitalized for or convalescing from an illness or injury incurred in active service, must submit a petition for re-employment by no later than 90 days following the completion of the active service or period of hospitalization. For employees returning after an absence of more than 30 days, if through no fault of the employee, it is unreasonable or impossible to file the required petition within the designated time, the

employee should file the petition no later than the first full calendar day on which submission becomes possible.

The period of hospitalization or convalescence may not exceed two years; however, the time can be extended if through no fault of the person, he or she is unable to reasonably report or petition the employer within the designated time frames.

A person who fails to report to the employer within the time period specified does not automatically forfeit re-employment Rights, but is subject to the employer's policies and practices pertaining to unexcused absences from work.

The following times are not included in the calculation of the five-year service limit:

- any period of active state service required to complete an initial period of obligated active service;
- any period for which the employee was unable to obtain release orders;
- any period during which the employee was ordered by an official specified in the statute to acquire additional training;
- any period of active service performed because of a state emergency declared by the governor or a national emergency or war declared by the president of the U.S. or the Congress; or
- any period of federal active duty described in 38 U.S.C. § 4312(c)(1) to (4).

Benefit Rights: A re-employed person is entitled to the seniority or other rights and benefits determined by seniority that the person had on the last day of employment before the person's active service began, plus all seniority and other rights and benefits determined by seniority that the person would have had if continuously employed with the employer.

A person absent from employment because of active service is considered to be on furlough or leave of absence while performing the active service and is entitled to receive all rights and benefits not determined by seniority that are generally provided by the employer to employees having similar seniority, status, and pay who are on furlough or leave of absence under a contract, agreement, policy, practice, or plan in effect on the day on which the active service began, or that is established while the person is performing the active service.

An employer may require a person on furlough while performing active service to pay the employee cost, if any, of any benefit that is continued, to the same extent that other employees who are on furlough or leave of absence are so required.

Exceptions: An employer is not required to re-employ an employee if:

- the employer's circumstances have so changed as to make the employee's re-employment impossible or unreasonable;
- the position of employment was for a brief, nonrecurrent period, and there was no reasonable expectation that the position would continue indefinitely or for a significant period of time; or
- in the case of a disabled person, the accommodations, training, or effort required to re-employ the employee would pose an undue hardship for the employer.

Re-Employment Rights: If the active state service was for less than 91 days, the employer must promptly place the employee into a position that the person would have had if the service leave had not occurred. If the employee is not qualified for the position, the employer must make reasonable efforts to qualify the employee. If those efforts fail, then the employee is entitled to return to the job held prior to the service leave.

If the active state service was for more than 90 days, the employer must promptly place the employee into a position that the person would have had if the service leave had not occurred. If the employee is not qualified for the position, the employer must make reasonable efforts to qualify the employee. If those efforts fail, then the employer will return the employee to the job held prior to the service leave, or to a job of like seniority, status, and pay.

If the employee returns with a disability that was incurred or aggravated during active state service, the employer must make reasonable efforts to accommodate the disability, but if the employee is still not qualified to perform the duties of the job in which the person would otherwise be entitled, then the employer must place the employee in any other position that is equivalent, or if that is not available, to the nearest approximation consistent with the employee's circumstances.

Prohibited Actions: An employer may not discharge or otherwise discriminate against any person for attempting to enforce, or for assisting in any action to enforce, a right pertaining to re-employment under the law.

Employers are prohibited from delaying or attempting to defeat re-employment rights by demanding documentation that does not exist or is not readily available at the time of the demand.

Employees who were absent for state service for more than 30 days but less than 181 days may not be discharged without cause within 180 days of the date of re-employment. If the service was for more than 180 days, discharge cannot occur without cause within one year of re-employment.

Enforcement: For violations, complaints may be filed with the adjutant general who will attempt to resolve complaints. If the employee chooses not to ask the adjutant general for assistance, or the adjutant general declines to pursue the complaint, the employee may file a complaint with the Department of Workforce Development. The complaint will be treated in the same manner as employment discrimination cases.

Remedies/Penalties: An employer that fails or refuses to reinstate an employee following active state service as required, may be ordered:

- to take such action as will fully vindicate the rights and benefits of the employee;

- to compensate the employee for any loss of wages, salary, or other benefits suffered because of the failure to provide re-employment rights or benefits;
- to pay the employee, as liquidated damages, an amount equal to the lost wages, salary, or other benefits, if the failure to provide re-employment rights was willful;
- pay the costs and reasonable actual attorney fees of the employee.

(*Wis. Stat. § 321.65, as amended by 2007 Wis. Laws 200, effective March 29, 2008*)

WYOMING

Summary: State law provides employment status and benefit protections to employees during active military duty or training.

Coverage: Public and private employees who are members of the armed forces, Army National Guard, Air National Guard, Commissioned Corps of the Public Health Service, or any other group designated by the president in time of war or emergency. Coverage applies to these individuals when performing duty on a voluntary or involuntary basis including active duty for training, initial active duty for training, inactive duty training, full-time National Guard duty, absence for fitness examination for duty, and state active duty by the National Guard called out by the governor.

Discrimination Prohibited: Employers are prohibited from denying any person initial employment, re-employment, retention in employment, promotion, or any benefit of employment because of qualifying military service. Similarly, employers may not discriminate or take adverse action against a person who acts to enforce rights to military leave, antidiscrimination, and re-employment, regardless of whether that person has performed military service.

Military Leave: An employee who leaves employment to perform service in the uniformed services must be treated as being on a military leave of absence during the period of service, provided that he or she applies for re-employment in accordance with these provisions.

Employees performing qualifying military service may at their discretion use any amount or combination of credited accrued annual leave, paid military leave, vacation, or compensatory leave while on military duty. Such employees shall continue to accrue sick, annual, vacation, or military leave while on military duty as if continuously employed.

Salary Continuation: Employees may receive paid military leave at the employers' discretion. Employers that provide paid military leave must pay employees uniformly and may not deduct from an employee's paid military leave any cost of replacing the employee during such leave.

Re-Employment Rights: Employees completing qualifying military service are entitled to re-employment rights and benefits within 10 days of application for re-employment, provided:

- the employee or an authorized military officer has given advance written or verbal notice of service to the employer;
- the cumulative length of the absence and all previous military absences does not exceed five years; and
- if the military leave was less than 31 days, the employee reports to work or submits an application for Re-Employment not later than the beginning of the first work day following the completion of military service plus an additional eight hours for travel; if military leave lasted more than 30 days but less than 181 days, not later than 14 days after the completion of military service; and after completion of military service for employees on military leave for more than 181 days, not later than 90 days.

Employees who are unable to meet the reporting deadlines through no fault of their own are required to report as soon as possible.

The five-year limitation on cumulative military leave does not include any service:

- that is required beyond five years to complete an initial period of obligated service;
- during which employees were unable, through no fault of their own, to obtain orders releasing them from military service before the expiration of the five-year period;
- performed to fulfill additional training requirements determined to be necessary for professional development or for completion of skill training or retraining; or
- performed by employees who are ordered to or retained on active duty in time of war or national or state emergency.

Employees who are hospitalized or convalescing from an illness or injury incurred in or aggravated by military service shall report to employers not later than the beginning of the first work day following their release from hospital plus eight hours' travel time (if military leave was less than 31 days) or submit an application for re-employment no later than 14 days (if military leave was more than 30 days but less than 181 days) or 90 days (if military leave was more than 181 days) after release from hospital.

A recovery period may not exceed two years. The two-year recovery period shall be extended by the minimum time required to accommodate circumstances beyond an employee's control that makes reporting within the guidelines impossible or unreasonable.

Employees who fail to report or apply for employment or re-employment within the appropriate time do not automatically forfeit their entitlement to re-employment rights and benefits; however, they are subject to the established policies and general practices of their employers with respect to absences from scheduled work.

Employees are not required to notify an employer of their intent to apply for re-employment if the notice is precluded by military necessity or is otherwise impossible or unreasonable.

An employee completing qualifying military service of more than 30 days must provide, upon request of his or her employer, documentation to establish that the application for re-employment is timely; that the length of service did not exceed the applicable limits; and that the employee was honorably discharged.

Employees reinstated in employment after completing qualifying military service may not be discharged without cause within one year after such restoration. The employees are entitled to all seniority, rights, and benefits they would have accrued had they been continuously employed.

Exceptions to Re-Employment Rights: Employers are not required to re-employ employees if the employer can demonstrate that:

- its circumstances have so changed as to make Re-Employmento impossible or unreasonable;
- re-employment would impose an undue hardship on the employer; and
- the employment was of a brief, nonrecurrent nature and that the employee could have had no reasonable expectation that the employment would have continued indefinitely or for a significant period.

Retirement Rights: Employees who apply for re-employment following release from service or discharge from hospitalization incidental to service are entitled to receive credit for such military leave toward vesting and computation of benefits in the applicable retirement system, pension fund, or employee benefit plan. These employees shall not receive more than a total of four years of military-service credit in such plans.

Remedies/Penalties: The district courts of Wyoming have jurisdiction to require employers to:

- comply with the military leave, re-employment rights, and antidiscrimination provisions of the law;
- compensate employees for any loss of wages or benefits suffered by reason of an employer's noncompliance with the military leave law; and
- pay employees an amount equal to the amount of lost wages or benefits as damages if the court determines that

an employer's failure to comply with military leave law was willful.

Any compensation awarded shall be in addition to and shall not diminish any other penalty rights and benefits.

(Wyo. Stat. Ann. §§ 19–11–101 to 19–11–113, and 19–11–121, as amended by 2007 Wyo. Sess. Laws 23)

USERRA DATA RETENTION REQUIREMENTS

Question	Answer	Comments	Citation
What Information Has to Be Kept (information type)	USERRA contains no specific requirements for the retention of particular documents. The following documents are those that are suggested for retention: 1. Notices of leave requests; 2. Military orders provided; 3. Communications with employee while on leave; 4. Requests for reinstatement; 5. Military discharge papers; 6. Documents regarding any benefits provided to the employee while on leave. Additionally, employers should retain hiring documents related to positions that become open while an employee is on military leave for which the employee may qualify.		38 U.S.C. §4301 *et seq.* 38 U.S.C. §§4312–4315

	Employers should also retain documents regarding an employee's participation in any pension/401(k) plans while the employee is on military leave to demonstrate the benefits the employer may need to pay into the plan (if a defined benefit plan) or that the employee may be able to contribute to the plan (if a defined contribution plan). Finally, any documents regarding claims of discrimination or retaliation on the basis of military service should be retained.	38 U.S.C. §4316 38 U.S.C. §4311
What Form to Keep Information in	No particular form of information is required.	
How Long to Keep Information (length of retention)	USERRA contains no statute of limitations. In addition, USERRA prevents a court from applying any statute of limitations to USERRA claims. Thus, no time limit can be accurately stated.	38 U.S.C. §4323(i)

(continued)

Question	Answer	Comments	Citation
Where to Keep Information (retention location)	No specific requirement.	Records may be requested by the DOL as part of an investigation into a complaint under USERRA.	20 C.F.R. §1002.289.
Who Keeps Information	Covered employers.		38 U.S.C. §4303(4).
Who Has Right of Access to Information	Department of Labor officials investigating a complaint under USERRA.		20 C.F.R. §1002.289.
Privacy Issues	USERRA contains no privacy restrictions.		
Possession, Custody, and Control Issues	None		
Any Specific References to Electronic Data	No		

TABLE OF CASES

References are to chapter and footnote number (e.g., 10: 85; 11: 98 refers to footnote 85 in Chapter 10 and to footnote 98 in Chapter 11).

INDEX

References are to chapter and section numbers (e.g., 10: I.B.3.a refers to section I.B.3.a of Chapter 10).